D0458145

The Presidency of FRANKLIN DELANO ROOSEVELT

AMERICAN PRESIDENCY SERIES

Clifford S. Griffin and Donald R. McCoy, Founding Editors
Homer E. Socolofsky, General Editor

George Washington, Forrest McDonald
John Adams, Ralph Adams Brown
Thomas Jefferson, Forrest McDonald
James Madison, Robert Allen Rutland
James Monroe, Noble E. Cunningham, Jr.
John Quincy Adams, Mary W. M. Hargreaves
Andrew Jackson, Donald B. Cole
Martin Van Buren, Major L. Wilson
William Henry Harrison & John Tyler, Norma Lois Peterson
James K. Polk, Paul H. Bergeron
Zachary Taylor & Millard Fillmore, Elbert B. Smith
Franklin Pierce, Larry Gara
James Buchanan, Elbert B. Smith
Abraham Lincoln, Phillip Shaw Paludan
Andrew Johnson, Albert Castel
Rutherford B. Hayes, Ari Hoogenboom
James A. Garfield & Chester A. Arthur, Justus D. Doenecke
Grover Cleveland, Richard E. Welch, Jr.
Benjamin Harrison, Homer B. Socolofsky & Allan B. Spetter
William McKinley, Lewis L. Gould
Theodore Roosevelt, Lewis L. Gould
William Howard Taft, Paolo E. Coletta
Woodrow Wilson, Kendrick A. Clements
Warren G. Harding, Eugene P. Trani & David L. Wilson
Calvin Coolidge, Robert H. Ferrell
Herbert C. Hoover, Martin L. Fausold
Franklin Delano Roosevelt, George McJimsey
Harry S. Truman, Donald R. McCoy
Dwight D. Eisenhower, Chester J. Pach, Jr., & Elmo Richardson
John F. Kennedy, James N. Giglio
Lyndon B. Johnson, Vaughn Davis Bornet
Richard Nixon, Melvin Small
Gerald R. Ford, John Robert Greene
James Earl Carter, Jr., Burton I. Kaufman
George Bush, John Robert Greene

The Presidency of

FRANKLIN DELANO ROOSEVELT

George McJimsey

UNIVERSITY PRESS OF KANSAS

Published by the University Press of Kansas (Lawrence,
Kansas 66049), which was organized by the Kansas
Board of Regents and is operated and funded by Emporia
State University, Fort Hays State University,
Kansas State University, Pittsburg State University, the University
of Kansas, and Wichita State University.

Library of Congress Cataloging-in-Publication Data

McJimsey, George T.
The presidency of Franklin Delano Roosevelt / George McJimsey.
p. cm. — (American presidency series)
Includes bibliographical references and index.
ISBN 0-7006-1012-X (cloth : alk. paper)
1. United States—Politics and government—1933–1945. 2. Roosevelt, Franklin D.
(Franklin Delano), 1882–1945. I. Title. II. Series.
E806.M46 2000
973.917'092—dc21 99-055956

British Library Cataloguing in Publication Data is available.

Printed in the United States of America

10 9 8 7 6 5 4 3 2 1

The paper used in this publication meets the requirements of
the American National Standard for Permanence of Paper for Printed
Library Materials Z39.48-1984.

To
Sandra and Anne

CONTENTS

FOREWORD

The aim of the American Presidency Series is to present historians and the general reading public with interesting, scholarly assessments of the various presidential administrations. These interpretive surveys are intended to cover the broad ground between biographies, specialized monographs, and journalistic accounts. As such, each is a comprehensive work that draws upon original sources and pertinent secondary literature yet leaves room for the author's own analysis and interpretation.

Volumes in the series present the data essential to understanding the administration under consideration. Particularly, each book treats the then-current problems facing the United States and its people and how the president and his associates felt about, thought about, and worked to cope with these problems. Attention is given to how the office developed and operated during the president's tenure. Equally important is consideration of the vital relationships among the president, his staff, the executive officers, Congress, foreign representatives, the judiciary, state officials, the public, political parties, the press, and influential private citizens. The series is also concerned with how this unique American institution—the presidency—was viewed by the presidents, and with what results.

All this is set, insofar as possible, in the context not only of contemporary politics but also of economics, international relations, law, morals, public administration, religion, and thought. Such a broad approach is necessary to understanding, for a presidential administration is more than the elected and appointed officers composing it, since its work so often reflects the major problems, anxieties, and glories of the nation. In short, the authors in this series strive to recount and evaluate the record of each administration and to identify its distinctiveness and relationships to the past, its own time, and the future.

The General Editor

PREFACE

This book portrays the presidency of Franklin Delano Roosevelt in two ways. First, it describes the major features of its domestic and foreign policies and the circumstances in which they took place. Second, it places Roosevelt's presidency in a specific historical context, which it calls "pluralism."

The book approaches its first objective by describing Franklin Roosevelt in the years before he took office and then narrating the inception of his New Deal during the first one hundred days of his term. It then divides various features of the New Deal into economic and social programs and programs for the use of natural resources. Organizing the chapters in this fashion clarifies events that would have collapsed into incoherence in a conventional historical narrative. The following chapter discusses the political nature of Roosevelt's presidency. In many respects, this is the most important chapter in the book. Without the ability to win elections and influence Congress to enact the legislation he proposed, Roosevelt's presidency would have merited only a passing notice. Because he was elected by overwhelming margins and carried so many congressmen with him, he was able to become one of the most influential legislative leaders in our history. At the same time, his popularity and large electoral triumphs, which resulted in his unprecedented and unique election to four terms, highlighted the weaknesses and failures of his political judgment. Politics, then, is the best standard for measuring Roosevelt's presidency. Placing the chapter earlier, however, would have disrupted the continuity between the "Hundred Days" and the subsequent New Deal.

The chapter on Eleanor Roosevelt is a unique feature of the volumes in this series, but few readers will be surprised by its presence. At the time, everyone realized that Eleanor Roosevelt was a major figure in her husband's presidency, and recent scholarship continues to enlarge her significance. The chapter includes brief portraits of three other prominent women in the New Deal: Frances Perkins, Mary "Molly" Dewson, and Ellen Woodward. Each was active in specific areas of concern to Eleanor: labor, political organization, and relief for the unemployed. Writing about them enlarges our understanding of the issues that were important to Eleanor and illustrates that women were more important in the presidency of Franklin Delano Roosevelt than in any of its predecessors.

The following chapters on the transformation of the New Deal during Roosevelt's second term and U.S. entry into and participation in World War II are presented in conventional narrative form. They show a politically weakened president emerging as a world leader whose efforts to rebuild the international order were cut short by his death.

The book's second objective is to place the presidency of Franklin Delano Roosevelt in its historical context. Although it is common to discuss the influence of Roosevelt's presidency, especially its expansion of the role of the national government in American economic and social life, the approach here is to see his presidency functioning in its own time. It broadly characterizes that time with the word "pluralism," an intellectual outlook that emerged in the 1920s and that informed approaches to organization and problem solving. As presented here, pluralism was multidimensional. It assumed that social relationships were or could be harmonious, but because such relationships were always changing, harmony required constant adjustments and decisions, each of which created a new reality that required other adjustments and decisions. Pluralism also favored a widespread sharing of decision making and saw leadership as facilitative rather than directive.

Pluralism characterized the presidency of Franklin Delano Roosevelt. It should be emphasized, however, that pluralism is not just this author's device for explaining the sprawling, many-faceted nature of the New Deal and the complexities of Roosevelt's design for an international order. As defined in these pages, the ideas of pluralism were characteristic of the 1930s and 1940s. As the book's conclusion indicates, this form of pluralism soon fell out of favor and is no longer accepted as a way to improve social conditions.

One result of emphasizing pluralism has been to direct attention away from the issues of social and economic class that are so prominent in much recent New Deal scholarship. The Roosevelt presidency taught those who wished to profit from its example that bureaucracy, operated by "flexible," "democratic" (that is, pluralistic) methods, was best able to solve social problems. The lessons were essentially political and administrative rather than social or economic. For a moment, they even surpassed the lessons of Keynesian fiscal policy—that government deficit spending could pull a nation out of economic slumps—which World War II spending appeared to justify. Of course, these issues were important aspects of Roosevelt's presidency, but they were manifestations of policies that were pluralist in nature. For example, the New Deal protected labor's "rights" by general principles of legislation that were given substance by worker elections and the bureaucratic decisions of the National Labor Relations Board. The New Deal formulation of spending emphasized a strategy of coordinating capital, labor, and consumption. In these and other policies, pluralism was an underlying principle.

My most obvious debt is to the many scholars whose works I relied on. I cited the most prominent ones in the notes and bibliographical essay, and I regret that space limitations kept me from crediting them all. The combination of industry and intelligence that these scholars brought to the study of Roosevelt's presidency both simplified and immensely complicated my job. These scholars have summarized and interpreted mountains of primary source material, but in the process, they have offered so many distinct insights that I was unable to do justice to them all. For this shortcoming and any others, I freely take responsibility.

Specific thanks go to Professors Patrick Maney and Homer Sokolofsky, who read the entire manuscript and provided helpful suggestions for its improvement.

I want to thank my colleagues in the Department of History at Iowa State University. My principal intellectual debt is to Professor Alan I. Marcus, who is an outstanding scholar in many fields largely because he has an unsurpassed ability to discover and describe the intellectual configurations of the past. Professor Hamilton Cravens helped me understand the intellectual background of the New Deal in the literature of the social sciences. Professor Joseph "Jay" Taylor helped me understand New Deal policies toward Native Americans and the use of natural resources. Professor R. Douglas Hurt helped with important aspects of New Deal agricultural and land-use policy.

A special thanks goes to Cherlyn Walley, who was my research assistant at a critical stage in completing the manuscript. Her speed, accuracy, and ability to find just the right quote or source were invaluable.

Carole Kennedy, the world's greatest secretary, lightened my administrative duties as chair of the history department so I could progress with this book.

I owe a profound debt to Dr. Leo Milleman and Dr. Larry Oteman, whose concern and skill made possible this book and, indeed, life itself.

I also thank Rebecca Knight Giusti of the University Press of Kansas for editorial guidance that improved the manuscript's accuracy, consistency, and exposition.

I am not sure I will ever find adequate words to thank Fred Woodward, director of the University Press of Kansas, for his helpfulness, good nature, and, above all, patient understanding. No author could wish for a better person to work with.

I dedicate this book to my wife, Sandra, and my daughter, Anne. Neither contributed specifically to the book, but in many ways they have enriched my spirit and made both my scholarly life and, indeed, life itself a joy to experience.

ABBREVIATIONS

AAA	Agricultural Adjustment Administration
AFL	American Federation of Labor
BEW	Board of Economic Warfare
BIA	Bureau of Indian Affairs
CCC	Civilian Conservation Corps
CES	Committee on Economic Security
CIO	Congress of Industrial Organizations
CWA	Civil Works Administration
FERA	Federal Emergency Relief Administration
FSA	Farm Security Administration
FTC	Federal Trade Commission
NAACP	National Association for the Advancement of Colored People
NAM	National Association of Manufacturers
NDAC	National Defense Advisory Commission
NDRC	National Defense Research Committee
NIRA	National Industrial Recovery Act
NLB	National Labor Board
NLRB	National Labor Relations Board
NRA	National Recovery Administration
NYA	National Youth Administration
OPA	Office of Price Administration
OPM	Office of Production Management
OSRD	Office of Scientific Research and Development
OWM	Office of War Mobilization

PWA	Public Works Administration
RA	Resettlement Administration
REA	Rural Electrification Administration
RFC	Reconstruction Finance Corporation
RPAA	Regional Planning Association of America
SPAB	Supplies, Priorities, and Allocations Board
STFU	Southern Tenant Farmers Union
TERA	Temporary Emergency Relief Administration
TNEC	Temporary National Economic Committee
TVA	Tennessee Valley Authority
USDA	United States Department of Agriculture
WPA	Works Progress Administration
WPB	War Production Board
WSA	War Shipping Administration

FRANKLIN ROOSEVELT IN THE SPOTLIGHT

The United States census of 1930 described a nation of nearly 123 million persons. That number represented a modest increase over the previous census and indicated that the country was settling into a period of stable growth after steady declines in immigration and birthrates. In less than thirty years, the center of the nation's population had swept across southern Ohio; for the past twenty years, it had crawled along in southwest Indiana and was expected to cross into Illinois during the next decade.

But it was not going to be a normal decade. Immigration declined nearly 90 percent, and the birthrate fell off by over a third. When the decade was over, the population had grown by less than half its previous averages. The population center was still in Indiana. The population's pattern had also changed. In a nation that had previously been moving from the farm to the city, the rate of urban growth had fallen off by 70 percent; rural nonfarm growth had stayed about the same, and farm growth had increased slightly.[1]

These numbers were a response to a shock of uncertainty and fear that undermined Americans' confidence in their society. We now call that shock the Great Depression, a severe and prolonged time of high unemployment, low wages and prices, closed businesses, and ruined banks, a time when the nation's ability to produce not only slowed but dramatically declined. These were socially created difficulties, but most Americans did not blame their society; instead, they blamed others and even themselves. Voices rose against "the big money men," "dishonest . . . men at the head of this government," "good-for-nothing loafers," "bad managers," "poor providers," and so on. Persons evicted from their homes and apartments or foreclosed off their land lost both pride of ownership and pride in themselves. Such persons often contemplated suicide and occasionally did it. Here and there, resentments flashed into violence. On a freezing March day in 1932, protesting workers marched on the Ford Motor Company to be met with tear gas, dousing from fire hoses, and gunfire from the police. Four of the protesters were killed. A mob of Iowans abducted a judge who was conducting foreclosures on farm properties, threatened his life, and halted the proceedings. New Yorkers stormed two bread trucks and distributed their contents among themselves.[2] In Washington, U.S. Army soldiers attacked a group of war veterans who had marched to Washington to lobby Congress to pay them a bonus.

Many avoided such sufferings, but even they saw the signs of uncertainty: apple and shoe-shine stands multiplying on city streets, strangers coming to their doors to ask for odd jobs soon after the freight trains had come through, lines that stretched for blocks at a place that had announced it was hiring, vacant storefronts, men and women sleeping in parks and under bridges and searching through trash and garbage cans. Who would plan a family when there were so many listless, hollow-eyed children in the schools, when so few jobs were available, when farm prices and factory wages returned so little for weeks and months of hard work?

More and more Americans diverted their energies from producing to surviving. Clothes were stitched and mended again and again, mothers extended meals with watery soups, farmers who could not sell their corn burned it for fuel. When fathers could not find work, mothers and sons went looking; daughters often stayed home to mind the house. People took their silverware and china to pawn shops and secondhand stores, explaining that the items were "just some extra things they had been intending to get rid of." The proprietors nodded and played along.

Such examples could be multiplied indefinitely—as they were among the 123 million Americans of the early 1930s. Indeed, this was what made them important. These experiences were common enough that they produced the result indicated by the census returns.

The social choices that affected the census results were reflections of fundamental weaknesses in the structure of American society. Although it was primarily an economic phenomenon, the depression was the product of weaknesses in American institutions. The triggering event was a crash in the stock market. In October 1929, the stock market, which had climbed steadily all year to astronomical levels, plunged in a series of free falls; by the middle of November, half the value of the stocks that made up the industrial index had been wiped out.[3] The stock market collapse put great pressure on the nation's financial system, comprising banks and investment houses (often called "investment trusts"). Many of the investment houses, which made their money by buying and selling stocks, went down in flames, taking their clients' money with them. That left the nation's finances in the hands of a banking system that was not well prepared to deal with it. One component of the banking system was the Federal Reserve, composed of a central bank and member "national banks" that could draw on the central bank to maintain their capital and stay in business. In addition, there were large regional banks, such as the Bank of New York. Although they were members of the Federal Reserve System, they competed with it for prominence, especially by loaning out money. During the heady days of rising stock prices, much of this credit went into the stock market, where it was wiped out by the crash.

Although such a drop would have been bad enough, it would not have been a disaster if the nation's economic structure had been strong enough to absorb it. But it was not. The reason was that the third banking system, representing two-thirds of the nation's banks and about 40 percent of bank capital, consisted of relatively small, independent institutions that served a local, often rural, market and were no stronger than their local economies. Essentially, they depended on farm prices to stay in business. But during the 1920s, farm prices had been low and rural economies fragile. Rural and small-town bank failures accounted for over 80 percent of all failures during the decade. Rural economies depended on demand from the industrial cities and foreign countries. But two features of American economic practice had weakened these sources of support. Although American manufacturing productivity had increased dramatically during the decade, American wages had not kept pace. Some workers prospered, but their numbers did not grow enough to absorb the increased production, and the vast majority of workers did not keep up. This meant that American production was increasing while American consumption was stagnating. The nation had developed a mass production economy without mass consumption. Sooner or later, stock market crash or not, the economy was headed for trouble. Seeing their sales declining and their inventories accumulating, manufacturers cut production and laid off workers. This, in turn, reduced demand in the city for farm commodities and put pressure on rural banks as farmers failed to repay loans and cut back their purchases at local stores. The stage was set for a productive, prosperous economy to run in reverse.

The domestic economy might have found some relief from international trade, but it too was fragile. During the 1920s, the United States had begun to loan money to Germany so that it could make reparations to Britain and France, which used those payments to repay their war debts to the United States. In other words, American credit was supporting European economies by relieving them of the burdens caused by the war. If the United States withdrew its support, the European economies would weaken or collapse, thus drying up their markets for American products. Supplementing these loans were additional credits advanced by large American banks, principally the Bank of New York. These credits helped maintain the international gold standard as the basis of foreign trade and provided money for Europeans to buy American products. Loss of this credit would both depress trade and endanger the gold standard.

This was where the American stock market proved especially decisive. Even before the crash, American banks had been cutting back their foreign loans to profit from rising stock prices. When the crash came, American banks either failed entirely or called in their loans and decreased lending so they could stay in business. In rural areas, this created a locally destructive cycle in which banks foreclosed and dumped their holdings on the market for whatever they might bring, while anxious depositors, unable to get loans and worried that their banks might fail, withdrew their deposits. Internationally, the cycle was about the same; as American banks cut back their loans to Europe, European banks failed, and their governments abandoned the gold standard.

Lacking markets, American business began laying off workers. Some firms tried to cushion the shock with severance pay, company loans, production planning, and unemployment insurance funds, but the depression overwhelmed their efforts. Although there was no recognized authority to estimate the size of unemployment, the reality of growing joblessness manifested itself in the increasing pressure on the nation's social welfare agencies.[4]

Before the twentieth century, relief for the poor had been administered by a combination of private charities and local government agencies, principally towns and counties. Early in the new century, however, states had begun to establish welfare boards, and by 1930, every state provided for the poor to some degree, primarily in the form of "pensions" to widows with children. Throughout these years, the private charities kept their distance, fearing that involvement with the state would compromise their efforts to improve techniques of social service and anxious to keep political patronage and corruption from infecting their work.[5] During early years of the depression, private charities strove with energy and imagination to help the unemployed. Their campaigns to raise money for relief set records, and relief spending by cities, towns, and counties similarly mounted. New York City's total relief expenditures, both private and public, increased from $13.6 million in 1930 to $79 million in 1932. In theory, this permitted relief allowances of $6.6 million per month at a time when good estimates were that wage losses because of unemployment totaled $80 million to $90 million per month. During this time, the share of relief provided by public agencies far outdistanced that supplied by private agencies.[6]

But the public welfare agencies were also losing the battle of relief. Local jurisdictions depended on property taxes, and their authority to borrow money was sharply limited by state law. As property values and business activity declined, revenues fell off. Financially pressed citizens opposed new taxes. Local governments became increasingly unable to help those who were suffering. Local jurisdictions often compounded the problem by requiring that individuals lose all their wealth before they could qualify for assistance. Thus continued the downward spiral of destitution and demoralization. At its national convention in 1932, the American Association of Social Work, the nation's largest society of private welfare organizations, called for welfare assistance from the federal government.[7]

American churches struggled and survived, but with many casualties. Churches with new mortgages lost their properties. Between 1930 and 1934, collections fell off by half. Different Christian denominations fit the depression into their core theology. Mainline churches called it retribution for sin and preached repentance, but they suffered from their identification with dominant cultural values that were now being called into question. Roman Catholics looked for redemption through suffering and pointed toward the better life in the hereafter. Their numbers increased, although more slowly than in the previous decade. It was the Fundamentalist churches, which saw the depression as a forerunner of the Second Coming of Christ, that prospered. Church membership increased modestly overall, but the Fundamentalists made great gains. Pentecostal and Holiness sects preached faith in God's love for the individual and relief of his or her cares, and their membership grew because of it. Such messages represented the churches' best efforts against the depression, since their resources were far too skimpy to meet the economic need. Indeed, even before the depression, the missionary spirit of the majority Protestant churches had been in decline.[8]

American schools also struggled and survived. The growth in the number of public schools, which had been dramatic since 1910, was reversed. School districts continued to rely on local funding for their support, but state and federal appropriations made up a larger proportion. Still, attendance remained constant, and graduation rates increased by over 50 percent. The income of the nation's colleges and universities dropped steadily between 1930 and 1934, especially from state and local support and from tuition. Colleges and universities tightened their belts by not replacing retired faculty, reducing the starting salaries of those they hired, lengthening the time before promotion, promoting without salary increases, and freezing the overall salary scale. Schools delayed maintenance and construction, reduced library purchases, and cut back support for faculty research. Student enrollments declined by nearly 10 percent. At the same time, public attitudes toward higher education remained positive. In 1937, a study by the American Association of University Professors concluded: "The same motives that drew students to the colleges and universities six and seven years ago still draw them. . . . No other institution has appeared with which young men and women can so readily identify themselves and derive the personal satisfactions that such identification brings."[9]

Local service clubs proved resilient, their membership falling off sharply during the early years of the depression but rebounding to new highs by the end of the decade. For the most part, clubs such as Rotary, Kiwanis, and Lions provided their members a safe respite from the nation's economic trials and worries.[10]

The underlying structure of American political life was its party system. The national tradition of two major political parties was by now long established. Although occasionally challenged by "third-party" or "reform" movements, the fundamental system remained intact. During the late nineteenth century, voter support, almost exclusively male, had run high. This was especially true in urban areas, where social and ethnic diversity created a variety of issues and elections were often decided by a few votes. After 1896, voter participation declined. Reformers injected state regulation into the voting process. Registration requirements, literacy tests, and longer residency requirements all complicated citizens' access to the polls. Voting rates plunged further after the Nineteenth Amendment gave the vote to women, most of whom had no tradition or experience with voting. Still, a major feature of voting was wealth. Historian Paul Kleppner estimated that an additional $1,000 in per capita income would increase voting in a given county by over 46 percent. Also significant was generational change. The children of late-nineteenth-century voters went to the polls at substantially lower rates than their parents had. But more than anything else, the decline in party competition undermined voter participation. The northern industrial cities began voting heavily Republican. In the southern states, the drive to exclude African Americans from politics produced all-white Democratic slates that faced little opposition on election day.[11]

The national consequences of this party configuration had been a decade of Republican domination. In the three presidential elections from 1920 to 1928, the Republican candidate had carried so many states by landslide margins that the Democratic Party was left with little hope of recouping at the next election. In Congress, Republicans enjoyed a margin of twenty-five to fifty seats in the House and (with the exception of a three-vote margin between 1927 and 1929) fifteen seats in the Senate.

The American institutional configuration defined the problems of society and suggested some opportunities for addressing them. The nation's business structure seemed incapable of correcting itself. All the optimistic predictions for a short downturn had proved false, and conditions seemed to be worsening. The widespread suffering and anxiety and the large pool of previously inactive voters suggested the possibility of a popular groundswell that might invigorate governmental institutions to address the crisis. But any approach, whether by government or by other means, would be shaped by certain assumptions about social relationships, problem solving, and leadership. These assumptions can be called pluralism.

Pluralism had emerged in the 1920s. Best defined by the theories of social scientists, pluralism was a departure from earlier assumptions that society could be organized in a fixed and hierarchical fashion in order to "solve" society's problems. Pluralism assumed that life was too complex, varied, and dynamic to be so organized. The core values of pluralism did not look for final solutions but rather a continuous process of decision and action, action and decision. Similarly, they downplayed the role of expertise, reducing the expert from the leader who knew all the answers to the facilitator who helped others improve their answers. They forsook confidence in the ability of experts to predict certain effects from certain causes. Fundamentally, they abandoned the belief in large systems, in the idea that a society and its parts could be connected in chains of causes so that the particular led inevitably to the general, to a single point that embodied the essence and purpose of the parts. What was left was a society of parts that interacted with one another and formed larger wholes, but did so in unpredictable ways. This meant that there was no large truth, no paramount leader, no foreseeable future, no long run. It meant that social analysis needed to understand the parts, to look at the grass roots, the small society. It meant that societies developed in ways that were essentially historical, that were peculiar to time and place.

It did not mean, however, that there were no larger truths or wholes. There were, but they were formed through historical processes and assumed shapes that were unique to particular times. Noted political scientist Luther Gulick used the metaphor of the Venus de Milo. This famous statue was composed of many small grains of sand. But the grains did not form a larger grain of sand, they formed a particular work of art. The whole formed by the grains was greater than the sum of its parts. And the whole was different from other statues created at other times. Pluralism's political analysis treated government and society as continually interacting and being changed by those interactions. Chicago sociologist Robert Park, who in the 1920s developed an influential school of urban sociology, put it this way: "The thing which distinguishes an organism from a mere aggregation of individuals, or parts, is the capacity for concerted action—the disposition of the parts, under certain conditions, to act as a unit."[12] It was this ability to act as a unit that made it possible for groups of persons to form wholes that were greater than the sum of their parts.

The vocabulary of pluralism defined terms such as *region, community, commonwealth,* and *federation*. These terms suggested a collectivity, but one whose parts either retained an important degree of autonomy or formed a larger whole that was different from other wholes.

As a guide to government policy, pluralism called for government to serve as a coordinator that facilitated problem solving by bringing together various perspectives, teams of experts who could address the multidimensional features of a given situation. Government policy could not be too general, centralized, or prescriptive. It had to value local conditions; its goal had to be to empower and enable those at the local, or grassroots, level to join for a common effort. Social units that worked in this way would prosper.[13] The expression of pluralism in the nation's political experience would be the presidency of Franklin D. Roosevelt.[14]

Franklin Roosevelt was born to the seventh generation of Dutch immigrants whose last name means "rose field." An ancestor, Nicholas, had moved up the Hudson River from Manhattan to trap furs and trade with the Indians, a career that prospered and expanded. When Nicholas returned to New York, he became prominent in business and politics. The following generations of Roosevelts showed that they were devoted to their community, ready to protest intrusions on its interests, and equally determined to preserve the social order from which they prospered. They invested well, kept their noses clean politically, and displayed something of a family talent for marrying well. A particularly fortunate marriage to a sister of William Aspinwall, who was to become one of America's wealthiest merchant princes, led to the birth in 1828 of James, whose business ventures in coal and railroads gained him comfortable wealth.

Comfort seemed to be the measure of James. He married a daughter of his mother's first cousin and in 1865 relocated the family to Springwood in the southern part of the village of Hyde Park, New York. He established gardens, raised crops, imported dairy cows, and eventually produced enough to pay for the upkeep of a place in New York City. He became a vestryman and warden of St. James Episcopal Church and a manager of the state hospital, and he promoted the local public schools. After his wife died, his son moved nearby and introduced him to Sara Delano. She was nearing twenty-six, a slender, dark-eyed young woman with strong features. Had she chosen, she could have been something of a beauty, but instead she held herself in a manner that conveyed strength of character, serious purpose, and proper breeding. These were qualities honored and expected by her father, whom she adored and whose stern, narrow, judgmental views she never questioned. Sara and James married on October 7, 1880. They circulated in the closed, privileged world of their mid–Hudson River society and traveled to Europe. James doted on "my Sallie" and was attentive to her welfare. Sara was pleased by his attentions; deferred to him, as was the fashion of the day; and pursued her role as mistress of their home with bustling efficiency. In the spring, Sara became pregnant. On the evening of January 29, she began a prolonged and excruciating labor that almost ended tragically when the doctor administered too much chloroform and literally had to breathe life into her newborn son by mouth-to-mouth resuscitation. Both son and mother soon recovered, and before James staggered off to catch his first sleep in more than twenty-four hours, he noted the arrival of "a splendid large baby boy," whom they would name Franklin Delano Roosevelt.

From the first, James and Sara incorporated Franklin into their lives. Sara breast-fed, bathed, and dressed him for the first year. They carefully selected nursemaids who accompanied them on their rounds of outings and travels. When he was a year and a half they visited Campobello Island, just across the Canadian border off the coast of Maine, and decided to establish a summer home there. A few months later they enrolled their son as a prospective student at the newly planned Groton School. They permitted Franklin to develop his interests and to play with others his age but expected him always to be a "gentleman," courteous, self-controlled, and dignified, tolerant and friendly toward his inferiors but careful never to descend to their level. He developed a gentlemanly deportment that often concealed a painful shyness and a fierce competitive spirit. If he was awkward in others' presence, he was determined to beat them in any competition. Among his peers, however, he asserted his authority, always giving orders because, as he explained to his mother, who was concerned that he was too bossy, "if I didn't give the orders, nothing would happen!"[15]

The young man became a collector, beginning at age nine with postage stamps and continuing with birds' eggs and nests and eventually the birds themselves. An enthusiastic shooter, he set out to kill and mount an example of every species in Dutchess County, and by the time he was through he had collected some 300 specimens. He kept a careful record of his ornithological findings until he gave up the hobby in 1896; he was an avid stamp collector for the rest of his life. He developed an abiding love of the sea and became a strong swimmer. In his studies, he showed an ability to master languages and to retain factual information.

In these ways, Franklin Delano Roosevelt emerged from his boyhood an excellent example of his culture. His world was filled with people who were used to getting their way. They were achievers, not because the world owed them servility or even deference, but because the things they were able to do made life better. When Victorian Americans spoke about wealth they often used the word *means,* which conveyed the idea that money gave one the ability to accomplish something. More than anything, James and Sara's generation was made up of takers and users. They contrived ways of getting minerals out of the earth and from them fashioning the sinews of material progress. More important, they were organizers who invented ways of systematizing their environments, inventing mechanical contrivances whose parts meshed and that complemented other contrivances to create a world of convenience and power. They were also inventors of organizations, large bureaucratic structures that concentrated power at a central point and projected its interests and influence over vast areas. Theirs was a confidence of people who knew what they were doing and knew that it was for the common good.

From his early years, Franklin acquired a firm religious faith, taught by the Episcopal Church, that Jesus Christ had died to redeem the sins of humankind and that God had endowed the human soul with the ability to do good so that after death good persons would go to heaven. He was an optimist, based on his faith that God had created an order in the world that rewarded faith, goodwill, and effort. Essentially, Franklin Roosevelt sought to achieve the proper structure of power.

At age fourteen he entered Groton Academy. He compiled a very good academic record, performed poorly at sports, and seemed a bit too argumentative to some of his classmates. From there he enrolled in Harvard College. During his first term, his father died. Sara was devastated by the loss of the man to whom she had become thoroughly devoted. In his stead, she turned her affections and support to Franklin. Here was the first important power relationship that Franklin had to manage. A competitive person who believed that things worked best when he gave the orders, he was not inclined to yield to his mother's every direction. Yet he was a loyal, loving, and dutiful son who had limited himself to such independence as his parents had permitted him. And so he developed the art of appearing to yield to her and disguising his own purposes. If his deceptions failed, however, he would avoid conflict by giving up his position.[16] Part of his strategy was to convince her of his manliness. At Groton and again at Harvard, he tried out for the football team. Failing to make the varsity, he played for the scrubs and peppered his letters home with comments on his various injuries, showing his hope that she would accept his growing to manhood.

At Harvard he offended some by his easy assumption of a superior social status and his soft, eager-to-please manner. But others knew him as a hard worker who took advantage of his opportunities, sympathized with the underdog, and wanted to be of service to society. He worked hard on the college paper, the *Crimson,* writing editorials encouraging more spirit at football games, more democracy in campus elections (that is, less slate-making by social clubs), and fire protection in the dormitories. Notably, he encouraged everyone to broaden their acquaintanceships, to learn more about their fellow students.

During his latter college years, Franklin met his fifth cousin, Anna Eleanor. In the fall of 1903, they became privately engaged. Sara disapproved of Franklin's choice and might well have disapproved of his choosing any woman over her. But Franklin prevailed against his mother's various attempts to delay the marriage, and on March 17, 1905, he and Eleanor were married. The bride, both of whose parents had died years earlier, was given in marriage by her uncle, President Theodore Roosevelt. After their honeymoon they returned to New York, where Franklin attended law school at Columbia University. Children rapidly followed, and by 1916 the Roosevelts were a family of seven.

Admitted to the New York bar in 1906, Roosevelt was hired by a prestigious city firm. By this time, however, he had decided that his career was to be politics. His first opportunity came in 1910 when the Poughkeepsie Democratic leadership offered him the chance to run for the state senate from Dutchess County. Accepting what seemed an impossible assignment, Roosevelt proceeded to carry on a vigorous campaign. Covering his district in a motorcar, something that no previous candidate had attempted, Roosevelt concentrated on the normally Republican farmer vote, denouncing the corrupt bossism of the state and local Republican Party organization. It was a Democratic year, but Roosevelt showed his own particular strength by emerging as the leading vote-getter on the ticket.

In Albany, his politics combined economic justice for the farmer with upstate distaste for city bosses. He tussled with New York City's Tammany Hall machine and supported a Progressive agenda that included low-cost loans to farmers, cooperative marketing, the conservation of natural resources, and the direct election of U.S. senators. Chairing the senate's Forest, Fish, and Game Committee, he collaborated with Gifford Pinchot, who had recently become the darling of Progressive conservationists in a struggle over resource management within the Taft administration, to revise the fish and game laws and to establish better forest management and fire protection policies. His aversion to Tammany blinded him to the ways in which the city Democrats were developing alliances with working people and, from those alliances, labor policies and welfare legislation. He failed to show up for the critical vote establishing a fifty-four-hour workweek for women and children—a misstep that caused the bill's major proponent, a labor reformer named Frances Perkins, to think him a poor choice for governor sixteen years later. Along the way, he made several tactical blunders, from which he gained an appreciation of Tammany's practical skills and the virtues of not alienating his political party base.[17]

During this time his political ideas began to emerge. He essentially accepted the New Nationalist version of Progressivism, preached by "cousin Ted" in his campaign against the reactionary Republican Old Guard. The liberty of the individual, he said, had to give way to the liberty of the community, which in turn would no longer be defined by the sum of the wants of the population but by "scientific," rational leadership that assumed a basic harmony of interests in the community. Although they were sketchy and imperfectly stated, Roosevelt's ideas assumed that the good society was composed of functional groups, that each person had a role to play, and that it was society's job to give that person a chance to play it. The means to this end was regulation by government, and regulation was to be based on expert knowledge of humanity and society. Social knowledge determined the function of each person and group. In a sense, it determined the value of that person or group in the system of society. Regulation encouraged that group to act reasonably in carrying out its role so that the social system would work efficiently.

In 1912, Roosevelt's Progressivism led him to support Woodrow Wilson for the Democratic nomination. During his own campaign for reelection, he acquired the services of journalist Louis McHenry Howe. Gnomic, wizened, and asthmatic, and with a perpetually dirty-gray face and slovenly clothes liberally sprinkled with ash from an ever-present cigarette, Howe had become one of New York's most knowledgeable political journalists. He had long been searching for someone he might groom for the presidency, and when he met Roosevelt in Albany, he believed that he had found a likely man.

Roosevelt won reelection, but before he could serve, Wilson appointed him assistant secretary of the navy. Arriving in Washington, Roosevelt plunged into making the Navy Department more efficient. He molded his traits into tools of executive leadership. His assets were his energy, nimble mind, boldness, tactical flexibility, and self-confidence. He had the courage of a gambler to take risks on the future. He was impatient with abstractions and focused on the particulars of the present situation, was little inclined to self-examination or circumspection, did not lack audacity, and was quick to break with traditions if they would frustrate immediate objectives. He wanted more freedom to act decisively. He personally investigated blunders and failures, separating lines of authority, and reassigned jurisdictions. The navy would be as compartmentalized as everything else in the well-ordered Victorian home. He backed away, however, when labor objected to the introduction of the "Taylor" principles of scientific management into the navy yards, claiming that they would exert too much pressure on the workers and eliminate too many jobs. Now his goal was to produce a first-class navy, not to advance social or economic reform. He fell out of step with his chief, Josephus Daniels, as well as with President Wilson and a majority of the cabinet, by supporting an aggressive naval strategy to advance American interests, but in the process he won the confidence of the officer corps. He supported American intervention in Haiti to prevent European penetration of the Caribbean. When he visited Haiti he winked at the slave-labor methods by which the marine commander had built roads, called all Haitians who resisted American authority "bandits," and contented himself with seeing what his conquering army commanders wanted him to see and accepting their interpretations at face value. When the United States declared war in 1917, he displayed the Roosevelt family talent for entrepreneurship. He was impatient with procrastination and fiddling with small details. He was capable of large vision and of developing ways to achieve it. His principal objective was to create large amounts of naval craft to meet any contingency. He was a builder and a strategist—a taker and a user after the traditions of the "robber barons." His efforts also showed his stubbornness, his perseverance. He was a determined person. He employed his own architect and gave him a free hand in advising navy construction.

During this time he had an affair with Lucy Mercer, whom he had employed as Eleanor's social secretary and occasional housekeeper. In 1918, when he was recovering from influenza, Eleanor learned of the affair. Devastated, she offered Franklin a divorce, but Sara would not hear of it and threatened to cut him off if he left Eleanor. Divorce would have ended his political career; the Fundamentalist Daniels would have fired him, and the scandal would have hounded his every public act. Caught between love and political ambition, he resolved the conflict by lying to Lucy that Eleanor would not divorce him.[18]

As the war ended and the presidential election of 1920 approached, Roosevelt and Howe began planning his presidential prospects. They mapped out a program of regulation of securities and railroads, highway construction, consumer cooperatives, labor's right to organize, profit-sharing, tax laws to prevent profiteering, and borrowing to finance public works as a safeguard against depression. The convention nominated James M. Cox of Ohio, with Roosevelt second. He campaigned vigorously, stumping the Midwest and the Plains. During the campaign, he acquired the services of a secretary named Marguerite "Missy" LeHand.

After Cox lost the election to Republican Warren G. Harding, Roosevelt spent several months defending his record as assistant secretary against partisan Republican queries. Finally, in July 1921, he traveled to Campobello

Eleanor and Franklin Roosevelt on the south lawn of their Hyde Park estate, August 16, 1933. Hyde Park was always more of a home to Franklin than to Eleanor. (Franklin D. Roosevelt Library)

to be with Eleanor and his children. After a particularly strenuous day, he was taken by a violent chill. After a restless night, he awoke to find that his legs barely functioned. As the day wore on, the pain grew worse. He knew that there was something very wrong.

What was wrong was poliomyelitis, which, accompanied by a raging fever and immense pain, deprived him of movement and dignity. It was a crisis that demanded all his resources and those of Eleanor and Louis Howe. They attained a proper diagnosis from a New York physician, who predicted a complete recovery, and bent their efforts to a regime of determined cheerfulness. Throughout the disease and its agonizing, frustrating, hope-denying course, Roosevelt exhibited great strength. He never complained about his pain and remained optimistic that he would fully recover. He believed that some of his muscles had survived the attack and could be "educated" to do the work that would restore him to normalcy. He rejected pity and treated others just as he had when he was well. He frankly acknowledged his condition, throwing back the covers to show his sons his withered legs, and giving them a lesson in anatomy by pointing out the various muscles. The savagery of his early symptoms had shaken him, because he had been helpless. During his months of relative inactivity, he continually asserted, against all evidence, that he was improving and would fully recover.

For the next years, Roosevelt concentrated on regaining his health. As he recovered, he found ways to battle and outwit his infirmity. He devised ways to fish, climb stairs, take books from the shelf, walk with leg braces and crutches, and ride horseback. When swimming in the warm waters off Florida seemed to help his condition, he looked for a location that he could visit regularly. That turned out to be Warm Springs, Georgia, an old, run-down health resort. Hoping to establish a national center to treat polio, Roosevelt invested heavily in its development. Eventually, the facility attracted other sufferers from the disease, whom Roosevelt welcomed and encouraged. Although he gained the ability to walk with a cane, with someone supporting him on the other side, only when swimming or sailing was he entirely free of his confining disability.

No one can say how, or even if, Roosevelt's condition affected his personality or his outlook on life. It seems clear that he feared being trapped in an enclosed space, such as an elevator, or being trapped in a fire. He also relished showing that he could overcome his limitations, especially by manipulating the hand controls on his motorcar to drive wildly about his Hyde Park estate, frustrating reporters and on one occasion terrifying Prime Minister Winston Churchill. He empathized with fellow polio victims and consistently did what he could to lift their spirits and look to the future with optimism. Once when he was governor, Roosevelt interrupted a tour of facilities along the state's canal system to speak with a boy whose leg was in a brace. A trooper helped the boy aboard the canal boat. Roosevelt examined his brace, showed him his own braces, and encouraged the boy to do his exercises and not become discouraged. "You can get along as well as your friends," he said, "in everything except running and jumping." The boy hugged and kissed Roosevelt and insisted on getting off the boat without assistance. At Warm Springs, Roosevelt mingled with the patients, accepting them, treating them as "normal," helping them overcome their doubts, fears, and shame.[19]

The most obvious trait brought out by Roosevelt's illness was his inner courage. Somehow he had developed a sense that, left to himself, he could master any challenge. Whatever might befall him, he would still be Franklin

Delano Roosevelt; nothing could alter or damage his inner core. Perhaps this belief had been shaped by the secure and loving nurture of his parents, perhaps by his comfortable advantages in the steady social order of the Hudson Valley, perhaps by his simple but unshakable religious faith.

What seems more problematic is the idea that his experience with polio enlarged his social sympathies. He acquired the social assumptions common to his era and class, but he seems not to have depended on them for his inner security. He could assume that most blacks would be servants but was not shocked by those who were not. He could tolerate and even enjoy anti-Semitic remarks but would not shun Jews as friends or collaborators. Throughout his life he would occasionally ascribe character and personality traits to ethnic groups and would appear to accept generalizations about a people's "national character," but he would never allow these alone to guide his sense of a just domestic or world order.

Anyone who tries to understand how polio affected Roosevelt's personality or character runs into the same problem when trying to understand how any of his experiences affected him. For all his inner strength, Roosevelt never developed a capacity for real intimacy. His inner self did not depend on others. Thus, he did not leave behind a true record of his inner nature: he composed no memoirs, and his private letters and occasional journals and diaries are notable for their consistent blandness. It seems clear that he needed people, but he needed them to help him accomplish his purposes. His personal attachments came and went. Because he had great inner strength and because he was able to convey strength to others, many people became devoted to him, and he could count on a core group that would work in his interest. It may be that polio enhanced this inspirational quality, but there is no way of telling.

During the early years of Roosevelt's illness, Louis Howe took charge of his political fortunes and enlisted Eleanor as his aide. Together they visited political rallies, gathered political information, and guarded his public image. As Eleanor broadened her acquaintance with these things, she made it a point to educate Franklin about them. Thus, Roosevelt, who had begun as a good-government reformer and moved to a business-efficiency Progressive, moved more and more into line with Tammany Hall reformers who wanted to provide for the safety and welfare of the state's working people. These sympathies led him to support Al Smith, the reform governor, whom Roosevelt nominated at the Democratic National Convention in 1924.

Throughout the decade, Roosevelt struck the pose of the party regular, bidding for party unity and harmony. He was so successful at this that when Smith won the nomination in 1928, Democratic leaders believed that Roosevelt had to run for governor if Smith was to carry New York.

After a hesitation that was based on his belief that holding office would delay or even end his recovery, he accepted. Conducting a vigorous campaign in which he emphasized state issues that focused on agriculture and labor, he was narrowly elected in an overwhelmingly Republican year. Aware of Roosevelt's concern for his recovery, Smith had assumed that Roosevelt would be a figurehead governor whose moves would be directed by his aides and by Lieutenant Governor Herbert Lehman. But, encouraged by Eleanor, Roosevelt immediately grasped control of his own administration. It was the beginning of ill feeling between him and Smith. Facing Republican majorities in both houses of the state legislature, he suffered many defeats but used the time to appoint an able staff and to cement relations with the Democrats in the legislature.

In Albany, with his hands on executive power for the first time, Roosevelt established his credentials as a left-of-center reformer. Facing a Republican-controlled state legislature that was almost certain to defeat or water down his proposals, he used special commissions to publicize the need for laws that favored farmers and workers. For agriculture he was able to get through measures on tax relief (which shifted the burden from poor counties to rich counties) and pest control. As farm prices remained low and the hardships of the depression hit rural areas, he acquainted himself with the "domestic allotment" proposals of agricultural economists M. L. Wilson and Rexford Tugwell. He combined land reform with conservation by securing funds to purchase marginal farmland for reforestation. He advocated the development of public power from the proposed development of the St. Lawrence River and state ownership of transmission lines.

During the early stages of the depression, Roosevelt sat back and hoped that optimistic predictions of a quick recovery would come true. He even postponed recommendations for tighter regulation of the state's banking system until the collapse of the Bank of the United States created a public outcry for action. Later, as evidence mounted that conditions were worsening and that local and private resources were nearing exhaustion, he acted. He recommended unemployment and old-age insurance and convened a regional governors conference to discuss the idea. At his recommendation the legislature created the Temporary Emergency Relief Administration (TERA) to provide "home relief," payments that the unemployed could use to purchase necessities to maintain a basic standard of living, and "work relief" in the form of employment projects that would pay cash wages. Roosevelt appointed a board of directors and named Harry Hopkins administrative director. Under Hopkins's guidance, TERA upgraded relief standards in the towns and counties and had such a good record that when Roosevelt and the legislature recommended its continuation with a $30 million bond issue, the voters overwhelmingly approved.[20]

In the meantime, Roosevelt was increasing his stature in the Democratic Party. When he moved to Albany, he balanced his appointments between supporters of former governor Al Smith and his own people. He brought in many who would move with him to Washington: Raymond Moley, Samuel Rosenman, Frances Perkins, and James Farley. Gradually, he drew away from Smith. In 1930, when Roosevelt was reelected by margins that exceeded any of Smith's, it was obvious that the two would part company. As the popular governor of the state with the most electoral votes, Roosevelt had become presidential timber with a claim on the prize that Smith, the defeated candidate in 1928, wanted. The two engaged in a statewide test of strength when Smith opposed a constitutional amendment that would authorize Roosevelt's reforestation projects. When the measure passed with 58 percent of the vote, Smith disingenuously declared that he was through with politics, and his supporters undertook a campaign to undermine Roosevelt's candidacy. By early 1932, Smith was a declared presidential candidate, and Roosevelt was going to have to fight for the nomination.[21]

Roosevelt faced his own political liabilities. No man with a serious physical disability had ever sought the presidency, and his opponents were certain to question his stamina. As a Wilsonian internationalist who had supported the United States' membership in the League of Nations, he was open to attack from the powerful Hearst press. For some reason, a few journalists, including columnist Walter Lippmann, were inclined to dismiss him as a lightweight, as a pleasant fellow with no edge, despite his record of achievement and liberal policies. More tellingly, he found himself embroiled with Tammany Hall, this time over evidence of corruption in the mayoral administration of Democrat James J. Walker. The issue was important to Roosevelt, since Al Smith was strong in the Northeast and he needed to pick up support in the South and West, which looked with great suspicion on any presidential hopeful with Tammany Hall connections. His political career seemed to be circling back on him. In 1911 he had attacked Tammany and bungled; now another bungle might be politically fatal. For a while he temporized, drawing fire from the press, the liberals, and upstate leaders. As spring turned into summer and the convention neared, the Tammany issue lay unresolved.[22]

Roosevelt did not let such matters divert him from his quest for the presidency. Louis Howe and James Farley set up a correspondence operation with Democrats around the country. A team of specialists pronounced Roosevelt physically fit. He announced that the United States should stay out of the League of Nations because it was taken up with internal European problems. He made speeches and radio talks criticizing the Hoover administration on various grounds. He worked with organization leaders in the South, the Midwest, and the Plains, picking up enough delegates to have a majority when the Democratic convention gathered in Chicago.

Roosevelt's problem was that under the convention rules it took two-thirds of the delegates to nominate a candidate. With Al Smith strong in the Northeast and Speaker of the House John Nance Garner of Texas holding his home state and California, there were enough votes outstanding to stymie his bid. To do this, however, his opponents needed to hang together long enough to convince the delegates that Roosevelt could not win and to start them drifting away in search of a more viable candidate, who most likely would have been Newton D. Baker, Wilson's secretary of war, a confirmed internationalist, and an economic conservative.

And so it might have happened. Convening in the evening, the delegates sat through the night as the nominating speeches droned on. It was dawn before the first of three ballots was taken, all of which showed Roosevelt well ahead and gaining, but still about ninety votes short of the nomination. When the convention adjourned and the exhausted delegates staggered out, it was obvious that the next ballot would be the last for Roosevelt. Farley and Howe decided to stake everything on turning Garner and approached Congressman Sam Rayburn, Garner's floor manager, who promised to "see what can be done." Both Garner and Rayburn were party men who had gone to the convention thinking that the choice would be Garner or Roosevelt.[23] They feared nothing so much as a deadlocked convention. Garner authorized Rayburn to switch his delegates to Roosevelt. When Rayburn reported back that Texas would not switch unless Roosevelt took Garner as vice president, Garner accepted, willing "to do anything to see the Democrats win one more national election."[24]

From the first, Roosevelt had decided to put the spotlight on himself. He rejected the tradition by which presidential nominees were advised of their good fortune by a committee of party leaders and boarded a plane for Chicago. There on July 2 he addressed the cheering delegates. To everyone—businessmen, farmers, investors, home owners, the unemployed and destitute—he promised support and relief. In the spirit of having broken with tradition, he pledged "a new deal for the American people." The words "new deal" were old and shopworn, but the next day when Sam Rosenman spotted an editorial cartoon with an airplane flying the banner "New Deal," the campaign and Roosevelt's presidency gained their identity.[25]

By the time of his nomination, Roosevelt had assembled a team of advisers who came to be known as his "Brain Trust." Recruited by Roosevelt's counsel Sam Rosenman, they were college professors associated with New York's Columbia University and its associated women's school,

Barnard College. Its principal figure was Raymond Moley, professor of public law and veteran of urban reform politics. It also included Rexford Guy Tugwell, professor of economics and an expert on agriculture and economic planning, and Adolf Berle, professor of law and an authority on corporate organization and finance. On the periphery of this core circulated influential businessmen and politicians, most notably Bernard Baruch, a wealthy speculator and self-styled authority on government finance and organization. During World War I, Baruch had headed the War Industries Board, which allocated materials for war production and balanced military and civilian claims on the economy. From this experience, he had attained an impressive reputation that subsequent scholarship has failed to sustain. Prominent political advisers included Senators James Byrnes of South Carolina and Key Pittman of Nevada, chair of the Senate Foreign Relations Committee.

The job of the Brain Trust was to provide ideas that Roosevelt could shape into a direction for his presidency. Because he was so accessible and so encouraging to those who presented ideas to him, some came to believe that they were engaged in a struggle for control of his thinking. But they were mistaken. Roosevelt was neither an absorber of information nor a coordinator of others' views; he was a taker and a builder who took ideas and people, tried them out, and found some useful place for them.

Roosevelt's method was to press his advisers and other interested parties to agree among themselves. He would encourage all viewpoints by saying that he was keeping an open mind, but when the time came, he would insist on a final statement that represented a consensus rather than a victory for only one side. This method established a direction of policy but embraced sufficient complexities and ambiguities to allow for adjustments to circumstances. It also often frustrated the advisers, especially the college professors used to having their way in discussions of ideas. "We never could really talk to Roosevelt," Tugwell recalled, "we had to talk with him. If we did not catch his interest, he would shift to another subject; if we did, it became a dialogue. . . . It might be only when I thought it over afterward that I knew he had not been convinced. It was an exchange, but there was not often any conclusion. . . . But all our talk was so fair and friendly that there was never a time when defeat was so definite that I finally gave up."[26]

In one sense, Roosevelt's methods aided decision making. Any decision made with the expectation that it could be easily changed could be easily made. Nor at this stage was it necessary to fix the details of public policy. During this formative period it was more necessary to establish a general direction than to establish a specific program.

Policy decisions went hand in hand with political calculations. Roosevelt's political base was in the southern and western states, which during hard times had suffered the most and had been most hospitable to economic reform. During the Brain Trust deliberations, Roosevelt spoke of reforming the Democratic Party into a "progressive" party under a South and West alliance. Still, Roosevelt was wary of assuming a progressive stance too early. Progressives, he believed, were too individualistic. Their efforts lacked coordination and solidarity; they were good fighters, but not good soldiers. The conservatives knew how to stick together, and this kind of discipline caused Roosevelt to avoid moving too rapidly.[27]

Politics also gave Roosevelt an ideological direction. Hoover's campaigning on the theme of American individualism encouraged Roosevelt to accept ideas that stressed cooperation, planning, and long-term solutions.

Roosevelt drew political lessons from Woodrow Wilson. Wilson's mistake, he believed, had been to waste his political capital too early in his administration. Thus Roosevelt was inclined to develop a comprehensive reform package and not to concentrate on only a few projects.

Although there was much flexibility and room for maneuver and adjustment in Roosevelt's planning, certain directional lines emerged. Roosevelt's rejection of Hoover's individualism inclined him to look for ideas that emphasized relations among groups and institutions and that viewed society in structural terms, as parts whose relationships needed to be readjusted. His desire not to move to the left too rapidly caused him to sympathize with ideas close to the heart of Baruch and his allies, such as balancing the federal budget. This suggested an opposition to federal bureaucracy and coercive federal programs, balanced by a willingness to create temporary emergency agencies to combat the depression, as Wilson had done to prosecute the war effort. A South and West political alliance suggested a concern for debtors, since schemes for debtor relief had been their historic response to hard times. This led to proposals to raise prices to producers by liberalizing credit and to use governmental power to control speculation and stabilize economic activity.[28]

The contribution of the Brain Trust was to shape these ideas. They began by accepting the trend in the American economy toward domination by large producers. This structure, they believed, should be reorganized so that more Americans could share its wealth. To a degree, they were all "planners" who were willing to use the power of government to accomplish their ends. Most favored a "targeted" approach, with specific government policies aimed at specific industries or economic sectors. They differed on points of emphasis. Tugwell argued that the supply of goods was adequate for prosperity and wanted to increase consumer demand by increasing farm prices and industrial wages. Berle wanted to induce an overall rise in prices to pay off the burden of debt and unfreeze assets. In the end, these differences mattered less than the Brain Trusters' ultimate objective of establishing a stable and socially just economic order.[29]

This approach sat well with Roosevelt, who wanted to combine ideas and begin a process. The risk he ran was that he might appear inconsistent and contradictory, giving both the public and his own advisers the idea that he was indecisive and unable to lead.

It was this aspect of his strategic thinking that provided the opening for Rexford Tugwell. The key considerations, Tugwell argued, were not levels of debt, prices, or wages but the relationships among them. Thus, rail rates should be coordinated not only with steel prices but also with textile and chemical prices. All should be taken as part of wholes and run together. "If all . . . industries were able to bring pressures on each other," he once declared, "if they bargained, made mutual arrangements, and so really related themselves to a whole market complex, an equitable situation might be restored."[30]

It was Tugwell's ability to think in terms of larger wholes that enabled him to contribute the key conception of balance: that a healthy economy needed various healthy sectors. This pointed Roosevelt's thinking toward those sectors most in need and toward the problem of American agriculture. He began with the idea of raising farm income and then moved to rural and regional planning. Inclined to romanticize rural life, he thought that the only way to deal with massive urban employment was to relocate city folk to the countryside. Rural improvement would provide jobs as well as a better environment.[31]

By 1932, the debate over farm policy had produced three variations. The most popular, known by the names of its congressional sponsors Senator Charles McNary and Representative Nils Haugen, called on the federal government to establish tariffs to discourage foreign competition and to purchase surplus crops to sell overseas, thus leaving American farmers free to sell at good prices in a protected market. Another approach, called "cost of production," would simply have the federal government fix the cost of farm products at a level that guaranteed farmers a profit. A third, called "domestic allotment," would regulate production by paying farmers to reduce their output. Underlying these approaches was the problem of farm credit, which was aggravated because land banks did not want to take responsibility amid such high failure rates. They argued that only higher prices would solve the problems. Different solutions were proposed, but all advocated more government subsidies for credit.[32]

The farm policy issue, then, epitomized the New Deal's dilemma. On the one hand, Roosevelt and his Brain Trust wanted coordinated policies that established mutually supportive relationships among the economy's different sectors. This was an approach for long-term prosperity and economic stability. On the other hand, farmers and farm organizations favored policies that would raise farm prices and provide easy farm credit.[33] Roosevelt's willingness during the campaign to appeal to all factions and ideological positions served the political purpose of attracting the largest possible following. Once in office, however, he would have to make choices. And in making those choices, Roosevelt would be defining his presidency essentially by losing supporters. Such a course was common to the administrations of active presidents. What was also common to successful and active presidents was their ability to maintain a political base on which they could govern. This task would come to Roosevelt's presidency sooner than he might have expected.

Roosevelt designed his campaign speeches to address the key issues facing the nation and to suggest politically viable approaches. The political necessities of campaigning inevitably caused some distortion of Roosevelt's views but did not break their essential lineaments. In keeping with his desire to see things in interrelated wholes, he attempted to present a central message of coordinating and balancing the economy by increasing farm incomes while restraining the ability of large producers to fix prices. At the same time, he believed that campaign strategy required him to speak to the needs of individual Americans, whose priorities were to earn a living and provide for their families. This, he believed, required him to speak in ways that suggested individualism. Further pressures in this direction came from economic conservatives such as Bernard Baruch, who wanted no tinkering with the gold standard or government intervention in the economy. Pressure on the other side came from the need to establish a base from which to attack Herbert Hoover. During the campaign, Hoover appealed to American individualism, charging that Roosevelt would use big government to regiment people's lives, while Roosevelt consistently suggested ways that government policies could alleviate the crisis.

During his campaign for the nomination, Roosevelt had outlined a number of important themes. He continually spoke in terms of relationships. He would restore rural purchasing power by increasing farm prices, protecting farm property from foreclosure, stimulating foreign trade, and attending to "ten or a dozen vital factors." When he spoke about Thomas Jefferson, he praised him for being "one of the first to recognize the community of interest between the shipowner in New York and the boatman on the upper reaches of the Ohio . . . one of the first to preach the interdependence of town and country and . . . to bring to the crusty conservatism of . . . the eastern seaboard the hopes and aspirations of the pioneer."[34]

Roosevelt rejected Hoover's claim that foreign economic problems were causing the depression. Indeed, he charged that Hoover's policies caused foreign economies to weaken and collapse. The causes of the depression were domestic, according to Roosevelt, and these problems needed to be addressed by a national agreement and leadership willing to engage in "bold, persistent experimentation." His role would be "to compose the conflicting elements of these various plans, to gather the benefits of the long study and consideration of them, to coordinate efforts to the end that agreement may be reached."[35]

Roosevelt continually emphasized that his calls for national unity did not mean government control, as Hoover was charging. He attempted to manage the distinction between "cooperation" and "regimentation" by attacking business actions and government policies that sacrificed the interest of consumers for high prices and profits. Indeed, he charged that the true regimentation of the American economy had been directed by "an informal group, an unofficial group, amounting to an economic Government of the United States." He zeroed in on "speculation" and "concentrated economic power," specifying the utility companies and the securities traders. He attacked the Republican Smoot-Hawley tariff for protecting business from competition and stifling the trade on which small business depended. He attacked the "haphazardness" and "gigantic waste" of the nation's economic growth, especially the "unjustified" investment of capital in enterprises that turned out "products far beyond the capacity of the Nation to absorb."[36]

Roosevelt suggested specific policies. He would control speculation by requiring "truth telling" by securities traders, regulating "holding companies that sell securities in interstate commerce," requiring "more rigid supervision" of the national banks, and separating investment banking from commercial banking. His policy for agriculture proposed conducting a national soil survey to determine which lands were most suitable for agriculture, reducing the farmers' tax burden, expanding farm credit, and lowering tariffs to promote trade. He proposed reducing the difference between farm income and expense by instituting tariff protection that would increase prices without provoking foreign retaliation. The plan would be self-financing and use "existing agencies" and "be decentralized . . . so that the chief responsibility for its operation will rest in the locality." It would also be cooperative and voluntary. Similarly, he proposed a national transportation policy and national and state development and regulation of electric power.[37]

On September 23, Roosevelt stated his views most sweepingly at the Commonwealth Club in San Francisco. His topic was, as he said, not politics but government. Roosevelt proposed an economic social contract based on the principles of the Declaration of Independence—life, liberty, and the pursuit of happiness—updated for the modern economic order. He briefly reviewed the rise of centralized government in Europe, the threat of despotism that it produced, and the reaction of the American colonies, resulting in American independence and the struggle between Thomas Jefferson and Alexander Hamilton to see whether the individual or the state would dominate. Jefferson's victory and the subsequent triumph of individualism led in the late nineteenth century to a conflict with the industrial revolution and its concentrations of economic power. As long as the American frontier provided individual opportunity and industrial production was too small to satisfy everyone's demand, the system worked well enough. But as the new century dawned, conditions changed. The frontier ended, and Americans faced the power of corporate wealth. Theodore Roosevelt thought of breaking up the large concentrations of power but soon realized that he would first have to distinguish between "good" and "bad" ones. Woodrow Wilson realized that the great threat to American individual liberty was the concentration of financial power, but before he could move effectively against such concentrations, the war took up his energies.

Now, with the frontier gone and concentrated wealth sharply limiting opportunity, the nation was "steering a steady course toward economic oligarchy, if we are not there already." This defined the problem of the age: not to discover more or to produce more, but to learn how to manage the existing system in order to adapt "existing economic conditions to the service of the people." The task, as Roosevelt saw it, was to figure out how to promote cooperation for the general welfare. A right to life was a right to earn a living. To secure this right, government had to "restrict the operations of the speculator, the manipulator, even the financier." Roosevelt hoped that "the responsible heads of finance and industry" would learn to subordinate their individual ambitions and work for the common good. Government should stand ready to regulate the behavior of those who did not. Thus, liberty and the pursuit of happiness were possible only through cooperative action and the avoidance of anything that threatened the liberty or happiness of others. It was government's duty to preserve the "balance" that protected individual liberty. The whole process would be long and slow, not achieved by overnight schemes. "Government," Roosevelt declared, "includes the art of formulating a policy and using the political technique to attain so much of that policy as will receive general support; persuading, leading, sacrificing, teaching always, because the greatest duty of a statesman is to educate."[38]

Building cooperative relationships by "persuading, leading, sacrificing, teaching"—these were the pluralistic values by which Roosevelt hoped to guide the nation out of its economic miseries. The strategy of the Brains Trust was not so much to integrate its economic strategy into a grand design for the entire economy as to propose ways to address the problems of each major sector—as Roosevelt put it, "to right specific troubles of specific groups without, at the same time, inflicting hardships upon other groups."[39]

Roosevelt followed this approach with a series of speeches on federal spending, unemployment relief, and the specific economic problems of cities, foreign investments, railroads, public utilities, and real estate mortgages. In each he applied the principles he had earlier stated: economy in government through reorganization, private cooperation and planning, necessary government regulation, and recognition of the obligation to prevent human suffering. His prescriptions were somewhat general and vague on the details of how they would be carried out, but that was because there was no way to predict the kind of Congress he would be dealing with. (Although the House of Representatives had a Democratic majority, the Senate was still Republican, and there were no guarantees that the election would change this. During the campaign, Roosevelt stressed how he had been able to work with the Republican majorities in the New York state legislature.)[40]

Election day, November 8, 1932, produced a landslide for Roosevelt and the Democrats. Roosevelt carried every state south and west of Pennsylvania and received 57 percent of the popular vote; the electoral vote was 472 to 59.

The presidency was his, but he would have to wait for it. The presidential term would not begin until March 4, nearly three months down the road. During that period, Roosevelt remained active, winding up his governorship, traveling to Warm Springs, and visiting other locations to deliver speeches. In the meantime, Congress would reconvene in December. Even before that, however, President Hoover received a request from Great Britain to consider revising the schedule and amount of its war debt payments. Claiming that the reaction of Congress to any recommendation on war debts would be influenced by "the views of those members who recognize you as their leader," Hoover invited Roosevelt to confer with him on that subject and on pending international economic disarmament conferences. Hoover hoped to get Roosevelt to agree to link the debt question to the larger issues of economic decline. In his mind, this meant an agreement between the United States and Great Britain to maintain the gold standard, which had been the basic measure of international trade. Roosevelt insisted, however, on separating the debt question from other economic questions.[41]

The result was two meetings, one toward the end of November and the other on January 20. In each, Moley opposed the Hoover approach of linking war debts to a general consideration of economic conditions. Moley also opposed Hoover's suggestion that Roosevelt join him in naming members of a special commission to consider war debts. These responses showed that Roosevelt wanted more freedom of action in his own administration and did not want to commit himself to Hoover's view that the depression had foreign causes. At the same time, Moley's insistence on separating war debts from general economic problems followed the strategy outlined during the campaign of separate treatment for different economic sectors. Moley's responses showed that Roosevelt preferred to look for domestic solutions to the nation's problems.

The fundamental problem, however, was that Hoover wanted Roosevelt to cooperate with him but had no intention of cooperating with Roosevelt. Hoover was suspicious of any member of his cabinet, such as Secretary of State Henry Stimson, who was willing to negotiate with Roosevelt evenhandedly. Beyond that, Hoover was so convinced of his own views and so hostile to Roosevelt's that he believed that the only way to avoid "a complete financial debacle" was for Roosevelt to abandon his New Deal program. Roosevelt's only choice was to refuse.[42]

Leaving Washington, Roosevelt traveled to Muscle Shoals, Alabama, site of a World War I nitrate plant and subsequently a centerpiece in a national debate over the development of public power. Accompanied by Senator George Norris of Nebraska, a progressive Republican who had led the public power forces, Roosevelt endorsed Norris's vision and added his own ideas of social reconstruction, anticipating what would soon become the Tennessee Valley Authority. From Muscle Shoals he went through Montgomery and then to Warm Springs, where he conferred with the British ambassador about the upcoming Washington conference on war debts. Then he was off to Jacksonville, Florida, for twelve days of fishing and relaxation in the waters off Florida and the Bahama Islands aboard the yacht of Vincent Astor. On the evening of February 15, the yacht docked in Miami, where it was met by various Florida officials and party leaders, as well as his 1920 running mate, James M. Cox, and Raymond Moley. Accompanying Roosevelt were his bodyguard and, as they had since the election, six Secret Service men. Riding with the mayor of Miami, he led a motorcade to Bay Front Park, where some 10,000 people had gathered to see him. Among the crowd was Joseph Zangara, a brick mason recently arrived in Miami from Paterson, New Jersey. Short, barely over five feet, and dark, he stood in the crowd wincing at the stabbing stomach pains that had tormented him for years and nursing a hatred for all those who held political power. In his pocket he carried a .12-caliber revolver he had recently purchased at a pawnshop for $8. He had come to shoot and kill Franklin Roosevelt. He was a few rows back in a set of benches, and at the moment, people standing in front of him blocked his view.

Meanwhile, Roosevelt was bantering with reporters, telling them he had locked up the ship's log to keep them from snooping into it. The crowd was good-natured, and as the motorcade entered the park, they cheered loudly. Crowded by cameras and microphones, Roosevelt sat on the back of his seat of the open car and delivered a short, bland speech, promising to spend more time in Florida. As he finished, those standing in front of Joseph Zangara began to sit down, and he took the opportunity to stand on the bench. Roosevelt concluded his remarks, and newsreel cameramen asked him to turn around and repeat them. Roosevelt refused and slid down the seat. Mayor Anton Cermak of Chicago walked up for a brief chat. A man approached with a long telegram. Just as he was presenting it to Roosevelt, something popped like a firecracker. Roosevelt jerked backward and then, apparently realizing what was happening, set his jaw and turned in the direction of the shots. In the crowd a woman had grabbed Zangara's arm, but the revolver's stiff trigger action and Zangara's strength pulled his arm down and he kept firing. In a few seconds, before a policeman was able to knock him to the ground, he had emptied his five-shot weapon. Each bullet found a victim. Two were hit in the head, one in the abdomen, one in the hand, and Mayor Cermak in the chest.

At once the Secret Service ordered Roosevelt's driver to get him out of the crowd. As the car lurched forward, Roosevelt ordered the driver to stop and to have the mayor placed in his car. Cradling Cermak in the proper position for a person with a chest wound, he felt for a pulse, which at first was not there but suddenly started. Roosevelt continued to support him, all the while saying, "Tony, don't move—keep quiet. It won't hurt if you keep quiet." At the hospital, doctors credited Roosevelt with saving Cermak's life. Roosevelt waited until he had talked to all the victims, except for a woman who had been rushed to surgery. He returned to the yacht at about 2 A.M.

To all observers, Roosevelt had acted with remarkable courage, both in his cool response to Zangara's attack and in his calm presence of mind in helping Mayor Cermak. He recounted the incident to the press in a straightforward fashion, showing a remarkable eye for detail—additional evidence that the danger had only sharpened his senses. At the hospital and later on the yacht, his friends looked for signs of a delayed stress or panic reaction. They saw none, nor anything to compare to their own ragged nerves. Moley later wrote of Roosevelt that night that he "had never seen anything more magnificent."[43]

During the incident, Eleanor was in New York, addressing a club for employees of the Warner Brothers motion picture company. She heard the news from the butler when she arrived back at her apartment. Showing no emotion, she remarked, "These things are to be expected." She placed a call to Franklin and reached him at the hospital. "He's all right," she said, putting down the receiver. "He's not the least bit excited." She showed some concern about how to tell Franklin's mother, who was next door. After assuring Sara that all was well, Eleanor was on her way to Ithaca to deliver a speech.[44]

Two days later, Roosevelt was back in New York to complete the job of choosing his cabinet. Hoping to be a president of all the people, a national healer and conciliator, he looked across the political spectrum, hoping to embrace conservative Democrats and progressive Republicans. He also looked for a regional distribution and wanted to build support in Congress. He wished to recognize Roman Catholics, but, wary of the religious bigotry that had characterized Al Smith's campaign in 1928, he wanted no more than two in his cabinet. Unlike Abraham Lincoln, who had sought to include a cross section of his own party, Roosevelt excluded his major rivals for the nomination; this ruled out Smith and Baker. In key policy areas he wanted individuals who had the expertise and respect of others in their fields. For secretary of agriculture he chose Henry A. Wallace, a major farm journalist, pioneer in developing hybrid seed corn, and major figure in agricultural economics (which put Tugwell in his camp). Roosevelt enjoyed drawing the political contrast between Henry the Democrat and his father, Henry C. Wallace, who had held the same office in the Harding and Coolidge administrations and had opposed Hoover's farm policies. Clinching Wallace's nomination was the support of one of the nation's more influential farm organizations, the Farm Bureau Federation. He also wanted a woman in the cabinet, continuing the precedent he had set as governor by appointing Frances Perkins as New York State industrial commissioner. Because secretary of labor was the cabinet post most closely related to welfare and relief, specialties in which women had become prominent, Roosevelt looked for a woman to fill that post. When Mary "Molly" Dewson, chair of the Democratic Woman's Committee, pressed him to nominate Perkins and reminded him of her committee's work turning out the women's vote, he agreed.[45]

Roosevelt had considered appeasing Bernard Baruch's conservative wing of the party by appointing Senator Carter Glass of Virginia secretary of the treasury. Glass was a longtime advocate of banking reform, but he was also devoted to the gold standard and would take the job only if Roosevelt would keep the United States on gold. Unwilling to commit himself, Roosevelt turned to William H. Woodin, a fellow New Yorker with extensive experience in banking and railroads. Above all, Woodin was a Roosevelt loyalist who could be expected to support his chief's wishes.

Two other cabinet posts lined up Senate support for Roosevelt's foreign policy. For secretary of state, Roosevelt chose Cordell Hull of Tennessee, a U.S. senator whose overwhelming popularity with his colleagues could be expected to ease the approval of treaties and other foreign policy initiatives. Roosevelt further strengthened his foreign policy base in the Senate by appointing Senator Claude Swanson of Virginia to be secretary of the navy. Swanson's appointment opened the way for Senator Key Pittman of Nevada, who had worked hard for Roosevelt and had been a political adviser to the Brains Trust, to assume the chair of the powerful Foreign Relations Committee.

In order to include progressive Republicans, Roosevelt had to engage in political juggling. Roosevelt had wanted to nominate progressive Republicans to head the Departments of Interior and Justice. His preference for secretary of the interior was Senator Bronson Cutting of New Mexico. Cutting had supported Roosevelt in the election, had a long and consistent progressive voting record, shared Roosevelt's Groton and Harvard background, and was his fourth cousin. The senator had also sponsored public works legislation, and Roosevelt intended to give Interior authority over public works projects. Cutting thought about the offer for a month and then refused.[46] Roosevelt next approached Senator Hiram Johnson of California, who also refused, but Johnson suggested that Roosevelt consider Harold Ickes, who was in town to be considered for Indian commissioner. Apparently without investigation or forethought, Roosevelt jumped at Ickes, who had been a Bull Moose Progressive supporting Theodore Roosevelt's third-party bid in 1912.

For attorney general, Roosevelt considered Philip LaFollette, former governor of Wisconsin, especially attractive. He was the son of Robert M. LaFollette, the long-term progressive governor and U.S. senator from Wisconsin and Progressive Party candidate for president, and the brother of Robert M. LaFollette, Jr., a progressive Republican senator. But before he could make the offer, Roosevelt believed he had to approach Democratic Senator Thomas J. Walsh of Montana, who had gained fame uncovering the oil scandals of the Harding administration and had loyally supported Roosevelt's bid for the nomination and presided at the Chicago convention. Unexpectedly, Walsh accepted Roosevelt's offer but died on his way to Washington for the inauguration. This necessitated last-minute searching that resulted in the choice of Homer S. Cummings.

Roosevelt paid purely political debts by filling the Commerce post with Daniel Roper of California (the state that had set in motion the swing to his nomination) and War with George Dern of Utah, a disappointed aspirant for vice president. It was a foregone conclusion that Roosevelt would nominate James A. Farley, his political operative in Albany, to be postmaster general, the richest patronage office in the cabinet.

As the cabinet nominations fell into place, the nation's banking system began falling apart. The economy's backward cycle was continuing. Banks holding depressed and worthless securities, owed by persons unable to pay, were feeling additional pressure from the nation's continued reliance on the gold standard. As other nations abandoned gold, speculators began purchasing gold in anticipation that the United States would follow suit and the price would rise. The loss of gold to the speculators further depressed prices and weakened the banks' ability to pay their depositors. By the time Roosevelt docked in Miami to face Zangara's attack, anxious depositors, many old, many unemployed, many fearful about their future, were withdrawing their deposits before the banks closed their doors for good. In order to head off the complete collapse of their banking systems, governors were declaring "bank holidays," closing the banks or limiting their actions to protect their assets.[47]

Hoover continued to pressure Roosevelt, this time to support any action the president might take to save the banking system and to promise to support the gold standard. Roosevelt responded that Hoover could do what he chose on his own authority. On March 3, the day before the inauguration, Hoover invited Franklin and Eleanor to tea, along with his financial advisers, and made one last plea for cooperation. Roosevelt evaded, saying that he would have to consult with his advisers. The occasion ended frostily.[48]

Roosevelt was to assume the presidency at noon on March 4. He and Eleanor arrived at the White House about 11 A.M. The awkwardness between him and President Hoover continued during the drive to the Capitol. After the swearing-in ceremonies, Roosevelt, now president, stood at the podium for his first official act. He began his inaugural address by assuring his audience that the nation "will endure as it has endured, will revive and prosper." Thus his first assertion, his "firm belief," was "that the only thing we have to fear is fear itself." Fortunately, the nation's material resources were sound and abundant; they required only the right spirit and the right organization to restore prosperity. He then undertook a summation of his fundamental campaign message: the need to redistribute population away from the industrial centers, to increase agricultural prices, to unify relief activities, to integrate transportation, and to undertake "a strict supervision of all banking and credits and investments" to provide "an adequate but sound currency." He went on to stress the interdependence of American life at home and abroad. He assumed that the normal constitutional powers would be adequate for the task, but if Congress failed to do its part, he would ask for "broad Executive power to wage a war against the emergency, as great as the power that would be given to me if we were in fact invaded by a foreign foe."[49]

He had assumed power and proclaimed responsibility. He had put himself in the spotlight. If America was to have a new deal, it was up to him to make it happen.

2

★★★★★

A HUNDRED DAYS

The United States that Franklin Roosevelt had addressed and now set about to lead was a nation in fear. From various corners came warnings of anger and unrest. The chairman of the National Steel Corporation had testified before the Senate Finance Committee that "practically all the people have suffered severely, and are worn out not only in their resources but in their patience." The head of the United Mine Workers declared that "the political stability of the republic is imperiled." Senator Robert Wagner, Democrat of New York and a fighter for relief for the unemployed, worried that "we are in a life and death struggle with the forces of social and economic dissolution." A few months earlier, an instructor at the Milwaukee State Teachers College had told a labor audience that the same extremes of wealth and poverty that now existed in the United States had caused social revolutions in the past. He urged the workers to prepare to take over the nation's basic industries and run them to produce life's necessities for the people. Not only working people were feeling restive. In Iowa, Milo Reno, the head of the Farmers' Holiday Association, proclaimed that "the farmers of the Mississippi Valley are in a desperate way, not only financially but in the matter of morale." In an effort to reduce supply in order to increase prices, corn and hog farmers picketed highways to keep farm products from the market. Reno's organization called for a "holiday" to withhold crops from market until farmers were guaranteed the "cost of production." The mayor of Sioux City described the movement as "a protest against an unbearable economic situation" and warned, "it would be a mistake to minimize the dangers." In a small rural district in north Texas, Sam

Rayburn, chair of the House Committee on Interstate and Foreign Commerce, later to be majority leader and Speaker of the House, was hearing about the "great amount of unsettlement among the voters this year. . . . There is more dissatisfaction this year among the masses than each of us have ever known. They are clamoring for reduction in taxes, reduction in expenses, and thisism and thatism. In other words, Mr. Rayburn, there is a general feeling to oust every man in office, and we are apprehensive." "When we arrived in Washington," recalled Raymond Moley, "terror held the country in its grip."[1]

In 1933, it was not difficult to recall the nation's history of depression unrest: how mass meetings had called for public works and other forms of relief for the unemployed, how "industrial armies" had marched on state capitals and on Washington itself to dramatize their desperation, how bloody riots had accompanied strikes, and how spokesmen for "agrarian radicalism" had rallied farmers to demand nationalization of the railroads and fundamental changes in the nation's money system. Now with farmers blocking roads in the Middle West and veterans clashing with troops in the nation's capital, the conditions for more unrest and violence seemed to be at hand. For much of his first term, Franklin Roosevelt, who had warned the nation against fear, would operate in its shadow. But he had asked for the job, and now he had to begin to do it.

In a magazine article in December 1932, Roosevelt called for a program to increase farm income and reduce farm debt, develop a national transportation policy, provide cheaper electric power, and restore foreign trade. This was a policy that aimed essentially at reducing the costs of production and distribution and expanding overseas markets. He also called for reducing the cost of government through less bureaucracy and more efficient management.[2]

As to the means of accomplishing these objectives, Roosevelt seemed inclined toward Progressive views of a government active in the economy. But the depth and complexity of the economic crisis and the changed perceptions of his time meant that his methods would be importantly different. Roosevelt was a Progressive, in that he believed that wise national policies could improve society, but beyond that he stood on new ground. In keeping with the Brains Trusters—and, for that matter, Herbert Hoover—he believed that society was composed of a complexity of interdependent interests. What he wanted to do was to achieve an economically healthier relationship among those interests. In many ways, his conception owed less to Theodore Roosevelt and Woodrow Wilson than it did to James Madison, who in the *Federalist Papers* had defined the general welfare as a concert of interests. (Madison, it might be argued, had raised the concert of interests as a justification for representative government and not a prescription for curing economic ills, but as we shall see, Roosevelt's conception also pointed in this direction.)

Behind Roosevelt's analysis lay an assumption that a modern economy was naturally interrelated. This explains his emphasis on power, transportation, and foreign markets. These sectors were all vital connecting links in the nation's economy. Indeed, confidence in interdependence radiated throughout Roosevelt's conception of government and society. All things could be reconciled and harmonized if one had the wit and will to achieve it. This was why Roosevelt so often asked people with apparently conflicting views to "weave" them together and why he often placed individuals with opposite views in the same organization. He had supreme confidence in his ability to persuade people to cooperate with one another. This was why those who were able to accept "reality" and to compromise fared better with him than did those who held fixed or doctrinaire views.

Roosevelt had promised bold leadership and decisive action, and the depression immediately gave him the chance to deliver. Although many Americans and all bankers believed that finance was too mysterious a science for all but the experts to understand, the vast majority of depositors knew that when securities and real estate lost value and when shops and factories closed their doors, their money, which the bankers had invested and lent to these instrumentalities, was being lost. As a result, they sought to protect themselves by withdrawing it. Such "runs" and the threat of them had caused banks to protect themselves by closing their doors, actions sanctioned by states that declared bank "holidays." By the time Roosevelt took his oath of office, forty of the forty-eight states had declared bank holidays. All but a handful of the nation's banking capital was in suspended animation. Elsewhere, those with claims on American gold, especially those in foreign countries, were vigorously exercising them. The result was an alarming flow of gold out of the banking system and out of the country. Capitalism was all but completely paralyzed.

Roosevelt entered office no fan of the American banking system. Irresponsible finance, he believed, had contributed mightily to the nation's economic turmoil. He considered most bankers selfish and grasping. Given a free hand, he might have preferred to reform the nation's currency rather than to restructure the banking system, but the bankers and their state governments had forced him to act. The night of his inauguration he ordered Secretary of the Treasury Woodin to prepare emergency banking legislation. The next day he forbade further transactions in gold, proclaimed a national bank holiday, and called Congress into a special session beginning March 9.[3]

Woodin enlisted the aid of Raymond Moley. At the Treasury they found that holdovers from the Hoover administration were working along Roosevelt's lines. The two paramount problems were how to identify banks that were sound enough to reopen and how to provide enough currency for them to operate. Moley and Woodin discovered that Hoover's secretary of the treasury, Ogden Mills, and his assistants had developed substantial plans for closing the banks and reopening the sound ones but were stuck on how to increase the amount of currency. This problem Woodin solved by adopting a proposal to issue notes based on the assets of the banks. The currency would be Federal Reserve notes and would be "money that looks like money." After Roosevelt approved the outline, Walter Wyatt of the Federal Reserve Board drafted the bill. The bill was then taken to Senator Glass, who rewrote it, changing the procedures for collecting gold and expanding the responsibility to turn in gold to private bodies as well as public. More important, he exempted state banks from federal licensing, leaving that to state authorities.[4]

When Congress assembled, the banking legislation was ready. "Here's the bill," announced House Banking Committee chairman Henry B. Steagall as he marched down the House aisle, waving a bill still slightly damp from the printer. "Let's pass it." Thirty-eight minutes later the House complied. The Senate, a more deliberative body, considered the legislation into the early evening before passing it. Roosevelt signed it a little after 8:30 P.M.[5]

Roosevelt had said that the nation needed action. Working with materials provided by the Hoover administration, he had supplied it. His success was a triumph of neither originality nor liberalism (the banking bill employed thoroughly conservative principles) but one of executive energy rapidly applied. Ten weeks later, Harry Hopkins would make headlines by distributing relief funds that Hoover's Reconstruction Finance Corporation had approved for the states but not yet distributed.

Roosevelt had also said that the nation needed to abandon fear. Now he addressed the psychological dimension by holding the first of weekly press conferences and by delivering a national radio address—later known as a "fireside chat"—to explain the banking legislation to the people. Aided by his extremely able press secretary Stephen A. Early, he tightly controlled the press conferences, telling the reporters how to use the information he gave them. At the same time he displayed his extraordinary gift for personal relations, looking directly at the reporter he was responding to, establishing eye contact, and, with a theatrically mobile face, conveying understanding, sympathy, concern, seriousness—whatever the occasion seemed to require.[6]

After banking, Roosevelt turned to reducing government expenses. The issue of economy in government centered on the need to balance the federal budget, something that orthodox thinkers believed necessary to guarantee a sound currency, which was a precondition to stimulating investment and employment. The recovery formula looked toward restoring prosperity through international means. A sound national currency was a step toward stabilizing international exchange rates, reducing war debts to a manageable level, and reducing trade barriers to stimulate commerce.[7]

Few adhered to this doctrine more strongly than Lewis W. Douglas. A representative from Arizona and heir to a copper fortune, Douglas had served on the congressional committee that, during the lame-duck session, had produced a bill to balance the federal budget by cutting expenditures. The bill gave the president sweeping powers to reduce expenditures and reduce government employment. Douglas believed that a combination of these measures would cut $900 million from a deficit of $1.2 billion. Roosevelt picked Douglas to be his director of the budget, the administration's chief fiscal officer. Douglas accepted Roosevelt's offer only after extracting a promise that Roosevelt was committed to economy and a balanced budget.[8]

The economy bill proved more popular with Douglas than with Congress. Parliamentary maneuvering passed it in the House, but only with the aid of Republican votes. In the Senate, Republicans opposed the sweeping powers the bill conferred on the president, and members of both parties balked at its serious cut in veterans' pensions. But Roosevelt was unwavering, using his patronage powers and introducing a popular bill legalizing beer in order to win over key votes.[9] He also placed Douglas at the center of things, referring all executive orders and agency proposals to him for duplication and expenditure. Douglas became part of Roosevelt's "bedroom cabinet," which met with him in the mornings to plan the day's work. As the weeks rolled by, Douglas slashed millions from agency budgets in a relentless quest to restore investors' confidence in the soundness of the dollar.[10]

But, as many of Franklin Roosevelt's associates were to learn, they had been summoned to serve him, not the other way around. When Douglas brought in the economy bill draft, Roosevelt said that he wanted to include $300 million for a Civilian Conservation Corps (CCC). Aghast, Douglas said that Roosevelt could not go in two directions at once; Congress would not pass such a bill. Roosevelt agreed.[11]

Roosevelt had made the relief of agriculture his top recovery measure. But now he sought a broader constituency than his Brains Trusters. He would accept no bill opposed by the major farm leaders. This promised to be no easy task, since the major farm groups had developed their own programs, most of which called for the national government to fix a domestic price on farm products and to dump the surpluses abroad, preferably by arranging trade agreements with other nations. These measures were supplemented with the historic American solution to agricultural discontent: currency inflation. In February, the farm leaders arrived in Washington to discuss the farm program. Under the leadership of Wallace, the group produced a report that outlined the Agricultural Adjustment Administration (AAA). They met with Roosevelt and read their report, which he accepted without comment, and pledged their support to him. The bill was then drafted in consultations that brought in others, including Baruch and key members of Congress George Peek, Cotton Ed Smith, and Marvin Jones. Roosevelt refused to make a final decision on whether the bill should include processing taxes. The bill was drafted to appeal to the conservative farm groups, assuming that the liberals would have to go along. The House passed the bill rapidly, but in the Senate it bogged down with efforts to attach currency inflation to it.

Originally the AAA gave the secretary of agriculture the authority to contract with farmers to reduce production and to arrange contracts between farmers and processors to increase farm prices. The program would be self-financing (and in accord with the Economy Act), being paid for by a tax on processors. The bill also permitted taxes on competing products, both domestic and foreign. In order to get support for different wings of the party, it gave the secretary great discretion in writing rules for carrying out the program. These means were designed to restore farm income to "parity," meaning the balance between urban and rural purchasing power that had existed just before World War I.[12]

The "parity" standard bowed in the direction of those farm leaders whose objective was simply to increase farm income without reforming the structure of agriculture. The early conception of the domestic allotment was designed to encourage farmers to create associational networks that would cooperatively administer it. But other interests had to be conciliated, particularly those associated with Bernard Baruch. Chief among these associates was George Peek, a former farm equipment manufacturer who had crusaded for government subsidies for agriculture. Peek and Baruch were interested in permitting farmers to reduce acreage and to market cooperatively abroad while processors operated through trade associations to fix prices and pass along their costs to consumers. They wanted a bill written by the processors for the processors. As the debate progressed in the Senate, Secretary of Agriculture Wallace became convinced that Baruch's support was needed to pass the bill. This led Roosevelt to promise to appoint Peek to oversee the farm program once the legislation passed. To satisfy a key southern senator, a section was added to reform the farm credit system.[13]

The most controversial issue in the farm bill arose from demands for currency inflation. Various senators presented their favorite methods, and debate continued until it became clear that none could succeed. At that point they combined them into an amendment sponsored by Senator Elmer Thomas of Oklahoma. It now appeared that inflation would inevitably pass. The Thomas amendment horrified Douglas, but Thomas provided the administration with a perfect response by presenting his amendment to Roosevelt in draft form, emphasizing that the bill gave the president discretion to use any one of the inflationary methods—or none at all—and inviting him to rewrite the text. Agreeing to accept the amendment, Roosevelt turned over its redrafting to Moley and Senators Key Pittman of Nevada and James Byrnes of South Carolina.[14]

Other and more substantial revisions were successfully pressed by Douglas and his coworker, banker James P. Warburg. Warburg had come up with a plan to capitalize the war debts by using them as a sinking fund, the interest on which would be used to purchase U.S. government obligations, the interest from which would purchase more obligations. Warburg called this plan the "Bunny" because it would magically make the war debts question disappear. Moley and Douglas were attracted to the plan as a way of heading off the inflationists in Congress while addressing an important international aspect of the depression. Moley and Douglas thought of it as a way to "reform" the gold standard without abandoning it. They seized the Thomas amendment and amended it to limit the president's authority to issue paper money. Warburg and Douglas believed that they had restored monetary sanity. Immediately, Roosevelt put out the word that he did not intend to use his new inflationary powers.[15]

For a time, Douglas and Warburg seemed justified in their optimism. When Roosevelt had turned the Thomas amendment to their ministrations, he had announced that he was taking the United States off the gold standard. Then he immediately held a series of conferences with world leaders to explore how "to get the world back on some form of gold standard."[16]

Overshadowed during these days but nevertheless fundamental to Roosevelt's agenda was relief for the unemployed. Roosevelt was determined to provide work for at least some of the nation's 12 million unemployed. His own preference was to provide federal employment for young men by having them perform conservation work in national parks. Only Douglas's objections had prevented him from attaching it to the economy bill.[17]

While Roosevelt developed plans for his forest army, others were seeking more comprehensive federal approaches. Working with progressive senators LaFollette, Wagner, and Costigan, Secretary of Labor Frances Perkins worked out proposals for public works and grants to the states to fund unemployment relief. Indeed, Perkins opposed Roosevelt's idea of paying young men $1 a day to work on conservation projects, fearing that the low wage would bring down the price of other labor. But Roosevelt was determined to go ahead with his plan for a civilian forest army. The result was a series of meetings that combined the proposals into a single initiative on behalf of the unemployed. Of the three approaches, public works attracted the least support. Roosevelt was wedded to the conservation program, and LaFollette had convinced Douglas that federal aid for relief was needed. Since "direct relief," which simply provided the poor with a minimum standard of living, was less costly on a per-person basis, Douglas favored that over public works, which had high costs for materials. Roosevelt agreed with that thinking, and Moley also seemed willing to accept it. Roosevelt ordered that unobligated expenditures be held up to free as much existing money as possible for relief and the CCC. In order to coordinate the relief grants, Roosevelt asked Congress to create the position of federal relief administrator.[18]

On the same day he signed the AAA into law, Roosevelt signed the Federal Emergency Relief Act and appointed Harry Hopkins its administrator. This legislation was virtually noncontroversial because the Hoover administration had already approved $300 million for loans to the states for relief. The legislation allocated $250 million in matching grants to states and $250 million in outright grants to states that could prove that they had exhausted their resources for relief.

Roosevelt took up a major program that would become known as regional development. In a process that represented a concert of interests, the Tennessee Valley Authority (TVA) seemed an inevitable creation. For years Senator George Norris, the famous Nebraska Progressive, had introduced bills for government operation of hydroelectric plants on the Tennessee River, on the theory that government rates would serve to measure the fairness of private utility rates. At the same time, southern congressmen wanted the nitrate production facilities at Muscle Shoals in northern Alabama to be converted to produce inexpensive fertilizer. Others saw the dams as a means of flood control and a weapon against soil erosion. Just prior to his inauguration, Roosevelt had visited the Muscle Shoals site and had extemporaneously promised to convert the entire Tennessee Valley into a laboratory of social planning, "tying in industry and agriculture and forestry and flood prevention, tying them all into a unified whole over a distance of a thousand miles so that we can afford better opportunities and better places for millions of yet unborn to live in the days to come."[19] Aiming to address the valley's rural poverty, Roosevelt hoped that the plan would enable the residents to develop small industries and a self-sufficient economy. His message to Congress endorsed the legislation creating the TVA as "national planning for a complete river watershed involving the many States and the future lives and welfare of millions." After a debate that focused on whether the TVA should have the power to put up its own transmission lines, Congress passed the legislation, and on May 18 Roosevelt signed it.

The TVA was Roosevelt's most unalloyed example of presidential leadership. It was a concept that he authored, proposed, and oversaw to passage. The bill closely matched his thinking about economic development and national planning. As a recovery measure, its regional scope restricted its effect. It was important, however, because it represented more clearly than any other New Deal measure Franklin Roosevelt's vision of American society. Roosevelt pictured Americans identified by some specific and distinct characteristic—in this instance, place. What Roosevelt was proposing to do was to align the various elements in this place, or region, so that they would produce an economy that provided a tolerable standard of living while still respecting the distinctiveness of the place and its people. Roosevelt related the TVA to his relief program by suggesting that the regional program might permit the people to "live soundly and in a self-supporting way until we can work our way into a new economy."[20]

Securities regulation benefited from congressional leadership and outside expertise. In the House, Sam Rayburn of Texas, chairman of the Committee on Interstate and Foreign Commerce, had crusaded for tough securities regulation since his days as a young congressman under Woodrow Wilson. A hard worker with ambitions to rise in the House hierarchy, Rayburn had labored faithfully to master his committee's subject matter and in the process had come to appreciate the kind of expertise that sharp eastern lawyers could provide. This attitude was unusual for a man who represented one of the nation's more rural districts and whose father had ridden in the Confederate cavalry with the famous raider Mosby. Somehow, perhaps because of his ambition to succeed, Rayburn had become a proud southerner but not a bigoted one. Later as Speaker, he would make famous the phrase "if you want to get along, go along." Now, in the midst of a legislative whirlwind, the person he felt he had to go along with was Franklin D. Roosevelt.[21]

Supplying the outside expertise was a coterie of Harvard-trained lawyers and their mentor. Although the "cooperation" and "commonwealth" approach had dominated the planning of the Brain Trust and the legislative thrust of the Hundred Days, early on there had been a vocal and influential group that wanted to subdue business with government power. A central figure in this group was Harvard law professor Felix Frankfurter. From the beginning Frankfurter had emphasized the need to stimulate consumer purchasing power. Suspending the antitrust laws and encouraging business "cooperation" would only hamper recovery by giving business more opportunities to raise prices and in other ways injure consumers.[22]

Roosevelt tended to evaluate the stock market in moral terms—how its dealings had thwarted and impoverished innocent men. During the weeks before he took office, he asked Samuel Untermeyer to draft securities legislation, but Untermeyer produced nothing of value. In the cabinet Roosevelt turned to Secretary of Commerce Roper, who recruited Huston Thompson, a former chairman of the Federal Trade Commission (FTC) and an ardent supporter of Wilsonian small enterprise, a man who was capable of affirming that big business threatened the futures of America's children. After looking over Thompson's draft and recommending one change, Roosevelt sent it to Congress, declaring that, among other things, the bill would restore public confidence in the stock market.

The fundamental feature of the Thompson bill was disclosure, forbidding the sale of securities not registered with the FTC. The bill made no effort to analyze the quality of stock issues or to protect consumers from weak or fraudulent ones. Many investors had welcomed a federal law to free them from the toils of myriad state regulations. They favored an antifraud law that would give the FTC the authority to investigate individual dealers suspected of illegal acts. Moley relayed these concerns to Rayburn, who asked him for writers who could draft a bill along these lines. Moley recruited Frankfurter and his young aides James M. Landis, Thomas G. Corcoran, and Benjamin V. Cohen. Their bill broadened liability to underwriters, distributors, and brokers instead of concentrating it on corporation executives. Although their bill came under attack from special interests, it passed the House intact, either because, Rayburn mused, it was so good or because it was so incomprehensible. As soon as this happened, Roosevelt called a White House meeting and endorsed it over the Thompson bill, which was pending in the Senate. (Roosevelt had intended to persuade Thompson to seek a compromise with the supporters of the Rayburn bill, but Thompson clarified the president's position by storming out of the meeting and refusing to work with the Frankfurter group.) The Senate then defeated Rayburn's bill and passed the Thompson bill.[23]

The scene then shifted to a House-Senate Conference Committee. With the help of Senate majority leader Joe Robinson of Arkansas, who favored the Rayburn bill, Rayburn gained the chair of the conference. But now Rayburn and Roosevelt encountered a new difficulty. Still battling corrupt alliances between government and business, Senator Hiram Johnson of California believed that the State Department often arranged sweet deals for American investors by bribing foreign governments to grant lucrative concessions and contracts to American financiers. Johnson proposed to create a special corporation to oversee these activities. The State Department, which had long considered it a normal and necessary function to aid American investors in foreign countries, protested that the amendment would confuse and snarl its activities. The problem was that Senator Johnson was a member of the conference committee, and Roosevelt was hoping to appoint him as a delegate to the World Economic Conference to be held in London in July.[24]

The result was a confusion of backtracking and covering, eventually resolved by Landis and Rayburn. Landis drafted a section that would defer Johnson's proposal's taking effect until the president deemed it in the national interest, and Rayburn presented it to him. To the amazement of all, Johnson accepted the revision. Then Roosevelt approved the formation of a private bondholders' council to supervise foreign securities trading so that the Johnson amendment would not go into effect. The resulting Securities Act required companies to disclose information when they issued new securities.[25]

Plans for industrial recovery were the last significant policy to develop. Many recommended centralized planning for industry, following the example of the War Industries Board, which had attempted to regulate industrial production during the world war. But Roosevelt showed little interest in centralized planning. When the president's uncle Frederic Delano proposed such a centralized federal agency, Roosevelt replied that the idea was ahead of its time.

Still, there were certain elements that, given the proper circumstances, might converge on an industrial policy. Roosevelt favored state regulation of wages and hours and had urged several state governors to recommend such action. Perkins favored regulating wages by creating federal "industrial boards" for each major industry.

Roosevelt also favored plans to spur the economy over the short term, especially plans that rejected government spending to restore prosperity. What attracted Warburg and Roosevelt was precisely the avoidance of spending. Warburg believed that a spending boom would cause inflation, weaken the bond market, and destroy investor confidence.

Also prominent were businessmen who advocated industrial self-government. Such proposals had been around for a number of years but in the 1920s had gained special support for those industries that were not participating so vigorously in the nation's spurt of industrial prosperity. These industries, supported by the American Bar Association and the National Association of Manufacturers, called for relaxation of the antitrust laws so businesses could combine to limit production. Prominent were producer goods industries and producers of undifferentiated products such as lumber, who complained that monopolistic buyers were holding down prices. They needed to combine to regulate production, their arguments ran, so they could balance the power of the buyers. Industry opponents included growing, specialized producers and volume sellers such as chain stores. When the depression arrived, the advocates of reform argued that combination would enable them to maintain employment and to protect small business from ruinous price cutting.[26]

In this atmosphere of uncertainty, Roosevelt delegated industrial recovery planning to Moley, who was too busy to focus on it. This meant that the momentum had to come from elsewhere, which turned out to be the Department of Agriculture. There, planners such as Hugh Johnson, Tugwell, and Wallace agreed that an industrial policy was needed to complement agricultural policy. Moley assigned Warburg to look into the subject. Worried about stimulating consumer spending and inflation, Warburg proposed government support for producer goods industries. But Moley believed that this formulation was inadequate and persuaded Roosevelt to set aside the matter until opinion had crystallized.[27]

One day after Warburg sent his recommendations to Moley, the Senate passed a bill by Senator Hugo Black of Alabama to limit the workweek to thirty hours. Roosevelt believed that the Black bill was unconstitutional and would depress purchasing power because it permitted businesses to reduce wages along with hours of work. It would also hamper seasonal industries, such as canning, which worked long hours for brief periods. But the Senate rejected his objections and passed the bill. Now Roosevelt realized that in order to forestall it he needed a substitute. Typically, he moved on several fronts. He authorized Secretaries Perkins and Roper to come up with a substitute bill and Moley to canvass various ideas on industrial planning. Perkins proposed amendments to the Black bill, creating industrial boards to guarantee wages and to regulate hours according to the needs of particular industries, but her proposal evoked vigorous dissent from Tugwell and the other economic planners in the Department of Agriculture, from organized labor, which opposed mandatory wages, and from Undersecretary of Commerce John Dickinson in response to pressure from business groups that wanted to clear the way for industrial self-government.[28]

In the meantime, Warburg had taken his proposal to Senators Wagner and LaFollette, who had been pressing for a large public works program. Warburg, who opposed public works spending as inflationary, convinced the senators that public works alone would not achieve recovery and that the country needed a more comprehensive approach. As his thinking developed, Roosevelt conceived of an industrial policy that would stabilize prices across a given industry so that consumers could support the largest number of firms and workers.[29]

This gathering of interested parties, along with press speculation that increased the public's expectation of an industrial policy bill, caused Roosevelt to authorize Wagner to move ahead. This shifted the momentum to Wagner. Wagner had made himself the focal point for various "planning" programs designed to limit the ruthless, cutthroat competition that continually depressed prices, wages, and employment. Wagner formed a group representing high finance, industrial trade associations, labor, and professional economics. Instead of allying himself with the American Bar Association and the National Association of Manufacturers, Wagner worked with economists from the Brookings Institution, who drafted a national economic recovery bill that authorized the federal government to permit minimum price setting in selected industries in order to maintain employment and wages. The bill would permit industries "affected by a public interest" to draw up codes to regulate production, pricing, and competition. A national authority would supervise these codes and regulate wages and hours while protecting the right of labor to organize and to bargain collectively without employer interference. The bill also included Wagner's pet plan for a public works program. The selective approach suggested that the legislation was designed to provide "startup stimulation" to the economy rather than to plan for overall supervision and regulation. Such an approach seemed in line with Roosevelt's thinking, which favored wages and hours regulation and some kind of quick economic stimulation.[30]

Wagner's bill focused the thinking that was evolving in Dickinson's group. Through the good offices of Frances Perkins, the two joined forces and early in May produced a Wagner-Dickinson bill for industrial planning. The process of drafting the bill, however, gave business an opportunity to press for industrial self-government. Displaying unprecedented unity, business groups, led by the Chamber of Commerce, swept aside the targeted "startup" approach in favor of comprehensive business control of markets, wages, and hours, with the authority to punish those who failed to abide by the agreements. By early May, business seemed on the verge of a major victory.[31] All the while, Moley had no idea what was happening. Pushed and pulled by his many responsibilities, he had accumulated some information about industrial planning but had not arrived at a comprehensive approach. He was near despair with the belief that he could not act quickly enough to thwart congressional action on the Black bill.[32] On April 25, he encountered Hugh Johnson, who had just returned to Washington, having been encouraged by Bernard Baruch to volunteer to draft an industrial policy bill. Moley readily accepted Johnson's offer, found him an office and an assistant, and dumped on his desk the various plans the White House had been receiving. But Johnson had not volunteered to synthesize others' ideas; he had come determined to advance his own. Within twenty-four hours he had produced a draft bill. Johnson's experience on the War Industries Board had convinced him that businesses always placed their own interests first and would serve a higher interest only when compelled. Unlike many spokespersons for industrial self-government, Johnson called for strong presidential authority, including the authority to license industry.

Johnson based his approach on the wartime analogy, treating the depression as a crisis that demanded extraordinary powers. But Moley disagreed, claiming that neither he nor Roosevelt wanted such powers. This meant that Johnson had to develop a more complex bill that included labor and consumer interests. To advise about labor, he acquired the help of Donald Richberg, a Chicago lawyer for the railroad brotherhoods. To stimulate consumption, he included public works and proposed that the federal government award contracts only to businesses that followed industrial policy.[33]

A decisive moment came on May 10. The House passed a version of the Black bill. Acting quickly, Roosevelt appointed a committee of Douglas, Perkins, Tugwell, Dickinson, Wagner, Johnson, and Richberg to work out a version of the industrial recovery bill.[34]

It was a critical moment, made to order for a decisive, strong-willed person to take charge. It did not require much expertise to guess that that person would be Hugh Johnson. In the conference, Johnson proved the driving force. As much as anything he infused the group with a crisis psychology that dismissed orderly, constitutional procedures as irrelevant and argued for a strong stroke of federal policy in the form of licensing and extensive presidential authority. This approach conflicted with Tugwell, who argued for a system of taxes to create a fund out of which the federal government would reward those firms that had complied with the code provisions.[35] But Tugwell failed to persuade the others. This meant that Johnson's licensing system remained the only effective measure to compel business compliance. Because Tugwell favored compulsion, he supported Johnson, and licensing wound up in the bill. Johnson also persuaded the drafters to apply the codes to virtually all industries and not just to the major ones, as Wagner had proposed.[36]

The emergence of the Johnson plan and the compromise committee of May 10 inspired a new effort by business interests. Obtaining Roosevelt's approval to confer with the committee, they objected to the federal licensing power and to the lack of import controls. Later, the National Association of Manufacturers (NAM) tried to eliminate section 7(a), which encouraged independent trade unions and collective bargaining. But Johnson held firm on licensing, and with Roosevelt's approval, Wagner's Senate committee upheld section 7(a).

The final product contained something for everyone. Government planners received licensing and vague supervisory powers, labor received a spur toward organizing, and business was given an opportunity to attempt to control prices and production (which the bill did not forbid). Roosevelt, seconded by labor, predicted that the bill would increase wages and employment.[37]

Meanwhile, the final piece of the legislation was being shaped by a debate over public works. Strong voices in the administration opposed public works spending. Douglas favored direct relief over public works, Roosevelt agreed with that thinking, and Moley also seemed willing to accept it.[38] Others such as Tugwell argued that public works were needed to create purchasing power and to create jobs for the unemployed. In Congress, influential senators LaFollette, Costigan, and Wagner favored public works in principle, and others of both parties saw the chance to create jobs for their constituents. This converted public works from a fiscal liability to a political asset.

In this situation, Roosevelt adopted Fabian tactics. Instead of opposing public works on principle, he criticized the expense of the proposed projects and reduced the appropriation from $5 billion to $1 billion. But Congress pressed the issue, insisting on a larger appropriation, and Roosevelt had to give in. Now the problem was how to finance the program. Discussions with Douglas convinced Roosevelt that the Treasury could afford to borrow the necessary funds if Congress imposed taxes high enough to cover the interest. After much consideration, Roosevelt proposed a national sales tax. But members of Congress, having recently opposed and defeated a similar proposal by President Hoover, persuaded the president to allow them to write their own bill.[39]

This meant that the bill proceeded through the tax and finance committees of the House and Senate, where conservative southerners occupied the chairmanships. Arguing against taxing "the little man," the House cut out the sales taxes and the Senate removed taxes on income in favor of taxes on banks and stocks.[40]

The resulting bill had something for business in the codes, for labor in organizing and collective bargaining, for planners in licensing, and for spenders in public works. Roosevelt then added taxes to pay the bonds used to finance public works. The taxes were mostly on consumption items (gasoline, sugar) and income from stock dividends. These had been recommended by Pat Harrison, chair of the Senate Finance Committee, and Robert Doughton, chair of the House Ways and Means Committee. They also persuaded Roosevelt to let Congress take the lead on new taxes in order to spare him a possible rebellion. In his message, Roosevelt associated the financing of the National Industrial Recovery Act (NIRA) to the repeal of Prohibition, which would restore liquor taxes. This linked the Democratic pledge to end Prohibition with his New Deal recovery program.

NIRA had been shaped by a process almost guaranteed to create as many problems as it could solve. It was essentially the product of self-interested parties with conflicting expectations. This meant that although the act was the work of many diverse and conflicting interests, it was not a compromise in which diverse parties each gave up something in order to participate in some greater good or at least in a mutually beneficial relationship. Instead, it was more in the nature of a truce in which each party was inclined to hold the others to strict observance while they maneuvered to improve their own positions. This situation had come about because the drafters had no common ground of agreement, no center of gravity around which to form a policy. Writing NIRA was a warning signal to Franklin Roosevelt and the New Deal.

At the same time that he was reordering his nation's domestic economy, Roosevelt was pursuing grand designs in foreign policy. He had entered office with ideas about adjusting the territorial disputes that had come out of the Versailles Treaty that ended the world war, reducing European tensions through disarmament, and adjusting tariff and currency rates to promote trade. He kept in office many of the career foreign service officers who had carried out Hoover's policies and appointed "internationalists" to important ambassadorships. Roosevelt also had a sense of the complexity of relationships, of putting together packages, making deals, "weaving" ideological opposites together. (This came at the cost of some political inconsistency, since during the campaign and the transition, Roosevelt had rejected Hoover's efforts to link these issues.)[41] But Roosevelt soon realized that if he was going to play in the big league he had to have his own hardball, and his was badly stitched. The United States had a credible navy but no significant land army or air force, and no inclination to develop either. Its domestic political leadership strongly opposed political commitments overseas. The major nations had long recognized this condition, and none had staked its foreign policy on good relations with Washington.

In such a situation, all Roosevelt could reasonably do was take small steps and launch trial balloons. Early in May the new chancellor of the German Reich, Adolf Hitler, unnerved the major nations by making warlike statements about Germany's intention to undo the Versailles Treaty and expand its territory. In response, Roosevelt issued a dramatic challenge to the disarmament conference meeting in Geneva to abolish offensive weapons of war, thereby securing an impregnable advantage for the defense. National leaders, including Hitler, applauded his words and went about their business. The president responded as best he could. He told the French that he did not expect them to disarm so long as Hitler was a threat. He authorized the U.S. representative at the disarmament conference to declare that his country stood ready to act with League of Nations members in the event of war and would pledge in advance to do nothing that would interfere with their collective steps to stop aggression. This pledge Congress promptly undermined by refusing Roosevelt's request to amend the neutrality laws to permit him to choose which belligerent power to embargo arms against. In the meantime, he did what he could to support any signs of cooperation among the major nations.[42]

During the depression, Roosevelt's most significant leverage was economic. The United States' position as a major commercial and creditor nation suggested that it had influence it could use profitably. But even here Roosevelt's room for maneuver was severely limited. Congress was unwilling to provide leeway on the debts, and Roosevelt was determined to manage the American currency in order to increase prices. As Roosevelt later wrote, there were two ways of moving out of the depression: reduce debts by bankruptcies and foreclosures until the amount of debt had shrunk below the value of property, or increase the value of property until it was greater than debt. He preferred the latter course.[43] Farmers and workers needed more money in their pockets so that they could purchase American products, and businesses needed to charge higher prices in order to make the profits to invest to create more jobs. And they all needed more money to pay off debts, which had been contracted during more prosperous times with a much weaker dollar.[44] Roosevelt's currency policies inhibited him from moving for lower tariffs. Increasing prices at home argued against importing cheaper goods from abroad. The agricultural legislation, for example, gave the president authority to increase tariff duties on commodities supported by the AAA. When Roosevelt approved the cotton program, he agreed to increase the duties on foreign cotton products.[45] Not surprisingly, Roosevelt did not want to press the tariff issue.

There was, of course, another side to the coin of economic nationalism. The less willing a country was to put its goods on the world market and to subject them to world prices, the more that country invited retaliation and trade wars. And many believed that not far behind a trade war would be wars of a substantially more destructive character. Within the administration, none voiced this position more loudly than Lewis Douglas.[46]

Douglas was not issuing a crabbed, self-interested warning. Hitler's rise to power signaled a real fear that unless strong countermeasures were taken, the Western world might be headed for another conflagration like the Great War, which all remembered and none wanted to repeat. (It was difficult to state as confidently, as Douglas was wont to do, that trade alone could overcome the territorial, ethnic, political, and other rivalries that so often contributed to national conflict. Douglas's comment that the abandonment of the gold standard signaled "the end of Western civilization" was more than most others were willing to concede. Nor was it so clear that other nations were as strongly wedded to free trade and the gold standard as Douglas was.)

In any event, Roosevelt had not closed the door to international economic cooperation. He had declared himself in favor of it but, predictably, had left the means vague, preferring the various nations to work out their own plans. The trouble was that other nations' plans were not likely to coincide with those of the United States. These possibilities were coming into focus at the World Economic Conference. In the spring of 1933, Roosevelt's decision to abandon the gold standard dominated everyone's thinking. The importance was easily understood. As long as the United States was on the gold standard, its bankers worried about currency fluctuations in nations such as Britain, which had gone off gold, while Britain believed that before stabilization could be achieved, prices would have to rise. What this meant, essentially, was that Britain wanted to set an exchange rate low enough to give it a competitive trade advantage with the gold standard nations. When Roosevelt took the United States off gold, his priorities became the same as those of the British. Thus, for all nations, on gold or off, the crucial issue was both the stability of exchange rates and their relationship. No country wanted another's exchange rate to be so low as to siphon off an "unfair" volume of trade. Nor did they want to see unstable or short-term fluctuations that would attract speculators who might, in turn, drive rates in disastrous directions. Of course, if a nation abandoned gold and then saw its currency drop in relation to others', that nation had less of an incentive to agree to any "stabilization" that would satisfy its neighbors.

Of the proposals for stabilization that were advanced, the most promising one came from the British, who suggested an international fund created by various governments and managed by an international agency that would make loans to national central banks. In its general features it resembled the special fund of bank notes created domestically by the New Deal's Emergency Banking Act. But when the British presented this idea, the United States backed away, citing domestic political opposition to sending funds to foreign governments, many of which were threatening to default on their past loans. Roosevelt's decision to abandon the gold standard immediately lessened his commitment to stabilization. When the United States abandoned the gold standard, the dollar began to fall and, as he had hoped, domestic prices began to rise. Roosevelt was eager to keep up the momentum. Stabilization became a long-term objective, devaluation a near-term opportunity. Stabilization was possible, he told Moley, only if it could be accomplished without shipping gold from the country and reversing the rise in domestic prices. Roosevelt hoped that the conference would limit itself to general statements and assign the hard work to committees, which would take time to reconcile the various national interests. Once that was done, the nations would have a base on which to build a structure of specific agreements.[47]

There was no way that either of these outcomes could be guaranteed, and as the conference proceeded, convincing evidence arose to the contrary. As soon as the conference opened, the delegates focused on currency stabilization, with the aim of stabilizing currency rates among the major economic nations. Roosevelt considered this a worthy objective but, along with Warburg and others, wanted stabilization to occur at a level low enough to support higher prices.[48] When the U.S. delegation to the World Economic Conference tentatively agreed to stabilize the dollar and the British pound for the duration of the conference, the dollar swung up in value, and the president rejected the proposal. Also, Roosevelt realized that even a "temporary" agreement would prevent him from using the means provided in the Thomas amendment to check such a rise. Fearing that the conferees did not understand his objectives, he dispatched Moley to London with instructions to increase the international price level. Then, in a statement he would later regret, he assured Moley that he would agree to a stabilization formula if nothing else would calm the gold standard countries. Shortly after Moley left, Roosevelt learned that the conference was beginning to move in the direction of adopting the generalities he favored, and he quietly explored ways to stabilize the dollar through the Federal Reserve Banks—a move that would have satisfied the worried delegates without tying his hands with an international agreement.[49]

Moley's trip to London galvanized the press and paralyzed the conference. Reporters searched for clues to his objectives, and currency markets gyrated wildly. (What Roosevelt expected Moley to accomplish has never been made clear. The president had firmly advised Moley that his objective was to raise world prices. At the same time, Roosevelt knew that Moley believed that for years the nations had been moving in the direction of self-sufficiency and away from interdependence and therefore saw little to gain from the conference. And Roosevelt had agreed to a temporary stabilization agreement, if necessary, to calm the anxious gold nations.)

At the conference, Moley accomplished what he believed to be the president's objectives. He secured a draft resolution that committed the nations to eventual stabilization. But to his dismay, Roosevelt interpreted the statement as an attempt by gold standard nations to force the United States to an early stabilization agreement. The president stingingly rejected the draft and the next day sent a public message to the conference deriding the delegates for catering to the "old fetishes of so-called international bankers" and chiding them for not endorsing the planning of national currencies to support purchasing power. The result was that the London conference ended in frustration, with everyone laying the outcome, for good or ill, at the doorstep of Franklin D. Roosevelt.

Many have speculated about the reasons for Roosevelt's decision, and there seems to be enough evidence to continue such speculation indefinitely. Roosevelt's rejection of the agreement contradicted not only his instructions to Moley but also his statements that spring to various European heads of state to whom he had pledged his devotion to currency stabilization. His reply distorted the content of the draft so seriously as to suggest that he had either failed to read it or suddenly changed his mind about stabilization. Such behavior suggested that special circumstances may have influenced his decision. First, Roosevelt was away from Washington on a sailing vacation to Campobello. Second, he was in the company of his Dutchess County friend Henry Morgenthau, who was spending a good deal of time preaching against the gold standard and in favor of a "commodity dollar." Third, on the night that he decided to reject the compromise draft, he had been irritated by disputes with Eleanor over minor domestic matters and was in no mood to make commitments he wanted to avoid. These facts provide interesting evidence for those who would like to find trivial explanations for historical events.

And indeed, such facts may, in some abstract, intuitive sense, explain Roosevelt's behavior. But such an explanation does not address the fact that the compromise draft included not one word about Roosevelt's priority of elevating world prices.[50] Instead, the draft stressed stabilization, making it appear that stabilization was an end in itself. Thus, it was at least possible for Roosevelt to conclude that, for whatever reason, Moley had elevated a secondary concern—a means to the end of increasing world prices—to an objective. (Of course, from Moley's perspective, it seemed that some compromise agreement was needed for the conference to continue and that the one worked out was sufficiently vague to commit the United States to no specific or immediate course of action. The president had indicated to Moley that he would be satisfied if the dollar stabilized at about $4.25 to the pound. When Moley arrived in London, the dollar was over $4.40. France and the other gold standard countries were panicked that they would be forced off gold. Moley now perceived that they no longer wanted any stabilization; they only hoped for some gesture that would halt the wild currency speculation that was so threatening.)[51]

It is an interesting question whether Roosevelt should have approved a stabilization agreement in order to cool a short-run speculative fever and then encourage more fundamental objectives such as increasing world prices, purchasing power, and living standards. In the form of an abstract either-or proposition, it lends itself to prolonged discussion. Treated as a historical question, however, it becomes more manageable. That is, it seems reasonable to look at the historical record to decide whether his methods were more realistically adapted to one course or the other. In the spring of 1933, Roosevelt was dealing with an emergency that needed immediate attention; still, most of the approaches he sponsored were the product of years of serious discussion and development, and the men who debated and formulated them represented interests with deep roots in the American social structure. Thus, there was nothing in the situation of the Hundred Days that made it impossible to think about long-term, fundamental objectives. Indeed, Roosevelt often discussed these objectives, and the measures he sponsored were designed fundamentally to alter the structure of many key market sectors, such as agriculture, banking, home ownership, and industrial production. The key element was not Roosevelt's long-range objectives but the particular methods by which he advanced toward them. Roosevelt adopted a legislative strategy that called on him to tackle problems piecemeal, as part of a stream of decision making rather than as elements of a fully rounded, logically defensible reform system. Once he had done this and adjusted to its rhythms, it became increasingly difficult for him to adopt "final" solutions that closed the door to future thought and action. This being the case, Roosevelt ought to have accepted some of the deals at the economic conference with the understanding that they were temporary, designed to settle the financial markets and perhaps serve as a basis for further planning. Whether such an approach would have worked, would have "saved" the conference, or would merely have spurred more demands for even longer-term agreements and assurances, no one can tell. But it would have clarified for those on the scene and for later historians the president's motives and his responsibility for whatever outcome emerged.

The larger significance of Roosevelt's action is subject to the same range of interpretation. Those who focus on the stabilization draft and compare it with Roosevelt's responses are properly struck by the president's gratuitous and overblown interpretation of it as a conspiracy against his recovery program. Certainly, this was the reaction of Moley, whose disbelief turned to sarcastic irony as he read Roosevelt's response at the American embassy. Others were less subtle, denouncing the illogic, arrogance, and impracticality of Roosevelt's declaration. One excellent student of Roosevelt, Kenneth S. Davis, has suggested that if Roosevelt had acted differently, the subsequent international order might have prevented World War II.[52]

Still, whatever may be said against Roosevelt's illogic and bad behavior, it is difficult to claim that he lost anything he could not afford to lose. Certainly he was not risking much political capital at home. The logic of the recovery program was turning him away from moves to reduce tariffs; Congress had weakened his ability to apply neutrality in a selective fashion and in no uncertain terms had let him know that war debts were not a subject even to be discussed. As Barry Eichengreen has argued, the World Economic Conference failed not because Roosevelt took the United States off the gold standard but because the participants had domestic political considerations that forced them to have different conceptions of how to solve the problem. The French could not give trade concessions, and without them Britain and the United States could not stabilize their currencies without running balance-of-payments deficits. Roosevelt's views on currency reflation mirrored those of the British, who were glad to be off the gold standard and were enjoying the flexibility of varying rates. Not surprisingly, they expected little from an international conference.[53]

In this situation, Roosevelt's only hope was to direct the conference toward an agreement on broad generalities. But the delegates refused to do this and insisted on finding ways to pin down the United States on the stabilization issue. The mild nature of the draft agreement might suggest that the Europeans wanted only a gesture of good faith from the president. But any claim they might have made in this direction was nullified when they interpreted Roosevelt's reaction as causing the breakup of the conference. Their action strongly suggested that once Roosevelt agreed to the draft, they were perfectly willing to pressure him for a more definite agreement. And Roosevelt had made it plain that this was something he was not willing to give.

The hectic pace of the Hundred Days, concluding with Roosevelt's decision for economic nationalism, rounded out the greatest production of legislation in American history. If it left many breathless and unsure how things would turn out, it at least bestowed on Roosevelt a critical advantage. By establishing his leadership, it kept him in the spotlight, where he wanted to be, and it presented him with a complete program of emergency measures with which to fight for economic recovery. Nothing could have better suited his experimental nature. He now had a full range of possible "solutions" and the opportunity to put them into effect. It would be hard to imagine conditions more favorable to a pluralistic leader.

3

STRATEGIES FOR ECONOMIC RECOVERY

The comprehensive nature of the Hundred Days legislation required Roosevelt to move on many fronts at the same time. His top priority had always been agricultural recovery, but NIRA and its administrative agency, the National Recovery Administration (NRA), had opened up possibilities for industrial recovery. These were to be the focus of his New Deal strategy.

New Deal policy makers believed that agricultural recovery and long-term stability depended on four approaches. To help farmers deal with the present emergency, they favored a program of government loans. For the longer term, they favored reducing trade barriers and opening markets to U.S. farm commodities. Until that could be achieved, however, they favored a national program to make agriculture more profitable. The essential means of doing this was to reduce production, first by land-use planning that would take marginal land out of production and turn it to better uses, and second by reducing the production of the major producers by a "domestic allotment" system. To these prescriptions Roosevelt added monetary inflation by tinkering with the value of gold.

Congress established three agencies to provide credit to farmers. The Commodity Credit Corporation loaned money to farmers on the security of their crops. The Farm Credit Administration reorganized local agencies and supplied them with additional resources to form cooperatives and meet production costs. The federal land banks extended mortgage credit to farmers. Under W. I. Myers, an agricultural economist at Cornell University, the administration developed a decentralized, voluntary system run by farmers. Roosevelt soothed Morgenthau's hurt feelings at not being named secretary of agriculture by naming him to head the new Farm Credit Administration.[1]

In the meantime, Roosevelt sought to provide immediate aid to farmers by manipulating the price of gold. When other nations, notably Great Britain, went off the gold standard, they devalued their currency by increasing the price of gold. This move had the effect of lowering the price of their exports by increasing the purchasing power of currencies, such as the U.S. dollar, still backed by gold. It also encouraged the exporting of gold to get the higher price and the hoarding of gold in anticipation of higher prices yet to come. Roosevelt responded to these pressures, but he especially responded to a decline in farm prices. Fearing that "marching farmers" might confront him with his own version of Hoover's Bonus Army, Roosevelt authorized the Reconstruction Finance Corporation, a federal lending agency established during the Hoover administration, to buy gold. The objective, he explained, was to raise prices so farmers and workers could more easily repay their debts and eventually achieve stability in "purchasing and debt-paying power" for years to come. Each morning he would meet with Morgenthau to set that day's price for gold, raising the price each day but varying the precise amount to confuse speculators. By buying in the American market, he had increased the U.S. price above the world price by the end of October, which meant that the dollar's purchasing power had increased abroad while declining at home. In order to increase world prices for American goods, Roosevelt now undertook to buy foreign gold. But his efforts were countered by British gold purchases and threatened by resulting instability in world trade. On January 15, 1934, Roosevelt asked Congress for legislation to permit him to fix the price of gold at no more than 60 percent of its pre-1933 price. Congress complied, and Roosevelt set the price of gold at $35 an ounce. From this time on, American policy was aimed at establishing a stable relationship with the major European currencies.[2]

Secretary Wallace wanted agricultural recovery to focus on the domestic allotment system, and here things got off to a lumbering start. Grouped around Wallace was a combination of old hands, New Dealers, and special agenda advocates. They were alike in being "agricultural fundamentalists," who believed that a healthy national economy depended on a healthy farm economy. The old hands in the U.S. Department of Agriculture (USDA), holdovers from the Hoover administration and housed in the Bureau of Agricultural Economics, wanted to use their knowledge of agricultural economics, land use, and demography to diversify and stabilize the rural economy.[3] They distrusted marketing agreements, which they saw as tools for monopoly pricing, and instead favored limiting production. Their principal objective was to increase commodity prices by signing farmers to production contracts.

The men around Wallace formed a kind of institutional shield that protected him from his somewhat eccentric personality. No one would argue against his reputation as one of the nation's foremost agricultural experts. As publisher of the nation's leading farm journal, *Wallace's Farmer,* he had helped form the study of agricultural economics and agricultural science, especially the development of hybrid seed corn. As a farm journalist he had experimented with various ways to improve agricultural production, including sponsoring the first corn-husking contests to improve the efficiency of corn harvesting. At the same time, Wallace had a peculiar streak. He was private to the extent of being unsociable. He approached life with a serious, humorless dedication to seeking the truth. His searches took him out of the mainstream and into the realm of mysticism, where he explored Native American religions and a movement called theosophy, which posited an Absolute Spirit that connects to the world in various ways, including investing every person with "a spark of divine fire." Through theosophy he met Nicholas Roerich, whom he adopted as a spiritual counselor and to whom he wrote a number of letters in which he referred to Roerich as "Dear Guru." These letters were to haunt much of his subsequent political life.[4]

The old hands strongly opposed the views of George Peek, the man Wallace appointed to head the Agricultural Adjustment Administration. Peek had ties to finance and industry and was backed by the Farm Bureau and the midwestern farmers. Perhaps more significantly, Peek was an ally of Bernard Baruch, a prominent figure in the early months of the New Deal. But Peek was not a Baruch bargain. He was aggressive, stubborn, opinionated, and determined to have his own way.

From the beginning, Peek and Wallace disagreed on the principal purpose of the AAA. Wallace favored the domestic allotment, with its emphasis on increasing farm prices by restricting production. Peek opposed all production restrictions and wanted to expand foreign trade through marketing agreements and to protect domestic agriculture with high tariffs. Peek wanted National Recovery Administration (NRA)–style marketing codes that were legally binding on the producers and the buyers. Such agreements would establish a two-price system—a high domestic price and a low international price—with export subsidies to help the United States "dump" its surplus production abroad.

Further tensions arose among the different elements in the New Deal agricultural structure. Wallace's general counsel, Jerome Frank, and his Consumers Counsel, headed by Frederick C. Howe and assisted by Gardner "Pat" Jackson, voiced a liberal-radical perspective that identified with farm laborers and tenants, the most impoverished in an impoverished and suffering sector. Frank and his crowd were largely city boys, fast talkers, aggressive, who did not take no for an answer. Bright, facile, and abstract, they were less interested in establishing a prosperous agriculture than in reforming rural society. In Frank's words, they wanted to use the "profit system . . . as a consciously directed means of promoting the general good." Specifically, they wanted to limit the profits of middlemen (the distributors and processors of agricultural commodities) in the interest of enlarging consumer demand. They would do this by licensing all buyers of agricultural products with agreements to set prices and by checking other marketing agreements to be sure they protected consumer interests. They had a certain amount in common with the USDA regulars, who wanted to use agricultural economics, land use, and demography to diversify and stabilize the rural economy, but they struck hostile sparks because their priority was to help the rural poor.[5]

From the beginning, the fundamentalists took charge.[6] Wallace and Peek moved smartly to reduce cotton production. Over 98 percent of cotton farmers signed contracts and removed over 4 million bales from production, almost all by plowing under cotton that had been planted that spring. When favorable weather produced a larger crop than the AAA had antici-

President Roosevelt presents the first government check for reducing cotton acreage under the Agricultural Adjustment Act to William E. Morris of Nueces County, Texas, July 28, 1933. (Secretary of Agriculture)

pated, the administration offered loans to the farmers in return for deeper acreage reductions.

The complexities of the agricultural economy guaranteed that no government program would operate free from criticism. For example, southeastern cotton farmers worried that the more productive southwestern farmers would get a greater benefit from a crop reduction program, shippers and dealers worried about the loss of business, and some economists worried that cotton loans at levels above market prices would only encourage extra production.

Other complexities bedeviled the corn-hog program. Drought conditions in the Middle West had reduced the expected corn crop to manageable levels, but, as with cotton, it was necessary to reduce the hog supply by slaughtering many that had already been shipped to market. As a result, the government purchased over 6 million pigs, many of them underweight and suitable for processing into grease and fertilizer. Another 2 million hogs were purchased and processed into meat for persons on relief. As a program of economic relief, the emergency effort worked well. Producer income increased by 10 percent; packers kept the lard as a credit against their taxes.

In the fall of 1933 the AAA initiated its corn-hog contract program. The contracts committed farmers to reducing their corn acreages by 20 to 30 percent of their 1932–1933 planting and their hog production by 25 percent in return for guaranteed benefit payments. Cattle and dairy producers worried that the farmers would convert their idle acres to pasture and raise cows in competition with them.

More important, complications in managing the programs caused irritating and politically embarrassing delays. AAA officials had to form local committees to write the contracts, sort out relations between landlords and tenants, and investigate complaints that farmers were overstating their base acreages or hog production numbers. In the end, only 25 percent of corn farmers and 60 to 70 percent of hog producers signed benefit contracts.

In contrast, the wheat program went into operation relatively smoothly because the wheat farmers associations had worked with the administration to write and staff an acreage reduction program. The main problem arose between winter wheat producers, who marketed early and received the highest prices, and spring wheat producers, who marketed late and suffered from drought and a price drop caused by large European harvests. Radical farm leaders such as Milo Reno in Iowa and Governor William Langer of North Dakota called for guaranteed prices for farm commodities (a program called "cost of production"). Langer attempted to keep his state's wheat off the market, citing a state law against selling any commodity at less than its cost of production.

In the dairy industry, the diversity of products made management difficult. In fact, if the industry itself had not asked for AAA assistance, the administration might not have approached it. Not surprisingly, the producers' initiative paid off; the AAA permitted them to write their own plan that allowed dairy associations to negotiate marketing agreements with distributors subject to AAA approval. In operation, the program proved a nightmare. Small retailers and chain stores demanded to sell milk products below the licensed price; small producers complained that the big ones had set base prices too low to drive out competition. Wallace concluded that the only reasonable course was to limit milk production. The problem was that the dairy associations and the distributors favored marketing contracts with licensed prices. The National Cooperative Milk Producers' Federation resurrected the McNary-Haugen formula by asking Congress to mandate government purchases of surplus milk to be dumped overseas or distributed to relief clients. As the production control program went in effect, AAA officials feared that it would be their biggest headache.

For the tobacco farmers, the major headaches were low prices, large stocks of low-grade tobacco, a multitude of tobacco varieties, and surplus stocks. The program emerged from sessions with growers and their representatives and from advice by agricultural economists in tobacco-growing states. It proposed to reduce production by half and to divert low-grade varieties to noncommercial uses. The program depended on the cooperation of the producers. When producers signed up in large numbers, the buyers agreed to pay higher prices. The result was short-term support for tobacco that resulted in stability for the industry by 1935.

In the rural South, landowners were squeezing out tenants and sharecroppers to pay off their creditors and reduce their operating costs.[7] The condition of tenant farmers was especially desperate. Often receiving less than $50 a year, their living standards plunged to primitive levels. Houses crumbled, clothing tattered. Without soap, hygiene suffered and sickness spread. Children missed school because they were needed to work in the fields or because they were sick.

The cause of the tenants was taken up by the Southern Tenant Farmers Union (STFU). Led by a combination of liberals, socialists, and traditional agrarian reformers, the STFU called for government ownership of land to protect tenant rights and for collective bargaining between tenants and landlords. With the support of Norman Thomas, the Socialist candidate for president in 1932, they publicized how landlords victimized their tenants by evicting them or withholding their fair share of AAA payments.

Resolving all these conflicts demanded administrative acumen. In the fall of 1933 there was a brief flurry of bureaucratic infighting between Peek and Wallace for control over AAA rule making. Peek won the first round by appealing to Roosevelt, but early in December, when Wallace refused Peek's plan to subsidize butter exports, Peek resigned. Now free to move forward without Peek's interference and carping, Wallace developed a flexible structure that combined grassroots participation, interest-group representation, and federal supervision and rule making. As a result, the main thrust of his program was to organize production, not the social relationships in agriculture. Local production committees were staffed by persons from the most prominent agricultural institutions: the extension services and the land grant colleges.[8] They favored the approach of AAA administrator Chester Davis, who replaced Peek in 1934. Davis believed that the fundamental task of agricultural recovery was to raise farm prices. That done, there would be no tenant-landlord problem. He also was determined to preserve the network of landlords, universities, extension service agencies, and powerful southern congressmen on which the AAA structure had come to rest.[9]

Davis and the liberals became engaged in a struggle for supremacy. The liberals had gained access to Wallace through Assistant Secretary Paul Appleby, who acted as gatekeeper for Wallace and screened his sources of information. Early in 1935, an explosive situation developed in northeastern Arkansas as the STFU faced off against planters and law officers and rumors flew that an AAA investigator was about to issue a report supporting the tenants.[10] In Washington the liberals decided on a showdown with Davis. In February 1935, they attempted to write AAA contracts to guarantee security to tenants. Existing contracts required landlords not to reduce the *number* of their tenants, they could change their tenants each year as they saw fit. Frank now reinterpreted the clause to require landlords to maintain the same tenants, and Appleby dispatched a telegram to the cotton committees announcing the new interpretation. This provoked an outcry from cotton planters and convinced Davis that Frank and Appleby were conspiring to force him to defend the planters. Believing that the provision would subvert the 1934–1935 cotton program by discouraging planters from participating, Davis promptly fired Frank and his followers. Wallace, who had been told that Davis was the only person capable of running the AAA, approved the firings for "administrative reasons." Roosevelt, who had earlier been warned by powerful southern congressmen that if he played ball with the liberals he would get no more farm legislation, allowed the dismissals to stand.[11]

Still, the issue of rural poverty did not go unnoticed. In 1933–1934, when almost 15 percent of rural families were on relief, four agencies were involved, representing a wide variety of interests from banking to practical farming to social science. When an issue developed this much staying power, Roosevelt looked for an agency for it. In April 1935, he created the

Resettlement Administration (RA). To head it he appointed Rex Tugwell, who used the agency as a laboratory for social experimentation.

Tugwell's projects provoked opposition from landlords, processors, brokers, and consumers, who wanted to maintain the system under which the rural poor formed a surplus labor pool, and from real estate interests that resented federal competition for development land. Against such opposition, which was well represented in Congress and was being propped up by the AAA, the RA had few resources. Tugwell's reputation as a left-wing "dreamer" was frequently hurled against his programs and incorporated into the anti–New Deal litany of bad management practices. The rural poor had little political muscle, often residing in states that required a poll tax receipt to qualify to vote. Attempts by the RA to pay poll taxes for its clients drew howls of protest. In 1935, a year in which Roosevelt was focusing on social security, work relief, labor, and tax policies, Tugwell could not develop the necessary presidential support.[12]

Meanwhile, the AAA moved in two directions. With Roosevelt's support, Wallace argued for expanding America's farm markets by reducing national trade barriers. Until that happened, AAA policy makers experimented with programs to determine the most efficient use of farmland and the appropriate amount of production for existing markets.[13]

Assuming that a stable and prosperous rural economy would be a consumer economy, the administration moved to provide electric service to rural families. In 1933, some 90 percent of farm families lacked electric service, effectively cutting them off from the previous decade's major advance—the application of electric power to methods of production and the manufacturing of electric appliances for American consumers. The basic obstacle had been the unwillingness of private utilities to provide service to scattered and in many cases low-income customers. Regional support for electrification had been building during the 1920s. North and South Carolina had established state authorities to provide electric service. In several midwestern states, farmers had organized electric cooperatives to establish the necessary purchasing power. A number of forces combined on behalf of rural electrification: public power, rural cooperatives, state experiments, and the TVA, which provided power to a cooperative formed by business and farm interests in northern Mississippi.

In 1933, Roosevelt created by executive order the Electric Home and Farm Authority, which made credit available to farmers to purchase electric appliances. The authority thus subsidized retail sales of refrigerators, radios, stoves, and light fixtures. The success of the program and the success of the electric cooperatives inspired Roosevelt to recommend a $100 million appropriation to purchase power lines for rural Americans. In May 1935, he created the Rural Electrification Administration (REA) with Morris L. Cooke, a longtime advocate of rural electrification, in charge. He later authorized the REA to lend money for self-liquidating projects. Cooke looked to the private utility companies for cooperation in constructing the facilities but found them unwilling to do anything but ask for an astronomical amount of money to provide services at astronomical rates. The battle for legislation regulating utility holding companies further alienated them from the federal government. In the end, Cooke had to sell rural electrification as a work-relief project.[14]

For several months, Cooke struggled unsuccessfully to get private and municipal power companies to join his system, but their unwillingness pointed the administration toward consumer cooperatives. Eventually, legislation subsidized cooperatives, but in a way that encouraged private power companies to provide service. At first the private companies fought the REA, often building "spite lines" that cut out the REA from the more lucrative rural markets. Gradually, however, the companies realized the potential of the rural market and began to take on their share. By World War II, some 1 million farm customers had been added to the electric service rolls at payback rates that imposed almost no cost to the taxpayers.[15]

Electric service brought far-reaching benefits to America's farms. Stoves, sewing machines, vacuum cleaners, and water pumps lightened the burdens of housework; refrigerators stored perishables that provided a balanced diet; radios improved civic awareness and provided entertainment; farm mechanization increased with the addition of separators, tools, and milking machines. Electric service made possible new industries: sawmills, lumberyards, slaughterhouses, grain elevators, canneries, and the like. In short, it brought self-sufficiency and diversification in greater measure than all the plans and programs of the New Deal social reformers.[16]

It still remained to grapple with the complexities of the farm problem. During Roosevelt's campaign for a second term, the thrust of farm policy took on a coherent form. The central issue was whether American agriculture would accept some kind of collective solution to its difficulties or would continue to be guided by its historic traditions of individual property rights and the cultural values that assigned success and failure to a farmer's ability to "manage." Hearings in the summer of 1937 revealed that Congress sympathized only with higher prices and farm ownership. This meant that rural "planners" had to focus on programs that aimed at higher prices, individual landowning, and "modern," "efficient" farming. They recognized the importance of prices and ownership, but they also realized that these alone could not provide economic stability. A more complex approach was needed, one that addressed the farmers' costs of operation and their relation to the larger national economy. This meant increasing farmer "efficiency," or increasing the productivity per farmer, which meant more mechanization, taking marginal land out of production, better conservation of soil and water, and a better balance between crop and livestock production. It also meant fewer farmers and finding jobs for the displaced in the industrial cities. This required industrial prosperity and an urban population that would benefit from the lower prices produced by "efficient" farming. This, in turn, justified the New Deal's program for industrial labor. Minimum-wage legislation would lift up the poorest third of industrial workers, and improved conditions for the rural poor would remove them as low-wage competitors. Thus it was necessary to oppose regional wage differentials, but also to accept regional variation: that different regional conditions would require distinctive approaches, and that regional societies were most susceptible to fully integrated solutions.[17]

Such an approach implied an integrated national policy that could address unique regional conditions and respond to changing economic conditions. In 1935, Wallace revived his idea of an "ever normal granary." He considered it important to the national interest to have grain reserves in times of shortage. The conception was analogous to theories of government fiscal policy based on alternating periods of surplus and deficit, depending on the state of the business cycle. It was a way of providing stability over time, a method of managing change.

Along with the ever normal granary, the New Deal developed a pluralistic defense of its farm program. Higher farm prices, the New Dealers argued, increased farmers' purchasing power to buy products manufactured in cities. Cutbacks in production simply reduced sales to nonexistent foreign markets while leaving sufficient production for home demands. Reductions in agricultural production were small compared with those in industrial production, suggesting that farmers were still producing enough to make their commodities affordable to urban customers. And the AAA could just as easily increase production when market conditions changed. Reciprocal trade was seen as helping farmers and opening markets. The AAA contracting system was defended as democratic, run by local committees of farmers and participated in by overwhelming majorities who signed up voluntarily. Nor did the New Deal back away from its relief policies, which aided farmers and their families in direst need, or its credit policies, which gave farmers capital to revive their operations.

These objectives were to be achieved by the methods of pluralism. The Soil Conservation and Domestic Allotment Act of 1936 adopted a multifaceted approach, employing voluntary conservation, allotment payments, soil quality, and crop variety in varying combinations to determine the benefit payment. Crops were cataloged according to how much they depleted the soil. Farmers were compensated for planting soil-building crops.

Under Howard Tolley, the administration was decentralized, with offices established in each state, where contracts were made and programs were supervised. One contract was written per farm. Thus it was no longer necessary to divide the nation into commodity groups, and the administration became more regional in nature. Outside experts were hired to travel around the country and examine the program. Efforts were made to solicit farmers' opinions. The USDA drafted a soil conservation district law to enable farmers to form local agencies that could interact with state and federal governments. A two-thirds vote on a given conservation practice would bind all members of the district.

Interests continued to clash, however. Mainline administrators believed that the RA was only propping up inefficient managers; the Farm Bureau and some tobacco and cotton farmers wanted a centralized program. When the AAA reorganized soil conservation committees to accommodate the land grant colleges, it aroused the suspicions of the extension services and the Farm Bureau.

No clashes were more severe than those over the future of tenant farmers. When Congress considered legislation to support tenants' buying land, Roosevelt appointed an executive committee of liberal reformers who made sure that the STFU had its say. The committee recommended a basket of reforms, the most important of which called for the government to purchase land and to hold title while the tenants acquired the knowledge and skills to manage it efficiently. But the conservatives on the House Agriculture Committee would have none of it and in the end provided only a token sum to be loaned to tenants who had the right "character" and enough cash for a substantial down payment. The best that Roosevelt and liberals could get out of the legislation was the opportunity to reconstitute the Resettlement Administration as the Farm Security Administration (FSA). Under the leadership of Will Alexander and other liberals, the FSA doled out only a pittance of loan money but provided pockets of economic and social opportunity for the disadvantaged. In the South, blacks and whites served on FSA committees and benefited equally from its services. The FSA continued the RA's experiments in social reform, establishing cooperative communities. All these activities brought forth the usual conservative denunciations.[18]

A more profound problem for the New Deal was to link the prescriptions of its planners to the aspirations of the citizenry. It was often too easy to overlook the priorities of those whose lives would be changed by the planners' prescriptions or to focus too narrowly on the interest of one group of clients. Americans might favor a social and economic commonwealth (or some expression of it such as "neighborliness" or "community spirit"), but their definitions of it and how best to achieve it might be light years apart. Most critically, it was easy to overlook the preference of commercial farmers for higher prices instead of social reorganization.[19]

Given the opportunity to choose, American farmers chose a narrow definition of their self-interest. A 1938 poll found farmers opposed to the Works Progress Administration (WPA) and relief in general, to labor unions, to government spending, and to the AAA. They generally favored banking legislation, the REA, farm credits, and surplus storage. The same year, Wallace reorganized the USDA, replacing Tolley with "Spike" Evans, a man who spoke the language of the practical farmer and scoffed at the "brains trusters" in the colleges and government agencies.[20]

In its various forms, New Deal agricultural policy had a mixed but generally beneficial effect. Least successful were its attempts to control markets directly and to reform rural society. Its attempts to raise farm income through loans and production controls were more successful, though in a limited fashion. These programs operated as minimum stabilizers, akin to minimum-wage laws that reduced the flagrant exploitation of labor, or retail price maintenance laws that limited the worst abuses of cutthroat competition. Prices for corn, wheat, and cotton remained between 50 and 60 percent of parity through the 1930s. But this still represented an increase over unsupported commodities, which declined relative to parity. Analyst Theodore Saloutos concluded that loans on storable staples effectively supported prices; price supports of perishable products were too costly because of the high price support ceiling and resulted in wasteful and conspicuous dumping procedures; marketing agreements worked for milk and some vegetables but did not provide for adequate consumer interest; and price deficiency payments substantially increased returns to farmers—40 percent for cotton, 20 percent for wheat.[21]

Because the New Deal farm policy aimed principally at raising farm prices, it could do nothing about farm costs of production and thus could not affect the profitability of agriculture. Nor could it guarantee consumer demand or affect the distribution of income in rural America. In the absence of expanded trade, the only recourse was for the government to become a buyer of last resort. The Commodity Credit Corporation was accumulating large stocks of grain as security for its loans and might have been swamped, as Hoover's Federal Farm Board had been, if the war had not swollen demand.[22]

The "parity" price standard further limited the flexibility of New Deal policy. Farmers received federal loans in return for production controls. In theory, the relation between these two could be adjusted indefinitely to market conditions. In practice, however, this did not happen. The parity standard, which fixed prices according to a historical standard, became a kind of talisman for agricultural policy makers. Farmers and their representatives insisted on continuing supports near the parity level. During good times, the price supports had little work to do, and in bad times, they helped keep farmers in business. Perhaps their most important effect was to provide a measure of stability while other forces—mechanization and chemical applications—transformed farming.

The New Deal program for industrial recovery began with a premise similar to the program for agricultural recovery: the need for a partnership between government and business. In contrast to the programs for agriculture, which operated from a base in the Department of Agriculture and employed the administrative machinery of the extension services, land grant colleges, and agricultural societies, any program for industrial recovery would have to be built from the bottom up. It would not be an easy task, since, as in agriculture, the nation's industrial structure presented many complexities and opportunities for conflict.[23]

The industrial provisions of NIRA hoped to reconcile a number of previously conflicting groups and agendas. Labor was given hope for mass organization and collective bargaining, business for price and production controls, competitive industries for more cooperation, weak industries for protection from technologically based competition, and small merchants from mass distributors. A number of economic theories and ideological preferences supported these positions. The act itself was vaguely worded and provided no specific direction. In this sense it was an ideal vehicle for experiments in cooperation; in another sense it provided a new field of struggle, a new medium of competition. It joined a considerable list of formulas that over the years had attempted to resolve conflicts by creating a structure that was capable of attracting support and thereby channeling discord into practices that the interested parties would agree were "fair," "reasonable," or "democratic" or was capable in some other way of persuading the parties to participate and to abide by the outcome. This was essentially Roosevelt's approach. He wanted the NRA to overcome the "abuses" and "unfair practices" of the business system so it could restore "self-regulation . . . the American method." Donald R. Brand characterized the "spirit" of the NRA as "voluntarist."[24]

Such a formula had to overcome the views and habits of those who saw the world rent by irreconcilable conflicts: management and labor, agriculture and industry, big business and small business, rich and poor, producers and consumers—the list could go on indefinitely. It also had to contend with those who thought that "competition" was the best regulator of business conduct.[25]

Another difficulty was that, although everyone knew what the NRA was supposed to do, no one knew how it was supposed to do it. Congress had given the NRA no clear mandate for procedure. This meant that the agency had no solid legislative authority to employ in the code-writing process; it could not encourage compliance by pointing to legislative objectives and methods. Roosevelt suggested that the NRA's mission was essentially restorative, to "stabilize" the "factors which make for the prosperity of the Nation, and the preservation of American standards."[26]

If no one knew how the NRA was to operate, everyone knew who was responsible for its operation. Congress had made the NRA solely responsible to the president, who was given the power not only to appoint the administrator but also to determine the structure and function of the agency. In this sense the NRA was to carry out the president's economic policy instead of the laws of Congress.

In carrying out his responsibility, Roosevelt pursued two not necessarily compatible objectives: speed and voluntarism. His approach dictated a passive administrative structure and dynamic leadership capable of inspiring volunteer spirits. Displaying his taste for federated decision making, the president appointed one administrator to head the NRA, and over him placed a review board of cabinet members. Roosevelt's idea seems to have been that the administrator would manage the NRA and the board would determine policy and ensure that the codes reflected that policy.[27]

But, as the New Deal was to demonstrate time and again, the dynamic element in its administrative structure was not its system of cooperative decision making but the flair, decisiveness, courage, and tenacity of one member of that system. In the case of the NRA, this turned out to be the man Roosevelt chose to head the agency: Hugh Johnson.

From the first, Johnson recognized that the success of NIRA depended on how it was administered. Given the ambiguities and conflicting expectations the legislation embodied, it was a prescient observation. On the surface, Johnson seemed to have the needed qualities. His brand of industrial self-government included necessary government compulsion to stop cutthroat competition; his administrative style relied on the maximum use of executive authority and discretion. Earlier experience on the War Industries Board had equipped him with the only practical experience then existing in the United States. His close association with Bernard Baruch suggested that his appointment would appeal to conservative Democrats.[28]

But Johnson had other more problematic traits. He had an impulsive, bullying streak and a flair for colorful, overblown language. A West Point graduate, he had spent much of his time on remote army posts writing western stories for pulp magazines and acquiring a drinking problem. He had always acted as a subordinate (Baruch called him "my number three man"). Nor was his estimation of his responsibilities particularly reassuring: "This is just like mounting the guillotine on the infinitesimal gamble that the ax won't work."[29]

It soon appeared to Johnson that the guillotine was well oiled and fully operational. On the day Roosevelt announced his appointment to the cabinet, the president also announced that he was giving direction of Title II (the public works section of NIRA) to Secretary of the Interior Harold Ickes. (The move came from Roosevelt's belief that public works spending was not necessary for recovery and would only unbalance the budget.) Ickes's appointment devastated Johnson, who believed that public works were needed to provide the purchasing power to pay for higher industrial wages and profits. He immediately talked of resigning. When Frances Perkins informed Roosevelt, the president told her to "get him over it."[30]

No sooner had Johnson calmed down and decided to stay than his fundamental approach was undercut. During the drafting of the industrial legislation, Johnson had argued for strong government authority over business, but as he was preparing to go into operation, he was warned that too strong an assertion would lead to court challenges that might well cause the Supreme Court to rule NIRA unconstitutional. Warily, Johnson adopted an approach of encouraging voluntary cooperation from industry.

Given his traits and the circumstances, Johnson's achievements were little short of stunning. Hitting the ground running, he began negotiations with the cotton textile industry while NIRA was still being debated. Prodding here, nudging there, showing a fine sense for compromise opportunities, Johnson orchestrated a code agreement by early July. Then, pleased with his handiwork and what he now perceived as the virtues of cooperation, he assigned the industry representatives who had drafted the code to administer it. When Roosevelt suggested amendments to strengthen government oversight of the codes, Johnson turned them over to the committee with assurances that he would accept whatever they supported. He then presented their revised draft to Roosevelt and persuaded the president to accept it. Johnson had taken the first step toward private domination of industrial recovery.

In mid-July, when the code-making process seemed to be slackening and the markets had suddenly turned soft, Johnson proposed a campaign to persuade industry to sign up by identifying the NRA with patriotism. For a time, the administration was skeptical, fearing that ballyhoo was no substitute for better economic news. But Johnson persisted, and later that month the NRA "launched a furious assault on the nation's conscience and eardrums." Marching under the banner of "the Blue Eagle," outlined on a white field and clutching symbols of industry, Johnson and his supporters praised consumers who bought products of code-regulated industries and denounced the "slackers" who preferred "rugged individualism" to "intelligently planned and controlled industrial operations."[31]

Johnson's parades and banners were just what Roosevelt wanted. The president stayed out of the code-making process, preferring instead to act as a cheerleader for the experiment in industrial cooperation. To a degree, he pictured the campaign in the same light as the mobilization of the Great War, an opportunity for millions of Americans to march shoulder to shoulder in goodwill and against a common foe.[32]

Johnson had first targeted the ten major industries for code making, and negotiations followed a pattern similar to those in cotton textiles. NRA code making followed an intricate path of discussion, negotiation, and review. This process occasionally produced some high-level revisions by Johnson and Roosevelt, who were especially concerned with the large public-interest issues involved in a given code. But this happened only in industries that were less concentrated or more competitive to begin with, and where one unit was likely to see a gain for another as a loss for itself. This meant that the vast majority of code-making decisions never came under higher-level review. In some ways this was desirable, since otherwise the Washington people would have been swamped with more information than they could have digested.[33] Occasionally supported by Roosevelt, Johnson talked tough to industry but wound up giving it what it wanted. Big Steel got the open shop, Big Oil the power to fix prices. The automobile industry had to drop the open shop from its code but retained a merit pay clause that amounted to the same thing. With Roosevelt's help, Johnson won major concessions from the coal operators to the mine unions, but at the cost of dividing the industry into myriad regional groups, which made enforcement difficult.[34]

From these practices flowed the theory that the codes were essentially self-enforcing, since they had been voluntarily agreed to by the members of a given industry. Those members had only to learn the details of their rights and duties, after which the majority would enforce general compliance by persuasion and only in the rarest cases by government force. Some of this spirit was encouraged by the circumstances under which Johnson attempted to complete the code-making process. Johnson soon realized that there was not enough time to negotiate separate codes for the hundreds of business groups and that a spurt in industrial production during the summer of 1933 was fueled in part by expectations that the coming restrictions and labor provisions of the NRA codes would increase costs. These realizations caused him to try to complete the code-making process quickly in order to stabilize industry before the production spurt died out and more workers were laid off.[35] What came out of the code-making process was essentially a victory for the management-employer view of industrial self-government. Tugwell's idea of a cooperative economic commonwealth and Roosevelt's of industrial reemployment and higher wages were discarded or overshadowed. This happened because neither the law itself nor Johnson had set definite objectives for those who drafted the codes. Indeed, Johnson argued strenuously against attempting to regulate industry by general rules. This meant that in the day-to-day negotiations to write the codes, the preferences of the NRA negotiators were crucial, and most of them were businessmen who shared Johnson's vision of industrial self-government and therefore placed the highest priority on agreement with one another rather than with representatives of labor and consumers. Unless by some magic of the marketplace prosperity suddenly returned, the NRA was bound to become the storm center of economic and political discontent.[36]

Such discontent was not long in manifesting itself. By the fall of 1933, the spurt of industrial recovery had vanished, and farmers, workers, and other consumers were faced with higher prices that either reduced the gains they had made or simply added to their burdens. When Johnson tried to stimulate the economy with an October "Buy Now" campaign, people snapped back: "What With?" In the meantime, rivalries with other government agencies, especially the Department of Agriculture, over supervision of the food processors, along with business dissatisfaction with the red tape and complexity of NRA regulations, were swelling the agency into the biggest political target in the New Deal.

Within the NRA structure there were spokespersons for alternative points of view, most notably in the Consumers' Advisory Board headed by Mary Rumsey. But Johnson was bent on industrial self-government and ignored their warnings and complaints. The best Rumsey could do was to persuade Johnson to schedule special price hearings for January 1934. The hearings were a turning point. When its members temporarily refused to accept evidence of price setting, antitrust senators led by William E. Borah of Idaho and Gerald Nye of North Dakota vigorously attacked the NRA for fostering monopoly and squeezing the small businessman.[37]

In short, it was proving all but impossible to raise prices by structural means without generating political opposition too strong to resist. In 1914 the noted Yale economist Walton Hamilton had written that "examination reveals in our scheme of prices an admirable mechanism for preserving this economic organization. Rising prices attract capital, labor, or goods; falling prices repel them."[38] Increasing prices had been a central objective of Roosevelt and the New Deal. Now, however, it was clear that both Johnson and big business were seeking this objective and, in the process, stirring up a political whirlwind. The result was that Johnson became a captive of his own actions. He had sincerely wanted to balance prices and wages; he urged business to consider its long-term interests by absorbing some of the administrative costs of the NRA and not passing them along. But because he favored voluntary action, he had no resources to deploy when business refused. Nor was it always easy to distinguish code formulas that encouraged collusion and monopoly from those that encouraged cooperation and "fair competition." Inevitably, Johnson lost control. He issued orders that he later rescinded. He uttered statements that he later retracted. He decided to form a special board to hear complaints from small business and then arranged for the noted defense attorney Clarence Darrow to head it. The board's report castigated the NRA for promoting monopoly and called for a return to competition enforced by the antitrust laws.[39]

In one of the more ominous signs of the early New Deal, controversies broke out between the NRA and other recovery agencies. The Department of Agriculture complained that rising prices were wiping out the benefits of the farm program, the Public Works Administration complained about rigged bids for its construction projects, the Federal Emergency Relief Administration saw its relief funds being soaked up by higher prices. Near the end of May 1934, the Darrow Board issued its stinging report. Johnson dismissed the charges but continued to fumble. In June 1934, NRA economists issued a directive prohibiting monopolistic pricing, but when the existing business code authorities complained, Johnson ruled that it applied only to future codes.[40] Since almost every industry had been signed up, the directive was a dead letter.

Responsibility for this state of affairs was easily assigned. As 1934 wore on, Johnson's "hard-driving," "no-nonsense," "practical" approach to business problems had given way to his "temperamental incompetence," eccentricity, and dictatorial qualities. In late summer, as the congressional and state election campaigns were getting under way, Roosevelt obtained Johnson's resignation and replaced him with an administrative board. The adjustment failed to solve the agency's difficulties, however, and as the next session of Congress considered whether to continue its existence, criticism poured in from all corners. Small business and consumer groups charged that it promoted monopoly; big business complained of "government regimentation"; labor felt betrayed by an administration that spoke of protecting workers' rights but did little to enforce them. In this setting, Roosevelt again found himself faced with orchestrating a consensus among competing groups. With his encouragement, a revised bill leaning in the direction of competition and limiting the scope of NRA authority was making its way through the House when the Supreme Court unanimously declared the original act unconstitutional. Immediately, the movement to revive it dropped as dead as a doornail.[41]

Of all the New Deal's efforts to revive the economy through cooperation, the NRA was the most conspicuous failure. Like previous catchall formulas, it paid a high price for being unable to satisfy conflicting expectations. It might be easy to conclude that the NRA failed because it tried to accomplish something that American society as a whole did not want accomplished. The combination of decentralized, weakly structured industries, the number of small businesses, and the ideology of competitiveness was so strongly ingrained that it could defeat any political effort against it. Still, from the perspective of Franklin D. Roosevelt's presidency, one needs to ask why an administration that deeply desired to engender cooperation to meet a dire emergency could not set up an administrative system capable of harnessing the energies of the industrial system more successfully.

The NRA had operated on the assumption that the public good was the product of negotiation and endless adjustments among varying interests. To a limited extent, this process worked. Manufacturers of parts and tools for the automobile industry, for example, negotiated a code similar to that of the auto industry in order to coordinate their work schedules. After complex discussions, the NRA recommended a code of uniform hours. But it failed to provide a forum in which the different interests could meet on equal terms. The result was a process that gave advantages to big business and to management.

Essentially, the NRA (and the New Deal) never discovered how to weave business profitability into the general social welfare. At first glance, this was a daunting challenge. In setting prices, for example, producers have to estimate their costs and their sales. "The difficulty of discovering a basis for making such estimates applicable to all units of an industry has resulted in the establishment of formulae that often have no bearing on the situations of many members." The principal problem is that costs vary with the volume of sales; greater sales stimulate more production and lower unit costs. This cannot be predicted and presents an insurmountable problem when trying to devise a formula to determine a "fair" price.[42] The New Deal shied away from setting up a state system that would make these determinations. Without price management, however, the NRA was blamed for price increases and for promoting "monopoly."

The NRA had a differential impact on American business. In sectors where a few producers dominated the industry, private interests were able to dominate the codes and delegate broad powers to the code authorities. In more competitive sectors, smaller producers tended to want government intervention in the code process to protect them from the larger producers.[43] The result was a crazy quilt of business arrangements, accompanied by continuing struggles for dominance of the code authorities.

Probably nothing damaged the NRA so much as its failure to produce economic recovery. A brief upward turn in the summer of 1933 rapidly disappeared. For the next year and a half, performance was sluggish. In 1935 a study of fifty-nine cities indicated that a family of four needed $900 a year for an "emergency" standard of living and $1,200 for a "subsistence" standard at a time when unskilled workers—the vast majority of the working population—were receiving between $600 and $800 a year.[44]

It also seems fairly clear that Franklin Roosevelt contributed to the failure of the NRA by his own ambiguous attitudes. On the one hand, he favored "fair" competition, "reasonable" prices, and "living" wages. On the other hand, he wanted to achieve these by voluntary cooperation and believed that the one thing needed for economic recovery was higher prices. He also favored quick action by a government agency that was newly created, that lacked a clear mandate and firm legal authority, and that had neither precedent nor experience to draw on.

Over time, Roosevelt and Johnson both tried to make up for these handicaps. Roosevelt increased Johnson's autonomy, and the NRA developed a structure that better suited broad policy making by a central administrative authority staffed by professional "experts" instead of businessmen volunteers. As this process went forward, many of the NRA's original business supporters turned against it and began characterizing it as "autocracy and bureaucracy."[45] During 1934, many of them had retreated to the traditional clichés of laissez-faire individualism. The Democratic Party victory in the fall elections temporarily muted their criticism, but by the spring of 1935, they were militantly attacking Roosevelt and the New Deal. This would do no political damage to Roosevelt's presidency, but it would subvert his desire for cooperation between government and business.

Business animosity was not simply a response to growing statism in the NRA. While it pressed for cooperation with business, the New Deal was simultaneously applying strong regulatory and antimonopoly policies to other sectors. Securities regulation had been the first achievement along this line, and its advocates—Cohen, Corcoran, and Landis—remained on the scene. Ickes had given Cohen a job as counsel to the National Power Policy Committee, where Cohen was assigned to draft a bill to control holding companies in the electric utilities industry. By 1934, many studies had demonstrated that through elaborate systems of fees and a bewildering variety of stock certificates, holding companies were milking the operating companies that actually delivered electricity to consumers and that kept themselves solvent by charging those consumers unnecessarily high rates. Cohen's bill proposed to reorganize the utilities into economically rational and regionally integrated systems, eliminating any holding company structures that could not meet this test. The Treasury Department proposed simply eliminating the holding companies. Roosevelt personally favored abolishing holding companies but, demonstrating his preference for weaving together differing views, combined the objectives of regional integration and abolishment of holding companies. Thus, the bill that went to Congress contained a so-called death-sentence clause to eliminate the stacking of holding companies and a proposal to integrate the industry into regional systems on the basis of technical efficiency.[46] Hearings began early in 1935 and by the time the bill reached the House floor in February, the industry and other business leaders had thrown up the barricades. Industry spokesmen, led by Wendell Willkie, president of Commonwealth and Southern, called the bill unnecessary and a step toward government control of the industry. Alarmed customers flooded congressional offices with letters and telegrams. Industry lobbyists outnumbered members of Congress. In March, Roosevelt came out for the bill and in June stood firm behind the "death sentence." Aided by some administration vote trading, the bill squeaked through the Senate but met a tidal wave of opposition in the House. Industry spokesmen rumored that Roosevelt had become insane, and the lobbying and letter-writing campaigns intensified. In July, the House removed the death-sentence clause.[47]

Then the legislative course changed direction. A special Senate committee chaired by Hugo Black of Alabama exposed the utility companies' lobbying efforts, which included sending hundreds of telegrams signed with names copied out of city directories and used without the individuals' permission. In the White House, Frankfurter proposed a compromise to permit holding-company control of one utility system, and Congress went along. Roosevelt grumbled that "Felix sounds just like John W. Davis," but he signed the bill.[48]

By early 1935, business opposition to the NRA had crystallized into a strategy of attacking administrative government in the courts. Taking advantage of the NRA's lack of a well-articulated legislative mandate and unable to reverse the trend in its administrative evolution toward greater independence from business and toward a more regulatory posture, the NRA's business opponents sought to subvert it where it was most vulnerable. In this they were often aided by the Roosevelt administration's Department of Justice, whose antitrust lawyers disliked the NRA's purpose and whose attorney general, Homer Cummings, wanted to keep control of all federal legal business.[49] They were more firmly supported by a number of Supreme Court decisions that had circumscribed federal economic regulation with the principles of laissez-faire economics. Also, NRA lawyers were following a strategy of suing small businesses for code violations, thus focusing important decisions on companies that the courts might easily find to be outside the jurisdiction of the national government.[50]

In January 1935, the opponents won an early victory when the Supreme Court declared unconstitutional the NRA code for the petroleum industry. Independent producers had wanted government price fixing to stabilize the industry. In order to prevent this and to minimize government power, the major oil producers had established a buying pool to maintain prices by purchasing "excess" oil and, in effect, offering guaranteed markets for all those who joined the pool. Secretary Ickes, who administered the oil code, then permitted the oil producers to set production quotas, with penalties for those who produced more than their quota. But some producers continued to flood the market with "hot oil," and prices declined. Ickes then established an elaborate screening system to detect hot oil. He was reconsidering the buying program when the Supreme Court in *Panama Refining v. Ryan* declared that NIRA's delegation of power was too vague to permit Ickes to do what he was doing. Congress responded by specifically delegating him the authority, and the oil companies undertook another buying pool to stabilize the market.[51]

For some time, various New Deal measures had been under constitutional attack, including NIRA. Different federal jurisdictions had found both for and against the act, and because of the complex issues the legislation raised, the administration had difficulty deciding which case to appeal to the Supreme Court. At length it was decided to advance a case in which a small kosher poultry business in New York City had been convicted under the NRA's live poultry code for selling diseased chickens and filing false sales reports. The appeal had been denied by the circuit court, which upheld the constitutionality of NIRA. The case was argued before the Supreme Court early in May and decided on Monday, May 27. Speaking for a unanimous Court, Chief Justice Charles Evans Hughes declared that NIRA had unconstitutionally delegated legislative powers to the executive and had attempted to regulate intrastate commerce, since the company sold all its poultry in New York City. Although the decision did not specifically deal with NIRA's labor provisions, the Court declared that they were inseparable from the regulatory powers it had invalidated and thus overturned them as well. (The Court, however, let stand the public works title of NIRA, under which the Public Works Administration [PWA] had been functioning.)

In striking down NIRA's labor provisions, the Court subverted a national labor policy that had developed ambiguities and contradictions similar to those of its industrial policy. The act specifically granted labor the right to organize unions freely, separate from employer influence. It failed, however, to prescribe the relationship between any such labor organization and company management.[52]

Responsibility for NRA labor policy fell to Donald R. Richberg, a Chicago lawyer who had represented railway unions and had drafted the Railway Labor Act of 1926 and the Norris-LaGuardia Act of 1932, both important legal advances for trade unions. Like Johnson, Richberg firmly believed in a business-government partnership to manage the economy. He differed from him in possessing greater political savvy, which he used to undermine Johnson's authority. Johnson and Richberg interpreted section 7(a) as meaning that the NRA was to encourage worker participation in union formation but was to be neutral as to the kind of union formed. Indeed, the NRA seemed to welcome a plurality of labor groups, believing that all should be represented and no one should have exclusive power to represent all company workers. Soon after the legislation passed, the NAM appealed to Johnson to rule that the law would not upset existing collective bargaining arrangements. The next month in the automobile code, Johnson and Richberg ruled in favor of proportional representation as opposed to majority rule and thus kept open the door for company unions.[53] They followed this position to the extreme conclusion that NIRA did not deprive workers of their right to bargain as individuals.[54]

These policy decisions might not have caused problems if the codes had boosted wages and purchasing power, but they did not. As summer turned into fall and prices rose, salaries lagged behind. It soon appeared that the only chance to strike a satisfactory balance would be through bargaining between labor and management.

From a business standpoint, the NRA attempted the impossible. It wanted business to increase wages and reduce hours faster than it increased prices. This would have worked if demand had increased. Then the increased production that resulted from higher wages would have reduced unit costs and maintained profit margins. But in a depressed economy, it was difficult for any businessman in a code industry to see this as a likely result. The "natural" reaction was to see higher wages as simply additional costs that would have to be paid for by spending cash reserves, economizing elsewhere, or raising prices. There is some evidence that businesses were holding large cash balances but no evidence showing the size or adequacy of those balances or, more important, how long any temporary market stimulation could have operated before being overtaken by rising costs.[55] In this situation, business was almost certain to resist any pressure to increase wages.

Still, the pattern of resistance was uneven. The main opposition to unionization came from the heavy industries. In those with less capitalization and more reliance on labor, unionism was seen as a stabilizing element whereby bargaining would establish a wage floor that would put pressure on "price chiselers" who "gouged" labor and set "unfairly low" prices. Wage stability was a method of recovery.

Thus one key to the success of NIRA was the ability of its labor provisions to stabilize the most competitive, most labor-intensive industries. There seemed to be some reason for optimism. In the needle trades, unionization under the NRA code made previously unorganized shops strong supporters of minimum wages. The problem was that unionization did not spread very widely, and nonunion shops could hire from the large pool of the unemployed. New shops arose to compete with the union ones. Suburban communities were less unionized than the central cities. Home work and price chiseling continued. Still, the major producers called for continuing the NRA because it had brought some stability.[56]

In the coal industry, regional differences and falling prices unraveled the code. Loud and persistent operators' protests caused the NRA to allow lower wage scales in southern mines. Coal prices continued to decline through 1935, the code doing nothing to stabilize industry competition. Dissatisfaction provided the opportunity to propose a special code. It was the threat of a nationwide coal strike that finally caused Congress to enact the legislation that created an NRA for the coal industry. Roosevelt signed the legislation in mid-August 1935.[57]

In cotton textiles, the code authority was dominated by management and permitted unions only to submit grievances to it. The advantage of the minimum wage was offset by production cutbacks and decreases in hours worked. The result was a series of wildcat strikes rising to the threat of a general strike. Roosevelt appointed a special board, which ruled for management on wages and hours issue and undermined the United Textile Workers' efforts for a nationwide organizing campaign.[58]

The issue was becoming not just whether organized labor could win its independence from management but whether it could find a voice within the structure of the NRA. Experience suggested the need for a more assertive labor movement. Some labor leaders, such as John L. Lewis of the United Mine Workers, declared that "the government wants you to join a union" and aggressively sought to sign up workers. Employers responded by forming company unions to deny workers independent representation or simply defied worker demands. The most dramatic result was a wave of strikes that quadrupled the number of lost man-days over the average of the previous six months.[59] Responding to these difficulties, Hugh Johnson and Roosevelt formed a National Labor Board (NLB) composed of three representatives from labor and three from management and chaired by Senator Robert Wagner.

The appointment signaled Wagner's emergence as a major influence in the New Deal. In his third term representing New York, Wagner had a distinguished career of public service and a record of seeking better conditions for workers. An experienced legislator, he relied on his able staff to flesh out the details of legislation while he spent his energies moving bills through the Senate. Although a "liberal" ideologically, he declined to join progressive coalitions, preferring to work within the structure of respect and authority that existed in both the Senate and the Democratic Party. In this cooperative manner, Wagner, who had served as a justice of the New York Supreme Court, hoped to build the NLB into a supreme court for labor, adjusting disputes through mediation and developing formulas and procedures that eventually would produce a "common law" of labor relations. The board got off to a good start, settling nearly 90 percent of cases that came before it. It first major victory came when it persuaded the hosiery mills in Reading, Pennsylvania, to permit workers to choose their bargaining agent through a secret ballot.[60] Still, the NLB operated on limited capital and had to contend with growing hostility from employers and the unwillingness of Johnson and Richberg to impose unions on unwilling employers.

In November 1933, the NLB suffered a major setback when the federal courts refused to issue an injunction against Wierton Steel for defying its rulings.[61] Roosevelt's attempt at voluntary compliance was failing. Parades, banners, and pronouncements might work 90 percent of the time, but the remaining 10 percent was a loose end that might unravel the whole ball of yarn. Roosevelt tried unsuccessfully to talk Wierton into accepting the NLB ruling. With more businesses following Wierton's lead, labor unions pressing for action, and some congressmen charging that the NRA was failing, Roosevelt issued a series of executive orders supporting the board's exercise of authority. But he required the NLB to forward all cases of noncompliance to the NRA for final action. The problem with this was that Johnson and Richberg opposed the NLB's position that a union that received a majority vote should represent all workers. Instead, they favored "proportional representation," which would have created "majority" and "minority" unions in a single shop. This set the stage for a showdown within the administration. On March 1, 1934, Wagner introduced a bill designed to stabilize industry by preventing strikes. Its heart listed various "unfair" employer practices that inhibited workers from freely choosing an independent union. It empowered the NLB with full legal authority to protect worker rights, including the principle of majority rule.[62]

As the Senate hearings got under way, events intervened in the form of a threatened auto workers strike. It was a decidedly awkward situation. Paralyzing the nation's most important manufacturing industry could easily paralyze the New Deal's recovery program. The New Deal needed the automobile industry much more than the industry needed the New Deal. The issue on which the industry drew the line was majority rule. In his haste to sign the automakers to a code, Johnson had assured them that they could keep the open shop, and Roosevelt had agreed. Bypassing the NLB, he appointed a special board that ruled in favor of "proportional" representation, emphasizing that the key element in a union election was free choice and not majority rule. Freedom of choice, Roosevelt predicted, would create the opportunity for a new form of labor-management cooperation. On questions of seniority, the president argued that workers with families should be given priority, along with consideration of their length of service or their productivity. He also established a special Automobile Labor Board to manage disputes. The board spent most of its time seeking voluntary resolutions instead of issuing orders, most of which favored management. The American Federation of Labor protested and withdrew from presenting cases to the board. When the time came late in 1934 to renew the automobile code, Roosevelt consulted only management. The new code strengthened the automakers' authority over wages and hours. This outcome appeared to reverse all the steps that had been taken in favor of independent labor unions since NLB's inception.[63]

Roosevelt's actions indicated two lines of policy toward labor. The president wanted both to keep the NRA machinery at the center of his industrial recovery program and to make himself the arbiter of labor disputes. In this sense he did not have a "labor policy" but rather a recovery policy that favored peaceful relations between management and labor, with himself as the chief peacemaker. Roosevelt did not have clear-cut views on labor. He did not think of labor as a counterweight to business; he sympathized with the powerless position of the workers and blamed management for selfish, autocratic, and manipulative tactics. He especially disliked management's refusal to bargain with workers. He thought of himself as holding the balance between the two. In other words, he opposed the idea of industry and labor collectively bargaining with each other. Above all, he wanted to stop anything that hindered economic recovery.[64]

During the auto strike, Roosevelt and Johnson used the threat of Wagner's bill as a club to obtain the industry's compliance with their settlement. Still, Roosevelt thought of the bill as another, stronger tool for mediation rather than as a means to establish collective bargaining. As industrial disputes continued to threaten both the NRA labor policy and economic recovery, Hugh Johnson concluded that labor peace was needed, and only Congress could provide the authority to accomplish it. This shifted attention to Wagner's labor dispute bill, which was designed to give the NLB the power to deal with what he thought was management's selfish determination to work around section 7(a). On April 20, 1934, he initiated a series of conferences on the bill. But management hotly opposed the bill, and congressmen wanted to avoid the issue until after the fall elections. The revised bill limited the NLB to intervening only in cases of threatened strikes, did not ban management from initiating company unions, and cut out penalties for employers' not negotiating with certified unions. Roosevelt seemed willing to press the bill in this form, but Wagner sought to amend it. The resulting uncertainty caused Roosevelt to withdraw his support, fearing that the controversy might cost the party in the fall elections.

Then new events intervened. As prices rose and the New Deal fuddled with arrangements that turned out to support management, labor leaders took matters into their own hands. Minneapolis truckers went on strike when employers, in violation of their NRA code, refused to negotiate with the teamsters local. In late May, violence left two dead; in July, two more died when police fired at unarmed strikers manning a roadblock. The Farmer-Labor governor, Floyd B. Olson, called out the National Guard and established martial law; after several weeks, he persuaded management to settle with the union.

On June 12, in the shadow of a threatened steel strike, Roosevelt called an emergency meeting at which he dictated what became Public Resolution No. 44, a joint resolution of Congress permitting the president to establish a system of labor boards independent of the NRA. When the bill passed, Roosevelt created the National Labor Relations Board (NLRB), composed of three persons who represented neither business nor labor. His purpose, he explained, was to achieve industrial peace and not to promote trade unionism and collective bargaining. He also created special boards for dock, steel, and textile workers.[65]

In July, violence erupted on the San Francisco docks, followed by a general strike. Hugh Johnson showed up and denounced the strikers as communists. More violence against the strikers followed. City officials called for federal troops, but Frances Perkins advised Roosevelt, away on a cruise, to ignore them. Eventually, both sides agreed to submit their case to the federal board Roosevelt had created under Public Resolution No. 44. In October the board awarded the union most of its demands.[66]

But Roosevelt's policy only created more tension. Early on, the NLRB accepted majority rule and collective bargaining, as the NLB had done a year earlier. Now the test would be whether the new board would have any better success than its predecessor in enforcing its ruling. It soon became clear that nothing was going to change. In the words of labor historian Melvyn Dubofsky, "the NLRB made its rulings; employers ignored them; Johnson and Richberg continued to thwart the board; and Roosevelt, as usual, equivocated."[67] Only when employers' arrogance reached the point of their not showing up for NLRB hearings did the government bring suit to enforce a board ruling. But the government lost the case, and Roosevelt, still equivocating, moved in the direction of confirming labor policies under the NRA codes—that is, leaving the subject to Johnson and Richberg.[68]

Again, Senator Wagner intervened by introducing another version of his labor relations bill. This one established the NLRB on a permanent basis and affirmed its powers to establish employee-controlled unions and to protect their right to bargain collectively with employers. More clearly than the earlier version, this bill was designed to affirm and defend workers' rights. Indeed, it no longer accorded the NLRB any authority to mediate labor disputes; the board would only protect the right of labor to bargain collectively. The response from the White House was all but mute. Frances Perkins testified for the bill but seemed most interested in locating the NLRB in her department. Still, the bill sailed through the Senate Labor and Education Committee, arrived on the floor early in May 1935, and passed sixty-three to twelve.

Up to this point, the sticking feature of such legislation had been Roosevelt's unwillingness to intervene in the NRA's codes. By this time, however, it appeared that the NRA had run its course. On May 24, Roosevelt called a meeting at which he endorsed Wagner's bill and ordered the interested parties to compose their differences on this premise. A few days later, the Supreme Court invalidated the NIRA, removing any motive for further hesitation.[69]

Roosevelt at once made the Wagner bill a top administration priority, and in July the House passed it on a voice vote. At the same time he appointed a coordinator for industrial cooperation to encourage industries to maintain code standards voluntarily, including the labor provisions of section 7(a) of the now-defunct NIRA, but administrative complications caused the arrangement to fail. Congress also passed its own code for the bituminous coal industry.[70]

The passage of the Wagner Act completed the evolution of the New Deal's industrial policy, which had begun amid the complexities of the New Deal's pluralistic attempt to create a whole greater than the sum of its parts through the interactions of interested members of a given economic sector. The idea of the early New Deal was to have the national government create agencies that would assist private institutions in developing structures and procedures for channeling market forces into constructive, cooperative paths. Now the Wagner Act departed from the goal of helping employees peacefully settle disputes with their employers to one of helping employees decide what kind of representation they wanted. Since the act outlined specific employee rights that employers were not to interfere with, it made more sense to define this process as employer versus employee rather than employee versus employee, thus establishing a protected sphere in which employees could function by "democratic" means.[71]

In one sense, the evolution indicated the weakness and failure of pluralistic assumptions, for the milling about that followed NIRA had produced not so much a cooperative commonwealth as a series of struggles for power. Those struggles had in turn redirected industrial policy toward establishing protected areas for the nation's economic groups. Thus management had come to dominate the codes, and labor had been forced to rely on the willingness of President Roosevelt to intervene on its behalf. This could be seen, as some analysts have been inclined, as a step toward a "broker state" of "corporate liberalism," in which the government made itself the protector of the nation's interests and invited those interests to bid for its favors.

There is little doubt that Roosevelt had wanted some form of cooperative commonwealth, and to this extent, his policies worked against his wishes. At the same time, however, it seems clear that what was evolving in the New Deal was not so much the failure of pluralist democracy as its transformation from the ideal of friendly cooperation to a new form of economic enfranchisement in which separate groups were given the means to organize their interests democratically. The motive for the transformation had come from labor's attempts to organize under section 7(a) of NIRA.[72] The Wagner Act's theory of collective bargaining was that justice consisted of enforcing agreements between parties that had an equal chance to bargain with each other. The law would be neutral regarding the parties' interests and objectives, apart from the opportunity to bargain and to agree. In this sense it would give workers a "free choice" of association in choosing representatives as bargaining agents, and it would promote "industrial democracy" by giving workers a sense of self-worth, freedom, and participation in the social process.[73]

The New Deal created a public sphere in which labor determined its own course by democratic means. The result was to provide workers a democratic environment in which free speech established competing appeals for their support. This was part of the New Deal emphasis on elections and free choice. Early on, the NLRB took the position that the Wagner Act required complete neutrality on the part of employers toward union representation. Employers could engage in no antiunion activity whatsoever, including speech. Employers had no legitimate interest in whether their employees joined a union. Thus all management statements, even it true, were considered objectionable. But it placed no restrictions on union speech, leaving it to the workers to evaluate union claims. Thus the NLRB never evaluated union claims for truth. Its only interventions were to punish statements that a particular union was favored by the NLRB or another government agency. In this, it wanted to protect the reputation of the government for objectivity and fairness.[74]

The Wagner Act was a contribution to the grassroots process by which the New Deal was moved toward an "underconsumptionist" interpretation of the depression. During the drafting sessions with Senator Wagner, Leon Keyserling, who worked on the legal staff of the NLRB, justified the legislation by arguing that the lack of mass purchasing power was a burden on interstate commerce. When he introduced the bill in the Senate, Wagner emphasized how prices, profits, and dividends had soared while the purchasing power of wages had actually declined. It was this "failure to maintain a sane balance between wages and industrial returns" that was endangering economic recovery.[75]

The result was a kind of corporate bargain in which management accepted certain labor "rights" and labor leaders conceded certain management powers and the right to a "fair profit." Labor and management joined to support peaceful collective bargaining, the welfare state, and overseas expansionism. The problem was that only industrial workers benefited from these reforms. Farm workers, service employees, and others formed a secondary labor market that increased with the decline of industry as the country's economic base.[76]

The New Deal's strategy of economic balance was assuming a definite form. The national government was encouraging economic interests to organize to achieve benefits such as acreage reduction payments or the right to bargain collectively. Its goal was not so much reform, in which government regulated or planned the nation's economic course, as it was stability, upon which the nation's economic interests could shape their own destinies. In this sense, the New Deal was true to the pluralistic assumption that social orders developed historically.

4

STRATEGIES FOR SOCIAL RECOVERY

As the New Deal programs for agriculture, industry, and labor matured, they focused on ways for these major economic groups to solve their problems "cooperatively" or "democratically." As the New Deal advanced, it moved away from "national" solutions toward "group" solutions and to a definition of citizenship that included identification with a social group. Such democratic group self-government could satisfy individuals' desire for self-expression and control of their lives and might also develop the habits and virtues of democracy in the mass of the people.[1]

This was part of the process by which Franklin Roosevelt sought to "multiply the number of American stakeholders," in effect using government policy to create a new social contract that emphasized the decentralization of wealth and industry and the multiplication of home owners, stockholders, and landowners, as well as the chance to enjoy the fruits of economic and technological progress. This would be the answer to the closing of the agricultural frontier and an antidote to the poison of social discontent and revolution produced in those who had neither hope nor property.[2]

As the "associational" framework of the 1920s had provided an economic framework for group democracy, the sociology of the 1920s had provided a geographical framework for group democracy. By the 1910s, social scientists were classifying areas as regions, emphasizing climate, vegetation, geographical features, animal life, historic development, and culture. Particular elements were less important than the belief that they combined to create a distinctive area, or "region." But—and here was the key element in regional thinking—regions themselves were part of a larger national whole. "Regionalism," wrote Howard Odum, a professor of sociology at the University of North Carolina who had pioneered the idea, "assumes first, last, and always a totality composed of the several area and cultural units, a great national unity and integrated culture in which each region exists as a region solely as a component unit of the whole."[3] Regional thinking assumed that the United States was made up of diverse peoples, climates, soils, and so forth but rejected the idea that such diversity necessarily led to conflict. Instead, regionalists claimed that ways could be found to combine these elements so that the nation would grow stronger, along with the happiness and well-being of all its individual citizens. Odum liked to contrast the humane, personal culture and "instinctive" democracy of the small towns with the impersonal, mechanistic "super-civilization" of modern industrialism.

Accompanying regionalism was an interest in getting "back to the land," a phrase indicating a movement from the city and town to the farm. Farm life promised a measure of self-sufficiency and personal independence, qualities the depression was curtailing in industrial and commercial centers. Studies later in the decade would indicate a population trend in this direction, and the 1930s stood in contrast to the advancing urbanization of society. At the time of Roosevelt's taking office, however, interest in the movement depended on the writings of journalists, independent economists, social critics, charitable societies, and President Roosevelt himself.

Many advocates combined regionalism and back-to-the-land values as an alternative to industrialization and urbanization. In *I'll Take My Stand,* published in 1930, twelve southerners, mostly literary persons associated with Vanderbilt University in Nashville, Tennessee, called on the nation to return to a small-community society based on individual workmanship and a culture that valued leisure and accepted a modest, uniform standard of living. The southerners called themselves "agrarians," because such a society would be "close to the soil"; they essentially wanted to turn American values away from mass production and consumption and toward membership in communities that recognized and valued individual worth. In *The People's Choice,* published in 1933, the popular sociologist Herbert Agar called for breaking up all large concentrations of wealth and widely distributing property so that people could live in more manageable, more democratic communities. (Agar was by no means an "agrarian," believing that the scale of modern technology, not its existence, needed to be controlled. It was not the goods turned out by mass production that were socially evil but the financial and business practices that accompanied mass production. For example, automobiles ought to be produced in many small plants rather than in huge factories and teeming metropolitan cities.) An important collective expression of this sentiment was the Regional Planning Association of America (RPAA), a small group of economists, architects, and city planners who contributed to various state, local, and national planning projects. Drawing from turn-of-the-century sociology, the RPAA planners sought to "survey" or identify the environmental, social, and individual needs of a given population and then find ways to develop them to form a harmonious community.[4]

Franklin Roosevelt shared many of the agrarians' values and purposes. As early as 1913, Roosevelt had suggested that suburban farms would help alleviate urban problems. Throughout his life Roosevelt favored linking country and city by institutional devices and rural and suburban planning. He often expressed his belief that in varying ways country life was a superior existence. In 1931 he had suggested offering the unemployed a few acres and the cash and equipment to "put in small food crops." As governor of New York he proposed a full-scale land-use program to include natural resources, public utilities, and settlement. His basic hope was to join agriculture and industry as part of a broad program of regional planning. In 1932 he congratulated the work of the Regional Plan Committee of New York City for having "opened our eyes to new vistas of the future." He wanted to create new rural communities with an industrial component. He saw planning as a way to avoid the topsy-turvy manner in which the nation had grown. Roosevelt included a provision for greenbelt towns in the executive order creating the Resettlement Administration. But Roosevelt's approach was to upgrade rural life through projects such as shelterbelts that would bring rain, rivers, and forests that would, in turn, attract settlement and provide economic opportunity. The president was not interested in promoting rural settlement for its own sake.[5]

At heart, Roosevelt wanted to find new ways to combine country and city. He spoke of how the end of the agricultural frontier had closed off America's "safety valve" for its industrial population and how it was now necessary to administer the nation's resources to create "a real community of interest" among all elements of society and thereby to create new "safety valves." Democracy, Roosevelt declared, depended on prosperity for all, which could be promoted by the government's helping to distribute property more widely.[6]

While the theorists pondered, debated, refined, and polished, the New Dealers provided laboratory cases to work on. Of these, the most promising was the Tennessee Valley Authority. Two RPAA members joined the TVA staff, and another RPAA member, Stuart Chase, publicized the undertaking. Although the TVA had originated in the Progressive desire to develop public power, Roosevelt had broadened the legislation to include regional community development activities. The president thought of the

TVA as a "social experiment" that combined the development of the region's physical and human resources. Resource development would bring more than prosperity; it would bring schools, radios, telephones, and other attributes of social and cultural progress. The first chairman of the TVA, Arthur Morgan, firmly shared Roosevelt's vision. His plan was to create a series of independent communities based on decentralized industries and cooperative means of production, distribution, and marketing, and drawing on the resources that forestry, soil conservation, and electric power could provide. The focal point and example of cooperation was to be the planned community of Norris (named for Senator George Norris of Nebraska, a longtime champion of the TVA concept). The area was characterized by a lack of capital, technological underdevelopment, self-sufficient farming, geographical isolation, a high birthrate, and much out-migration. People lived not so much in villages as in loose clusters of houses connected by bloodlines. Less than 4 percent of the homes had electricity. Kinfolk acquired farm tools by bartering with one another. To promote the project, Arthur Morgan took up residence in Norris.[7]

Intended for a population of 10,000, Norris was designed for single-family houses on small acreages with a central shopping area and a surrounding greenbelt. The TVA built a modern school and provided health services. The residents took up a few cooperative activities, such as a local credit union, but the ultimate promise failed to materialize. Most of the original residents came to build the dams and left when the work was completed. Those left behind gradually formed a town government and then cut the town off from the TVA. The community development projects faded away, and Norris became a bedroom suburb of nearby Knoxville. The population never reached much beyond 3,000. Although neither Norris nor the other planned communities of the TVA fulfilled the dreams of the regionalists and small-community advocates, they provided opportunities that their residents would not otherwise have had.

Other imperatives drove the development of the TVA. Its multipurpose design included electricity generation, flood control, and fertilizer production. From the beginning, such larger-scale purposes dominated the TVA's agenda. Priorities for dam construction, recreational uses, and soil conservation took precedence over providing for displaced families. An overscrupulous adherence to legal conventions denied displaced tenant farmers any compensation. The displaced also had to overcome the emotional stress of leaving homes that they and their forebears had inhabited for generations.[8] In 1934 Roosevelt had toured the TVA sites and praised the residents for taking matters into their own hands in deciding how to use the project's bounty. "This is not coming from Washington," he declared. "It is coming from you. You are not being Federalized."

Taking him at his word, the people of the valley chose cheap electricity and fertilizer as opportunities to enter the commercial, consumer economy.[9]

As a result, industrial and commercial enterprises occupied the mainstream of TVA activity. They provided opportunities not so much for creating new agencies as for expanding the reach and scope of existing ones: the land grant colleges, agricultural experiment stations, shippers and haulers. This was the context in which the TVA created benefits and opportunities. North Alabama farmers increased their yields by purchasing cheap fertilizer, while local businesses flourished with access to river transportation and cheap electricity. The TVA also encouraged trade unionism and provided regional libraries and recreational areas. The valley never developed the economic base on which the relocated residents could build significantly new lives. The only established agencies to suffer were the private power companies, which were forced out of the area by the TVA's public service. By 1940, the TVA was the largest producer of electric power in the United States. After World War II, the authority decided to make electric generation its principal activity. Thus, when it reached the limit of its water power resources, it turned increasingly to steam power generated by coal. By 1954, steam power had outpaced falling water as the source of electric power, and by the 1970s, the TVA was under criticism for environmental pollution.[10]

This raises the issue of President Roosevelt's leadership. There is much evidence that Roosevelt wanted the TVA to be a social experiment to improve living conditions and opportunities for "forgotten" Americans. But the president accepted vague, multipurpose legislation and appointed a board whose members represented different priorities. He then gave only fitful attention to the project. In essence, the president made the TVA a kind of "grab bag," putting it at the mercy of the most artful grabbers. Perhaps this is what one can expect from the pluralistic, decentralized, democratic polity. In any case, this is what America got.[11]

In targeting special groups for projects of social benefit, the New Deal gave special attention to Native Americans.[12] By 1933, American Indians had the deepest and most oppressive poverty of any group in the United States. American policy, adopted a generation before in the Dawes Act, had sought to assimilate Indians into white society by encouraging individual landowning, education in the culture and useful knowledge of white society, and the substitution of Christianity for native religion. Behind this program was the Bureau of Indian Affairs (BIA), one of the oldest and historically one of the national government's least effective agencies, which interpreted this mission as keeping Indians from intruding on the social and economic lives of white Americans. This and occasional attempts by white interests to deprive the Indians further had brought forth criticism and calls for the reform of Indian policy from organizations such as the Indian Defense Association as well as individual reformers. A 1928 study by the Brookings Institution, prepared by lawyer and political scientist Lewis Meriam, had widely attacked BIA performance and called for significantly increased resources. President Hoover had appointed persons sympathetic to reform to head his Indian affairs agency, but they had run into bureaucratic and congressional opposition and incurred the criticism of the man who was emerging as the principal spokesman for Indian reform, John Collier.

Trained as a social worker, Collier had attempted to create a sense of community and mutual support among New York City's immigrant population. Experiencing frustration, he and his family moved to California. When he accepted an invitation to visit the Pueblo Indian settlement in Taos, New Mexico, he found his ideal: a society that balanced ideological, ecological, social, and aesthetic values, a society that was based on sharing and cooperation. His admiration for Pueblo life took a political turn in the early 1920s when he emerged as a spokesman for the opposition to a bill in Congress to legitimate non-Indian claims on Pueblo lands. Now he used the Meriam report and subsequent reports and investigations to campaign for a radical, Indian-centered departure in national policy. With Secretary of the Interior Harold Ickes's dogged backing, Collier won Roosevelt's approval as commissioner of Indian affairs.

Collier later described his approach to Indian policy reform as discovering, regenerating, or creating purely Indian societies and providing them with self-determination, freedom, and the means to succeed. This program of "responsible democracy" recognized Indian diversity and depended on continuous research to succeed in action. His approach sought to create a balance between a separate Indian ethnic identity and Indian assimilation into white society. Collier wanted Indians to gain independence and develop their culture in ways that both strengthened their own social order and established an economic base within American market capitalism. Indian arts and crafts were central to his program. Collier hoped that over time Indian craft works would become commercially successful while at the same time preserving Indian cultural identity.

Collier organized his bureaucracy in typical New Deal fashion, favoring decentralization and variable responses to different local settings. His goal was to promote cooperation between his office and the Indian communities. This approach gave Indians more direct contact with the national government and input into its operations than ever before. Collier planned that at some point the Indians would take over the duties of the Interior Department.[13]

Collier began by frontally attacking the established system. By a series of executive actions and successful appeals to Congress, he removed opponents and abolished programs of individual landowership, Christianization, and paternal supervision. In their place he proposed that Congress enact an Indian Reorganization Act that would end the policy of assimilation and enable Indians to form self-governing corporations that would assume control of their own finances, culture, and property and administer their own justice, with necessary government support.

As soon as his plans became known, Collier found himself at the center of a storm of protest. Indian rights organizations split, bureaucrats dragged their feet, Christian missionaries charged that he was endorsing paganism, and many Indians worried that Collier was sending them "back to the blanket." Not for the first time, Americans faced the fundamental question of what was "best" for the Indians: assimilation into the dominant white society and culture, or promotion of the Indians' ethnic identity. To Collier, it seemed obvious that assimilation had produced only poverty and demoralization and that encouraging ethnic identity would revitalize the Indians with a sense of purpose and collective strength and creativity. To his critics, it seemed that he was denying Indians the chance to "modernize," to "progress," and to succeed as individuals according to the standards of the dominant culture. To them, Collier's self-government was a plan for Indian segregation and an isolated, limited existence.[14]

Collier responded by holding a series of "congresses" with Indian tribes, after which he proposed amendments that would protect private lands from confiscation. Powerful senators demanded further amendments, and in its final form, the bill permitted a variety of exceptions, most notably giving the tribes the opportunity to reject its provisions by a referendum. Still, the bill stopped the individual allotment system and provided some funds and legal protection for implementing Indian self-rule.[15]

The referenda began in the fall of 1934 and continued into 1936. They produced mixed results. A majority of tribes and Indians accepted the new law's provisions, but 40 percent of those voting opposed it, and only half the tribes that voted approval also drew up charters of self-government.[16] The most notable rejection came from the Navajo, who resented a program to reduce their sheep herds in order to protect their land from overgrazing.

The Navajo's response deserves close attention, because it illustrates the complexities of New Deal pluralism. The first element was Collier's own sincere desire for a better life for the Navajo and all Indian people. He firmly believed that self-determination would put the Navajo on the road to a better life. Naturally, he interpreted his objectives in light of contemporary experience, which in the Southwest was heavily influenced by the drought and the dust bowl.

Added to this was the creation of the Soil Conservation Service under Hugh Bennett, a forceful and persuasive advocate of erosion control. Another complicating element was the Taylor Grazing Act, designed to protect western rangeland from the soil-destroying effects of overgrazing. To this was added the "regionalist" assumption that the resources of a given area ought to be coordinated to provide for the welfare of the whole. And underlying all these elements was the New Deal faith that planning by "experts" and regulation by government could create a better life for all.

In the case of the Navajo, these elements created an urgent sense that Navajo sheep raising needed to be severely curtailed and regulated to control the disastrous soil erosion on Navajo lands. This erosion not only jeopardized future Navajo livelihood but also threatened to send tons of topsoil down the Colorado River. This would eventually silt up Boulder Dam, which had been built to supply water and electric power to southern California.

The problem was that the Navajo considered sheep raising central to their well-being and way of life. Although other concerns influenced their vote against reorganization, the most prominent one was their resentment of the sheep reduction program. Here was a classic example of New Deal pluralism's producing friction instead of harmony and of Collier's failure to understand the variety of Indian experience and social order. Collier responded by chiding the Navajo for rejecting the benefits of reorganization and pushed ahead with the sheep reduction program. Because of the Navajo's prominence among Indians and the American public, their rejection severely damaged Collier's credibility.

In the meantime, Collier strove to tidy up his system. He secured special legislation for the Indians of Alaska and Oklahoma, who had been excluded from the original act. A strong supporter of Native American culture and economy, he sponsored the Indian Arts and Crafts Act of 1935, which established a board whose purpose was to encourage the production of Indian artifacts for market while protecting the indigenous Indian culture from commercial exploitation. The program was a notable success. With Collier as chairman and René d'Harnoncourt as manager, the Arts and Crafts Board pursued its twin objectives of vitalizing Indian art and providing a way to combat the depression. "Indian arts and crafts obtained a solid and continuing acceptance by government officials and, more important, by the general public," concluded Francis Paul Prucha, "in considerable measure because of the work of the board."[17]

Collier moved along similar lines in Indian education, closing boarding schools that had removed children from their families and educated them in the ways of the white world. He established community day schools based on "progressive" educational thinking that encouraged students to advance at their own pace and to learn skills that helped them master their own environment. At the same time, in keeping with New Deal federalism, the national government transferred many Indian children to state and local schools under an act that allowed states to enroll Indian children. By 1938, over twice as many Indian children were in state and local schools as in community day schools. The transition from boarding schools to day schools was awkwardly managed, harming educational opportunities for a substantial number of Indian children.[18] When war came, however, many Indians left for military service or better jobs and began to demand an education that would prepare them to benefit from opportunities in white society.

Indians probably benefited more from the New Deal's short-run programs than from Collier's fundamental reforms. Collier and Ickes vigorously pursued an Indian New Deal to relieve economic suffering. CCC, Civil Works Administration (CWA), and WPA programs put Indians on New Deal payrolls; soil conservation and irrigation projects stimulated Indian agriculture and a balanced program of grazing. Through the Resettlement Administration (later the Farm Security Administration), Indians acquired some 900,000 acres for their own use, three times the amount provided in the Indian Reorganization Act. The Indian Service protected forestlands from overcutting, and the timber industry boomed in response to World War II demand.[19]

When Collier resigned in 1945, he left behind an ambiguous legacy. His efforts on behalf of Indian self-determination contributed to the New Deal's emphasis on social groups having a say in their own future. His drive to uproot the allotment and assimilation system without appreciating its benefits and the degree to which many Indians had accommodated to it and profited from it caused him to create hardships and bad feelings that a more complex view could have avoided. In the same fashion, although he believed that Indian tribes possessed a wholesome and creative traditional culture that the proper political circumstances could revitalize, he established a rigid political system within which various factional rivalries flourished. No doubt a more flexible system that would have permitted Indians to experiment with forms other than the tribe would have been more successful. This was especially troubling, since more than any of his predecessors, Collier had emphasized research into Indian ways of life and called on anthropologists for advice.[20]

At the same time, it is difficult to ascribe all the difficulties of Collier's reforms to his own naive vision of a unified Indian culture or his simplistic white-versus-red political analysis. Collier's administration of the Indian Reorganization Act permitted Indians to set their own course. If this course led to internal squabbles and power struggles, it served Indian society no worse than such struggles served white society. Nor was Collier ever given a free hand to pursue his objectives. Congress narrowed the scope of his reforms, most notably by limiting his ability to consolidate Indian lands, and grew increasingly suspicious of his efforts. Senators Burton K. Wheeler of Montana and Dennis Chavez of New Mexico, both powerful committeemen on Indian affairs, were outwardly hostile toward him. After 1935, Congress froze his funding except for emergency relief dollars, leaving him to scrabble for money from other agencies. Collier's encouragement of Indian arts and crafts provided an economic base for some of the tribes. And there was a natural friction between Collier's goal of Indian self-determination and New Deal relief programs that provided emergency support within a framework dictated by Washington. At the same time, Indian awareness of the New Deal willingness to respond to the distressed led to the organization of a "pan-Indian" movement, which, through the National Congress of American Indians, provided a forum for Indian voices of reform. The Indian Claims Commission, another Collier innovation, provided a mechanism for a practical response to Indian interests.[21]

Other less ambitious and visible community projects were carried on by the Federal Emergency Relief Administration (FERA), the Resettlement Administration, and the Division of Subsistence Homesteads. In a section sponsored by Senator John Bankhead, a back-to-the-land supporter from Alabama, the National Industrial Recovery Act appropriated funds for settling people on subsistence homesteads. Roosevelt assigned this responsibility to Harold Ickes, who set up the Division of Subsistence Homesteads within the Department of Interior. Those associated with the project envisioned clean, convenient, neighborly small towns, essentially rural but possessing modern household amenities and permitting a standard of living many social rungs above the dreary, constricting circumstances of rural poverty and removed from the soulless manipulations of industrial managers. The vision of the community builders ran contrary to the forces that were transforming American agriculture into a mechanized, chemically dependent business enterprise that responded to market forces. At root they wanted to sustain the mixed society of rural America by setting up small towns and light industry. Their faith was in the power of the region to integrate town and country by developing a shared awareness of the region's peculiar needs. Such communities would be self-sustaining and not dependent on government handouts. At their finest they would turn American culture away from excessive individualism and materialism. M. L. Wilson, who headed the subsistence homestead division, thought of a society similar to that of New England in the 1830s, where rural dwellers combined farm and factory work near water-powered mills, each providing for the needs of the other. Seeing grassroots participation as essential, Wilson only accepted projects submitted by the people who would inhabit the community. A viable community needed from twenty-five to one hundred families. Others would be taken in after a rigorous examination of their qualifications. The federal government would provide credit at 4 percent over thirty years.

Limited funds permitted only demonstration projects, one of which drew the interest of Eleanor Roosevelt: Arthurdale in West Virginia. A fumbling effort by Louis Howe, eager to remain Eleanor's champion, skyrocketed housing costs and attracted hostile journalists and congressional suspicion of "competition with private enterprise" and limited its chance to develop a business foundation. In the end, it limped along with a furniture factory. At no time was more than a third of the population employed in local industry.[22] Other problems arose. Labor unions complained that some projects were sponsored by corporate employers who used government credit to set up company towns. Farm organizations and processors worried that the settlements would be too self-sufficient and weaken agriculture's ties to the market. Farmers feared competition from new producers. Some theorists decried the prospect of creating a permanent peasant class in America.[23] During its brief existence, the subsistence homestead division established thirty-four communities containing over 3,000 housing units.

While the subsistence homestead division was about its work, the Rural Rehabilitation Division of FERA was carrying on similar projects. FERA began twenty-eight communities containing over 2,400 housing units. In the spring of 1935, Roosevelt combined them into the Resettlement Administration and appointed Rex Tugwell to head it. The RA thus became the administration's major force for community development. It had responsibility for moving farm families from submarginal land to productive land, upgrading farms in "borderline" condition, and aiding displaced persons who had been turned off their land or discouraged by urban living.

No fan of subsistence living, Tugwell wanted to provide the displaced and aimless a place in the mainstream of social development. His idea was to provide people with property and the benefits of modern technology. His purpose was not so much to send people back to the land as to transform the land. Thus the RA provided its communities with equipment for commercial farming. It also encouraged suburban settlement in greenbelt towns near major urban centers.[24] If enough city dwellers could be enticed to these towns, the slums could be torn down and the land made into parks. The greenbelt towns were the RA's version of the TVA's Norris—havens of economic stability, pleasant living, and community spirit. In the end, the RA built three towns: Greendale near Milwaukee; Greenhills near Cincinnati; and Greenbelt, Maryland, near Washington.

The greenbelt towns suffered from an awkward legal status. They wound up the wards of a kind of bureaucratic joint custody that resulted in overlapping bureaucratic jurisdictions, often causing comical arrangements such as shared responsibility for cutting the grass. Two of the three communities housed populations too small to sustain cooperative enterprises. Like any business operation, the co-ops needed entrepreneurial leadership to sustain themselves, something a community ethos neither discouraged nor promoted. Like any New Deal program, the greenbelt towns sustained partisan criticism. The press inflated the cost of the houses and trumpeted bureaucratic interference, such as a regulation prohibiting dogs in Greenbelt, Maryland.

Both the "experts" and "the people" had their doubts about the communities. Professional city planners differed over the merits of the communities, many preferring to concentrate on developing neighborhoods rather than entire communities. Many Americans disliked the prospect of mixing individuals of varying social and economic backgrounds, preferring economic, social, and racial separation. This was what the planners' emphasis on the neighborhood endorsed.[25]

The New Deal communities were bound to fail, in the sense that they could provide neither a wide-ranging solution to the depression nor a direction for the long future. In the short term, their funding was too limited, their expense too great, and their administration too complex to be implemented on a grand scale. The American people, as represented in Congress, were unwilling to countenance community building by the government, regardless of how "decentralized" or "democratic" it might be. The communities brought relief to the few thousands who occupied them and to the many more who built them, and to a small degree they relieved the pressures on other welfare agencies and programs. For the longer term, they lacked the resources necessary to sustain the "planning" ethos that had created them. Internal social and political structures did not support the cooperative commonwealth the New Deal planners had envisioned. Most settlers wanted security rather than the chance to live experimentally. Inevitably, the forces of American capitalistic, mixed-enterprise society exerted themselves, and the communities fell into the general pattern of American suburbanization. That many survived in this form and even prospered suggests that they were another of the New

Deal's achievements in reinforcing and advancing the American way of life.[26]

Faulty logic and political conservatism had limited the New Deal community programs. The resettlement economists believed that manufacturing and exploitative industries moved naturally to population centers adjacent to natural resources. If these centers were located in rural areas, industry would be attracted by low property taxes, rents, and wages. But historical experience had long suggested otherwise. The South, which since Reconstruction had pursued such a strategy, had remained a region of tenant farming and part-time industrial work. Congress supported subsistence homesteads as a temporary way of absorbing urban unemployment and taking some of the pressure off concentrated urban industries. Still, congressmen hesitated to promote government competition with private industry and forced the president to scale back the program, characterize it as "subsistence" homesteading, and incorporate it into NIRA. The product was a vague piece of legislation that gave the president wide latitude. Roosevelt took only a passing interest in the communities, briefly touring Greenbelt shortly after his reelection and recommending the project to the rest of the nation.[27]

In January 1937 the RA became part of the Department of Agriculture, which decided to liquidate the subsistence homesteads gradually. But instead, the department transferred them to the newly created Farm Security Administration. The homesteads were eventually liquidated by various remaining federal property credit agencies.

The several thousand families helped by the New Deal community projects were a tiny fraction of the nearly 18 million Americans who needed some degree of assistance in the spring of 1933. Although he considered the programs to support agriculture and to promote industrial cooperation the fundamental means of restoring prosperity, Roosevelt recognized the need to provide for those with immediate needs. FERA was his major instrument for this purpose. To head the agency, he nominated the man who had managed his Temporary Emergency Relief Administration in New York State, Harry L. Hopkins.

An experienced professional social worker, Hopkins had considerable experience directing large welfare organizations, principally the Gulf Division of the American Red Cross and the Tuberculosis and Health Association in New York City. A past president of the American Society of Social Workers, he was thoroughly committed to professional standards of social work, which had been most highly developed in the eastern states, especially in New York. At the same time, he realized that the federal government had never undertaken so massive a relief effort. Thus, although he made headlines by rapidly distributing relief funds committed but not spent by the Hoover administration, he approached his task cautiously. "I am experimenting with this fund in various parts of the country," he announced to the U.S. Conference of Mayors. "If you don't agree with me, it is all right. You may be right and I may be wrong."[28]

Congress had appropriated $500 million to FERA—$250 million to be allocated to the states in matching grants of three federal dollars for each state dollar, and $250 million to be granted outright for special situations. Hopkins spent his early weeks pressuring the states to set up professional welfare systems and to contribute their share of relief money. He especially bristled at attempts by governors and mayors to run their relief organizations as patronage plums, in some instances "federalizing" or taking federal control of state systems he considered more political than professional.

Hopkins also tried to persuade the American people to accept the federal government's role in relief. In radio addresses he referred to the unemployed as "fine hardworking, upstanding men and women . . . the finest in America" and declared that they were entitled to support as a right of citizenship. He encouraged Americans to understand that the unemployed did not want to be on relief, that they took all possible steps to avoid it, but their responsibilities to their families left them no choice.[29]

Hopkins expected that his relief activities would be temporary, providing support until the New Deal's recovery programs became effective, but they failed to perform. Farm prices improved slightly but remained low, and the NRA lurched along, producing only worrisome price increases without significantly increasing employment. At the same time, Ickes's Public Works Administration moved slowly as he struggled with the complexities of federal and state jurisdictions and the shenanigans of private contractors. By October, many were predicting an unemployment crisis during the winter.

In response, Hopkins and his chief aides, Aubrey Williams and Jacob Baker, proposed a federal program of work relief. In contrast to FERA rules, the new program would employ any person who was unemployed and not require that he or she qualify for state assistance. It would also employ people directly rather than working through private contractors. Funded in part by $400 million transferred from Ickes's PWA, the job of the CWA was to employ 4 million workers from December 1, 1933, through February 15, 1934.

Working at lightning speed, Hopkins converted his FERA operation to the CWA and ordered its members to develop projects and hire workers. By early January, 4.25 million were on the payroll. Projects emphasized construction: roads, sewers, waterworks, and public buildings. Hopkins also allocated money for "white-collar" projects: public art, archives organization, editing, and translating.[30]

For Hopkins and his relief staff, the CWA was a tonic experience, showing them the possibilities of a federal work relief program. It seemed to confirm the wisdom of pluralist decentralization, as FERA's federal structure worked effectively to put people to work. In a discussion of how to set up local committees to represent consumer interests, he chimed in. He favored a unified administrative system in Washington that could deal directly with national concerns of a long-term nature. For temporary, emergency matters, such as relief, he favored a decentralized structure of local committees, staffed by volunteers or administered by the states. He thought that the CWA was less expensive and less administratively demanding because local committees ran it, with his administration simply paying the bills. Otherwise, the administration would incur large costs and be charged with creating a political machine.[31]

From President Roosevelt's perspective, the administration of the CWA was less important than its long-term implications. The CWA was popular nationally, and Congress had no trouble supplementing its funding to carry it into April. But Roosevelt was wary of the program. Continuing the CWA into the summer, he believed, would cost too much and would "become a habit with the country." Disliking its cost and preferring to rely on his other initiatives to combat the depression, he permitted the program to go no further. "We want to get away from CWA as soon as we can," he declared.[32]

Roosevelt might want to get away from the CWA, but he could not get away from relief. During the rest of 1934, unemployment adjusted seasonally but showed not signs of a major decline. Neither did the complexities of the relief situation. As with other parts of the New Deal, federal relief confronted the Roosevelt's administration with the fundamental tension between the American tradition of individual self-reliance and the needs and purposes of an orderly, efficient, modern democratic society. The CWA experience had suggested that government jobs—"work relief" for cash wages—both raised the morale of the poor and provided society with useful services and products. But the cost of materials, tools, and supervision made work relief more costly than traditional "home relief," which usually provided clients with vouchers for specified items. The object of relief was to carry clients until they could find private employment. This suggested that relief wages should be lower than those in the private sector. But Roosevelt and Hopkins did not want to set wages so low that they in effect subsidized sweatshop employers or offended organized labor, which insisted on a "union" wage scale. Many, including Hopkins, shared Roosevelt's desire not to encourage Americans to rely on the government for employment. But the reliability of government work and the rigorous standards used to qualify for relief encouraged those on the rolls to stay there.

For a while the administration tried a middle approach. The CWA was ended and FERA allowed to run a modest work program. Relief workers were to be "cleared" from the rolls when seasonal jobs such as cotton picking opened up. Workers on strike were declared eligible for relief.

Most important, Roosevelt wanted to help the unemployed. The nation, he declared, should not tolerate a "large army of unemployed." No American should expect to remain permanently on the relief rolls. Thus, after the fall elections had returned sweeping Democratic majorities, the president called in Hopkins, Ickes, and Secretary of the Treasury Henry Morgenthau to plan a work relief program. When the new Congress convened, Roosevelt asked for $4.8 billion to help the unemployed. When Congress complied, he set up a committee of Hopkins, Ickes, and chairman Frank Walker to administer the funds. Within the administrative setup, Hopkins was given charge of a new agency that would screen project applications regarding employment. The agency was to be called the Works Progress Administration (WPA). At the first meeting, Roosevelt made it clear that he wanted the money spent primarily for employment. This gave Hopkins a natural advantage, since Ickes's PWA had emphasized substantial construction projects with high costs of materials, whereas Hopkins's FERA and CWA had favored light, labor-intensive projects.

Not surprisingly, the relief program turned into a struggle between Hopkins and Ickes. Although their varying emphases on employment distinguished their approaches to unemployment relief in the eyes of President Roosevelt, at bottom their differences were ones of organizational approach. Hopkins favored a decentralized, "federal" system in which the central administration provided funds and general rules and the local administration provided a variety of projects, skills, and supervision. Ickes, who constantly worried that such decentralization would invite inefficiency and corruption, favored a centrally administered system.

At a September conference in Hyde Park, Roosevelt chose between the two, allocating the lion's share of the relief balance to Hopkins. From that time forward, the WPA would be the New Deal's symbol of hope for the unemployed. As the NRA faltered, the WPA also became the means by which the New Deal touched the lives of the depression's largest constituency.[33]

The WPA carried out its mission with a federal structure. Local agencies, often partially funded with "sponsor" contributions from city or county governments, proposed projects; the state and federal agencies approved them; and Washington supplied the funds. Unlike the CWA, the WPA required that at least 90 percent of project workers come from the relief rolls. (The other 10 percent supplied necessary skilled labor or supervision.) The pay scale depended on the level of skill and ranged from $60 to $100 a month, a rate that was above mere subsistence but supposedly lower than comparable private employment. An early controversy with union labor in New York City resulted in the WPA's paying the "prevailing wage" rate, which for a forty-hour week would have exceeded WPA wage guidelines. In order to keep the wage rate at the union level, the WPA had to reduce the hours of work, a practice that hampered many projects and created pounding administrative headaches. Wary of criticism and unwilling to drive government finances too deeply into the red, Roosevelt juggled WPA funds so that its employment rolls fluctuated wildly, reaching a high of 3 million in 1936 and falling to 1.4 million eighteen months later. By the time it was abolished in 1943, it had employed some 8 million people, one-fifth of the nation's workforce.[34]

Along the way, headaches abounded. Politicians tried to incorporate the WPA into their patronage system. Republicans charged that its projects were of little or no value and that its employees "leaned on their shovels" instead of working. Critics invented the word "boondoggle" to describe the typical project.

In these somewhat unpromising conditions, the WPA carried on. Its workers built thousands of miles of roads and streets and improved drainage systems, public buildings, parks, and recreational facilities. Despite critics' efforts to embarrass and humiliate them, its members reported high levels of job satisfaction.

Although most WPA projects were manual labor, the agency conducted a number of "white-collar" projects. The Writers Project produced the American Guide Series. Designed as tour guides of the states and major cities, the books contained much local history and popular culture. The Federal Arts Project decorated hundreds of public buildings, often with murals that depicted the history and major work of the locale. The Federal Theater Project employed producers, directors, stagehands, and actors and introduced many to their first live theater. The Federal Music Project put on symphonic and choral performances in various locations.[35]

The WPA projects were expressions of social and cultural pluralism. The construction projects met local needs for transportation, recreation, and public service. The arts and literature programs evoked local history and culture. The most dramatic example was the Federal Theater Project's production of *It Can't Happen Here.* A warning against dictatorship, the play was written by the famous novelist Sinclair Lewis and Jack Moffitt. Federal Theater administrators decided to present the play with a splash, opening in twenty-one theaters in seventeen states simultaneously on the night of October 27, 1936. Nothing like this had ever been done before in the history of theater. But the key feature of the play's production was the various forms in which it presented its message. In Seattle the play opened in the black section of the city and emphasized the danger of dictatorship to minorities. Birmingham staged the play as a political rally. In Brooklyn-Queens the locale was a neighborhood street corner. The Yiddish production effected a surrealistic set threatened by encroaching darkness. The Broadway version omitted a concentration camp scene; the Yiddish version included it.[36]

Of the New Deal's various achievements, the WPA is one of the most difficult to judge. It was a unique effort that occurred in unique circumstances. Never before or since has the national government undertaken to employ so many people simply because they qualified for relief assistance. Never before or since has the nation experienced an economic crisis as severe as that of the 1930s. In one sense it represented a culmination of an approach that professional social workers had long advocated—that work rather than charity benefited both the recipient and the larger society, and that cash wages encouraged independence and responsibility, which society's middle-class values especially honored. In this aspect of its experiment, the WPA was bound to succeed because, contrary to the derision of its political and ideological opponents, the WPA was helping people who had held paying jobs and who had managed money as family breadwinners. Thus it did not assume the task of training or retraining workers; it made use of skills they already possessed or could easily acquire. This was one particular value of its white-collar projects, which relieved many of the unemployed from having to perform manual labor, to which they were not suited.

Still, the WPA's success was severely limited. Its appropriations and fluctuations prevented it from helping more than a third of the unemployed, and often less than that. Its effort to help as many as possible further strained its resources, so that over half of its unskilled workers received less than what the WPA itself defined as "an emergency standard of living."

Nor was it clear that the WPA contributed to economic recovery. Following its mandate to maximize employment, it spent most of its money for wages rather than materials. This limited the "indirect" or stimulating effect it could have on private business—a point that Harold Ickes made often and without success. A study conducted in 1940 concluded that Ickes's heavy construction projects created up to twice as many jobs as they directly employed, whereas WPA projects created less than 20 percent of the number they directly employed.[37]

But spending to stimulate private employment did not interest Roosevelt, in part because it did not fit his budget objectives. Always a partisan of a balanced federal budget and a fierce critic of Hoover's deficits, Roosevelt was determined to keep spending and revenues in line. However, he made an exception for relief for the needy. In his mind, this meant that federal spending that exceeded revenues would have to help those on relief. This belief was strongly and insistently pressed by Henry Morgenthau, his secretary of the treasury and Dutchess County neighbor. From the beginning, Morgenthau had argued that Hopkins should have control of the works program because he could get money into the hands of the unemployed. Hopkins lent his support to this. "The people we are handling," he declared, "are the people who don't eat unless we give them relief." Together they persuaded Roosevelt to make the WPA the New Deal's exclusive provider of relief and thus the only agency entitled to run the government into the red. It was not, however, an entitlement that the president was inclined to grant much latitude to.[38]

Of course, it could be argued that stimulating private development would produce both the employment and the tax revenues that would bring recovery and a balanced budget. But this would have taken the form of a long-range approach, to which Roosevelt was unsympathetic. Instead, he wanted his administration to support those in immediate need.

There were points to be made on Roosevelt's behalf. It made humanitarian sense to support those who had suffered through the years of the Hoover administration and the sputtering of the NRA. Nor was it crystal clear that Ickes's kind of "indirect" stimulation would prove any more effective than the indirect methods of the Hoover administration, now so widely derided as trickle-down economics.[39]

The most compelling advantage of WPA work relief was its political value. Surveys showed that approximately 80 percent of WPA workers voted Democratic. Because the WPA operated through a federal system that encouraged local government participation, it provided opportunities for local officials to benefit. Some local and state politicians tried to use the WPA as a patronage machine by controlling administrative appointments and pressuring workers at election time. One especially embarrassing incident occurred in a Kentucky senatorial primary, when WPA workers were told to support the incumbent Alben Barkley against Governor A. B. "Happy" Chandler.[40] For the most part, however, Roosevelt and Hopkins fought off such political interference, and the politicians learned that the best politics of work relief was to provide good jobs that produced tangible civic benefits. Sometime in 1936, Florence Kerr, whom Harry Hopkins had appointed to supervise WPA women's projects in the Midwest, visited a sewing project in Kansas City, Missouri, and saw that the women did not have enough sewing machines and many of them had nothing to do. At once she marched into the office of the city Democratic boss, Tom Pendergast, and told him to come up with 200 machines. When he hesitated, she wondered aloud what might happen if a reporter from the *Chi-*

cago Tribune (the nation's most fiercely reactionary, anti–New Deal mass circulation newspaper) visited the project and wrote a story about its sorry condition. She got the machines. She also showed Pendergast that it was good politics to run a program that provided useful, productive work for unemployed women.

"Wasn't that blackmail?" asked Mrs. Kerr's interviewer in 1974.

"No," she replied, "I think it was a good move."[41]

New Deal relief politics operated by good moves like hers. Of course, no moves—good, bad, or indifferent—were going to spare the administration charges of using relief for partisan advantage. "Who is going to vote against Santa Claus?" groaned one anti–New Deal mayor. Polls showed that by a margin of 55 to 25 percent, public opinion was that "politics" played a part in handling relief.[42]

Because of its political prominence, the WPA illuminated the ambiguities and complexities of Franklin Roosevelt's presidency. Its relief effort was little more than a palliative, reaching barely one-third of the unemployed. Its contribution to economic recovery was negligible. Its improvised nature, squabbles and compromises with organized labor, congressional restrictions, uncertain funding, and external patronage pressures encouraged inefficiencies and invited public skepticism. When he was getting ready to run for a second term, Roosevelt expected the Republicans to attack "WPA inefficiency, and there's plenty of it."[43] The Republicans mounted such an attack, but it had little effect.

In the end, the WPA proved itself a dynamic force in Franklin Roosevelt's presidency. It survived its limitations and fought through its obstacles. Its greatest source of strength was Roosevelt's own determination to help the unemployed directly and to substitute work projects for debilitating and demoralizing "relief." Roosevelt's leadership plus the imagination and drive of Hopkins and his staff revolutionized the national government's role in aiding the unemployed. They provided an unprecedented approach to an economic crisis of unprecedented proportions. Roosevelt's willingness to accept deficit spending for work relief gave Hopkins the chance to advocate government "spending" and the stimulation of consumer demand as strategies for coping with hard times. Thus, when hard times returned in the fall of 1937, Roosevelt could draw on a body of economic thinking that could supplement the structural reforms he had previously favored.

The political complexities of the WPA also balanced out in its favor. Civic groups, local and state officials, and congressmen applied for its funding. Its construction, artistic, educational, and literary projects became sources of local and regional pride, as well as sources of personal satisfaction to those who participated in them. Polls showed that 80 percent of WPA workers supported Roosevelt.[44] Many of these were African Americans.

In localities where it was possible, the WPA employed people without regard to race. At a time when African Americans were the last hired and first fired and when many white Americans assumed that black Americans deserved a low standard of living, the WPA became the third largest employer of African Americans.[45] Thus, it was not surprising that as Roosevelt's first efforts at economic recovery failed or produced puny results, Hopkins and his work relief projects should gain prominence, or that Roosevelt should consider Hopkins a possible successor in 1940.

In June 1934, as the CWA was phasing out, Roosevelt appointed a commission to propose a system of social insurance. The idea that government might provide resources to support the old, the unemployed, and the sick had been around for a generation. In the United States its most prominent expression was federal pensions for war veterans, most notably those who had served in the Union army during the Civil War. During the early years of the century, some states had enacted "widows' pensions" to provide for widowed mothers. Otherwise, the record was skimpy: in 1928 only six states had laws for old-age pensions, and all of them permitted counties to opt out of the system. Pension laws had originated as an outgrowth of relief for the poor, and in some states pensions were administered by relief officials or were adapted to relief practices and standards. By the end of the decade, however, the trend was to consider pensions a separate activity and to remove pensioners from the jurisdiction of the poor laws.[46]

Previous thinking about social insurance had been influenced by the relative prosperity of the early twentieth century and by the Progressive desire for efficiency. Attention had centered on stabilizing markets for production and for labor. This had promoted the idea of "labor exchanges" that kept workers continuously employed by directing them to job openings. In 1933 the Wagner-Peyser Act had reestablished the United States Employment Service, which had first been established during the Wilson administration to help meet the demands of wartime mobilization. During the 1920s, however, attention had centered on stabilizing industry through management techniques that would reduce seasonal fluctuations in the demand for labor and control inventories to keep production lines in continuous operation. Some companies established unemployment insurance funds to limit employee turnover, discourage strikes, and support mass purchasing power.[47] The problem with these plans was their narrow scope. Industrial pensions covered only 14 percent of workers and less than 7 percent of the potentially dependent elderly. Most of these programs disappeared during the depression. This, combined with the general crisis in relief, turned attention to national solutions. The exception was business, which continued vociferously and actively to oppose any government system of pensions.[48] Thus by the middle of the decade, the topic of social insurance had come to be understood as government support for those unable to help themselves and as a method of stabilizing labor markets and providing business with an experienced and loyal workforce.

Further discussion about social insurance was limited by the terms of these alternatives. One approach, defined by the objectives of business efficiency and stabilization, was for businesses to create "reserve" funds that states would hold to pay to workers who were laid off. This system, which was adopted by Wisconsin, maintained the capitalistic emphasis on individual distribution and offered security without affecting the distribution of income. In contrast, some economists and social workers believed that business stabilization plans could not adequately protect workers against all possible risks and favored spreading the risk by creating an insurance "pool" to which all employers would contribute.

Roosevelt's action began with the introduction of legislation to encourage the states to adopt unemployment insurance programs. Earlier debate had revealed differing opinions on how such a system should operate. Organized labor distrusted government pensions and preferred to establish them through collective bargaining. Others favored a reserve system that would create a pool out of which would be paid uniform benefits. Others wanted a true insurance system that would pay people according to the amount they had contributed. Roosevelt's message establishing the commission envisioned joint state-federal funding and administration but was vague on other details.[49]

The mobilizing force behind social insurance was the Townsend movement, the brainchild of Dr. Francis Townsend, a retired physician in California. By 1934, there was a Townsend club in nearly every congressional district. Advocating a pension stipend of $200 a month—twice the average monthly earnings—and direct payment from the government's general revenues, the Townsend plan's simplicity made it especially powerful politically, although it was distasteful from a fiscal standpoint. Roosevelt needed a New Deal alternative. "Congress," he declared, "can't stand the pressure of the Townsend Plan unless we have a real old age insurance system."[50]

Although Roosevelt withheld his ideas about social insurance, he had strong preferences. He looked at social insurance essentially as a longer-term relief program, in contrast to the works program that was meeting immediate needs. Over time, social insurance would help to stabilize employment by giving older workers an incentive to retire. Like work relief, he wanted the funding for social insurance to be "off budget" and "self-liquidating." This translated into a reserve fund supported exclusively by contributions from beneficiaries and operated on "actuarially sound" principles. A program financed out of general revenues, he believed, would be easily expanded by popular political influence. In selecting the members of his Committee on Economic Security (CES), he purposely chose welfare experts with records for "good government" and "fiscal responsibility." Roosevelt also preferred to give the states an important role in the program.[51]

The committee followed Roosevelt's wishes. The moment of decision came when Harry Hopkins, who had been declaring in speeches that the opportunity to work was a fundamental right of citizenship, proposed the same right to a government pension. The committee, which was determined to keep the government from giving direct grants to its citizens, voted him down. When CES members wavered to the extent of proposing some supplemental funding out of general revenues, Roosevelt demanded that they eliminate it.

Once it had been decided to have a social insurance program that met special needs, various interests sought to turn it to their advantage. Especially concerned were small businesses, which wanted to avoid the costs of the program, and southern economic and political interests, which wanted to maintain white supremacy and the low wage structure of their region. Such opposition gradually gave way, however, to the strong political demand for some kind of system and the corresponding desire to avoid its costs. It was better to join the movement and try to divert it into harmless channels than to forsake it to those who might not consider one's interests. These desires led to pressure to require employee contributions. A proposal to exempt employers whose private plans met or exceeded federal standards failed when private insurers backed out of the market. Roosevelt blocked proposals for means-testing benefits, which would have limited benefits to the most destitute elderly.[52]

Like most other New Deal programs, social security combined federal and state responsibilities. The Wisconsin representatives on the CES persuaded the committee to permit states to collect unemployment compensation by means of payroll taxes to which employees and employers would contribute equally. Contributions would be made on a tax-offset basis, whereby states meeting federal standards could continue to operate their systems. Old-age assistance was a national program, but Congress eliminated a requirement that states meet a minimum standard of payment to recipients. The original bill required states to apply civil service standards when selecting administrators, but Congress insisted on opening the system to patronage. In the end, the only hope for those who wanted the system to be administered by independent civil servants was to have the Social Security Board persuade the states.[53]

From a fiscal standpoint, the Social Security Act was astonishingly regressive. Its payroll taxes took money out of the hands of working people, many of whom were hard-pressed. By giving businesses an incentive to compensate for their employment taxes by raising prices, it amounted to a national sales tax. "I guess you're right on the economics," Roosevelt commented when Tugwell pointed out this last feature, "but those taxes were never a problem of economics. They are politics all the way through. We put those payroll contributions there so as to give the contributors a legal, moral, and political right to collect their pensions and their unemployment benefits. With those taxes in there, no damn politician can ever scrap my social security program."[54]

The contradictory objectives of the bill were soon apparent. Roosevelt had wanted an actuarially sound system based on the "reserve" principle of acquiring a large fund that would earn returns to pay the benefits. Social scientists on the board favored the reserve because it would "depoliticize" the system by funding it out of investment income instead of congressional appropriations. The original act provided for this, but on sober second thought, it appeared that there was no way to guarantee that the fund would always be large enough. Sooner or later, payroll taxes would have to be raised or general revenues drawn upon. In the meantime, the Townsendites attacked a program that was not scheduled to pay benefits until 1942. The result was the creation of a special advisory committee, proposed by the Senate Finance Committee and appointed by the committee and the Social Security Board, which recommended giving up the reserve proposal and adopting a pay-as-you-go system that would pay benefits out of current revenues and reduce the reserve fund to a much smaller "contingency" fund. At the same time, the scope of the fund was enlarged to include payments to survivors and dependents.[55]

The legislation also bowed to the nation's cultural politics. It excluded agricultural and domestic workers, who had historically been subject to their employers' personal protection. Amendments in 1939 established a system of survivors' benefits that assumed that women were dependent on men's wages and, in fact, penalized two-income families and single persons.[56]

Social security benefited greatly from the political savvy of its architects. At every turn they avoided partisan wrangling, co-opted their critics, scripted favorable questions and comments for supportive congressmen, and sold their program to the public as an "insurance" program that preserved individual self-reliance. It adopted a "regional" organizational structure, which it employed to publicize its virtues in ways that pleased local constituencies. In these ways it operated as a typically successful New Deal agency, administratively flexible and politically aware.[57]

The significance of the Social Security Act reached far beyond its early formulation. Unlike the temporary, emergency programs, it established a category of "social rights" for unemployed and elderly Americans. In so doing it made it possible to extend these rights to previously excluded groups. It dropped "social security" into the mainstream of the United States' equal rights tradition. Central to the American political experience, the equal rights tradition had made it politically respectable for persons and groups to claim rights that had been granted to others but denied to them. Although such claims did not always succeed—and in some cases were honored and then reversed—they have more often than not been able to mobilize a political constituency that eventually made them legitimate.

New Deal social programs combined small experiments, temporary relief, and long-term security. Their results mirrored those occurring in economic recovery. The New Deal was providing opportunity and security under certain "rules" that emphasized fairness and democracy but whose decentralized nature permitted considerable latitude to shape their outcome. As things turned out, Americans preferred a better standard of living, the chance for useful work, associations with persons like themselves, and a patriarchal social order. Such an outcome was perhaps not inevitable, but given the New Deal's pluralistic methods, it was a most likely one.

5

★★★★★

RESOURCES FOR RECOVERY

Franklin Roosevelt often characterized himself as a farmer. Whenever he got the chance, often to divert a conversation or to evade an issue, he would dilate on Dutchess County agriculture. Toward the end of his second term he spoke about retiring to Hyde Park to get back to his "trees," by which he meant his experiments with different varieties and the care he gave to their development. In this sense, Roosevelt considered himself a conservationist. In 1935 he declared: "We think of our land and water and human resources not as a static and sterile possession but as life giving assets to be directed by wise provision for future days. We seek to use our natural resources not as a thing apart but as something that is interwoven with industry, labor, finance, taxation, agriculture, homes, recreation, good citizenship." The goal of its wise use was to improve future living standards for all Americans. He understood the word "forestry" to mean "not merely the acquisition of land that has trees on it and the maintenance of that land in a state of nature for a thousand years to come. The land ought to be used. The trees ought to be used. Certain areas, of course, should be applied to public recreational purposes, but the other areas, the tree crop, should be used just as much as a crop of corn or wheat."[1]

Roosevelt's remarks placed him in the camp of conservationists who sought a proper "management" of the nation's resources, as opposed to "preservationists," who sought to protect them from private entry and exploitation. This was not to dismiss his aesthetic appreciation of nature, for he could marvel at the natural beauty of Glacier National Park, which he opened in 1934. Still, his inclination, strengthened by the needs created by the depression, was to develop a resource policy that would improve human living standards. These were his favorite "conservation" projects. He was a great fan of water management projects, especially dams in western states. Such projects as the Grand Coulee and Bonneville Dams on the Columbia River and Boulder Dam on the Colorado would provide electric power and water for irrigation, improve navigation, and promote settlement and economic development.[2]

As Roosevelt moved into his presidency, his resource ideas grew more complex. Increasingly, he spoke of the interrelations of resource development. Early in 1934 he established a cabinet committee to look into the creation of a "non-political, non-partisan" planning commission to study "the whole area of the United States, and the easiest way to do this is by watersheds." The commission would study the dangers to life and property, the economic development of the region, and how much population the region's resources could support. The commission would develop a list of projects in their order of importance, and out of this would come a legislative program.[3] In July, Congress established the National Resources Board, charged to report on "all aspects of the problem of development and use of land, water, and other national resources, in their physical, social, governmental and economic aspects."[4]

The board's goal of developing "integrated, regional" plans for resource management was a national extension of Roosevelt's version of the Tennessee Valley Authority. Leaving aside TVA's role as a "social experiment" (which has been considered elsewhere), Roosevelt thought that the project would provide the region with the electric power necessary to spur economic development. Key to his approach was the desire to "democratize" electric power by combining public development and "regional" management and distribution with the reorganization of private power networks into "regionally integrated" systems, whose rates would be influenced by competition from public power. In order to carry out this strategy, he found it necessary to attack the holding company structure in the utility industry.[5]

When he was governor of New York, Roosevelt had acquired a knowledge of electric rate making, which he considered largely a matter of proper accounting.[6] As worked out with TVA's directors, the authority would provide power in certain targeted areas and from that develop a base rate, or "yardstick," that would become a measure of the fairness of private rates. Working in a hurried atmosphere and liberally mixing accounting with guesswork, the directors proposed rates that were less than half those being charged by the private companies. They followed by creating an agency to provide low-cost loans to residents to purchase household electric appliances. The result was skyrocketing purchases of the appliances, increased demand for electricity, and volume discounts to consumers in the form of lower rates.[7]

Roosevelt continued the momentum for public power. The PWA began loaning money to local jurisdictions to build public power systems; Roosevelt created the Rural Electrification Administration, began his attack on the utility holding companies, and introduced legislation to publicize private rate schedules.[8] There followed a protracted, convoluted, and publicly noisy series of discussions between the TVA and the region's private utility, Commonwealth and Southern, headed by a man named Wendell Willkie. As one episode followed another, it became increasingly clear that public and private power, at least in the Tennessee Valley, were not going to mix. The TVA won one competition after another for rich local markets, which used PWA money to set up public systems; other private companies sold out to the TVA. In 1938, Roosevelt resolved a feud between the TVA's major proponent of public power, David E. Lilienthal, and its advocate of cooperation with private companies, Arthur Morgan, by firing Morgan. Willkie saw that he had no recourse but to sell his properties to the TVA. From that time on, the TVA expanded its influence, which included ruling electric power policy with an iron hand.[9]

The TVA's ability to persevere through these difficulties overshadowed the complexities, frustrations, and unique circumstances of its development to qualify it as a model for other such projects. Nowhere were these projects more popular than in the states west of the Mississippi River. During his campaign swing through the Pacific Northwest in 1932, Roosevelt had promised to provide the region with hydroelectric power. After his election, the PWA provided funds to construct a dam across the Columbia River. Construction began at once. During the ensuing four years before its completion, parties and interests debated its manna. Democrats wanted a Columbia Valley Authority, modeled on the TVA, with differing ideas about whether it should serve the entire Pacific Northwest or be limited to the dam's transmission area; the Army Corps of Engineers, which was building the dam, and the Bureau of Reclamation, which had responsibility for developing land and water resources, squabbled over controlling the power supply.

The debate continued into 1937, when Roosevelt proposed a plan along the lines of the TVA: public power marketed separately from private power and favoring public and cooperative customers, and a "civilian agency" established in the Interior Department to market the power. To placate the War Department, which bitterly fought for the Corps of Engineers, the final bill gave it control over producing the power, with the civilian agency in charge of distributing it and setting the rates.[10]

Bonneville's development followed the TVA's in complexity, frustration, and delay—only the details were different. One unique complication was having to work with Harold Ickes, who limited the agency's development and supported a poor administrator for too long. Gradually, the mission of the project drifted away from the multipurpose social experimentation of the TVA to that of simply supplying public power. Then, international crisis and war scuttled the principle of independent public power; the War Production Board ordered all public and private systems to be connected in a single grid.[11]

Roosevelt's program for Bonneville was his last attempt to establish a national policy. As he was outlining his requirements for the Columbia Valley, he was backing away from a proposal by Senator George Norris to blanket the country with regional authorities. Instead, he proposed to establish seven other regional agencies that would submit resource plans to a new Department of Conservation that he was asking Congress to establish as part of a general reorganization of the executive branch. The result was that he never articulated an administration policy on public power but proposed instead to allow a complex of legislative and administrative rivalries to decide the issue.[12]

Roosevelt's power policy again revealed the essential dynamic of pluralism. By establishing a framework for public power and then countenancing and facilitating different strategies for implementing it—and, in the process, accepting necessary compromises—Roosevelt permitted policy to develop along a socially and politically "natural" course. Given his preference, which he often announced, of embedding New Deal reforms in local institutions so that subsequent administrations could not undo them, this was probably inevitable. Whether this policy ultimately "failed" or "succeeded" depended on the views of those who, then and since, have looked at it from multiple perspectives. What seems indisputable, however, is that the policy established the role of public power and brought millions of Americans into the dominant culture of production and consumption.

In addition to supplying electric power, the New Deal reconfigured land-use patterns in western states. On the Plains, a decade of agricultural exploitation had created a ticking bomb in the form of loosened soil and persistent winds that swept over vast flat, treeless expanses. All that was required to touch off the bomb was dryness, which the generally arid climate usually produced. In the 1930s, the bomb went off with a vengeance. Record high temperatures, prolonged and unrelieved by rain, and swirling winds caused the land to disintegrate. In April 1935, winds in Colorado and Kansas carried aloft so much dust that the day turned to night. Cattle suffocated, and people huddled indoors, snatching choking breaths through wet handkerchiefs. The storms continued through 1936 and 1937, often depositing dust as far east as Washington, D.C. The New Deal responded on many fronts. Henry Wallace's Drought Relief Service purchased "surplus" cattle to reduce the pressure on remaining grasslands. It undertook a Land Utilization Project to purchase farmland and convert it to grassland. But neither effort, nor the AAA itself, succeeded in significantly reducing cropland acreage.

More successful was the Soil Conservation Service, whose chief, Hugh Hammond Bennett, energetically sold conservation with the promise of more efficient production and successfully organized soil conservation districts that were authorized to make binding conservation regulations. These programs saved some land and reorganized western rural society in favor of its greater landlords. Those who owned the most acres could retire them from cultivation, move off renters, collect an AAA payment, purchase machinery, and move off more renters. With the machinery they could undertake conservation techniques of contour plowing, terracing, and ditching.[13]

Supplementing these conservation projects was Roosevelt's proposal to reduce wind erosion by planting trees on the plains. Tugwell coordinated the effort, known as the Shelterbelt Project, and in July 1934, Roosevelt allocated $15 million in emergency drought relief funds to the Forest Service to start it. Farmer hesitancy, bureaucratic obstruction, and congressional skepticism delayed the project, which at first made only modest headway. In 1937, with WPA funding, its pace quickened. As the project, renamed the Prairie States Reforestry Project, gained popularity, the Forest Service adopted the AAA model to carry it out. With the assistance of county extension agents, the Forest Service appointed a committee of conservation-minded farmers who held meetings to discuss the best locations for tree planting and encouraged local farmers to cooperate. In 1942, at the behest of Congress, Roosevelt transferred the project to the Soil Conservation Service, where it lost momentum during the war emergency. By then, however, it had planted some 18,600 miles of trees and had enlisted hundreds of farmers in the effort for conservation.[14]

The administration followed a similar pattern in administering the Taylor Grazing Act of 1934. Designed to address overgrazing that was both causing soil erosion and diminishing the grasslands for livestock, the act federalized all rangelands and established grazing districts, in which forage would be leased to stockmen who had a previous history of using the land, and limited the grazing rights to specific boundaries. To aid the law, Roosevelt issued an order canceling homesteading in the West. In 1939 Congress created the Division of Grazing in the Interior Department. The head of the Grazing Service organized district boards of local stockmen elected by their fellow cattle ranchers to decide how to allocate grazing permits. This process aided ranchers who owned land adjacent to federal rangeland and caused essentially no drop in cattle grazing. The advisory boards often obstructed the service's efforts at land management.[15]

In the meantime, the Bureau of Reclamation was spreading its influence as an agent of economic development. It took charge of dam construction and became the keystone in the region's economic development. As more dams went up, the bureau took charge of western rivers and the distribution of their water. It completed the All-American Canal, which irrigated a million acres of desert in California, and provided a $24 million interest-free subsidy to Central Valley growers. It also undertook the Central Valley Project, which, with dams on the Sacramento River, would produce electric power and concentrate water for "efficient" allocation for irrigation and municipal water systems. Expanded agricultural production brought forth not only vegetables but also political supporters for the bureau.[16]

Elsewhere, the New Deal stepped in to manage the nation's oil resource. By 1933, the Texas and Oklahoma oil fields, at the time the largest in the world, were suffering a glut of overproduction. As the depression reduced prices further, the oil companies agreed to the need for production controls and let Washington know that they were ready for some form of national authority to take charge. The administration offered such control if the companies would sell off their pipelines in return. But the companies refused this trade-off, and in the end, Congress authorized the administration to set production quotas. Roosevelt named Secretary Ickes to administer a Petroleum Advisory Board under the NRA. Ickes allocated production quotas to the states for assignment to the individual fields and imposed penalties on those who shipped "hot oil" outside the quotas. His vigorous administration seemed to be working when the Supreme Court declared the "hot oil" provision unconstitutional and then followed by overturning the entire NRA. Congress then substituted an act that left regulation in the hands of the states.[17]

Judgments about the New Deal's resource policy depend on one's perspective. From the standpoint of true "conservationists," the New Deal leaned too much in the direction of those who thought that resources should be exploited for economic benefit. Even from the standpoint of those who wanted "efficient" resource management, the New Deal failed to develop a consistent and coherent policy of national supervision. Often its "management" strategies were attempts to bail out interests, such as the cattlemen and the oilmen, who were tasting the bitter fruits of their forebears' greed. Roosevelt might have taken the lead in developing a national power policy, but he was either more concerned with the social development of resource areas or willing to allow a policy to develop over time through the recommendations of "planning" agencies. This latter approach had a good deal to recommend it, for it would have indicated how well TVA-style projects might adapt to a given region. Such an approach might have avoided the effects of the flood control and development projects created on the lower Missouri River. Done largely at the behest of Kansas City commercial interests to develop the economy and traffic along the river, the Fort Peck and successive dams encouraged farming up to the riverbanks, which increased soil erosion and tributary stream erosion, lowered the water table, and damaged fish and wildlife. The projects increased the upper river's flow so that it became unsafe for barge traffic. Nor did the project stop flooding, which reached disastrous proportions in 1993.[18]

As with its other pluralistic strategies, New Deal resource policy sought to involve a variety of interests in determining how wealth would be created and distributed. Roosevelt continually argued for the policy that would benefit the greatest number of persons, and especially the disadvantaged. Having to work through a social, political, and economic system that favored the advantaged would always limit his achievements. In some instances, his administration was able to shape a course; in others, not. Power was generated, and economic opportunities created. The American West, which previously had been little more than a colony of the rest of the nation, gained a foothold for economic independence because of hydroelectric power.[19] Rangeland was better managed, and soil was conserved through tree planting. These were opportunities for people to take advantage of as they desired. Such opportunities typified the New Deal.

ROOSEVELT'S POLITICAL BASE

Franklin D. Roosevelt's presidency functioned within a political environment. That is to say that he depended on a popular vote as expressed through the electoral college system and a congressional vote in the coequal branches of the House and Senate. Since 1896, that environment had generally favored the Republicans, producing lopsided Republican majorities in seven of nine presidential elections and producing an untainted Democratic victory only in 1916, when Woodrow Wilson narrowly won a second term after defeating a deeply divided Republican Party in 1912. Republican and Democratic presidents had normally enjoyed their party's controlling both houses of Congress, the exceptions being 1911–1913 and 1931–1933, when Presidents Taft and Hoover had faced Democratic Houses (with Republicans still controlling the Senate), and during Woodrow Wilson's last Congress (1919–1921), when the Republican opposition controlled both houses.

Thus it was common for Americans in the first third of the century to vote for a national government that united the executive and legislative branches. This unity did not, however, mute or stifle controversy. Throughout these years, presidents contended with policy controversies born out of the nation's social and economic complexities and the abilities of political leaders to shape these complexities in ways that would help them win elections. These controversies assumed a political weight generally proportional to the strength of an issue's political leadership and/or popular support. These issues often shaped a presidency regardless of the intentions of the president. One thinks, for example, of Theodore Roosevelt's supporting federal meat inspection after the public outcry generated by Upton Sinclair's muckraking exposé of sanitary conditions in the nation's packing plants, or Woodrow Wilson's concluding his presidency by campaigning for a new international order after having entered it determined to spend his time on the nation's domestic agenda.

When we realize that Franklin Roosevelt was elected to four terms, that throughout his presidency he dealt with Congresses dominated by Democrats, that he began with a sweeping domestic agenda and died in the midst of carrying out a sweeping international agenda, and that his administration produced an enormous amount of legislation that reordered the nation's political economy, we can appreciate why a generation of successors measured their presidencies against his and why his presidency was a transforming moment in the history of American politics and government. To appreciate the nature of that transformation, we have to understand the political base that Franklin Roosevelt constructed to support his presidency. Roosevelt consistently sought to base his political appeal on himself, or, more precisely, on his ability to build a relationship of trust and confidence with the voters.

Roosevelt began his day with breakfast in bed, during which time he read several newspapers and held bedside conferences with people invited to discuss the day's business. Sometimes he made phone calls, occasionally to cheer up a sick friend or in other ways to lift spirits. After dressing with the help of his valet, he was wheeled to the Executive Office, where he went through correspondence with his secretaries Missy LeHand and Grace Tully. Next came meetings with scheduled visitors, screened by Marvin McIntyre and Louis Howe (later Edwin "Pa" Watson). He continued to confer at his desk during lunch and into the afternoon, taking time later for a swim in the White House pool. He then returned to the Oval Office to look through evening newspapers and to preside over a cocktail hour with his current inner circle; then came dinner with a number of guests. The day concluded with evening conferences, memos, letters, and messages. Bedtime was usually just before midnight.

Roosevelt was a great tinkerer and classifier. He crowded his desk with gadgets of all kinds. His mind seemed to process information in a similar fashion. He delighted in classifying and arranging data. He spent hours with his stamp collection. In card games he showed an excellent memory for what had been played. He amused himself with a complex game of solitaire with two decks and ten across. He often tried his hand at architectural design. Careful, patient analysis did not suit him. He liked to grasp issues by ear. When he read, he scanned. Most of his sources were familiar—newspapers, memoranda, dispatches—and he knew the tricks of reading them rapidly. He avidly collected facts, which he used to impress

Roosevelt at this cluttered desk with Grace Tully, Steve Early, and Marguerite "Missy" LeHand, May 22, 1941. (Franklin D. Roosevelt Library)

reporters, visitors, and cabinet members. Information alone never satisfied him; whatever he had he wanted to use.[1]

Roosevelt put his ability to concentrate on detail to excellent administrative use. In meetings with his National Emergency Council, an organization he had formed to gather information on New Deal programs, he displayed a remarkable ability to master a wide range of subjects and to ask appropriate and helpful questions about them. He was, indeed, an executive, able to sort through details, to see the relation between broad policies and day-to-day procedures. He scanned agency reports with an eye for problems, contradictions in logic, and omissions of fact. When vital information seemed lacking, he called for investigation. He was aware of the complexities of NRA wage rates, such as how a wage rate in a large plant might be too high for a small plant only a few miles away. In the same vein, he chided a delegation from the National Association of Manufacturers for never having studied the conditions they were taking political stands on.[2]

This side of Roosevelt's personality helped him make the most of his physical limits. He lived in a world of gadgets. Special hand controls enabled him to drive a car. A railroad car and C-4 airplane were specially outfitted for his comfort and special needs, including an elevator that lifted him in his wheelchair from the ground into the cabin. A specially designed wheelchair and elevator also enabled him to ride between floors in the White House.

Most of all, he liked to contrive administrative systems. His contrivances often baffled his contemporaries and puzzled scholars, who came up with the term "competitive bureaucracy" to describe his work. But this was probably not his motive. Any president or high-ranking executive knows that in one way or another, his or her administrators will compete with one another. The purpose of most administrative systems is to promote cooperation and harmony rather than conflict and competition. This was probably Roosevelt's motive. One of his more obviously "competitive" arrangements—the Ickes-Hopkins-Walker committee to manage the relief appropriation—actually assigned different responsibilities to the three main persons, with Walker given the responsibility for ensuring fairness to the others. It was not Roosevelt's design but Hopkins's ingenuity that enabled him to win control of relief and to make the WPA into the New Deal's banner agency.

The Ickes-Hopkins-Walker arrangement and many others like it (one of his arrangements in defense production had a certain person supervising himself) indicated that Roosevelt was essentially interested in managing people. Roosevelt measured people by an inner radar that was intuitive rather than rational. His written comments about others were usually bland and commonplace. His personal letters seldom went beyond characterizing others as "nice," "interesting," or "a bore." He preferred to describe or narrate rather than analyze. For the most part, he kept his observations on the surface. When he was more specific, he most often admired a person's useful traits. He praised people for their judgment, industry, or organizational skill. He especially liked those who had good judgment about their relationships, "a sense of proportion about [themselves] and others," and a sense of humor.[3] His preference for collaboration and agreement informed his judgment of those who worked for him. He directed one of his notable explosions of anger against someone who had violated his code. It came in 1943, in the wake of Sumner Welles's resignation from the State Department. Welles had been Roosevelt's most valued contact in the department and, like him, a gentleman of patrician background. Welles resigned following a scandal caused by reports that he had solicited sexual favors from a railroad porter. Prominent among those who had spread the story was William C. Bullitt, a man of similar social position and a long-time friend of Roosevelt and rival of Welles. Roosevelt summoned Bullitt to the White House and ordered him to stand in place and fixed him with a glare. "Saint Peter is at the gate," he began. "Along comes Sumner Welles, who admits to human error. Saint Peter grants him entrance. Then comes William Bullitt. Saint Peter says: 'William Bullitt, you have betrayed a fellow human being. YOU CAN GO DOWN THERE.'" With that he told Bullitt that he wished never to see him again.[4]

Through it all he was a cheerful optimist, capable of lifting others' spirits by showing them small kindnesses and sympathies, taking in their ideas and manners as part of life's continuing adventure and newness, as something to be treasured and enjoyed. He was not a Lincoln, who would memorize dark passages in *Hamlet* and compose prose poems about the ordeals and limits of the human condition. Roosevelt's style conveyed an urbanity and polish that revealed his eastern patrician background, but also a genuine warmth and delight. He loved people and was exhilarated by their company. More than anything he possessed an extraordinary sensitivity to others. He could sense their moods, especially those of despair, and was always eager to bolster them. "Bring it over to me, Henry," he said, sensing that his secretary of agriculture was struggling with some difficulty. "My shoulders are broad."[5] He was particularly sympathetic to the sick, seldom missing a chance to show his concern and to do what he could to lift their spirits with a call, a note, or a visit.

Somehow, out of the complex of his political and personal experiences, Roosevelt had come to think of human relations as essentially psychological. In discussing various measures of the nation's economic health with his National Emergency Council in 1935, he had concluded: "The important thing, in the last analysis, is the psychology of the people themselves. This is the first time I have been west of the Mississippi since 1932. The difference was perfectly apparent in the faces of the people. You could tell what the difference was by standing on the end of the car and looking at the crowd. They were a hopeful people. They had courage written all over their faces. They looked cheerful. They knew they were 'up against it' but they were going to see the thing through."[6]

It was that cheerful courage that Roosevelt sought to nourish. He himself conveyed an air of such confidence that those around him came to believe that he operated from some deep and profound qualities of character. Two who thought differently, and were in a position to have their views respected, were his wife Eleanor and his later confidant Harry Hopkins. Eleanor summed up her husband's character by referring to his deep and abiding Christian faith, which assured him that it was God's will that all should be well.[7] Hopkins's view was similar though secular. Once during the trying months of 1941, when American foreign policy was trapped between the public's desire to see the defeat of Nazi Germany and the desire to keep the United States neutral, Roosevelt had proclaimed American objectives to be the achievement of four freedoms: "Freedom of Speech, Freedom from Want, Freedom of Worship, and Freedom from Fear . . . everywhere in the world." "He wants to make the boys think he's hard-boiled," Hopkins observed to speechwriter Robert Sherwood. "Maybe he fools some of them, now and then—but don't ever let him fool you, or you won't be any use to him. You can see the real Roosevelt when he comes out with something like the Four Freedoms. And don't get the idea that those are any catch phrases. He believes them! He believes they can be practically attained."[8] His lack of cultural depth provided evidence for such beliefs. He had no interest in the fine arts. He read no "serious" books of fiction, history, or social analysis. His favorite tune was the simple, sentimental idealization of country life, "Home on the Range"; his favorite group recreation was poker, and his favorite hobby was stamp collecting. He enjoyed motion pictures, provided that they were neither too long nor too sad. Feature films were always accompanied by a cartoon, of which he particularly enjoyed Mickey Mouse.

Roosevelt's self-confidence had its limits. He chose his inner circle with an eye toward loyalty. Most persons who came to see him, he once told Wendell Willkie, wanted something. This made the presidency "a lonely job," he continued, and if Willkie ever found himself in it, he would feel the need for "somebody like Harry Hopkins who asks for nothing except to serve you."[9] As soon as he was confident of a person's loyalty, Roosevelt was willing to give him or her his support and encouragement, to the extent consistent with the demands of his office. Next to loyalty he valued a person's ability to get along with others. It was revealing that his happiest times in office were during the early-evening cocktail hour, which he always preferred to spend in the company of agreeable people. His commands to those of differing opinions to go into a room and reconcile their differences were both directives to accomplish a goal and tests of the individuals' character. Those who could not get along often found themselves on the outside. One exception was Harold Ickes, who seemed unable to get along with anyone and who periodically threatened Roosevelt with his resignation. Roosevelt, in the words of Arthur Schlesinger, Jr., "played Ickes like a violin," soothing, encouraging, and praising, realizing, perhaps, that Ickes's loyalty to Roosevelt and his desire to remain close to the seat of power were stronger than his ego.[10] Roosevelt sincerely disliked conveying bad news. From time to time, especially in 1944 when he was choosing his running mate, he would go to extreme lengths to avoid disappointing any of the aspirants, often inflicting more painful wounds than if he had acted directly.

There were, of course, elements in Roosevelt's methods that could be interpreted as cruel or uncaring. In the years after Roosevelt's death, Dwight Eisenhower observed that he had most disliked Roosevelt's callous treatment of those who served him (an observation that, coming from one whose job had been to send thousands to their deaths in battle, tells us a good deal about Eisenhower as well as about Roosevelt).[11] In 1944, Harry Hopkins observed that Roosevelt had never given him an assignment because he thought that Hopkins could do it; rather, he had given it to Hopkins because he wanted Hopkins to be the one to do it.[12] Roosevelt used people as instruments of state. As such, their value was based on the degree to which they could achieve a state purpose.

Roosevelt made the best of his own qualities. A designer and a tinkerer, confident of his objectives, he used people to achieve his ends. He enlisted those devoted to his causes and tapped their best energies. This is something that all persons in public life, and especially those with large and critical responsibilities, must do if they are going to succeed. Those who put the welfare of individuals above their public responsibilities—Richard Nixon comes to mind—often pay dearly for it. To Roosevelt, people were like the artifacts and gadgets on his desk. They were endlessly fascinating and important, but primarily so that he could arrange them and think about them when he wanted to. If he used people, he used them well and not badly.[13]

It was probably not the complexity of Roosevelt's beliefs that interested people but rather his strategic senses, his timing, his anticipation, and his ability to react and, above all, to maintain control. People in power are always the subject of conversation and at least casual analysis by those near them, and the longer and more successfully they hold power, the more intense the interest and the more clever and complex the analyses.

Here we approach the core of Roosevelt's achievement as a presidential leader. He had a deep understanding of power and how it could operate in a democratic political culture. Nothing illustrated this better than his penchant for putting antagonists face-to-face. During a session of the Brains Trust, he flabbergasted Raymond Moley by suggesting that he should take diametrically opposing ideas and "weave the two together."[14] In part, his complex administrative systems were devices to maintain his power by building in tensions that he alone could resolve, and in this sense, his methods were instruments of power. At the same time, they were opportunities for individuals to work out their differences and to move toward a larger synthesis. What this essentially meant was that the success or failure of a given program depended less on the organizational structure than on the qualities of the people who participated in it.

The qualities Roosevelt looked for in an administrator were similar to those he valued in his personal relations. He was willing to make appointments for political reasons, for "party balance," or to court sympathetic Republicans and independents. But he insisted on loyalty to him and honesty in doing the public's business. Remarkably, given the scope and complexity of the New Deal and later the wartime bureaucracies, no scandal touched any high-ranking administrator. (At lower levels, congressmen, governors, and mayors attempted to manipulate New Deal programs for their partisan advantage, occasionally with embarrassing results for Roosevelt's administration.)

To the extent that there was a flaw in Roosevelt's style of governance, it was in the disjuncture between his personal style and the needs of his office. His desire for harmony, his preference for encouragement and positive incentives, and his fear of making enemies often built up expectations that he could not fulfill, leaving people feeling that they had been manipulated. Roosevelt did what he could to soothe such hurts and often succeeded to the extent of submerging them.

Of course, he could never have succeeded with any of this had he not been so popular a president. The joke about Herbert Hoover's asking for a nickel to call a friend and being offered a dime so that he could call all his friends would have applied equally to Franklin Roosevelt if his popularity had sunk to the level of Hoover's. But as long as he remained popular, he could afford to manipulate the people around him. Acutely aware of this reality, Roosevelt strove mightily to maintain his political strength. This affected his personal relationships in complex ways. As issues and challenges changed, some advisers moved into his inner circle, and others moved out of it. Anyone whose actions embarrassed his administration or threatened the Democratic Party had to be removed or contained.

During most of his presidency, Roosevelt worked without a fixed team of advisers. Louis Howe, his first political mentor and troubleshooter, joined the White House staff but was soon moved to the fringes of the administration, largely as an aide to Eleanor. Roosevelt had long since absorbed Howe's lessons and was operating on a different plane. Now he was concerned with reordering the nation's economic system, something beyond Howe's talents for manipulating issues and spinning out slogans. He maintained a small staff of long-serving and deeply loyal persons: his personal secretary Missy LeHand, appointments secretary Marvin McIntyre, and press secretary Stephen Early.

Policy advisers came and went. Moley and Tugwell enjoyed a few months' prominence, but they were soon joined by Hopkins and later by

Cohen and Corcoran—all at odds with one another to some degree. Not until very late in Roosevelt's second term did Hopkins emerge from this group to become his closest confidant and troubleshooter. Among those who were more or less constant—Morgenthau and Ickes—Roosevelt consulted them and used them as sounding boards and as support for his own ideas, but he relied on them no more than he relied on anyone else.

Roosevelt's relation with such advisers depended on circumstances. He could be "influenced" by them, such as when Hopkins proposed a federal works program for the winter of 1933–1934 or Ickes proposed a party "purge" in 1938. But such "influence" usually amounted to a practical suggestion of moving along a track to which Roosevelt was already committed.

This is not to say that Roosevelt never needed advice and was at all times in command of a given situation. During his administration he experienced many periods of frustration and indecision. Such times seemed to have an enervating effect on him, and he would appear listless and inattentive.

Roosevelt's need for loyalty could also cause problems for him. As much as he commanded his own presidency, he continually needed the comradeship and support of a loyal inner circle. At first Eleanor and Howe had been his core supporters. Later came the Brains Trust, Tommy Corcoran, Harry Hopkins, and Henry Morgenthau, Jr. This meant that the quality of his decisions depended on the quality of the people on whom he chose to depend. Each relationship had its positive and negative outcomes. Corcoran and Ben Cohen proved able advocates for antitrust legislation and had their successes as congressional strategists. Corcoran's advocating the "purge" of 1938 contributed to a major blunder. Hopkins's success in advocating and carrying out high-employment work relief projects substituted short-term benefits and political gains for more substantial contributions to recovery. His mishandling the 1940 convention needed Eleanor's saving touch to avoid a major embarrassment. Then, his wartime service as diplomatic representative and administrative coordinator contributed mightily to Roosevelt's success. Morgenthau's fiscal conservatism reinforced Roosevelt's own instincts and prevented the New Deal from adopting a Keynesian economic policy. His conservatism better served the country during the war, helping the nation to achieve the lowest inflation rate and the most equal distribution of income during any of America's wars to date. Morgenthau's "plan" for the deindustrialization of Germany embarrassed the administration during the campaign of 1944 and brought Harry Hopkins back into the center of Roosevelt's circle.

At the center of Franklin Roosevelt's presidency was the man himself. He had a full range of emotions, which he seemed to wear on his sleeve. In moments of enjoyment he was boisterous and demonstrative. He would throw back his head and almost shout: "O, I love it, I LOVE it . . . don't you just LOVE IT!" During the evening cocktail hour he kept up a light-hearted chatter. In his dark and angry moods his face would redden and his jaw tighten. In conversation he could be endlessly charming, nodding, agreeing, being ever so thankful that his visitor had stopped by to share the fruits of his or her thinking. To Frances Perkins it seemed that he always looked for "the common denominator between him and everyone with whom he had contact."[15] He loved to josh with reporters, advising them how to write their stories, chiding them for not getting the point, even occasionally assigning one or two to wear a dunce cap and sit in the corner. But when the morning headlines or bylines were against him, he would become bitterly suspicious, detecting the dark motives of corporate greed or un-American ideologies.

Most of all, Roosevelt trusted his own judgment, especially his own sense of timing. At one time or another his advisers would find him audacious or timid—audacious when he had decided the time had come to act, timid when he was waiting for the right moment. Once he had decided to take action, he became stubbornly determined, even at the risk of failure and embarrassment. During periods of long frustration, while he waited for the opportunity to act, he could become lethargic and detached. He seemed to lose interest when he was not at the center and in control. On one occasion during a coal strike in the fall of 1941, he fell asleep at his desk while Missy LeHand read him a detective story.[16]

Roosevelt's trust in his own sense of timing kept even his closest advisers off balance. For long periods he would seem placid, stymied, or indifferent, then suddenly he would make a bold move. The first and second "hundred days" were conspicuous results, as were the Supreme Court plan, the nominations of Republicans Stimson and Knox to the cabinet, the Lend-Lease Bill, the announcement of an unlimited national emergency, the "shoot on sight" order against German U-boats, and the unconditional surrender doctrine. Most turned out well; others failed to have an effect or had a bad effect. At times he seemed to act impetuously, as though he had lost patience. The attack on the Supreme Court and the party "purge" were two notable examples.

His confidence in his sense of timing often prompted him to be secretive. The Supreme Court plan, his silence about his intention to run for a third term, and his silence on his vice presidential choice in 1944 were tactical examples. His arranging secret military collaboration with Great Britain and his promise to Churchill at the Atlantic Conference to wage war without declaring it were strategic examples.

Behind his self-confidence were his religious faith and his willingness to take responsibility. Roosevelt never thought of himself as a savior but

Roosevelt gives his characteristic wave in Ottawa, Canada, August 25, 1943. (Franklin D. Roosevelt Library)

as someone who had been given "a grand opportunity" to address the nation's problems.[17]

Often those who wanted bolder action from Roosevelt mistook his method of operating. Rexford Tugwell, a member of the Brains Trust and holder of a few less conspicuous posts, wrote widely and extensively on Roosevelt and his administration. Tugwell described Roosevelt's method: "He became conscious of it [the problem]. He sized it up. Something occurred to him. After a cautious interval he began to broach ideas to this or that associate or to someone called in for the purpose. His understanding broadened and deepened satisfactorily, and policy began actually to shape itself. He put someone or a group to work on detail or on verification, and presently there it was, ready for action." At the same time, Tugwell noticed something always unfinished or provisional in Roosevelt's style. "We never could really talk to Roosevelt," he recalled, "we had to talk with him. If we did not catch his interest, he would shift to another subject; if we did, it became a dialogue. . . . It might be only when I thought it over afterward that I knew he had not been convinced. It was an exchange, but there was not often any conclusion. . . . But all our talk was so fair and friendly that there was never a time when defeat was so definite that I finally gave up." Roosevelt approached a problem by pressing in a direction, always watching for a response, to which he then reacted. His approach was to "persuade rather than dictate, to approach rather than conclude." This method often caused him to change his means of operation, but not his objective. Still, to those who favored a more straightforward, decisive style of leadership, the result was often confusing, and it often seemed as though he was temporizing to the point of cowardice. (Frances Perkins, who had worked with him since his governorship, made sure that she had his approval twice before going ahead with a project.)[18]

Roosevelt's style fit with his sense of political reality. "A candidate might surprise the voters, but he must not shock them." A president "could educate in the interest of his program, but a candidate had to accept people's prejudices and turn them to good use." A president, he believed, had a limited amount of political capital and had to avoid spending it too early. To this he added his belief that progressive politicians were unreliable allies. Progressives were always willing to quit, but when it came to compromise, they stood on virtue and demanded more than was possible for their side. Roosevelt wanted to transform the Democratic Party into a "liberal" or "progressive" party, but he believed that he could not rely solely on the support of the progressives to achieve it. In some way he would have to transform the regular party organization. This meant that Roosevelt worked through the northern city bosses and southern agrarians, doing what he could to enlist them in progressive causes.[19]

His strategy for enlisting them was to create programs that brought tangible benefits to their constituents. Roosevelt believed in results. Policies that improved people's lives would translate into voter loyalty. Checks to farmers and the families of CCC workers, better relief to the unemployed, improved working conditions: these were the things that counted. To the degree that these programs mobilized the beneficiaries to participate in them by "democratic" means (voting in farm program referenda or union elections), they both strengthened the program and sent signals that guided the politicians.

Roosevelt followed an unsteady course in dealing with Congress. Early in his administration he worked closely with congressional leaders. All the major legislation of his first term was a product of presidential and congressional interaction, with Roosevelt following the lead of Congress as often as he led. The agricultural and industrial recovery acts were joint projects, as was the securities exchange act; the relief act and the utility holding company acts were largely congressional measures. When Congress was in session, Roosevelt spent three to four hours a day with members, talking about a variety of subjects. He was anxious to show a good face to Congress, to show that the New Deal was operating efficiently. Prior to the meeting of Congress in January 1935, he advised his agency heads to be sure to get their requests in before the middle of the month. Submitting "happy ideas" while Congress was doing its main business "delays the action of Congress . . . confuses the legislation [and] angers the members." To enhance coordination, he suggested that agencies hold small group meetings to exchange information. "It is getting together that counts more than anything else." Still, he cautioned against offending members of Congress. "All your money, my money, your existence and mine," he advised his agency heads, "is dependent on the Congress of the United States. There is absolutely no question about that. We have to conform with the appropriation and we have to conform with the law." Realizing that many congressmen were complaining about New Deal agencies' not hiring their political supporters, Roosevelt argued for a middle ground. It was all right to hire qualified people regardless of their political credentials and to refuse to hire unqualified friends of congressmen, but under no circumstances should an agency employ a person who had worked against the congressman or the administration. "Fire the fellow!" Roosevelt barked. "A few good examples of firing people . . . will be an awfully good thing."[20]

At the same time, Roosevelt valued his own relations with the public and wanted as much direct contact with it as possible. In a large part, he thought of his mission as educational. He wanted to show people the interrelatedness of his programs, how in general terms people could see the benefits of another's well-being. City folk could accept an increase in the price of pork chops if they were informed of the farmers' problems. He was hoping "to get away from the division between city and country. We are going to get away, in the same way, from a division between different regions of the country. . . . I am trying to emphasize the rounded picture, and I think every one of us has a definite responsibility in getting that rounded responsibility across in the next few months."[21]

Roosevelt disliked interference with his objectives. His tinkering and designing were for his own purposes and no one else's. He favored compromise as long as others were doing it. His openness to others, his conciliatory and encouraging approaches, his various councils, committees, and boards were devices for giving him the maximum amount of information, but they were not designed to let others make up his mind for him. In 1936 he would say that he was the issue, and that was the way he wanted it. Those who crossed him or interfered with his purposes did not last long. Some demonstrated their relevance to only one issue, and when that had been resolved, they were cast aside. If he found them operating against his political values, he discarded them, often in rough and obvious ways. He liked to say that he was "an old softy" who could not fire anyone. What he meant was that he disliked discarding the services of someone whose talents or interests were no longer a priority for him. Those who adapted themselves to his ways and put their energies into fulfilling his purposes could stay the course. In his eyes they showed loyalty, a quality that rated at the top of his scale. The best were the ones who provided advice and skill but not leadership or, in rare cases, had the ability to portray their leadership as a subcategory of his own.[22]

Roosevelt's shifting of his means should not give the impression that he was careless about them. The opposite was the case. When elections were coming up, he carefully briefed his administrators to "keep your tempers" and not be upset by charges and faulty press reports. He wanted to convey the impression that opposition and criticism were arising out of misinformation or misunderstanding, as well as "politics [and] pure cussedness." Near the beginning of a reelection year, Roosevelt's advice became more specific and detailed. His administrators should stick to their own business, not call anyone names, and use illustrations that were meaningful to the audiences they were addressing. Citizens of Massachusetts were not going to applaud a program that was helping citizens of Utah. In so doing they would be getting "down to the human element." He carefully planned his campaign trips, knew the details of his stops, employed his prodigious memory to project his charm and to appear at home. His speeches went through five to ten drafts before they were ready for delivery. In 1936 he arranged the gubernatorial tickets in New York and Michigan so that popular candidates would be providing coattails for his reelection.[23]

Nowhere was his meticulous planning more evident than in his attempts to manage the news. In the beginning, Roosevelt saw the relation between his administration and the press as less one of mutual hostility than one of comparative advantage. Reporters naturally sought to take advantage of one's ignorance. Typically, they would throw up a quotation from a source and ask for a response. If, for example, someone asked about his response to a statement by the American ambassador to Great Britain proposing a closer working relationship between the two countries, an approving response might worry the Japanese, and a disapproving one might worry the British or the ambassador. Instead of commenting, Roosevelt advised, one should always plead ignorance of the quote and ask for time to study it. He imposed a flat rule against anyone's commenting on a matter that affected another department. Also, one had to remember that in Washington there were no secrets. Leading columnists paid people to inform on government officials. Tonight's casual dinner conversation could be tomorrow's headline. Roosevelt and Steve Early set firm ground rules for press conferences, and Early carefully briefed him before each one. Early monitored the press conferences, often breaking in to say that a given statement was off the record, and he would even call a halt when he thought the time was ripe. He collected favorable comments for use in speeches. He controlled photographic coverage, firmly disallowing any pictures that revealed Roosevelt's handicap. Roosevelt carefully monitored control of the radio networks. He was fearful and angry when newspapers, most of them hostile to the New Deal, began to purchase radio stations. He influenced a decision by the Federal Communications Commission to require the Radio Corporation of America to sell one of its two NBC networks and to limit CBS's control over affiliate station time. He tipped reporters to news opportunities. Supportive congressmen were given favorable New Deal material to place in the *Congressional Record* and to mail, postage free, to their constituents. Roosevelt informed cabinet members of topics to include in their speeches. He also warned agency heads against spontaneous replies to reporters' questions, pointing out that the reporter might be implying something that was not true and that all answers should be based on sound information. Reporters appreciated the administration's help in locating the best source for a story, but this made it easier for the administration to manage the news.[24]

Roosevelt best combined his talent for influencing the news and keeping himself in the spotlight through his "fireside chat" radio broadcasts. These, along with all his radio addresses, were meticulously researched and rehearsed. The setting for the fireside chats was a White House room with a desk containing several microphones. Twenty to thirty invited guests arrived about twenty minutes before the broadcast and sat in folding chairs.

Ten minutes later, Roosevelt was wheeled in, carrying his text, his cigarette in a holder tilted at a jaunty angle. At a signal from the engineer, the announcer would identify the broadcast as coming from the White House and introduce "The President of the United States." Roosevelt would begin: "My friends. . . ." Newspaper and motion picture photographers would record portions of the speech that Roosevelt had selected. At the end, the stations would play the "Star Spangled Banner." The visitors would then crowd up to the president's table. After a short time they would drift away, and Roosevelt would retire for a snack and postmortem discussion of the speech with staff and perhaps a few invited guests.[25]

Roosevelt's greatest asset with the press was his popularity. Early in his administration, *Time* magazine referred to his "shriveled legs" and used similar terms to describe his paralysis. Readers complained so much that the magazine changed to describing how he had overcome his disability. But Roosevelt was no more successful in shaping public values than many other presidents. His heroic and cunning efforts to shape the news in favor of his plan to reform the Supreme Court failed to win over the press, the public, or Congress.[26]

Inevitably, Roosevelt found himself snarled in the Faustian bargain that all modern presidents make with the press. He had won the opportunity to use his magically persuasive powers to shape the news and to tell his side of things. But at the same time, he had opened himself to hostile interpretations of his programs and actions and, perhaps more important, to probing attempts to get behind his words to his meanings and intentions. This was to prove especially difficult in foreign relations, where Roosevelt wanted to oppose the spread of fascism more actively and the public feared the possibility of war. To a president for whom press criticism was almost obsessive, the difficulties of his position created a kind of garrison psychology. The result was a record of deception and half-truths that more than any other aspect of Roosevelt's presidency cast a shadow over his historical reputation. When the *Washington Post* broke the story that U.S. ships were convoying lend-lease supplies in U.S. waters, Roosevelt falsely labeled the story "a deliberate lie."[27]

As Roosevelt's confidence in the newspapers' ability to report public opinion waned, he turned to polling. Most of the polling was done to check the effect of news coverage. Roosevelt believed that most newspapers were biased and inaccurate and wanted to see whether the voters believed them. During the latter New Deal years he relied on Emil Hurja of the Democratic National Committee, but in 1940 he turned to Hadley Cantril of the Princeton American Public Opinion Institute. After Pearl Harbor, Cantril began to report directly to the White House. He regularly supplied the White House with polling results on a wide range of topics, from agricultural price supports to foreign policy to election prospects. Cantril categorized the vote by place and size of community, race, and gender. Prior to the 1944 election, he predicted that the African American vote would give Roosevelt the northern cities and that women would vote for Roosevelt more heavily than men. His reports on specific issue differences between Roosevelt and challenger Thomas Dewey—war leadership, planning for peace, domestic versus foreign issues—provided Roosevelt the chance to craft his messages to attract the largest support.[28]

To a degree remarkable among modern presidents, Roosevelt's tactics succeeded. There were in certain circles, however, feelings of intense bitterness, even hatred, toward Roosevelt and his works. Such persons, as we shall see, were never a threat to Roosevelt's holding office. But from time to time, they were able to direct his policy choices or to shift his political tactics as he tried to parry their influence.

All presidential administrations have their critics. Some come from the political party establishment; others are "fringe" leaders who consciously set themselves apart from the parties. One group that deserted Roosevelt during his first term was certain progressive Democrats with Woodrow Wilson loyalties. Loyal trustbusters who were inclined to believe that economic size and evil were proportional to each other, they were most offended by the NRA cartelization of business sectors. Most believed that government should play a role in coping with the stresses of the depression, but to those accustomed to the moralistic certainties of a Theodore Roosevelt or a Woodrow Wilson, Franklin Roosevelt's pluralistic, changeable methods suggested an unsavory kind of selfish opportunism, carried forward by government programs that substituted government checks for appeals to patriotism and humanitarian ideals. Essentially, they were reformers who preferred to change leaders rather than to change institutions, to elevate the moral discourse rather than to raise the living standards of workers and the poor. Programs that seemed aimed at the latter had the odor of social revolution. During a decade when dictators were menacing the peace and moral standards of the world, Roosevelt's focusing attention on himself and expanding executive authority suggested that he posed a threat to democracy itself.[29]

Predictable hostility came from business organizations such as the United States Chamber of Commerce and the National Association of Manufacturers. Thoroughly grounded in the sanctity of the gold standard and hostility toward organized labor and government regulation of business, these organizations and their spokesmen called for a return to "individualism" and an end to "experimentation." They denounced Roosevelt's "dictatorship," "government spending," "government debt," and "collectivism." Clinton L. Bardo, president of the National Association of Manufacturers, warned that unless the New Deal was removed, America would be destroyed "by a deliberate and well-timed rapid-fire and devastating attack by economic crack-pots, social reformers, labor demagogues and political racketeers."[30]

One particularly visible agent of this kind of opposition was the American Liberty League. Founded in 1934 by a bipartisan coalition of conservative Republicans and Democrats, the league included John W. Davis, corporation lawyer and 1924 Democratic presidential nominee; Nathan Miller, former Republican governor of New York; the du Ponts of the great Delaware business fortune; and Franklin Roosevelt's former ally-turned-competitor (and now antagonist) Al Smith. (The league invited Herbert Hoover to join, but since some of them had been Democrats in 1932, he sourly refused.)

These groups and their spokesmen were potentially important because they were vocal. They wrote newspaper and magazine columns, published books, organized public forums, and contributed to anti–New Deal candidates. Between August 1934 and November 1936, the Liberty League, by far the most prolific of the publicists, issued 177 separate titles and distributed 5 million copies. Whatever Franklin Roosevelt's other advantages, they did not include public ignorance of the men and ideas of his opponents.[31]

Three of Roosevelt's opponents the public got to know better than the others. Senator Huey P. Long of Louisiana had the firmest political base. Long had won power by employing populist rhetoric to defeat his state's corrupt alliance between machine politics and corporate wealth. Long combined a genuine class-conscious politics that provided state services to low-income persons regardless of race with a desire to crown his power with the structure of state authority. Elected to the governorship, he improved roads, built hospitals, increased funding for education, and adorned his labors with an imposing state capitol. With the aid of the state militia and a rubber-stamp state legislature, he bypassed the courts, discredited his opponents, and erected a system of power that forced all public and party leaders to bow to his will. All this he did with a flamboyant, southern folk-culture style that appealed to those with strong attachments to rural localities and who felt apart and alienated from the nation's social and economic mainstream. For them, Huey P. Long was a kind of political vigilante, willing boldly to acquire and to assert power in clear, direct, and unambiguous ways without regard to the procedures and customs that thwarted their sense of opportunity and justice.[32]

Elected to the U.S. Senate in 1930, Long immediately set his sights on the presidency. Projecting from his ideological base in southern populism, he proposed dividing large wealth and in January 1934 formed the Share-

Our-Wealth Society. It would provide every family with $5,000, a home, an automobile, and a radio; set up old-age pensions; impose limits on working hours; advocate federal purchase of agricultural surpluses and immediate payment of veterans' bonuses; offer free college to all qualified by IQ exams; and sponsor improvement and development construction projects. Long would seize all savings over $1.7 million.[33]

Superficially different but essentially similar was the appeal of Father Charles Coughlin. Beginning a series of radio addresses to raise money in his struggling suburban parish of Royal Oak, Coughlin became a broadcasting phenomenon, the most listened-to radio personality and recipient of the most mail of any American citizen. His message was a blend of Catholic social justice and diatribes against communism and socialism. During the early years of the depression, he directed his most hostile comments against individual greed, monopoly capitalism, and the concentration of wealth. After Roosevelt's election, he endorsed the New Deal but was soon moving beyond it to advocate his own panacea for the nation's economic ills: monetary expansion. More money in circulation, he argued, would stimulate demand while breaking the power of the Wall Street bankers.

Coughlin's popularity and political potential seemed formidable. Not only did he receive tons of mail; his word could generate torrents of mail to the White House. Coughlin's pains earned him the Roosevelt treatment. Visiting the White House, Coughlin was assured that the president would rely on his advice. The "radio priest" was neither the first nor the last person who took this assurance seriously. But to one who reduced politics to the power of the spoken word and whose words seemed more powerful than anyone else's, his awakening to the truth was especially rude. As it became increasingly apparent that Roosevelt wanted his support more than his advice, Coughlin moved from support to disenchantment to, inevitably, hostility. Just after the 1934 elections, Coughlin formed the National Union for Social Justice, his vehicle for influencing party politics and perhaps with the potential to become a third party.

The leadership of Dr. Francis Townsend appealed to a more specific constituency with a more specific agenda. An elderly physician who, after a struggling career in rural practice, found himself nearly destitute in southern California, Townsend concocted a plan to provide all senior citizens with a pension of $200 a month, provided that they retire from gainful employment and spend the entire amount before their next allocation. (This was an astonishingly large amount of money at a time when incomes averaged between $1,000 and $1,500 a year.) The Townsend plan's political appeal was remarkably powerful. It had several strengths: it was simplistic, it relied on a small tax of 2 percent of business transactions to provide funds for its elderly recipients, it corresponded to ideas for social insurance already under discussion, and it appealed to feelings of regard for the aged while mobilizing a constituency that usually voted in large numbers. From its base in southern California it spread to other state legislatures that urged Congress to adopt the plan. A petition drive drew the signatures of one-fifth of the adult population, "an exhibition of public support unmatched in history."[34] By 1934, Townsend had founded an organization to lobby for his plan.

The potential appeal of the Long, Coughlin, and Townsend movements disturbed the administration. A poll taken by the Democratic National Committee in the spring of 1935 showed Long with substantial strength throughout the nation, strongest in the South and weakest in New England. Outside of New England, Long's support failed to reduce Roosevelt's margin below a majority, although in the Middle Atlantic, Great Lakes, and farm belt states it reduced it to barely over 50 percent. The poll did not offer voters the chance to choose Coughlin, but enough wrote in his name for him to be included in the tallies. He added to the third-party potential, but not enough to change the overall picture.

The significance of the poll was the importance Roosevelt attached to it. Persuaded by Farley that Long might hold the balance of power in the next election, Roosevelt authorized strong steps against Long and his potential allies. Federal patronage, including control of relief projects, went to his political enemies. The administration looked into Coughlin's citizenship, finances, and political connections and explored the possibility of influencing the Catholic Church to get him off the air. Roosevelt inspired attacks on the Townsend plan. When he attacked back, Congress investigated and dredged up every unsavory aspect of Townsend's operation, from mismanagement to self-aggrandizement and outright greed. The hearings concluded with a grilling of Townsend, who cracked under relentless cross-examination and appeared ill informed and bumbling.[35]

Such activities may well have been a wasted effort. All three movements were essentially houses of cards, divided by the agendas of their local constituencies, plagued by opportunists, and ultimately subverted by the poor judgment of their leaders. It was especially telling that many of their supporters believed that they should work with Franklin Roosevelt and not against him. Nor was it clear how the specific programs of the three could be brought together.

Such, at least, would be the emerging realities of the protest movements. Whatever chance they might have had was destroyed in September 1935 in the rotunda of the Louisiana state capitol, where Carl Austin Weis, perhaps angered that the Long machine had removed his uncle from a state judgeship, fired a bullet into Huey Long. Although rushed to a hospital, Long suffered from incompetent medical attention and bled to death. His successor, Gerald L. K. Smith, cobbled together an alliance with Coughlin and Townsend that produced the National Union Party, which nominated North Dakota senator William Lemke for president. The result was a political fiasco. The National Union Party was rent by self-seeking, petty vendettas, narrow loyalties, poor financing, ballot restrictions, and erratic and ludicrous public behavior. In the end, the best the leaders could muster was prediction of a victory for the Republican nominee, Governor Alf Landon of Kansas. In the election, the Lemke vote represented fragments of the disaffected citizens groups that had rallied behind the disparate elements of protest.

In the end, only the Townsend movement could boast a positive achievement. Its vigorous lobbying persuaded the administration and Congress to include old-age assistance in the social security legislation, both in the original bill in 1935 and in the 1939 amendments to move up the first payments from 1942 to 1940 and to increase the federal share.

The common thread in the appeal of these three leaders was their support by vulnerable persons who placed their individual needs above those of the larger society—small businessmen, dirt farmers, the elderly, and those who were culturally offended by their society's march toward large, complex organizations, secular expertise, sophisticated political leadership, and a non-Victorian morality. In these respects they were not radically different from those who supported Franklin Roosevelt and the New Deal, especially after Roosevelt moved to the left and advertised himself as the opponent of the nation's "economic royalists." They differed primarily in the degree of their detachment from the American political system and in the intensity of their yearning for a single person who could cut away the complexities and obstacles of a pluralistic social analysis and replace it with the determination and power of a single person. Their desire for such leadership did not make them "fascists," "reds," or participants in some other kind of contemporary movement (although their leaders did not always realize that). At bottom, their values were traditionally American—a belief in capitalism, free enterprise, and success through individual effort; a personal moral code based on evangelical Christianity; and a staunch patriotism. Ten years later, countless more of their kind would be found on Omaha Beach than on FBI lists of subversives. At the moment, however, they demanded more of the nation's political system than the system could provide.

Among voters, Franklin Roosevelt drew strength from a variety of sources. Prominent among traditional Democratic voters, who voted Democratic without regard to their social and economic status, were northern white Catholics and southern whites. In 1936, 80 percent of northern white Catholics voted Democratic, in contrast to 52 percent of northern white Protestants.

In 1940, 62 percent of these Catholics identified themselves as Democrats, 68 percent voted for Democrats for Congress, and 70 percent voted for Roosevelt. Over 80 percent of southern whites voted Democratic. By way of contrast, only 31 percent of northern white Protestants identified with the Democrats, 34 percent voted for Democrats for Congress, and 39 percent voted for Roosevelt.[36]

Northern white Catholics and southern whites could provide a core of support, but they could not make the difference between winning and losing. In 1932 that difference was supplied by the anti-Hoover vote. In that year, the presidential vote shifted massively toward the Democrats among all groups of the population and in all regions of the country. At the same time, voters did not change their order of preferences: previous Republican groups and regions were still more Republican than other groups and regions; the Republican vote was simply a smaller percentage of the total vote than it had been in earlier elections.[37] In some areas, Roosevelt's margin was provided by additional voters—new and less frequent voters who had turned out to vote for him. Because the South was already voting overwhelmingly Democratic, the largest shifts occurred in the North, principally in farm areas and most strongly where local Democratic Party organizations were able to mobilize former nonvoters.[38] The priority Roosevelt's New Deal gave to agriculture was more than a continuation of his nomination strategy and his concern about rural radicalism; it was a response to the votes of rural Americans. Generally, then, traditional Democratic voters provided the base, and new voters provided the margin.[39]

The "mobilization" (that is, the turning out to vote) of new and previously indifferent voters was critical to Franklin Roosevelt's political base. Between 1928 and 1940, the number of voters increased more than three times the natural increase in the voting population. This mobilization was the largest in the twentieth century. Many of these new voters began voting against Hoover in 1932, but the majority of them began voting for the New Deal in the congressional elections of 1934, thus adding seats to the president's party for the first time (and, until recently, the only time) in an off-year election in this century. These voters tended to be first- and second-generation immigrants, young voters, the unemployed, and those on relief.[40] The vast majority of them registered as Democrats and identified with the party.[41] Between 1932 and 1938, the Democrats not only maintained their ascendancy in presidential and congressional races but actually gained votes while the Republicans lost votes.[42] Because the voting pattern was a northern Democratic majority and a southern Democratic majority, it made Franklin Roosevelt's presidency the first truly national presidency since the pre–Civil War administration of Franklin Pierce.

The overwhelming nature of Roosevelt's majorities masked a complex pattern of shifting loyalties. Between 1932 and 1936, northern rural voters began to drift away from the Democratic Party, while urban laborers moved heavily into it. Between 1933 and 1936, by far the largest shift to the Democrats came from workers and city residents. In 1934 and 1936 the Democrats gained votes in the nation's urban and industrial heartland, in states from New York west through Illinois and Wisconsin.[43] In the North, the vote assumed a class character. Because northern working-class white Catholics had previously voted Democratic in large majorities, it was difficult to distinguish class differences among them, but among northern Protestants, who had been weak supporters of Democrats, class differences were pronounced.

Professor Lizabeth Cohen has provided an excellent insight into the process by which Chicago workers interacted with the New Deal. Many, especially white ethnic workers, began voting in large numbers in the late 1920s. As New Deal programs began to affect their lives (insuring their bank deposits, offering credit to protect their homes, providing employment), they developed a faith in the state and in the state's role in providing welfare and security. Roosevelt's class-conscious rhetoric consolidated their allegiance to a leader who was fighting for them against local enemies. Organizing and fighting to form unions under NIRA and later the Wagner Act tightened the bonds of class solidarity. The Congress of Industrial Organizations (CIO), the driving force in the New Deal labor movement, promoted this solidarity. It gave members buttons to wear on the shop floor, organized bowling teams and other forms of recreation, delivered radio broadcasts, formed women's "auxiliaries," and established classes in home economy. Out of these struggles, workers, in conjunction with the skilled administrative structure of the CIO, put New Deal labor legislation into effect.[44]

In 1936 about 20 percent of Roosevelt's support came from voters who usually considered themselves Republicans.[45] Ideological preferences accounted for some of this shift. As the New Deal moved toward government regulation of business and support for organized labor, northern progressive Republicans moved into the Democratic camp. The shift of Progressives was most notable in North Dakota, Minnesota, and Wisconsin. In these states, Progressives had operated in an overwhelmingly Republican political environment. The only way Progressives could gain power was by controlling the Republican Party. This situation changed briefly when the 1932 surge to Roosevelt temporarily bestowed power on pre-depression Democrats. But those state Democratic regimes were inherently unstable, led by persons unaccustomed to exercising power and based on a "constituency" that had voted against the incumbent rather than endorsed his leadership. As the New Deal program unfolded, progressive Republicans followed different courses. In North Dakota they simply coalesced with the Democrats. Between 1933 and 1936, Wisconsin Progressives supported Roosevelt and then split into pro- and anti-Roosevelt factions. In 1938 the major progressive faction tried to form its own national party. After that failed, they formally allied with Roosevelt and the Democrats.[46] In Minnesota the rural Farmer-Labor Party became an urban party that cooperated with the New Deal. But the party collapsed with the death of popular governor Floyd B. Olson, and in 1938 the Republicans benefited from a surge that made them a strongly competitive minority in presidential voting and a majority party at the state level. A Democratic-Farmer-Labor coalition would not develop until the 1940s.[47]

Another complicating element in the development of Roosevelt's base was the tendency of some Republican voters to support Roosevelt without identifying with his party. Between 1933 and 1936, California voter registration showed no increase in either Republicans or Democrats, but Roosevelt's margin of victory in the state increased from 22 percentage points to 35 percentage points. Similarly, between 1936 and 1940, 42 to 44 percent of African Americans identified with the Democratic Party, and 67 to 71 percent voted Democratic. Between 1936 and 1940, 85 percent of Jews voted for Roosevelt, but in 1940 only 45 percent called themselves Democrats.[48] There was even some instability in the New Deal's working-class support, as 54 percent of semiskilled and unskilled workers identified with the Democrats and 68 percent voted for their candidates. One consequence of this lag in party identification was split voting for the president and Congress. Although the votes for Roosevelt in 1932 and 1936 produced large majorities in Congress, some 14 percent voted for Roosevelt and for a Republican congressional candidate.

During Franklin Roosevelt's first term, as urban and labor interests moved to the center of the New Deal, rural supporters moved toward the Republicans. Between 1932 and 1936, Democratic losses were concentrated in farm areas.[49] In every election after 1936, the Democrats lost ground in Missouri, Iowa, Kansas, Nebraska, and the Dakotas. These losses were enough to cause an underlying trend toward the Republicans. One result was to weaken conservative Democrats in the North or to reduce them to a fringe minority of predominantly Catholic voters in states such as Iowa.[50] In Minnesota the depression converted the essentially rural Farmer-Labor Party into an essentially urban party that cooperated with the New Deal and moved the party toward urban liberalism. This resulted in rural Minnesotans' moving back toward the Republicans.[51] It is surprising to realize that despite their overwhelming victories in the electoral college and heavy majorities in Congress, the Democrats struggled to win a majority of the regional popular vote in the northern states. In twenty-five elections in five northern regions from 1932 to 1940, the Democrats received a larger vote than the Republicans in only eleven. In 1938 and 1940 they led in only two out of ten.[52] Throughout the New Deal period, the Republicans were potentially a political force to be reckoned with.

All the complexities of ideological, social, and cultural shiftings and siftings contained one element that drew them all toward a common focus and arranged them in a pattern of striking clarity. That element was Franklin Roosevelt. No president since Abraham Lincoln had so dominated national party politics. Roosevelt's record was astonishing. In his four elections, his average margin of victory in the states he carried was just over 29 points. In the other states, his losing margin averaged just 8.4 points. In other words, he came much closer to carrying his opponents' states than they came to carrying his. In his first three elections, his margin in the electoral college was untouchable. If we consider a difference of less than 10 percentage points between a winning and a losing candidate to be a "close" election, only the election of 1944 was "close." With 266 votes needed for a majority in the electoral college, Roosevelt's challenger, Thomas E. Dewey, received 99 electoral votes and came within 10 points of Roosevelt in states with 250 electoral votes. Actually, the election was even closer than this. Dewey could have won by capturing the states Roosevelt carried by 5 points or less. In the other elections, however, the Republicans had no chance. In the election of 1940, the next "closest" election, Roosevelt won by fewer than 10 points in states with 71 electoral votes. But his opponent, Wendell Willkie, won only 82 electoral votes, leaving him 184 shy of the 266 needed for a majority. Roosevelt could have lost the vote in every one of the "close" states and still have won the election by a margin of 113.[53] In 1932 and 1936 his margins were much larger.

Franklin Roosevelt's declining margins in the electoral college indicate that his political base diminished. The most likely source of this voter decline was the 20 percent of Republicans who had voted for him in 1936 and subsequently drifted back to their party. This was especially true in the rural Midwest and made itself most strongly felt west of the Mississippi River in Iowa, Missouri, Kansas, Nebraska, and the Dakotas. By the mid-1940s, election-night commentators were hedging their predictions by cautioning listeners to "wait for the farm vote" to come in, which, all assumed, would register gains for the Republicans. Roosevelt's base also depended heavily on lower-income voters, whose turnout pattern was inconsistent. Whereas upper-income voters turned out consistently and increasingly voted Republican, lower-income voters turned out in large numbers in 1934 and 1936, when the economic issues between the parties were starkly apparent. After 1936, when the economy took a tumble on Roosevelt's watch and labor militancy disturbed his previous rural supporters, his vote fell off.[54] At the same time, however, it should be emphasized that in none of his four elections was Roosevelt seriously in danger of losing. Throughout he remained the nation's undisputed champion of presidential politics.

Roosevelt's second political base was his large congressional majorities.[55] These majorities resulted largely from Roosevelt's own popularity. The presidential and congressional elections closely paralleled each other. During the 1920s, the Democrats had been forced to rely on representation from overwhelmingly "safe" Democratic districts, largely in the South and in ethnic Catholic neighborhoods in northern cities. In competitive races against the Republicans, they usually won less than 40 percent of the time. From 1932 to 1940, however, they maintained their southern and urban bases, picked up additional "safe" seats, and won 57 percent of competitive races. During the war, their strength declined in both competitive and "safe" seats but still left them the "normal" majority party.[56]

The figure of Franklin Roosevelt loomed over the congressional races. Few Democrats could expect to carry a district not carried by Roosevelt. Between 1932 and 1944, Democrats won only twenty-five seats in districts that voted against Roosevelt (about four seats per election). During the same period, 145 Democratic congressional candidates (twenty-one per election) lost in districts that voted for Roosevelt.[57] The lesson was clear: in only the safest Republican districts could a candidate run against Franklin Roosevelt.

Not surprisingly, congressional Democrats came to associate party loyalty with loyalty to Franklin Roosevelt. Repudiating the president risked weakening the party and handing over the government to the Republicans. That, in turn, meant more than the loss of a program; it meant the loss of committee chairmanships and the opportunity, as a member of the majority, to design bills to serve constituent interests. (This constraint was especially powerful for southern congressmen, who, by virtue of having been elected throughout the 1920s, had the seniority to command leadership positions. Except for issues that challenged white supremacy and issues that benefited organized labor and working people in general, southern Democrats were loyal New Dealers.)[58] In the first session of Congress, over 90 percent of House and Senate Democrats voted with the president. Although this margin fell significantly over the next five years, in no session was Roosevelt's Democratic support less than 70 percent.[59]

It was easy for Democratic congressmen to vote for the New Deal, because its program bolstered so many constituent interests. The New Deal had something for everyone. At the same time, the New Deal gave the voters ways to express their support for specific New Deal programs. Farmers who voted to approve a commodity program under the AAA, workers who voted to organize unions under NIRA and the Wagner Act, communities that applied for WPA funding, home owners who took out government loans, and many others all gave their congressmen guides to their support for the New Deal. In most cases, that support was overwhelming.

As with voter preferences, congressional voting patterns shifted during the New Deal. During Roosevelt's first term, the Republicans had been seriously divided along regional lines. Eastern Republicans strongly opposed New Deal legislation, while westerners, especially Progressives and representatives of rural districts, supported its agricultural and business reform provisions. Gradually, however, western support withered. Republican losses in 1934 and 1936 reduced the Republican ranks to the most hardcore party faithful, and the New Deal's turn toward urban labor alienated farm-state representatives. Roosevelt's Court-packing proposal united the Republicans and enabled them for the first time to form a working alliance with conservative Democrats. The return of depression conditions in the fall of 1937 further encouraged them to mount a united front against Roosevelt and his party. When the 1938 returns dealt the president his most severe political defeat, they closed ranks against him. Meanwhile, the Democrats were absorbing the party's progressive wing. When Congress assembled in 1939, the Republicans were still a minority, but they were a more unified one with a conservative, anti–New Deal, anti-Roosevelt ideology and a record of having defeated the president in concert with conservative Democrats.[60]

Most Democrats displayed a consistent pattern of party loyalty independent of region. Newly elected members were somewhat less supportive of the New Deal than were veteran members, but both were strongly supportive. On key New Deal measures, such as agriculture, organized labor, and social security, party rather than region dominated voting. The South was the most consistently loyal, the Northeast the least. This split represented something of an agriculture versus industry split. Northeastern Democrats most strongly supported the NRA and most strongly opposed utility reform. There was some division between North and South over public housing, but the major break came over the Fair Labor Standards Act. The South feared that a national minimum wage would interfere with its attempt to attract industry with low wages. Still, by far the best test of support or opposition to New Deal legislation was partisanship.

Also helping the New Deal in Congress was the "institutionalization" of Congress, especially the House. By the 1930s, the committee system had come to dominate congressional business. Committee members based their reputations on achievements within their policy areas. This encouraged them to create and support administrative agencies that would implement their policies. Thus, Congress tended to pass laws that stated general objectives and left the details to the administrators.[61] Roosevelt's strong legislative leadership and the panic atmosphere of the Hundred Days made Congress all the more willing to underwrite executive authority. In agriculture, for example, a trend had developed in the 1920s for "commodity groups," producers of staple crops for market, to lobby for their interests in Congress. These organizations, such as the American Farm Bureau Federation, established close relationships with key congressional committees and pushed for legislation to raise farm prices. When the New Deal Congress passed the Agricultural Adjustment Act, which resulted in administratively determined formulas to raise prices for different commodities, it encouraged the commodity groups to specialize their lobbying efforts. Wheat had a lobby, cotton had a lobby, tobacco had one, potatoes, rice, and so on. The House Agriculture Committee realized that in order to carry on its business, it would have to establish subcommittees for the various commodities. The subcommittees, in turn, fell under the control of representatives from states that specialized in that commodity and who saw it as their mission to "protect" it.[62] This created a system that was invested in sustaining New Deal programs.

In short, nothing in what we might call the political structure (presidential voting and congressional representation) seriously threatened the New Deal.

Still, as the years passed, Roosevelt's popular and congressional support eroded. In 1933 and 1934, Democratic opposition to New Deal legislation had been trivial. Following the Democratic sweep in the 1934 elections, opposition to administration measures grew to 19 percent of House Democrats and 20 percent of Senate Democrats. After Roosevelt's overwhelming triumph in 1936, over 30 percent of Senate Democrats opposed him. Some of this erosion was caused by circumstances common to most previous administrations: the exhausting of patronage and, after 1936, the assumption that Roosevelt would not run again. The return of economic stability and the seeming success of the New Deal dissipated the crisis psychology that had forced many congressmen to line up behind the president. No longer nagged by fears of economic collapse and of mobs menacing the social order, congressmen were more inclined to stir their voices and their egos into the political mix. Beginning in 1935, the Supreme Court began to inspirit conservatives with its anti–New Deal offensive. The rise of business opposition and the New Deal's response in favor of organized labor, ethnic minorities, and city bosses alienated rural voters and their representatives. And, as the battles over the holding company "death sentence" and the wealth tax bill showed, congressmen disliked bills that forced them to choose between their contributors and their constituents.[63] In other words, as the New Deal assumed a more decidedly liberal character, its more conservative constituencies became less reliable.

Roosevelt shared much of the responsibility for worsening relations with Congress. During the early days of the New Deal, Roosevelt assiduously cultivated Congress, consulting with its leaders and key committee chairs, encouraging those with diverse and conflicting views, making its members feel part of the New Deal team. Such consultations invited negotiating sessions that were often tedious and frustrating but produced a unified party, a comprehensive program, and a string of smashing electoral victories.[64]

In 1935, however, Roosevelt began to treat Congress with careless indifference. To get the wealth tax act and the holding company "death sentence," he held Congress in session for a sweltering, non-air-conditioned summer. In the process he embarrassed Senator Pat Harrison, chair of the Finance Committee, by making it appear that Harrison was the one demanding swift action on the tax bill. Later, Roosevelt's gross mismanagement of the Court-packing bill irreparably damaged his relations with Congress, demolishing the myth of his invincibility and portraying him to the nation as erratic, stubborn, and wrongheaded.[65]

Following the Court-packing fiasco and the embarrassments and frustrations of dealing with a recurrence of the depression, Roosevelt committed another blunder by attempting to "purge" the party of prominent conservative congressmen. Although one motive of the purge was to strengthen support for pending New Deal legislation—to protect key administration supporters such as Senate majority leader Alben Barkley and to remove the obstructionist conservative John O'Connor, chair of the House Rules Committee—the principal objective was to create a liberal Democratic Party and, by implication, a conservative Republican Party. Although the purge achieved limited success, principally by defeating O'Connor, it was essentially a fiasco, not so much because it failed to elect a substantial number of New Deal liberals but because its few conspicuous failures reflected badly on Franklin Roosevelt. This was Roosevelt's own fault. When the effort to defeat Senator Gillette of Iowa failed, Roosevelt publicly took charge and led the campaign against entrenched senators in the Deep South, the least likely ground for victory. In primary campaigns, Roosevelt backed liberal candidates by channeling patronage to them, dispatching aides to campaign for them, and publicly praising them. In return, the candidates enthusiastically declared their support for the New Deal. It was the most energetic effort by a president to influence off-year congressional elections since Andrew Johnson's "swing around the circle" in 1866.

In contrast to 1866, which was a complete disaster for Andrew Johnson, Roosevelt's attempt to realign the party system produced mixed results. Although most southern conservatives were returned, most New Deal liberals in the rest of the nation were elected. The president and his New Deal were still the voters' choice, though at reduced margins. The major result of the purge was to illustrate the limits of party reform. In targeted areas, state party officials rallied behind the beleaguered incumbents, as did many of their Senate and House colleagues. Although the election results reduced the congressional Democratic majorities for the first time in Roosevelt's presidency, they left the party with a firm majority.

The 1938 elections also began a period of Democratic decline in Congress. In each of the off-year elections of 1938 and 1942, House Democrats lost 70 seats. Roosevelt's popularity in 1940 and 1944 produced small Democratic gains but still left the party with a net loss of 109 seats. These declines set the stage for the massive Republican triumph in the 1946 elections.

Roosevelt sought to institutionalize his popular and congressional majorities in the Democratic Party. Before assuming the presidency, Roosevelt had been a party man who sought ways to strengthen the party's organization and focus its programs. Roosevelt believed that the Democrats could succeed by offering the voters a choice on important issues. Downplaying cultural issues such as Prohibition, he emphasized economic issues such as public ownership of electric power. As governor, he had promoted social welfare and relief programs to treat the human miseries of the depression.

The New Deal program produced strains in the party by creating an administrative structure based on expertise instead of party loyalty. Relief administrator Harry Hopkins resisted efforts by state governors and congressmen to incorporate his welfare appointments into their patronage organizations. From the beginning of his term, Roosevelt and Farley were willing to give patronage to pro-Roosevelt, pro–New Deal Republicans. The hope, according to Farley, was to convert them into loyal Democrats; the potential difficulty was that it would alienate established party loyalists. At the same time, Roosevelt maintained his base with southern whites and northern city bosses. Pursuing such a strategy while attempting to swing the party behind a liberal economic agenda was bound to strain the party structure. The first signs appeared when the Senate required confirmation of any official whose salary was over $5,000, an obvious attempt to inject patronage politics into federal relief. After this, Hopkins declared that he was going to be "all political" in running relief, by which he meant employing only loyal supporters of Roosevelt and the New Deal. At about the same time, Roosevelt began to develop an inner circle of advisers that included Hopkins and Thomas Corcoran. Corcoran, who, in partnership with Benjamin Cohen, had drafted the legislation that broke up the utility holding companies, had led a successful effort to elect Alben Barkley Senate majority leader after the death of Joseph Robinson, using threats of reduced WPA spending against wavering key senators. Roosevelt was attracted to those who, like Corcoran and Hopkins, seemed to combine professional expertise with political savvy. As the New Deal tilted its programs toward urban labor and work relief, toward unions, blacks, and white ethnics, it further irritated its southern conservative base. As Roosevelt's political center of gravity shifted toward the northern cities, the president became more dependent on the urban bosses.[66]

It fell to the party's central organization, the Democratic National Committee, to seal the breaches in party unity. Under the leadership of national chairman and postmaster general James Farley, the national committee patterned itself after the New Deal by establishing special divisions, strengthening others, and undertaking special events to target separate groups. The party established special divisions for blacks, youth, and labor unions. The division for blacks, called the Colored Division, proceeded cautiously, wary not to offend white supremacist regimes in the southern states. Underfunded and not even incorporated into the permanent national committee structure, the Colored Division concentrated on black voters in northern states and a few southern cities. Throughout Roosevelt's presidency, more blacks voted for him than identified with his party. In contrast, the Women's Division, which had been established in the 1920s after women's suffrage, benefited from the vigorous and imaginative leadership of Mary "Molly" Dewson, as well as from the support of Eleanor Roosevelt. Similarly vigorous leadership molded the Young Democratic Clubs, made up primarily of college students, into a strong voice for liberal reform and provided Roosevelt with a forum for promoting liberal policies.[67]

The growth of industrial unionism under the New Deal was both an opportunity and a challenge for the national committee. The head of the Labor Division, Daniel J. Tobin, president of the Teamsters Union of the American Federation of Labor, wanted to bring all union political activity under his leadership. But the unions, especially those that emerged under the CIO, wanted to maintain their independence. One result was to keep the United States from developing a "labor" party along the lines of those in western European states. At the same time, the strategy recognized the party, ethnic, and occupational diversity of the labor movement. In 1936 the CIO formed Labor's Non Partisan League as an independent, pro-Roosevelt, pro–New Deal movement. The CIO leadership also attempted to play down its members' ethnic and racial sensibilities and to ally the labor movement with the New Deal's bureaucratic structure, as represented by the Department of Labor and the National Labor Relations Board.[68]

Roosevelt closely followed Democratic Party politics, maintaining an intimate knowledge of his support and opposition from within. During his first term, he flattered and cajoled party leaders, but during his second term, his attitude toward the party paralleled his attitude toward Congress. He became detached, determined to shape the party in his image of liberalism.[69]

As usual, the significance of an event was what people chose to attach to it. Roosevelt had undertaken Court reform and the party purge to convert the Supreme Court and the Democratic Party to New Deal liberalism. The aftermath of these events left him just as determined to persevere.

ELEANOR ROOSEVELT AND A NEW DEAL FOR WOMEN

Not all, but much of New Deal policy making was a traditional response to political pressures and political anxieties. The New Deal came into being because of the widespread suffering caused by the depression. But because the depression was widespread, it was easy to conceive of "solutions" to it in traditional categories such as "farmers," "workers," and "the unemployed," that is, in categories familiar to "reformers" and "social critics." At the same time, the depression caused a sense of crisis that created the occasion for determined groups and charismatic leaders to influence public policy. Concerns over marching farmers, striking workers, "Share Our Wealth" clubs, Townsendites, and the like all shaped New Deal policies. Any group that was organized, disciplined, determined, and in a position to cause his administration political embarrassment could inspire Franklin Roosevelt's desire to "do something" for it. American women lacked this kind of political base. They were too divided by race and class and too restrained by traditional cultural values to present a united front.[1]

By the time of the depression, the status of one-third of middle-class families depended on a second income, most commonly the mother's. But most women had no collective sense of their critical role. Working wives thought of their husbands as the responsible breadwinners. For most white families, a working wife was a stigma that they sought to avoid. By 1940, only 15 percent of all married women were working. Depression hardships focused attention on finding work and earning an income rather than on issues of equal pay and equal access.[2]

Although they lacked unity and political strength in the mass, American women still had political leverage. Since the turn of the century, elite, college-educated women had been forming networks of voluntary associations concerned primarily with social welfare issues. Often they had become useful agents and allies of "progressive" male leaders, such as Governor Al Smith in New York. Their influence in the presidency of Franklin Roosevelt would depend on their ability to gain a similar place in the New Deal. If they succeeded, however, they risked surrendering their agenda to a male power structure.

No one strove harder or with greater effect to promote a women's agenda and women's control over that agenda than Eleanor Roosevelt. In so doing she emerged as a major figure in the presidency of Franklin Roosevelt and as a First Lady in a class by herself.

When Franklin Roosevelt entered the White House, Eleanor was forty-five years of age, the mother of three boys and one girl, all grown. She had a strained, tentative relationship with her husband, the product of his having had an affair with his personal secretary during their years in Washington when he was assistant secretary of the navy. She had hated the prospect of his becoming president and upon his election had burst out to her friends that rather than become First Lady she would leave him and run away with another man.

What she most deeply hated and feared was the prospect of being shut up in the trivial ceremonial role of the First Lady—rounds of teas and luncheons, social gatherings, and "occasions." She had seen her predecessor, Lou Henry Hoover, herself a woman of education and independent achievement, caught up in such a role. Eleanor had spent too much of her life trying to avoid it, invested too much of her energy and character in moving beyond it.

Like her husband, she had been born into wealth. Unlike him, she had not been born into happiness. Her father, Elliot, the brother of President Theodore Roosevelt, had been an alcoholic; her mother, Anna, a fretful beauty given to social extravagance and a personal coldness.[3] By the time Eleanor was ten years of age, both her parents had died, and she went to live with her mother's mother.

Thus was established a threefold tension in her life among a need for love and security, a distaste for extravagance and self-indulgence, and a desire to break through to self-fulfillment, independence, and authority. Only gradually did the tension resolve itself toward independence and authority. In her family relationships and friendships, she encountered women who were weak and victimized and women who were strong and achieving. Sent to school in London, she blossomed under the tutelage of Marie Souvestre, who emphasized independence, social justice, and education and set an example of quick, subtle intelligence.[4] Then she returned to enter "society" and to marry her distant cousin Franklin, who adopted the role of traditional patriarchal husband who concentrated on his career and left it to her to discipline the children. Such trials and disappointments were compounded by Franklin's mother, the doting and domineering Sara, who sought to control their lives for her own satisfaction.[5] Eleanor tried to respond positively to her circumstances, but only at the cost of much frustration and pain. She tried to win the approval of Sara, who would never give it, and who probably saw her efforts as signs of weakness to be exploited. Eleanor sought to support her husband's career, first when he was a state senator and later as Woodrow Wilson's assistant secretary of the navy, only to be emotionally rebuffed by his affair with his personal secretary. Devastated, she offered him a divorce, but Sara, realizing that a divorce would ruin his political career, would not hear of it.

If ever a woman seemed doomed to a barren domesticity, it was Eleanor Roosevelt. But she persevered and fashioned a new life. She joined a circle of "New Women," social feminists who took politics seriously and worked for social reform. They enjoyed art, literature, and good food; they wore "sensible" clothes, cultivated emotionally satisfying relationships, and tried to view life holistically, as a work of art. The vigor, variety, and warmth of their society attracted her enormously. She realized how much she had lost in spending a lonely childhood.[6]

She capitalized on these associations and on Franklin's willingness to be helpful by purchasing a cottage near their Hyde Park estate and using it to produce furniture for the local market. She taught at a private school in the vicinity.

Most important, she became a figure in politics. She joined the League of Women Voters. She became active in the Women's Joint Legislative Conference; she edited the *Women's Democratic News* and participated in the Women's Division of the Democratic State Committee. These associations and her friendships drew her into a network of women's groups that campaigned for social and political reform. They raised funds, edited newsletters, moderated panels, disseminated information, toured for candidates and causes, and attended national conventions. They campaigned for civic improvement (sanitation, housing, mass transit, public parks and recreation), the welfare of youth (school lunches, school nurses, outlawing child labor), the rights of labor (unemployment insurance, workers' compensation, job safety), and consumer protection (pure food and drug legislation). They advocated protective labor legislation for women and children. They campaigned for the right of women to serve on juries. They proposed measures to eliminate waste and duplication in government. In 1924 Eleanor led a successful fight for women to nominate their own delegates to the national committee. She chaired the women's platform committee and named social activists to the membership. She emerged as a leader, although the all-male resolutions committee refused even to receive their recommendations. She now adopted a partisan stance from which she never retreated. At the same time, she sought to move the Democrats to the political left. When she became chair of the Women's City Club in 1927, she steered the agenda of the supposedly nonpartisan organization toward Democratic objectives. During the depression, she worked with the Women's Trade Union League, headed by Rose Schneiderman, to create recreational programs for working women and campaigned for better housing and better wages. She publicly supported strikers; she was less concerned about labor radicalism than about unemployment and bad working and living conditions. As conditions worsened, she called for changes in the economic system and less emphasis on ameliorative activities. She once confessed that if her husband had not been running for president in 1932 she would have voted for the Socialist candidate Norman Thomas.[7]

Necessary to her expanding interests and activities was her skill at management. Her mind sorted and organized myriad details. She planned and maintained complex schedules, always finding time to write personal letters that kept her from becoming "so much of a machine that you forget you have feelings." She followed dozens of political issues and the details of political campaigns.[8]

As a "social feminist," Eleanor perceived women as a distinctive class with their own interests and contributions to make. She believed that "equality" was something to be won by women as a group and not for them as part of a larger whole. She had been skeptical of women's suffrage and supported it as a way for women to state their claims more effectively. When the leading suffragette Alice Paul proposed an equal rights amendment to the federal Constitution, Eleanor opposed it, fearing that it would eliminate the "protective" legislation that women had achieved in the workplace. Instead of equal rights, women needed to achieve women's rights through organization and representation. Women needed to form trade unions and reform societies. They needed to form a women's division of their party and to claim places for themselves on party committees. Women needed to be valued for their special and unique qualities. In practical politics, she said, women did the day-to-day work, while men concentrated only on campaigns.[9]

She received considerable support from Franklin's personal political mentor Louis Howe. Howe accompanied and tutored her in public speaking. He told her to be prepared, to know what she wanted to say, to say it, and to sit down. But as she gained confidence as a speaker, she won over her audiences by more than mere technique. She succeeded as a speaker because she cared so much about people and could form an intuitive bond with her audience.[10] Her communications skills developed beyond public appearances. She began to write a magazine column and to give sponsored radio broadcasts.

She considered this time when she was not supporting FDR a "private" interlude, by which she meant time to herself. She never admitted any personal joy or skill at politics but kept it all in the conventional perspective of the dominant culture. During Franklin's recovery from polio, she assured him that when he was well and back in politics she would gladly subside into domesticity. In this way she accommodated herself to the double standard that permitted women an outside life only when they were single or attached to incapable men.

During these years of growth in politics and social reform, she supported her stricken husband. As they both struggled to regain their independence, they built separate but mutually reinforcing lives. They had a core of devotion to each other and a strong sense of how they could most profitably interact, although Franklin always wanted Eleanor to be more the domestic, supportive wife than she was inclined to be. For her part, she came to synthesize her personal and social evolution. She generalized her struggle for personal freedom as a struggle for social justice for all disadvantaged persons. She liked a sentence from a novel of the time: "Back of tranquility lies always conquered unhappiness."[11]

Their relationship contained a considerable degree of sexual politics. She became emotionally attached to Earl Miller, a handsome, athletic New York state trooper who was assigned as her driver and bodyguard. During Franklin's presidency, Miller had an affair with Franklin's secretary Missy LeHand, encouraged by Eleanor as a way of winning Missy away from a possible relationship with Franklin, and encouraged by Franklin as a way of separating Miller from Eleanor.[12]

In 1928 Eleanor first met Lorena Hickok, a reporter for the Associated Press who was covering New York politics. Smart, quick-witted, a good storyteller, and a savvy political journalist, "Hick," as she was called, was the sort of person Eleanor was ready for. They developed an intimate relationship. They were mature, experienced women who had been on their own and knew the score. They made their commitments to each other, shared what they could, pleased each other as they desired, and got on with their lives.[13] For the first years of the New Deal, Hick lived in the White House and provided Eleanor an emotional center of gravity.

In the context of her relationship with her husband, Eleanor's achievements created a dilemma for her. Knowing that Franklin's real vocation was politics, she had to encourage him to seek a political career so that he might escape a life of inner despair and helpless, pampered invalidism, which his mother preferred. But in helping Franklin to escape a life of self-indulgence and self-pity, she risked being trapped in the confines of an "official" life of ceremonies and domestic duties.

So it was that Eleanor approached Franklin's presidency with deeply ambivalent sentiments. Just after the election, a student in her history class said that it was grand to have the wife of the president for her teacher. Eleanor responded, "You mustn't think of me that way." During her first visit to the White House following the election, she refused to ride in a limousine and walked instead. As First Lady, she steadfastly and even angrily refused police protection, either from the Secret Service or from local police. She rode airplanes tourist class. She wore cheap dresses, used public transportation, and ate at drugstore counters. She seemed determined to go to great lengths to make people forget that she was their First Lady.[14]

But they would neither forget nor ignore. In the summer of 1934, Eleanor broke away from the official routine and joined Hick in San Francisco for a holiday. Hick had been traveling as an unofficial reporter for Harry Hopkins, sending him reports on social conditions in various parts of the country. Determined to get some peace and quiet, Eleanor had faced down reporters, refusing to tell them her travel plans and getting out of sight as soon as they left. There followed several days of sightseeing, visiting Eleanor's daughter Anna, and camping. But in San Francisco, someone saw Eleanor and tipped the press, and she and Hick had to make another hurried escape. Then in the little town of Bend, Oregon, Eleanor was recognized again and besieged. She came into their hotel room and threw herself on the bed. "Franklin said I'd never get away with it, and he was right!" she cried in anger and despair. "I can't." She now knew that henceforth she would be only the president's wife. If there was to be more to the role, she would have to create it.[15]

By 1934, she was well on her way to establishing that role. The public attention testified to her success at it. Hick had played a role, encouraging Eleanor to take charge of her role, first of all by holding her own press conferences. This she did, convening the first one, for women reporters only, on March 6, 1933, two days before her husband's first one. She stipulated no political questions and passed around candied fruits.[16]

Louis Howe arranged for her to visit the encampment of the Bonus Army, where she mingled with the veterans, visiting their quarters and eating in their mess. In an informal talk, she recalled her own wartime experiences and declared that she never wanted to see another war. She had found the veterans polite and friendly, she reported to her news conference. They were "grand looking boys," she said, with "a fine spirit."[17]

She was on her way to finding the compensations and balances that would make her role tolerable and fulfilling. Unable to find happiness in marriage, she attached herself to those New Dealers who best represented her ideals. Early on, she doted on Harry Hopkins, whose relief programs directly helped the poor. She was also attracted to social reformers like Tugwell. She appreciated opportunities to be where "human beings count for their worth and not for what they have." She developed a sense of duty that emphasized patience and grace in the face of disappointment. She developed loving friendships, but not attachments. "I love other people the same way or differently," she wrote to Hick, "but each one has their place and one cannot compare them." These differences meant that her friendships changed according to her own needs and perspectives.[18]

Not everything went so smoothly. In August 1933 she visited Morgantown, West Virginia, in the heart of the coalfields. She interviewed the miners and reported that she had found the makings of perhaps not a revolution but a protest party. Relief funds were exhausted. Crime had risen, including some petty theft to secure necessities, but also murder and suicide. The United Mine Workers had sponsored a number of strikes, communist organizers were at work, and there was much talk of "Reds," "radicals," and "Red agitators." After she reported to the president, he announced a subsistence homestead project for Morgantown. Wanting to do something to alleviate the misery for some while providing hope for others, she joined Louis Howe in the Arthurdale subsistence homestead project.[19]

The project got off to a muddled start. Hoping for a quick demonstration of success, Howe hurriedly arranged for housing that provided no protection against the winter cold. Eleanor then assumed a major role in the project. She named most of the project personnel. She urged businesses to establish factories in Arthurdale. She screened potential homesteaders and advised on choosing the school principal and setting up a children's clinic.[20] She hoped that the project's school would both improve opportunities for the residents and make them better citizens by teaching them about American government and providing a center of community life. Some complained that the schools practiced an advanced form of progressive education, and some parents objected and sought to enroll their children in traditional schools nearby. In 1936 the school was incorporated into the local school district.[21]

In response to criticism, Eleanor defended the effort as a cost of experimenting. Indeed, she considered Arthurdale a "laboratory" for determining "the highest level to which the family with an ordinary income can aspire." When given the opportunity to choose budgets for the project, she chose the most costly. She wrote that if Arthurdale were successful it could become a model for other projects to help solve unemployment and poverty in the industrial cities.[22]

If in the end Arthurdale failed to achieve her wishes for its residents, it demonstrated her commitment to better communities, better education, and a higher standard of living. It also showed a toughness of spirit that perhaps not everyone who knew her would have expected. She neither gave in to her critics nor deflected their attacks toward others. Her defense of the project demonstrated her emergence as a publicly committed social reformer.

Neither did she lose sight of her feminist objective to advance the social role of women. She worked tirelessly to have women hired into the federal bureaucracy. Postmaster General Farley estimated that some 4,000 women had won fourth-class postmasterships because of her influence. When the male journalists held a men-only gridiron dinner, Eleanor organized one for her and the female reporters.[23] She supported the appointment of Rose Schneiderman to the NRA labor advisory board and Mary Rumsey to its consumer board. She campaigned successfully to establish work camps for unemployed women. She warned against wage differentials for women in the NRA codes, but despite Perkins's assurances that they would not be permitted, the codes were rushed through with the differentials. She used her contacts with Ellen Woodward and Florence Kerr, who worked in Harry Hopkins's relief organizations, to argue for relief projects for women and a greater role for women in relief administration. Hopkins's agencies employed more women in high positions than any other in Washington. She publicized the work of women for social betterment by holding dinners and testimonials in the White House.[24]

Eleanor took a more active role in party politics. In 1940 she worked with other members of the administration to settle demoralizing factionalism in the California Democratic Party. Her role was to bring forward Helen Gahagan Douglas, talented entertainer and wife of actor and Democratic activist Melvyn Douglas. Helen Douglas had attracted Eleanor's attention when she visited Washington and discussed the conditions of migrant workers. As her association with Eleanor and Franklin deepened, her standing rose in the California party. Eleanor visited California to appear with her at political events. In return, Douglas patterned her career after Eleanor's example of practical political activism. In 1944 she ran successfully for Congress, the first Democratic woman to win that office.[25]

At the same time, in her voluminous published statements, Eleanor instructed women about their social duties and warned them of the risks of public life. She encouraged women to prepare themselves for office-holding, but warned that they needed to gain experience and accept the political challenges that men faced. The uncertainties of political life also

Eleanor Roosevelt, 1934. (Franklin D. Roosevelt Library)

demanded that women who went into politics have some work they could return to.[26]

Her emphasis on working opportunities for women and her long campaign for protective legislation for women and children caused her to oppose an equal rights amendment to the Constitution. Proposed by a branch of the women's suffrage movement, the amendment would have eliminated legal distinctions between males and females. Eleanor continually insisted that women were "different from men, their physical functions are different, and the future of the race depends upon their ability to produce healthy children." Instead of equality for women, she advocated justice. After women obtained justice, perhaps it would be time for an equal rights amendment.[27]

Her key to justice in gender relations was justice in all social relations. Jobs for women were the best guarantee of equal rights. Women should be active in unions, promote the common interests of labor and the community, and use their experience to promote their roles as useful citizens. Women should influence social conditions by objecting to the conditions under which goods are produced; a woman's conscience could affect the labor market. Women should be concerned that the excessive profits of milk distributors caused the underconsumption of milk by children.[28]

Her comments about women in general did not apply to married women with families. These women, she believed, should stay home and nurture their children. Married women should work only when economic conditions required it.[29]

She continually emphasized a mother's nurturing influence. As usual, it was a nurture that operated within a web of social betterment and social responsibility. Mothers and fathers should prepare young people for good citizenship. Women should support higher wages for teachers to reduce the money spent on arms.[30]

Nurturing meant teaching youth to measure up to standards of responsibility. Life should not be too easy. She admired people who fought against adversity. Youth might rightly complain about the lack of recreational facilities, but they should also take advantage of opportunities such as reading and group singing, which did not require elaborate equipment. Youth should volunteer for community service, which would improve the standard of living and gain them experience in democracy. In 1941, as the United States was instituting the military draft for young men, she came out in favor of compulsory community service for girls.

Her concern for American youth led to a suggestion to Harry Hopkins that resulted in the creation of the National Youth Administration (NYA). She actively supported the American Youth Congress and the Student Union. Such organizations, which supported federal welfare program and programs for youth, would promote good citizenship among the young. As she advised the American Youth Congress: "Organize first for knowledge, first with the object of making us know ourselves as a nation, for we have to do that before we can be of value to other nations of the world and then organize to accomplish the things that you decide you want. And remember, don't make decisions with the interest of youth alone before you. Make your decisions because they are good for the nation as a whole."[31]

She attempted to mediate between the enthusiasm of youth and her own sense of the practical. She urged them to be patient with the administration, predicting that the liberals would come to the fore. She warned them against getting too far ahead of public opinion and pointed to signs of conservatism that they needed to heed.[32]

Her greatest difficulty was in answering complaints about radicalism, including communist influence, in the youth movement. She excused their platforms as youthful impatience and as representing sentiments common to all young Americans. Those who worried about communist influence in this or any other movement, she frequently declared, should devote themselves to making capitalism work for the good of all. At the same time, she tried to exercise a moderating influence on their youthful spirit. When members of various youth organizations, including Joseph Lash of the American Student Union, were summoned before the House Un-American Activities Committee, she advised them to cooperate. As the hearing was beginning, she entered the room, immediately causing a sensation. The hearing turned into an exercise in courtesy on the part of the chairman, Joe Starnes of Alabama.[33]

Her most trying moments came in the wake of the Nazi-Soviet treaty of August 1939, after which communist influence in the youth movement led it to change from supporting the administration's anti-Hitler policies to condemning those policies and supporting isolation. In resolutions, the American Youth Congress opposed defense spending, vowed not to go to war, and supported the Soviet Union's invasion of Finland. The invasion and the Soviet takeover of the Baltic States had soured her on Stalin and the Soviet system. The defining moment came early in 1940, during a youth "pilgrimage" in Washington. Addressing a youth gathering on the south lawn of the White House, President Roosevelt dismissed the delegates' views as uninformed and dismissed their resolutions opposing American aid to Finland as "unadulterated twaddle." He called the Soviet Union "a dictatorship as absolute as any other dictatorship in the world." None of this sat well with the delegates, who had been kept waiting in the pouring rain. Some booed, but they were hushed. Later that day they cheered John L. Lewis's criticisms of the administration. This was enough for Eleanor. Henceforth she distanced herself from the Youth Congress. When members invited her to a meeting to discuss ways to oppose Hitler after his invasion of the USSR, she reminded them of their behavior in 1940 and declined. She would help individual members on a personal basis, but she would not work with them politically.[34]

In none of her activities did Eleanor Roosevelt swim against a stronger national tide than in her support of racial acceptance and toleration. In various ways, white Americans condoned, tolerated, or practiced white supremacy. The depression's hardships further encouraged bigotry, as whites sought to claim for themselves the crumbs left by capitalism and the opportunities offered by public relief.[35] She was an active supporter of equal opportunities for African Americans. She addressed conferences on equal rights and encouraged agencies to include blacks in their programs.

The touchiest political issue was federal legislation against lynching. The National Association for the Advancement of Colored People (NAACP), the nation's major civil rights organization, had undertaken several campaigns to raise funds to lobby for federal antilynching legislation, which was needed in the face of states' unwillingness to prosecute lynchers. Eleanor supported the campaigns and invited Walter White, executive secretary of the NAACP, to the White House to confer on that and other issues and to discuss the subject with Franklin, but the president was inclined to do little. When she raised the subject with him, he replied that southern Democrats controlled the major committees in Congress and would block every New Deal measure if he pressed for antilynching legislation. He was willing to say that he hoped such a bill would pass, but he did not press for it. In 1934 she asked his permission to speak at a rally protesting a brutal lynching in Florida, but Franklin refused to allow her.

Her husband's caution, the intransigence of Congress, and white America's racist values limited the scope of her aspirations but not her devotion to them. To the impatient and frustrated, she counseled patience and conciliation, arguing that times were changing and that too much pressure would cause a backlash. In many ways the situation was no different from that of other causes she had championed.

Unable to achieve grandly, she strove incrementally. She arranged an appointment to the National Youth Administration for the noted African American educator Mary McLeod Bethune. She toured African American schools, churches, and relief projects. She spoke at African American conventions and interracial meetings. She invited African Americans to White House receptions.[36] At a meeting of the Southern Conference on Human Welfare in Birmingham, Alabama, she had her chair placed in the aisle separating the black and white delegates.

Her most famous public statement against bigotry came in 1939, when she resigned from the Daughters of the American Revolution because the organization refused to permit the gifted African American opera singer Marian Anderson to sing in Constitution Hall. A Gallup poll showed that 67 percent approved and 33 percent disapproved of her resignation. Secretary Ickes, whose department had jurisdiction over Washington's national historic sites, proposed that Miss Anderson sing at the Lincoln Memorial. Her performance drew an audience of 75,000 and captured national headlines and newsreel footage.[37]

The Marian Anderson incident had political ramifications. Garner, Farley, and Wallace were invited to sign on as sponsors of the event. Garner tried to claim that he had not received his invitation, but Franklin leaked to the press that he had received one. It was an issue bound to harm Garner's presidential ambition by alienating the black vote in the northern states.[38]

Meanwhile, Eleanor's efforts were moving Franklin to action. He publicly denounced lynching as "murder" and had himself photographed with African American leaders. He nominated William Hastie of the NAACP to the federal bench and made the father of another NAACP officer an assistant attorney general. By 1941, the number of African Americans employed by the national government had more than tripled and had grown even more in the professional ranks. In 1934, Roosevelt responded to prodding by Harold Ickes, who worked closely with Eleanor on civil rights issues, to form a "black cabinet" of advisers on race relations. Eventually, the group grew to over forty and formed a network that united cabinet departments and New Deal agencies.

Such action had a reciprocal effect. Each step by the president on behalf of African Americans encouraged more of them to vote for Roosevelt and the New Deal. More black Democratic voters, who were especially important in key northern states, encouraged African American leaders and their White House ally, Eleanor Roosevelt, to pressure the president for more action. Franklin Roosevelt responded. Executive orders promised equal treatment for persons of all races. During his second term, the president supported antilynching legislation.[39]

Even the smallest steps on behalf of equal rights caused reactions that kept Eleanor and the White House in a perpetual state of damage control. Even small gestures on behalf of blacks brought forth storms of protest from white supremacists. The biggest damage control operation of all occurred over black demands to oppose discrimination in hiring for defense production. To head off a proposed march on Washington, Franklin sent Eleanor and others to New York, where they arranged for a conference between

Roosevelt and the protest leaders. As a result of the conference, the president issued an executive order forbidding discrimination.[40]

Eleanor's leadership provided a context for other New Dealers to advance civil rights. Harold Ickes's PWA projects built affordable housing for African Americans and established hiring quotas for them. Harry Hopkins's WPA similarly employed African Americans, and its Federal Theater dramatized civil rights issues. The Resettlement Administration and the Farm Security Administration allocated generously from their limited resources to help black sharecroppers.[41]

Eleanor provided a way into the White House for myriad voices. Her special constituency was the poor. She held daily conferences with relief administrator Harry Hopkins and asked him to do what he could for those who appealed directly to her. She testified before congressional committees on behalf of migrant workers and against discrimination in defense industries. She encouraged civic organizations by giving them an entrée to the president. These included the League of Women Voters, the NAACP, the National Public Housing Conference, the National Consumers League, and the National Sharecroppers Fund. She closely followed the progress of the National Housing Authority. Long a supporter of unions, she bristled when Vice President Garner advocated using force against a prospective demonstration by the Worker's Alliance, which organized the unemployed. If that happened, she snapped back, she would go down and join the demonstration.[42]

All the while, she was a voice to the American people on behalf of the New Deal. Although her comments appeared in numerous forms, they appeared most consistently and effectively in her daily column "My Day." After rejecting a request that she write a daily column on Washington social customs, she agreed to write a daily "diary" for United Features. The activity gave her a role and some control over her identity within the White House. She found that the writing came easily and that she was able to dictate it during her travels. Her publishers added necessary detail and saved her from careless expressions. She praised New Deal programs by reporting favorable comments from average Americans she had met, by making flattering remarks about New Deal administrators, and by writing favorably about such values as the right to work and the right to have material security. She also used her column to rebuff sniping by political opponents about personal matters within the White House. By 1938, her column was reaching over 4 million readers, competing with popular male columnists, and lagging behind only Walter Lippmann and Dorothy Thompson.[43]

In 1937 she wrote an autobiography. Published serially in the *Ladies Home Journal,* it appeared in the fall as *This Is My Story.* The articles and the book were a publishing bonanza, saving the fortunes of the *Journal* and winning rave reviews from the critics. Whether consciously or not, she reviewed a life that could have served as a metaphor for the journey of many American women who sought to transcend the social and personal difficulties of growing up female. Eleanor pictured herself as an ineffectual child, easily influenced by others, naive and romantic, bound by social convention, ashamed of her physical appearance, and terrified of "society." But her story was one of overcoming shyness, fear, dependence, and withdrawal from conflict and responsibility. She showed herself gradually taking control. She developed a passion for order. She became tolerant of others by being less willing to judge their behavior and looking for motives instead. She credited Franklin's political career, which brought her into contact with diverse people. She developed a sense of duty toward Franklin, not wishing to add to his burdens. Thus she developed a sense of her own ability to persevere in situations that had previously annoyed or frightened her. Franklin's bout with polio gave her more responsibilities and broadened her political and social contacts.

She ended the autobiography in 1924, with Franklin's return to active political life. By this time, she saw not only herself but also society in general liberated from the narrow social and moral conventions of her early years. Now, she believed, young people would have to take more individual responsibility because they could not rely on settled standards from the past. Not surprisingly, she saw the world in pluralist terms: "The lessons learned were those of adaptability and adjustment and finally of self-reliance and the developing into an individual which every human being must eventually do."[44]

And so it went—continual appeals for a life lived for service, a public that was defined by a network of shared responsibilities. Eleanor Roosevelt was not the first person to advocate such ideas, but no one who knew her story could gainsay the experience on which she based her lessons. She was a woman who had broken out of confining and demeaning circumstances by taking up social welfare and social reform. She had been besieged but never defeated, bewildered but never at her wits' end, wounded but never destroyed.

The next most prominent woman in Franklin Roosevelt's presidency was Secretary of Labor Frances Perkins. A college graduate, teacher, social worker, and social reformer, she had served as Al Smith's commissioner of industrial relations and held the same post when Franklin Roosevelt was governor. After Roosevelt's presidential victory, Molly Dewson organized a campaign to have him appoint Perkins the first female cabinet member.

Perkins and Harold Ickes were the only cabinet members to serve throughout Roosevelt's presidency. In contrast to the blustering, combative Ickes, Perkins was a dutiful, undramatic public servant who preferred formality to personality, negotiation to conflict, and expertise to politics. In her less obtrusive way she made her mark. She successfully countered Lewis Douglas, who feared unbalanced budgets, and kept a public works program in the National Industrial Recovery Act. She persuaded Roosevelt to transfer public works from Hugh Johnson, whom she considered a soft touch for grafters, to Harold Ickes. She operated the Labor Department with a practical efficiency, aiming to improve the quality and fairness of its service. She loosened restrictions on immigrants, reorganized the employment services, and enforced federal equal rights laws against segregationist governors. She strengthened the Bureau of Labor Statistics, appointing the extraordinarily able Isadore Lubin to head the agency. She established a division of labor standards, purged the Immigration and Naturalization Service of racketeers, and upgraded the Federal Mediation and Conciliation Service. She convened conferences to coordinate state labor legislation. Because of her leadership, many states established their own departments of labor. She established training programs for state factory inspectors; she produced instructional films on worker safety. She supported U.S. adherence to the International Labor Organization. Following favorable congressional resolutions, the United States joined in 1934. She worked closely with the organization and drew on its resources to develop American labor and welfare legislation.[45]

Organized labor viewed Perkins with suspicion, and with good reason. During her years in New York, she had believed that because trade unions represented so few workers, government laws and rulings rather than unions would better advance the interests of working people. This, combined with her retiring, soft-spoken demeanor, suggested that she could not cope with the hurly-burly of internal divisions and external combat in the labor movement of the 1930s. Indeed, she favored reasoned negotiation to combat and reacted equivocally to the radical tactics of the sit-down strikes. Still, she consistently stood up for labor's right to organize and blamed employers for any violence that accompanied workers' efforts to form their own unions. When, in the wake of the San Francisco longshoremen's strike, conservatives called on her to deport the radical union leader Harry Bridges, she refused. Her refusal and the late-1930s political tide against the New Deal led some members of Congress to call for her impeachment. After she appeared before the House Judiciary Committee, the impeachment effort fizzled.[46]

The hallmark of Perkins's approach to public service was her desire to promote cooperation through reason, trust, and mutual understanding. Because of this, she was distressed by conflict and often behaved indecisively in its midst. Throughout Roosevelt's presidency, she was unwaveringly loyal, although she disapproved of his demagogic tactics and actually preferred Al Smith, believing him to be more trustworthy than Roosevelt.[47]

Less bothered by controversy but determined to shape it to winning ends was Mary "Molly" Dewson. A graduate of Wellesley College, she had come up through the network of social betterment and reform committees. Actively supporting the Democratic Party during the 1920s because of its backing of welfare legislation, she was recruited by Eleanor Roosevelt to organize Democratic women for Al Smith in 1928. After Franklin was inaugurated, Eleanor had her appointed to the Women's Division of the Democratic National Committee. During her tenure, she built the Women's Division into a permanent part of the party structure, with its own headquarters and publication. She increased the number of women campaign workers to 73,000 in 1936 and 109,000 in 1940. She developed the reporter plan, whereby every Democratic county women's organization assigned a reporter to cover a government agency and to present facts to civic groups, clubs, and other organizations. By the summer of 1934, 5,000 women were signed up; by 1936, 15,000, and by 1940, 30,000. The goal

Two political pros: Mary "Molly" Dewson and Eleanor Roosevelt, January 8, 1941. (© CORBIS/Bettmann)

was civic education but also New Deal promotion. She held regional conferences to inform people about the New Deal. In 1936 she persuaded the national committee to give women equal representation on the national platform committee.

As her biographer, Susan Ware, notes, Molly Dewson's objective was "a feminist commitment to giving women a chance in public life, politics, and the professions." Her essential approach was a politics of difference. In her view, women were more strongly committed to social betterment and humanitarian justice. They worked with one another and concentrated on building relationships. They wanted security for the home, a chance for children, and peace. Her approach was to keep women's activities separate from men's and to rely on local organizations and local effort.[48]

Within the New Deal bureaucracy, no one fought harder for women than Harry Hopkins's assistant for women's programs, Ellen Woodward. A native of Mississippi, Woodward entered public life when her husband died and she replaced him in the state legislature. She organized a network of women's club leaders and civic promoters to boost better roads, schools, social centers, and welfare institutions. In 1931 Governor Theodore Bilbo chose her to represent the state at Hoover's conference on housing and home ownership. During the depression, she headed a state board to improve commercial transportation and helped found the state welfare conference. In 1932 she organized Mississippi women for Roosevelt and after his election argued for the appointment of women in the New Deal.

Thus her credentials as a politician, welfare administrator, and feminist were well established by the time Hopkins brought her to Washington. In none of these capacities did she fail to measure up. In appointing her state administrators, she insisted on loyalty to the New Deal and full-time commitment to the work. She battled stereotypes that women did not need relief but were dependent on men. She struggled to equalize pay for women on work relief. She set up an information service to respond to critics, saying that taxpayers had a right to know where their money was going. At the same time, she designed her information campaigns to promote the New Deal and to reelect President Roosevelt by identifying friends and enemies of the New Deal. In Mississippi she aligned herself with the powerful chairman of the Senate Finance Committee, Pat Harrison, instead of the race-baiting maverick Theodore Bilbo.

Woodward also attempted to combat white supremacy. Working with Eleanor, she convened a conference to discuss the issues of African American female administrators. Eleanor advised the delegates, who represented the National Council of Negro Women, to develop biracial women's committees in their local communities, where the major work had to be done.

Woodward's efforts were partially successful. During the CWA's demobilization, she persuaded Hopkins to order directors to keep women employed. Hopkins also ordered that women could direct combined women's and professional divisions and that women were to be employed regardless of whether they had small children.[49]

These were women who had fought battles for social improvement. They knew how politics and business worked. They understood power. They got along with men. They did not see men as the enemy per se; they saw them as people to work with and whose perceptions and policies ought to be enlarged and improved. Like so many women who came to the New Deal, they believed that their first priority was to do their jobs well. "Every woman who makes good on a job," wrote Ellen Woodward, "brings the day nearer when there will be no thought of sex but only of fitness in choosing public officials."[50]

Eleanor Roosevelt's appeals to women to become more active citizens, Frances Perkins's example of exercising the powers of cabinet office, Molly Dewson's efforts to enlist women in the political process, Ellen Woodward's struggles to keep women part of the relief agenda, and the efforts of all to bring more women into the sphere of public decision making had their effect. Women made headlines as insiders, their decisions affected the lives of millions, and they took the heat before congressional committees and the press. In proportion to the prevailing political winds, they were admired, despised, pitied, congratulated, rewarded, attacked, and defended. Their campaign to bring women into the national government paid some dividends. The percentage of female government employees rose from 14.3 percent in 1929 to 18.8 percent in 1939; the rate of women's employment increased at twice the rate for men. They were more likely to be employed in newly created agencies and were especially prominent in those administering welfare programs, making up 45 percent of the WPA.[51]

The achievements of women in the New Deal seemed proportional to those of the First Lady. They achieved incrementally but not grandly. In a sense, it is surprising that they achieved as much as they did, since the essence of the New Deal agenda was against them.

Thus, the success of women and African Americans would depend in large measure on their ability to make themselves a meaningful political force. By the end of the decade, it was becoming obvious that black Americans were on their way to achieving that status as a key element of the Roosevelt vote in northern states. American women, however, lacked these advantages. Although numerous, they were too divided by race, region, class, and culture to influence New Deal policies.

Signs of second-class status were everywhere. Contrary to Frances Perkins's wishes and expectations, NRA codes incorporated lower wage scales for women. Federal work programs underrepresented women (who received less than 10 percent of the jobs while representing 25 percent of the unemployed) and emphasized traditional skills such as sewing, canning, and managing nursing clinics. The most controversial was the Household Workers Training Program, which trained women for domestic service, an occupation that was in low repute and earned substandard wages in the private sector. African American women were especially disadvantaged. They were underrepresented on sewing projects, often sent out to the cotton fields at harvest time, and assigned lesser tasks and those requiring cruder skills. Much of the discrimination resulted from the sponsorship requirement, which made it hard to overcome a local culture of white supremacy. The Housekeeping Aide Project sent black women to work for white families, perpetuating the existing racial order. Latinas and Native Americans experienced similar treatment. Whites were disproportionately approved for relief and monopolized administrative appointments. Twenty-five percent of black women were on relief, but they made up only 2 percent of workers on WPA projects. WPA rules were more strictly enforced against blacks than against whites who refused to take private employment. Black women were assigned to fieldwork, while white women worked indoors.[52]

The policy of assigning women a traditional role of dependent housewife showed up most clearly in the social security legislation. The 1935 act discriminated against women by excluding the occupations they most often held and by penalizing occasional workers and those who moved from a covered occupation to an uncovered one—characteristics of female employment. The situation was even worse for black women and for blacks in general because of the large number of agricultural workers in the African American population. Amendments to the act in 1939 were centered on the family and not the individual wage earner and added survivors' insurance and aid to dependent children.[53]

How one added up women's gains and losses depended on one's perspective. In the static situation of the New Deal years, the gains were severely circumscribed. Women's opportunities were what men chose to provide. For Eleanor Roosevelt and her circle, any opportunity was better than none. They did not despair over half-empty glasses.

8

THE NEW DEAL REACHES ITS LIMITS

In the election of 1936, Franklin Roosevelt achieved one of the century's most smashing triumphs. Running against a moderate Republican, Governor Alfred M. Landon of Kansas, he carried forty-six of the forty-eight states and received just under 60 percent of the popular vote. Determined to make himself "the issue" in the campaign, he had aggressively challenged his opponents, calling them "economic royalists" and saying that he "welcome[d] their hatred." When he began his second term, the first one that began on January 20 under the Twentieth Amendment to the Constitution, observers had every right to expect that he would continue and enlarge on the New Deal. He intended not to disappoint them.

During the first half of 1937, Roosevelt introduced a comprehensive package that suggested a strong direction for the New Deal. He sent to Congress plans for long-range public works, flood control, and conservation projects in seven regions (the latter came to be known as the "seven little TVAs"). He proposed to reorganize the executive branch of government. He proposed national housing legislation to provide dwellings and subsidies for the poor and tax reform to shift the burden to those better able to pay. For the rural poor he proposed the Farm Security Administration. For urban labor he proposed national wages and hours standards.

These proposals indicated Roosevelt's determination to perfect the New Deal. But they also contained a sense of a new direction. During his first term, much New Deal legislation had been considered temporary, pertaining only to the depression emergency. Now Roosevelt was seeking to extend the long-range parts of the New Deal. His public works and flood control programs were designed to run beyond the congressional budget cycle. Thus it was clear that he wanted to shape the national government into an instrument for continued national development. He proposed to underpin his program with an administrative structure. In 1936 Roosevelt had appointed a committee of distinguished political scientists and public administrators, headed by Louis Brownlow, to develop a plan for reorganizing the executive branch. The President's Committee on Administrative Management (known as the Brownlow Committee) warned that the national government had developed a "fourth branch" in the form of "a haphazard deposit of irresponsible agencies." The committee proposed to put them under the supervision of a cabinet secretary. To institutionalize the New Deal, it further proposed a cabinet department of welfare and public works and recommended creating a permanent planning board in the White House. The proposals anticipated the New Deal's assuming a permanent form and thus needing the kind of coordination honored by administrative theorists of the time.

Before any of this could happen, however, Roosevelt believed that it was necessary to reorganize the Supreme Court.[1] Roosevelt's Court plan had begun with the ruling against the NRA and had gained momentum with subsequent anti–New Deal decisions. If he had a more complex understanding of his motives to reform the Court, he kept it to himself, much to the consternation of his friends, who could not fathom his reasoning, and to later scholars, who have enough trouble interpreting the documentary evidence. The NRA decision had set the president against the Court, and each subsequent anti–New Deal decision had brought cries of protest and demands that the president "do something." So there seemed ample reason to think that most of the country would be behind him. During the last year and a half of his first term, he explored possible ways of limiting or deflecting the Court's influence. He even encouraged sending cases to the Court to add more anti–New Deal decisions as a way of invigorating anti-Court backlash. Finding an appropriate way to "do something" was a puzzle. Many suggested some form of constitutional amendment to underwrite New Deal legislation, but the amending process was so lengthy and weighted so heavily in favor of minorities that it was rejected. As the discussions dragged on, the conclusion emerged that the problem lay not with the Constitution but with certain justices' construction of it. Although the decision against the NRA had been unanimous, many others had been by margins of one to three votes. This suggested that instead of changing the Constitution, one had only to change the membership of the Court. It was this perception that brought the suggestion from various sources that Congress enlarge the Court's membership. The plan finally agreed on and sent to Congress provided that when a justice who had served ten years chose not to retire within six months after reaching age seventy, the president could nominate another justice, up to a limit of six additional justices, or a total Supreme Court membership of fifteen.

The plan went to Congress with a special message on February 5, three days before the Court was to begin hearings on the constitutionality of the Wagner Act. At first it appeared that the plan would pass fairly easily. Both houses had overwhelming Democratic majorities, many of whose members had ridden to victory on Roosevelt's coattails. What Roosevelt had not calculated was the outburst of public hostility, which inspired the few opponents in the Senate. Sensing a groundswell against the administration, the Republicans decided to keep silent and watch the Democrats tear each other apart. Circumstances subverted the president's initiative. While the bill was in committee, the Court handed down a series of decisions upholding New Deal legislation. Then Justice Van Devanter, a sure vote against the New Deal, announced that he would retire at the end of the term. As the air went out of the crisis balloon, support for the bill sank. By mid-May, it was clear that the administration did not have the votes. At this point, Vice President Garner, who might have been brought in to shore up the southern conservatives, left Washington, in effect thumbing his nose at Roosevelt and the Supreme Court bill. Just afterward, the Senate Judiciary Committee issued a stinging report against the bill.

But people counted out Franklin Roosevelt at their peril. Roosevelt threw a large party for all congressional Democrats, turning on all of his considerable charm. The president and the Senate majority leader, Joseph Robinson of Arkansas, agreed to pare back the number of justices he could name to one a year. In the cloakrooms, the administration spokesmen and the party leaders turned on the heat. All observers now predicted the bill's passage. But at a critical moment in its consideration, Senator Robinson died. Without his leadership to keep them in line, key freshman Democrats deserted the administration. The bill went back to committee, from which it never emerged.

The political consequences of the Court fight were largely negative. The Court bill united the Republicans more successfully than any piece of New Deal economic legislation. It divided both Democrats and liberal reformers of both parties. It showed that the president could be beaten and that his popularity was not ironclad. Most important, it gave Roosevelt's opponents a master symbol to use against him: that he wanted to become a "dictator." In the international political climate of the late 1930s, in the time of Hitler, Mussolini, Stalin, and the Japanese militarists, and with the rise of fascist dictatorships in Latin America, the image was a potent one.

Although there was no direct truth in the image, it had a certain currency. Roosevelt had made the mistake of conflating his reelection with the popular will. He had seen himself as the nation's man of destiny. He had not taken account of the complexities of American voting behavior: how voters chose candidates for different levels of government, often expecting that they would have a certain independence, that they would be "their" congressman and nobody else's. Nor had he understood that people might cry out for him to "do something" without endorsing what he would do. In this regard, the president and the public were on the same page. No public outcry accompanied the Court's later swing behind the New Deal. The public seems to have been glad to see it. People did not want a new Constitution or a larger Court; they wanted New Deal decisions.

In the midst of the Supreme Court fight, Roosevelt presented the rest of his reform agenda, along with proposals to cut federal spending and balance the federal budget. Roosevelt's budget balancing made a certain amount of political and economic sense. During the 1932 campaign, he had consistently attacked President Hoover for not balancing the budget. Prices and consumer credit were increasing, and inflows of gold and capital from Europe were threatening to create more demand than American productivity could satisfy. These signs alarmed Secretary of the Treasury Morgenthau, the cabinet's most influential advocate of balanced budgets. Morgenthau was willing to accept the emergency measures that would benefit those who suffered from the depression, but he was determined to return the government to fiscal stability at the earliest possible date. On April 27, 1937, Roosevelt called for eliminating all unnecessary expenditures in order to eliminate the deficit. As word got out that the president was in a budget-balancing mood, the cabinet members, notably Ickes and Wallace, swung into line.[2] In October, Roosevelt warned Congress against increasing farm subsidies unless it could find the money. If Congress could not balance the budget, he would keep it in session "throughout the full year until they give me additional taxes to make up the loss."[3] But his warnings were soon drowned out by the reverberations of economic crisis. In August the economy recorded its sharpest decline in industrial production. On Friday, October 17, the stock market collapsed.

For the second time, Franklin Roosevelt faced a depression crisis, but now in decidedly different circumstances. This crisis would be a test of the New Deal's institutions. In 1933 Roosevelt had been able to select his Brain Trust and guide its deliberations in something close to an academic atmosphere. Now, however, the New Deal had developed bureaucratic and political interests and individuals who were seeking to entrench themselves. During the fall and winter of 1937–1938, advisers offered roughly three different approaches to the new depression.

One group wanted to stimulate recovery by increasing business investment. Its members, who included Morgenthau, Donald Richberg, and

Adolf Berle, wanted to stabilize business through the cooperative methods of the NRA, or a better version of it. The Business Advisory Council, pro–New Deal businessmen who advised the Department of Commerce, favored business cooperation, along with collective bargaining and federal wages and hours legislation.[4] They saw the economic downturn as a chance to restore the cooperative commonwealth constructed during the Hundred Days.

Other New Dealers believed that the recession resulted from monopoly business interests' keeping prices artificially high while holding down costs and wages. They sought to continue the theme of Roosevelt's reelection campaign by charging the hard times to "economic royalists." This group contained Secretary Ickes, the old progressive trustbuster, and a collection of economists and lawyers who favored more active government regulation of the economy. A key idea for them was the "administered price" theory, which had been advanced by economist Gardner Means in his 1935 book *Industrial Prices and Their Relative Inflexibility*. Means had argued that large businesses set prices independent of market conditions. This price fixing limited the returns to labor. The way toward recovery was a regulatory system that increased wages while holding the line on prices. The text for managing such a policy was James Landis's *The Administrative Process*, which argued that effective regulation needed to adapt the governmental machinery to the needs of the industry it regulated. Landis believed that it was no longer adequate for government to "maintain ethical relations of the members of society"; it was also necessary "to provide for the efficient functioning of the economic processes of the state." The device to accomplish this would be the administrative tribunal, which had the authority and the expertise to make up for the inability of the courts and legislature to keep up with the complexities of modern industrial development. It had the flexibility to adjust to new market situations and to efforts by business to thwart its objectives. Hedging and narrowing the powers of the administrative tribunal by legislation or judicial review, he argued, denied the agency the necessary flexibility to keep up with modern society.[5]

To the degree that the antimonopolists had a center of gravity, they clustered around Thomas Corcoran and Benjamin Cohen. Bright, inventive prodigies of Felix Frankfurter (hence the sobriquet "the happy hot dogs"), the two had made a splash drafting the securities and utilities legislation, which had been central to touching off business hatred of the New Deal. Himself a consummate actor, Roosevelt enjoyed Corcoran's energetic and entertaining personality. Corcoran played to Roosevelt's attentions for all he was worth, often representing himself to others as the president's special agent. It was a strategy that might promise short-term gains, but no one who knew Franklin Roosevelt would have recommended it for the longer term.[6]

The third approach recommended government spending to subsidize consumption. Its proponents argued that consumption drove a modern economy, and public spending was the most effective way to fight economic recession and stagnation. Although this thesis was later associated with the British economist John Maynard Keynes, it had quite respectable roots in American economic thought. The basic text was by Foster and Catchings, who argued that private and corporate savings, unequal incomes, and artificially high prices all affected aggregate buying power, which in turn was the engine of economic prosperity. Indeed, they claimed that private saving caused price fluctuations and a cycle of prosperity and depression.[7]

The spenders based their argument on the concept of the national income, or "the output of goods and services, measured in money." From there they developed their own version of the "mature economy" thesis. The nation's economic growth had first depended on new lands and, when those were no longer available, on industrial development in the cities. But in the early decades of the century, the decline in population growth caused a decline in demand for urban industrial production. Thus by the end of the 1920s, the national economy had reached its limits, explaining why a normal decline in the business cycle was so catastrophic.

Remedying this situation required a threefold strategy. The economic sectors with growth potential needed to expand production, the nation's human capital needed to be strengthened, and consumers needed more buying power. The recession of 1937 indicated that private capital could maintain neither economic stability nor growth. Thus it was up to the government to borrow and spend to stimulate both production and consumption. Production would be stimulated through spending on housing, recreation, roads, rapid transit, and conservation. Old-age benefits, aid to education and health, workers' compensation, unemployment compensation and relief, and wages and hours standards would stimulate consumption by redistributing income. Such a program should be financed through taxes, based on the ability to pay, and the elimination of tax shelters and loopholes. Such a program would create assets that would pay no return to society and thus neither burden the taxpayer nor compete with private enterprise. Nor should anyone have quailed at the suggestion of government support for the economy, since government had historically supported economic growth with generous land prices to individuals, land grants, and subsidies to roads, canals, and railroads.[8]

The spending argument had the political virtue of simplicity: it proposed a single remedy and a single objective. Increasing the national income to a certain figure would result in "full employment." Within the administration, key advocates of the spending thesis were Marriner Eccles, chairman of the Federal Reserve Board, and Lauchlin Currie, a Reserve Board economist. A November 1937 memo by Currie ascribed the causes of the recession to restrictive monetary policies. The memo became the central argument for a spending program and a glue among liberals. Among the New Dealers who were close to Roosevelt and who sympathized with the spending-consumption thesis, none was closer than Harry Hopkins, whose relief programs depended on government spending and who had often argued that relief spending stimulated recovery by boosting consumer demand.[9]

Among the three approaches, it was possible to combine the last two by defining antimonopoly and public spending as support for consumers—the first because it reduced prices, the second because it put money in consumers' pockets. On a more sophisticated level, it was possible to support antimonopoly and public spending by saying that the United States had attained a "mature" economy. The thesis held that American land had been used up, population growth had declined, and capital investment had stagnated. Since private investment could not be relied on, the government should stimulate consumption through spending and easing credit. Increasing purchasing power was becoming an attractive alternative to the complexities of antimonopoly.[10]

But theories were only as strong as their political muscle. At first, the vision of the cooperative commonwealth was ascendant. Roosevelt had always been the NRA's greatest fan. His anger and disappointment at its passing had been profound. Historians have explained the "reform" legislation of the "second hundred days" in part as a response to the Supreme Court's outlawing the NRA.[11]

And the economy was showing Roosevelt that he could not ignore the New Deal's political evolution. The rhetoric of the second campaign continued to echo in his ears. When Ickes handed him a note declaring that the administration was experiencing a replay of Andrew Jackson's war against the Bank of the United States, "except that big capital is occupying at this time the role of the bank," Roosevelt exclaimed: "That's right." He was even willing to speculate that Wall Street financiers had engineered the recession in order to discredit him.[12] In October and November he pointedly attacked monopoly.[13] At the same time, no one ought to have forgotten that the president had consistently supported Hopkins's relief programs and had been willing to unbalance the budget to pay for them.

When Roosevelt's preferences were hazy, political and economic events would be decisive. The aftermath of the Supreme Court fiasco left Congress in an edgy and hostile mood. Conservative congressmen began introducing bills to curb the National Labor Relations Board's ability to support union organizing. Nor was business willing to accept an NRA that would include organized labor as a partner. Indeed, business was not especially interested in budget balancing, which it rated behind lower taxes and weaker labor unions.[14] Business groups drove home their unwillingness to enter a partnership with the New Deal with sneers and gibes about "the Roosevelt recession." As one industrialist put it, "the depression was created in Washington and it will have to be cured in Washington by a frank acknowledgment of some mistakes that have been made."[15]

For a time, Roosevelt seemed willing to wait and watch. In November he proposed to Congress to reduce spending by $800 million for the next fiscal year and by $750 million for the following one. He convened a conference of business and labor leaders and met with them into February before realizing that they had nothing to offer.[16] But evidence of depression persisted. Relief rolls increased, and he had to ask Congress for a supplemental appropriation. He directed the Reconstruction Finance Corporation (RFC) to increase credit to borrowers who would increase employment.[17] Morgenthau's resolve to balance the budget weakened, to be replaced by his consistent desire to help those at the bottom of the social and economic ladder. Still, he rejected spending for its own sake as a way to combat the depression. The best he could recommend was specific policies targeted to specific commodities to either raise or lower their prices and bring supply and demand better into line.

All this tinkering and debate seemed fine with Roosevelt. On March 14, Morgenthau observed that he was "just treading water . . . to wait to see what happens this spring." Roosevelt replied: "Absolutely."[18]

Then, in April, the president reached a decision. He had gone to Warm Springs for some relaxation and had invited Harry Hopkins, who was in Florida recovering from surgery that had removed two-thirds of his cancerous stomach. Seeing a chance to advance the "spending" agenda, Hopkins had recruited a team consisting of his friend and relief colleague Aubrey Williams, economist Leon Henderson, and social policy analyst Beardsley Ruml to supply him with material to make his case to the president. Hopkins's timing was impeccable. The German takeover of Austria a month earlier had sent stock prices tumbling.

At Warm Springs, Hopkins argued that lifting the depression depended on increased productivity, which could be stimulated only by increased purchasing power, which depended on government spending. He based his argument on national income analysis, what today would be called the gross domestic product. In order to have full employment, his argument went, the national income (the money value of all goods and services) needed to be $80 billion. The analysis persuaded Roosevelt, who decided to ask Congress for additional spending. On the way back to Washington, he encountered two of the trustbusting school, who persuaded him to add antimonopoly to his recovery package.[19]

It was a decision in the classic Roosevelt mode: sudden, confident, and politically astute. With business hostile, the international situation threatening the stock market, Congress having recently passed an important wages and hours bill, and New Deal liberals carrying the day in congressional primaries, the president was ready to launch an offensive to advance liberalism both on the national agenda and within the Democratic Party.

In an address to Congress on April 14, 1938, Roosevelt used national income analysis to recommend additional spending. He blamed the renewed depression on overproduction caused by "certain highly undesirable practices," which he specified only as different in different industries. The key, however, was that consumption had not kept pace with production. At the same time, the price of basic raw materials such as copper and steel had risen more rapidly than either inflation or wage increases. He called for a partnership between government and business to move people into private employment, to equalize the tax burden, and to end monopolistic "practices" and "price fixing." He called for maintaining the New Deal reforms that had already been enacted. "Our immediate task is to consolidate and maintain the gains achieved. . . . Let us use the tools already forged and laid out on the bench." The current problem was the failure of consumer demand. This would be remedied by increasing the national income by increasing employment, and thus increasing tax revenues, and by reducing government expenditures.

He proposed $1 billion for the WPA, $175 million for the FSA, $75 million for the NYA, and $50 million for the CCC. These would avert layoffs among those in government service. He also endorsed loans by the RFC. He moved on to loosening credit by desterilizing $1.4 billion in gold and asked banking and securities agencies to simplify their procedures. For private enterprise he asked for an additional $300 million for the U.S. Housing Authority, $450 million in spending by the PWA, and authority to loan up to $1 billion to states and localities, the latter in no-interest loans. An additional $100 million would go to the Bureau of Public Roads, and $37 million to flood control and reclamation. This totaled over $2 billion in appropriations and $950 million in loans from the Treasury.[20]

In July, Roosevelt presented to Congress a "lend-spend bill," which would have authorized funds for "self-liquidating" construction projects. The funds were to be "off budget," that is, they would be considered in the same category as relief spending, as a temporary expedient to meet an economic emergency. But Congress defeated the bill.[21]

Roosevelt hedged his commitment to spending with certain qualifications. Although for the moment, at least, he seemed to have abandoned reviving the NRA and creating a business commonwealth, he still spoke the language of a government-business partnership. At the same time, his antitrust investigation by the Temporary National Economic Committee (TNEC) suggested a further faith in reorganizing the structure of the political economy, as did his praise for collective bargaining and farm subsidies. It was by no means clear that he intended to redefine the New Deal in terms of spending.

Still, Roosevelt had given the "spenders" greater weight in his administration. In June, prodded by reports from Harry Hopkins that the unemployment situation had become desperate, Congress appropriated $3.75 billion, $1.425 billion of it for immediate use by the WPA. Morgenthau and Eleanor got the president to release funds to buy milk for children in Chicago. That fall, he appointed a special board to advise him on fiscal and monetary policy. The membership was weighted in favor of spending, although, in typical Roosevelt fashion, he designated Morgenthau as chair.

An important result of the spending policy was to redirect federal housing policy. During his first term, Roosevelt had favored a program of extending credit to families to purchase their own homes. He opposed multifamily dwellings and refused to endorse public housing. Over the months and years, however, states and municipalities pressed Washington to support public housing, and New York's senator Robert Wagner regularly presented federal housing bills. In 1937 Roosevelt agreed to make housing legislation an exception to his drive for budget balancing and Congress passed the first United States Housing Act. It was substantially less than Senator Wagner had wanted. Rural Democrats reduced its funding and spread its resources over as many states as possible to keep the major cities from reaping all the benefits.

However underfunded and hemmed in by the phalanxes of Republicans and rural Democrats, the New Deal housing policy affirmed for the first time that the United States had become an urban nation and that the welfare of the cities was critical to the national welfare. As a result, urban matters assumed a higher profile. City planning commissions won renewed prominence, as did other projects to improve the quality of urban life.[22]

All was not sweetness and light. Roosevelt had asked Congress to equalize the tax burden according to one's ability to pay. When Congress returned a bill (some thought influenced by Bernard Baruch) that encouraged corporate tax avoidance and imposed a flat rate on capital gains, the president denounced it but allowed it to become law without his signature.

Roosevelt's shift to spending accompanied a shift of political strategy. He now asked Congress for funds to investigate the concentration of economic power. Congress complied and created the TNEC. Chaired by

Senator Joseph O'Mahoney of Wyoming, the committee began a slogging journey that eventually consumed three years and produced volumes of weighty reports. In the meantime, the Justice Department undertook a vigorous prosecution of the antitrust laws, producing some spectacular dissolutions until defense mobilization made big business seem to be in the national interest.[23]

The general appeal of antimonopoly, which could round up support in progressive urban and populist rural areas, indicated little more than Roosevelt's making good on the antibusiness rhetoric of the campaign. He indicated a more specific policy direction by sponsoring federal wages and hours legislation. The bill required all businesses engaged in interstate commerce to establish a forty-hour workweek and a minimum wage of forty cents an hour, with time and a half for overtime. Appearing in May 1937, it passed the Senate but arrived in the House in the wake of the Supreme Court defeat and the "Roosevelt recession." Sensing a weakened president, conservatives bottled up the bill in the Rules Committee, which was chaired by John O'Connor of New York, a longtime anti–New Dealer. Although such legislation had long been on the agenda of social reformers, it ran into opposition from southerners, who thought it was a northern ploy to price labor out of their market, and the American Federation of Labor (AFL), which had consistently preferred collective bargaining to government standards.

Thus, the bill became a test of strength between reformers and the AFL and, to a lesser degree, between the AFL and the CIO, which endorsed the bill. It also became a test of strength between reformers and conservatives in the Democratic Party. The specific battleground would be less in Congress than in the Democratic primaries. More than just this legislation was at stake. This was Roosevelt's first chance to reform the party by defeating conservative senators who had been elected in 1932, and he wanted to take advantage of it. He began by allowing surrogates to put administration support behind New Deal candidates, succeeding with Senators Lister Hill in Alabama and Claude Pepper in Florida. Pepper had campaigned for the wages and hours bill, and his victory had the effect of springing the bill out of the House Rules Committee and to ultimate passage. The final product was weak and ambiguous, filled with exemptions and silent on the question of regional wage differentials, which it left to the law's administrator.[24] It was the bill's politics rather than its economics that seemed promising to the New Deal.

But the political outcome was no brighter. Roosevelt achieved a few victories, electing Senator Alben Barkley in Kentucky and defeating O'Connor in New York City, but in other races he lost badly. In Georgia, South Carolina, and Maryland, the senatorial targets of his opposition survived by votes that gave Roosevelt's critics new resolve to test their strength.

One of the targets of this resolve was Roosevelt's proposal to reorganize the executive branch. As conceived by the advisory committee, reorganization meant giving the president authority for flexible management of his responsibilities. The plan was designed for a "strong" president who could master political situations but would need strong management tools to follow through. Such flexibility was in keeping with the needs of "democracy," something that had to be shored up in the troubled state of the world. Specifically, the plan called for strengthening White House management by permitting the president to appoint six special assistants, improving budget oversight, consolidating some 105 agencies into twelve departments, and creating an auditor general with the sole responsibility to report "illegal and wasteful expenditures" to Congress.[25]

Roosevelt invited Congress to participate in the reorganizing process, in the hope of avoiding charges of executive "dictation." It was a vain hope, which he himself subverted by presenting the reorganization package in finished form. The lawmakers were disinclined to be pushed around in this fashion, and they found a number of things they did not like. They most objected to the proposal to place all nonpolicy positions under the civil service system, outside of party patronage. Congress considered the executive agencies its own particular responsibility, and the ability to fund and manipulate them was one of its major prerogatives. Consolidating agencies would break the special ties and cozy relationships congressmen had established with certain agencies. Conservatives disliked the proposal to do away with the office of comptroller general, which, in the hands of a Republican appointee, had held up various New Deal projects. Still, on its first consideration, the House passed the bill with little change.[26]

When the Senate took up the bill, special interests rallied to oppose it, fearing that they would lose some privilege for lack of contact with their special agencies. They were aided by the alliances they had established with powerful congressional committees and their chairmen. A classic case was the Forest Service, which was part of the Department of Agriculture, which favored "tree farming" management that emphasized lumber production. Opposing this view was the Department of Interior, whose boss Harold Ickes disliked policies that involved the government with "the exploiters of our forests" and favored managing them for their aesthetic and recreational purposes. The reorganization plan proposed to create a Department of Conservation, and Ickes was determined to put the Forest Service in it. This led to a major tussle that had disastrous consequences for the bill, as advocates of keeping the Forest Service in Agriculture opposed not just the transfer but the entire bill. As they rounded up support from other forest "users," they created an opposition that worried even staunch New Deal supporters. Nor were all New Deal senators immune from partiality to their favored agencies. Senator Robert Wagner wanted to maintain the independent status of the National Labor Relations Board and the Housing Administration, both of which he had sponsored. When the Senate passed an amended bill in late March, it was by a single vote, with Wagner voting in the negative.[27]

Wagner's opposition was an indication that Roosevelt was in trouble again. As with the Supreme Court reorganization plan, executive reorganization seemed to threaten the institutional balance within the government. This was just the kind of issue that could break down barriers between "liberals" and "conservatives." Still, at the last minute it seemed that the bill could be saved if Roosevelt was willing to drop his request for a Department of Welfare, thus accepting a slap at Harry Hopkins. By this time, no New Dealer so irritated conservatives as Hopkins, who had made a reputation as a brash, sarcastic, and uncompromising liberal and Roosevelt partisan. Congress had started the 1937 session by earmarking Hopkins's relief funds and temporarily cutting his salary in half. When Roosevelt made it clear that reorganization would have to include the welfare agency, the House recommitted the bill to the Rules Committee, where it lay as the session and the 75th Congress ran its course.[28]

The next Congress, the most conservative and anti-Roosevelt one to date, finally passed a stripped-down version that omitted the Department of Public Works and Welfare. The bill did, however, create the Executive Office of the President and give him the authority to appoint six assistants and to submit to Congress plans for reorganizing departments. In his reorganization plans, which Congress failed to defeat, Roosevelt made up for Congress's slap at Hopkins by creating a Federal Works Agency and a Federal Security Agency, each containing a number of previous public works and social welfare departments. He short-circuited the congressional animus against Hopkins by nominating him for secretary of commerce.

In September 1939 Roosevelt completed the administrative reform process by issuing an executive order forming the Executive Office of the President. He divided the office into six departments, including the Bureau of the Budget, which he brought over from Treasury, and an Office of Emergency Management, through which he planned to coordinate American response to the recent outbreak of war in Europe. Although in an accompanying statement he said that he wanted to mold the Executive Office into "a compact organization," he failed to create an office of administrative management.[29] Thus he kept the oversight and coordinating responsibilities in his own hands. Roosevelt had acquired new resources and, as usual, had decided to use them as instruments of his political judgment. In the hands of so resourceful a chief executive, the potential value of these resources was sure to be magnified.

At the moment of the bill's final passage, May 9, 1939, no one could anticipate how events overseas were going to bring about an executive reordering that would dwarf the recent struggle.

9

★★★★★

FROM ISOLATION TO WAR

While he was attempting to rebuild the structure of his nation's depression economy, Roosevelt and other national leaders were also trying to shore up the crumbling structure of international relations. The causes of the international difficulty were the depression and the rise of militant fascist nationalism led by Germany and Japan, with an assist from Italy. Acting separately and later as allies, Germany and Japan unraveled the system of treaties that had limited armaments, guaranteed borders, established international buffer zones, and ultimately renounced war. Their final triumph was the Second World War. In the meantime, however, Roosevelt and others were engaged in a long and fruitless struggle to maintain the peace.[1] During his first two terms, the efforts to deal with fascism interacted with efforts to restore prosperity.

No task required more of Roosevelt's pluralistic skills than his foreign policy.[2] He had to find some way to combine his principles and objectives with his domestic priorities, congressional and popular attitudes, and the policies of other nations. Considered in the abstract, as simply a matter of presidential responsibility, Roosevelt's task was no different from that of any other president. It was the critical nature of his presidency, both domestic and foreign, that required an unusual measure of skill. Roosevelt's foreign policy combined a number of elements. By the time he entered the White House, he had withdrawn considerably from the interventionist assertions of American power and moral superiority he had declared during his tenure as assistant secretary of the navy. He still wished to maintain the United States' primary position in the Western Hemisphere, but he sought to do it by fostering a spirit of cooperation and mutual understanding. His preference for peace based on cooperation and interdependence carried over into his desire to maintain the peace through disarmament and free trade. He hoped to be able to target American economic power against those who most threatened the peace or, failing that, to support other nations' blockades or embargoes. In the meantime, he tried to create goodwill with potentially useful allies: in Latin America with a "good neighbor" policy, and in Eastern Europe by recognizing the Soviet Union.

At the same time, the American public seemed to be frightened by charges that international cooperation weakened American national sovereignty and security. Roosevelt was not entirely averse to such sentiments. Although he sought cooperation from smaller and weaker nations, he did not shy away from pressing his nation's claims to the other major powers. He desired partners, but he much preferred to be the chief one. His program to restore national prosperity pushed him further toward national sovereignty and the search for ways to help American business penetrate new foreign markets.

Public uneasiness and Roosevelt's own reservations had a strong political expression in the congressional "isolationists." These were a group of mostly western progressive Republicans and Democrats who wanted the U.S. government to concentrate on domestic reform and who distrusted alliances and partnerships, which, they argued, would result in the nation's being drawn into "other people's" quarrels. They even distrusted negotiations, which in their view always resulted in the United States' being outmaneuvered. Most isolationists were not pacifists. Indeed, they distrusted the institutions of international cooperation, such as the League of Nations and the World Court, which most pacifists supported as means of peacefully resolving international conflicts. Isolationists also favored military preparedness for defensive purposes.[3]

During the 1930s, the isolationists were powerful enough to limit Roosevelt's flexibility in shaping foreign policy. They criticized any of his efforts to cooperate with the League of Nations, even those on behalf of disarmament. They prohibited loans to governments that had defaulted on their war debts. They passed neutrality legislation designed to keep the United States from supporting any warring nation. They opposed letting Roosevelt make agreements with other countries that would lower tariff rates between the two, arguing that this delegated too much power to the president. Although they failed each time the "reciprocal trade agreements" legislation came up, each time their voting strength increased.

The isolationists' major effort was the Ludlow amendment, a proposed constitutional amendment named for Democratic Representative Louis

Ludlow of Indiana. The provision would have required a popular referendum before any declaration of war could have gone into effect. Proposed in 1935 and 1937 and debated until early 1938, the measure was the high point of the isolationist's ambition and a turning point in their ability to restrict Roosevelt's actions. Roosevelt publicly opposed the amendment and campaigned against it. On January 10, 1938, the day the House voted on bringing the amendment to the floor for debate, Roosevelt sent a letter to Speaker William Bankhead charging that the amendment would "cripple" the president's ability to conduct foreign policy and would actually encourage other nations to "violate American rights with impunity." Bankhead read the letter just before the vote, and the Ludlow amendment died in committee.[4]

But as with all pluralistic strategies, Roosevelt's were hostage to circumstances. His desire for collective security depended on the willingness of other nations to participate. His ability to lead depended on the willingness of the American people to support him. In this regard, the political misfortunes and miscalculations of his second term created a political structure that shaped his role in the growing world crisis. As things turned out, these circumstances presented Franklin Roosevelt with no good choices.

In Europe, Britain and France tried to maintain the peace by puttying the cracks Germany's Adolf Hitler was making in the system. For a time, the British and French tried to ally with Italy's fascist leader Benito Mussolini against Hitler. Britain responded to the Germans' rearmament by negotiating a naval treaty with them. When the Italians invaded Ethiopia, Britain and France opposed a blockade or economic sanctions against them. When Hitler marched into the previously demilitarized Rhineland in March 1936, the British and French managed a muddled and passive response that played down the seriousness of the event. The result of all these moves was to close off any avenues that Roosevelt might have pursued to support stronger actions against Germany.[5] Indeed, as much as anything, the Rhineland affair showed that among leaders of the world's major nations, only Roosevelt fully appreciated Hitler's threat to peace and believed that counterthreats of force were necessary to contain him. In Britain, the accession of Neville Chamberlain in 1937 failed to improve things. The Chamberlain ministry never had a clear and consistent view of Hitler's purposes, apart from realizing by early 1939 that he could not be trusted. But that was a different thing from realizing how to stop him, on which topic advice piled up in confused and contradictory heaps. The other reality was that the Europeans were looking after themselves and distrusting one another. The Soviets regarded British proposals for a united front against Germany as an effort to commit them to defending Britain without a reciprocal commitment from Britain. The German-Italian alliance of May 1939 convinced the Soviets that Hitler was aiming to advance to the west and not the east. From this moment the Soviets began to move toward a formal accommodation with Germany, confident that the Germans would see that it was in their interest to respond. As the British recorded one accommodation with Hitler after another, Roosevelt began to suspect that British policy was being controlled by the "Cliveden Set," a group of politicians and financiers not unlike the American Liberty League, which sought to influence Britain to strike a deal with Hitler for their mutual financial advantage. In return, the British ministry held a low opinion of Roosevelt, the New Deal, and Americans generally.[6]

The consequence of this situation was that the course of Roosevelt's diplomacy—and indeed of all American foreign policy during the 1930s—was replete with ironies. One of the lessons of the war that followed was that Roosevelt had been right all along and that a firm stance against the fascist powers would have been a wise course. To the extent that his opponents blinded the American public to the erosion of the world order, to the extent that they preferred bashing Franklin Roosevelt to developing constructive policies, and to the extent that they hampered their nation's psychological and material preparation for the war, their struggle with the president diminished their stature. At the same time, however, we need to remember that Roosevelt's foreign policy—however well it perceived the realities of Europe's direction, however clearly it understood that American security and the security of European democracies were interrelated, and however practical it was to provide diplomatic and later military support to those democracies—aimed at the same objective as his opponents: preserving the peace. In August 1936 Roosevelt declared that he hated war, and as far as anyone can tell, he meant it.

The problem with Roosevelt's formulation was this: the world situation in the late 1930s called for war and not for peace. Preserving the peace—which could only have meant prolonging it—would have kept Hitler in power. Can we really feel comfortable with such an outcome? We know that by 1938 the Nazis had begun work on an atomic bomb. We also know that Hitler's scientists went off on the wrong track, but would they have stayed there forever? More important, would the United States, having "contained" Hitler with a conventional arms buildup, have proceeded with its own atomic weapons program? Perhaps, but the outcome would have been far more problematic. A tie or a narrow margin by either side would not have dissuaded Hitler from plunging the world into a full-fledged nuclear exchange. Probably not Washington, but London, Paris, and certainly Moscow all would have been gone before Berlin, if Berlin went at all. This would have left Hitler astride a devastated Europe while the United States desperately rushed toward its own contribution to the holocaust that "real" history avoided. Maybe we do not need to give a full three cheers for the isolationists who helped Hitler discount the United States and push ahead with his plans to take Europe by any means necessary, but we might give them one and a half.

The two camps were those who wanted to preserve peace in the world by means of collective security, supported by an active, positive U.S. policy, and those who wanted strict and impartial neutrality. The first group, to which Roosevelt belonged, wanted neutrality laws that would give the president discretion to embargo support for belligerents. Roosevelt also looked beyond a distinctively American position, thinking of ways to bring collective pressure against Hitler's rearmament program, even going so far as to blockade Germany if it persisted in rearming. The other side was less concerned about world peace than about American peace. Its proponents favored cutting off all contact with warring nations and believed that President Woodrow Wilson's unneutral actions had led the United States into war against its best interests. At the moment of decision, the summer of 1935, the political momentum favored their cause. The prospect of war between Italy and Ethiopia raised fears of another escalating conflict similar to the one that had produced the Great War. Peace organizations flooded Congress with petitions for strict neutrality legislation. Roosevelt attempted delaying tactics, but failed. When it became clear that fighting for authority to name the target of an arms embargo would jeopardize his domestic reform legislation, he gave up the fight. The bill that passed and that he signed in August mandated an embargo against all belligerents. When Italy invaded Ethiopia, Roosevelt sought to use the law against it. He proclaimed the embargo at the earliest possible moment and instructed Secretary of State Hull to publicize its effects on Italy. In the end, however, he had to back away from discretionary powers, lest isolationists and Republicans charge that he was cooperating with the League of Nations.

The outbreak of the Spanish civil war gave Roosevelt a low-cost way to pursue his desire for peace while placating his isolationist critics. Although the civil nature of the conflict exempted it from the Neutrality Act, he adopted the law's sanctions as administration policy. He went to extreme lengths to cooperate with the British and French to promote nonintervention in the Spanish civil war, going so far as to request special legislation, which was passed, to prohibit arms shipments to Spain. Having made his bed, he found that he had to sleep in it. As evidence of German and Italian involvement in the Spanish conflict mounted, along with their atrocities against civilians, he considered applying the neutrality act's embargo against Germany and Italy but gave up the idea when Britain assured him that a fascist victory in Spain would not jeopardize its interests.

In August 1936, while he was considering his Spanish policy, Roosevelt gave a speech in which he emphasized his commitment to peace. Recounting his policy of fair dealing and cooperation in Latin America and his support for universal disarmament, he concluded with an emotional rendering of his own experience when he had toured the battlefields of Europe at the end of the Great War. "I have seen war on land and sea," he declared. "I have seen blood running from the wounded. I have seen men coughing out their gassed lungs. I have seen the dead in the mud. I have seen cities destroyed. I have seen two hundred limping, exhausted men come out of line—the survivors of a regiment of one thousand that went forward forty-eight hours before. I have seen children starving. I have seen the agony of mothers and wives. I hate war." What he meant, of course, was that he hated the thought of another European war. Isolating the butchery in Spain would satisfy that fear, as well as the fears of the American people. One should not underestimate the force of the American people. It was an election year, and Roosevelt knew full well that any gesture toward intervention would bring down not only the censure of the peace organizations but also round condemnation from his Republican opponent, who was being no less ardent in courting the peace vote.

After the election, Roosevelt traveled to Buenos Aires, Argentina, to attend the inter-American peace conference. Spreading goodwill along the way and meeting tumultuous crowds, he hoped to establish a permanent machinery for settling hemispheric disputes. But many South Americans, led by Argentina, remained suspicious of U.S. power, which might endanger their sovereignty or their own ambitions for influence, and nothing came of his efforts.

Still, Roosevelt continued to encourage hemispheric solidarity. He maintained relations with Mexico while exerting pressure and strongly protesting Mexico's expropriation of American oil interests. He won support at the Pan American Conference for a resolution opposing aggression by a non-American state. He supported military consultation between the United States and other American nations.

In the spring of 1937 Roosevelt looked over the European situation and concluded that the parties were looking to him to provide the leadership for peace. They wanted someone to come forward with "a hat with a rabbit in it." "Well," he declared, "I haven't got a hat and I haven't got a rabbit in it."[7] He conferred with Western leaders and sent Joseph Davies to Moscow to woo the Soviets toward the democracies. He wrote to Mussolini to support his expressed interest in arms control and to encourage him to participate in stabilizing the situation.

Renewed Japanese attacks on China raised new complications. The navy requested additional troops to protect American citizens, while isolationists demanded the withdrawal of all American troops and the application of the Neutrality Act to the conflict. Seizing on the fact that no war had been declared, Roosevelt permitted private vessels to trade with China at their own risk while forbidding any U.S. ships from doing so. But he was playing a weakening hand. The abortive effort to enlarge the membership of the Supreme Court had undermined his credibility and emboldened his critics. Then, late in the summer, the sharp recession found him struggling to deal with hard times that could be charged to his own account.

In an effort to reseize the initiative, he discussed making a dramatic speech that would highlight the need to isolate aggressors by denying them the "economic benefits" of membership in international society. He was thinking of cutting off trade, including raw materials, to aggressor nations. The result was a speech in early October in Chicago, where he called for the "quarantine" of aggressors. In his mind, he was calling for some form of collective action, but the international disarray, economic anxiety, and political contention made it impossible for him to have his way. He was soon on the defensive, trying to explain what "quarantine" did not mean. The issue plagued him when he agreed to participate in a conference of the nations that in 1922 had agreed to preserve China's independence and integrity. Various nations pressed Roosevelt to take the lead, but he refused, believing that he could not get too far ahead of American opinion and that initiatives that had once been hailed as "leadership" were now just as likely to be castigated as "dictatorship." Roosevelt's main problem was that he had no program for collective action. As long as the other democracies interpreted his statements as gestures toward leadership instead of invitations to collective action, and as long as he felt too constrained by public opinion at home, there was nothing he was prepared to do.

The December 1937 Japanese attack on the U.S. gunboat *Panay* seemed to open an occasion for action. Roosevelt contemplated economic sanctions and even a blockade of Japan. American political and public sentiment overwhelmingly opposed going to war. Anything Roosevelt did would have to achieve American objectives without bloodshed, and this was a guarantee he knew he could not give. When Japan apologized and agreed to pay reparations and to respect American rights in the future, he closed the book on the incident.

Much of the next year was taken up with the problem of appeasement. As the Chamberlain government in Britain sought to maintain peace by accepting German and Italian conquests, Roosevelt held back, not wanting to derail any prospects for a longer-lasting peace. He had continually looked to Europe to provide initiatives to which he might hitch American policy, and for the time being, appeasement was the only game in town. In addition, Roosevelt was giving his economic program top legislative priority. The outside world would have to fend for itself. Such seemed to be the case when France and the Soviet Union appeared willing to stand firm to protect Czechoslovakia from Hitler's demands. Roosevelt interpreted Chamberlain's response as a British commitment to fight for Czechoslovakia. But weakening his hand was the congressional backlash against the New Deal and anger at Roosevelt's "dictatorial" methods. This was, indeed, his dilemma. As he told the French, he could promise anything but "troops and loans."[8] Not surprisingly, he seized the prospect of a diplomatic settlement that would give Hitler his territorial demands as a satisfactory way to preserve the peace. Thus he pressed for what turned out to be appeasement's finest hour—the Munich Conference.

Roosevelt's response to the Jewish refugee crisis resulting from the Nazi pogroms was generous, within the restrictive terms of American immigration laws. He combined the German and Austrian quotas to increase the number of Jewish immigrants and called on other nations to cooperate in determining a policy to aid the refugees from Nazism. A conference actually took place, but participants demonstrated only a general unwillingness to act. New atrocities did nothing to soften attitudes or to open borders.

Continuing tensions forced Roosevelt to shift from diplomacy to deterrence. He sought to increase American warplane production and to find ways to supply planes to Britain and France. Even here he had to fight through a tangle of difficulties. The American military chiefs, unwilling to put the defense of a foreign nation ahead of defense of their own, objected to an emphasis on air production and favored a "balanced" program of military construction. Others, including Secretary of War Harry Woodring, opposed sharing America's latest technology with other nations, and American industry proved unable to meet production schedules.

At home, Roosevelt's leverage seemed weaker than ever. The congressional elections had returned enough Republicans and anti–New Deal Democrats to stymie liberal legislation and to embolden further critiques of his foreign policies. His own backing down and equivocating had done little to enhance his credibility. When he attempted to take the Senate Military Affairs Committee into his confidence to justify selling warplanes to France, one member leaked that he had defined America's frontier as the Rhine River. Although Roosevelt at first acknowledged this statement as a way of showing how American security was tied to that of the Western democracies, the outcry in response to the statement led him to brand the attribution "a deliberate lie" and to accuse his critics of endangering America's security.

Not even another act of bold aggression by Hitler could stir the United States. Hitler's taking over Czechoslovakia in March 1939 convinced Britain and France that the next German advance would be a cause for war. In

Washington, Roosevelt used the occasion to call on Congress to revise the neutrality laws to put all war supplies on a cash-and-carry basis. The assumption was that Britain and France instead of Germany would benefit from such a policy. For a time, Roosevelt considered pressing for a general repeal of all the neutrality laws, but word from Key Pittman, chair of the Senate Foreign Relations Committee, that even cash-and-carry would be difficult to pass dissuaded him. As the European situation continued to deteriorate, Roosevelt actively lobbied congressmen to get whatever revision he could. But senators seemed impervious. Most members perceived no threat of war. Blocked in the upper house, Roosevelt turned to the lower one, where the Foreign Relations Committee was more sympathetic. Even there, however, the best the administration could do was a bill granting the president discretion over trade to belligerents, except for arms and ammunition. Then the Senate Foreign Relations Committee, on the votes of two Democrats Roosevelt had tried to purge, defeated neutrality revision. A White House meeting with Senate leaders confirmed that revision was dead. It would take the outbreak of war in Europe to persuade the senators to change their minds.

In the Far East, Roosevelt found himself in a situation similar to that of the European democracies. In November 1938 Japan announced that it was creating "a new order in East Asia," in effect taking control of the region's political and economic relations. Japan specifically repudiated the Open Door policy, by which Western European nations and the United States had shared economic access to Chinese markets. Japanese policy seemed to call for a strong American response. Public opinion polls showed overwhelming support for an embargo of military shipments to Japan, and even Congress demanded action. China desperately needed aid, which the United States could supply relatively inexpensively. But again there seemed to be no good options. Aid to China might halt Japanese expansion and force Tokyo to reconsider its policies, but it might also lead to war. A more "moderate" policy, it was hoped, would encourage Japanese moderates to take a stand against the militant expansionists. In the end, Roosevelt compromised by giving the Japanese six months' notice that he intended to cancel their commercial treaty.

For a time, Roosevelt's action seemed to calm the situation in the Pacific. But in Europe, Hitler's war plans moved forward unchecked. On August 22 he concluded the Nazi-Soviet Pact, securing his eastern front to attack Poland. There followed several days of feverish discussions overlaid by a pall of inevitable catastrophe. The moment came on September 1, when German troops invaded Poland and Britain and France declared war on Germany. That day Roosevelt called a cabinet meeting and announced that the United States "was not going to get into war."[9] On September 3,

1939, Roosevelt addressed the nation in a fireside chat. He discussed the war in Europe and acknowledged American neutrality. However, he declared, he could not ask Americans to be neutral in thought. "Even a neutral cannot be asked to close its mind or conscience." Behind his words lay his belief that American neutrality and security depended on the defeat of Germany. To this end, he began to explore ways to help Britain and France. Again he focused on revising the neutrality legislation. He called a special session of Congress to revise the acts to permit munitions shipments on a cash-and-carry basis. Once again the same obstacles arose: a combination of partisanship, pacifism, and fear of war. But he persevered. He cooperated with the British and French blockade and harassed German shipping in American ports. He enlisted prominent Republican internationalists to speak up for neutrality revision. He laid plans with Vice President Garner to stop a Senate filibuster. In late October, cash-and-carry passed both houses—overwhelmingly in the Senate, close but comfortably in the House.

Roosevelt hoped that cash-and-carry would help the Western Allies. But limited cash reserves, the unavailability of American loans, and tight shipping restrictions limited American aid to a trickle. The American military chiefs also warned against shipping too many war goods when American defenses were so thin. (At the war's outbreak, the American military capability ranked just behind Switzerland's.)

As fall turned into winter, Roosevelt continued to walk a tightrope. He attempted to bring the Latin American states together to reaffirm their mutual commitment to hemispheric defense and to establish a "neutrality zone" to keep out belligerent warships. When, after the fall of Poland, the western front settled into a "sitzkreig," or "phony war," and Hitler called for peace, the president refused suggestions that he play the mediator's role. In early 1940, in order to save Britain and France from possible defeat, he explored possibilities for peace.

In the spring of 1940, the Germans' invasion of the Netherlands and Belgium and their move into France shifted the momentum to Roosevelt. Congress passed generous appropriations for defense. Voices called for a stronger effort for military preparedness and political unity. The problem was that such voices opposed aiding the Allies at the expense of American defenses. Roosevelt had always believed that the Allies were America's best defense. He had explored the possibility of assigning "surplus" armaments to the Allies, but not until June, when the public reacted to the impending collapse of France by supporting more generous aid, did he assign materiel to the Allies. It was too late. Italy's entry into the war made the French position hopeless. The result was a series of messages from the new British prime minister, Winston Churchill, declaring that the only thing that could keep France in the fight would be a U.S. declaration of war. Roosevelt could do nothing, and on June 22, France surrendered to Germany in the same railroad car in which Germany had capitulated in 1918. The newsreels recorded Hitler dancing a jig of triumph. American polls gave Britain little prospect of holding out.

The noose seemed to be tightening. Roosevelt had long been concerned for the safety of the Western Hemisphere. Now rumors of elaborate Nazi subversion plots and the danger of economic blackmail from Nazi control of European markets inspired him to renew his efforts on behalf of hemispheric solidarity. The results of the Pan American Conference were superficially satisfactory but still revealed a certain unease, a combination of distrust of the United States and fear of German power, that lessened the participants' willingness to put their full faith in Roosevelt. Although the conference gained more for the United States than it lost, there was less solidarity than Roosevelt thought the times required.

Meanwhile, Roosevelt and Hull steered a middle course in the Far East, trying to apply enough pressure to restrain Japan from war. Now to the mix were added stronger voices for action. In June Roosevelt had removed his isolationist secretaries of war and navy in favor of Republican internationalists. For secretary of war he nominated Henry Stimson, a crusty seventy-year-old who had served in that capacity for President Taft and had been President Hoover's secretary of state. For secretary of the navy he nominated Frank Knox, a Chicago newspaper publisher and vice presidential nominee with Governor Landon. At once both men became strong advocates of stern measures against Japan, including economic pressure and a show of naval strength. The two joined Secretary of the Interior Harold Ickes and Secretary of the Treasury Henry Morgenthau, Jr., in consistently urging vigorous measures.

As Japan refused to reestablish the Open Door policy and moved south into French Indochina, Roosevelt responded with growing firmness. By September, the United States had cut off all shipments of iron and steel scrap and was limiting shipments of aviation fuel. Roosevelt held back from a full embargo on oil, however, not wanting to push the Japanese to war. But these measures only pushed the Japanese closer to the Germans and Italians. On September 27, the three nations signed a mutual defense pact. Aimed at the United States, the pact was designed to keep the United States from picking its targets in either Europe or the Far East.[10]

Desperate cries from Churchill still occupied most of Roosevelt's attention. During the summer of 1940, the prime minister beseeched Roosevelt for destroyers from the "surplus" of the American fleet. Amid predictions of an imminent British defeat and congressional opposition to releasing any war supplies needed for American defenses, Roosevelt hesitated. Eventually, he agreed to trade fifty overage destroyers for long-term leases of

British bases in the Caribbean. It took some verbal gymnastics on both sides to publicize the deal. Churchill wanted the deal to appear to be unrelated acts of generosity on both parts; Roosevelt wanted it to fall within the cash-and-carry mandate of the neutrality laws. In the end, they agreed to a convoluted arrangement whereby Britain offered some bases as gifts and others in exchange for the destroyers. Congress, recognizing a good deal when it saw one, swung behind the president. Roosevelt announced the destroyers-for-bases deal during the early stages of his campaign for election to a third term.

Although the Constitution did not prohibit it, no president had served more than two terms. Of the thirty-five men who had served as president before Roosevelt, ten had been elected to a second term, half, including Lincoln, since the Civil War. In the hundred years before Roosevelt's first election, eight had run for a second term, and six had won. Not since 1876 and 1880, however, when the "stalwart" Republicans had wanted to nominate Ulysses Grant for a third term, had any president seriously considered making a bid.

In the usual course of events, Roosevelt would have given up the presidency and returned to Hyde Park, where he was planning to establish a library to house his presidential papers. The Nazi defeat of France, Britain's precarious state, and Japan's advances in Asia persuaded him to consider another term. In part, he decided to run because there were no good alternatives. He had encouraged Hopkins, but his ill health and unpopularity among party leaders ruled him out. The other possibilities were Vice President Garner, Secretary of State Hull, and Postmaster General Farley. Roosevelt ruled out Garner, a conservative who disliked the New Deal and was unacceptable to labor, and Farley, who stood well in party circles because of his attention to organization politics but had little foreign policy experience. The one candidate whom Roosevelt could accept, and behind whom the others could rally, was Hull. But Hull would do nothing without Roosevelt's blessing. In the end, only Farley persisted in seeking the nomination.[11]

Roosevelt's decision to seek a third term was hardly unexpected. Since 1939, Hopkins and Ickes had been publicly favoring a third term. All year, the press quizzed him about the third term, only to be put off with light remarks. If a decisive event clinched his decision, it was the Republican nomination on June 28 of Wendell Willkie. A native of Indiana but since 1929 a resident of New York City, Willkie had first emerged in the public spotlight when, as president of the Commonwealth and Southern utility company, he had opposed the TVA. But this was something of a minor detail in his overall political background, which had been Democratic and liberal. He had fought the Ku Klux Klan in Indiana, criticized monopolists in the utility industry, supported much of the New Deal domestic legislation, and opposed isolationism. His nomination, achieved in dramatic fashion by an amateur but effective organization at the convention, persuaded Roosevelt that none of the other Democratic hopefuls could be elected.[12]

On July 15, the Democratic National Convention opened. Roosevelt had chosen Chicago so that he could manage the proceedings through the Democratic boss, Ed Kelly. To convey information to Kelly, he had dispatched Harry Hopkins, with whom Kelly had worked closely and harmoniously when Hopkins was parceling out federal work relief. With Hopkins, he sent a statement to be read to the convention in which he declined to be a candidate. When he arrived, Hopkins determined that no one wanted such a statement read; it might lead the convention to nominate someone else. But Roosevelt insisted, agreeing only to postpone the statement a day so that the permanent chairman, Senator Alben Barkley, could read it. News that Hopkins had some kind of statement quickly spread. Hoping that Roosevelt might change his mind, Hopkins kept the contents to himself, stirring the anger of the delegates, many of them old-line party folk who had long resented his sharp-tongued New Dealism.

On the evening of July 16, a restless convention gathered to hear from its permanent chair. A polished orator of the old school, Barkley held his audience for half an hour. He then closed by reading Roosevelt's message: "The President has never had, and has not today, any desire or purpose to continue in the office of President, to be a candidate for that office, or to be nominated by the Convention for that office. He wishes in all earnestness and sincerity to make it clear that all the delegates to this Convention are free to vote for any candidate." Stunned, the delegates sat a long moment in silence, providing a perfect setting for what happened next. From loudspeakers placed around the hall there boomed a voice: "WE WANT ROOSEVELT." The voice, which belonged to Mayor Kelly's sewer commissioner, continued as delegates rose to their feet, first in small, scattered numbers, but ultimately in a torrential demonstration on Roosevelt's behalf. Whatever else they might think of Franklin Roosevelt, they knew that with him leading the ticket they would win. The next night, they overwhelmingly nominated him for a third term and turned to consider the vice presidential nomination.[13]

Just as he had planned to surprise the convention with his nomination ploy, Roosevelt planned to surprise the delegates with his vice presidential choice. Scouting the possibilities, he still hoped to attract progressive Republicans to his standard. His cabinet nominations of Knox and Stimson had been strong steps in that direction, and now he took another in putting forward his secretary of agriculture, Henry Wallace. Roosevelt sent word to Hopkins, who passed it along. It was the worst possible strategy. The delegates were already fed up with Hopkins's apparent arrogance in withholding Roosevelt's intentions, and now they were equally fed up with his conveying Roosevelt's choice of a former Republican and outspoken liberal. To some on the floor it seemed that they were on the verge of being fed up with Roosevelt.

One person sharing this concern was Frances Perkins, who phoned Eleanor and asked her to come to Chicago. Eleanor hesitated, but Franklin encouraged her. She flew out the next day and at once went to work calming hurt feelings. She visited with Farley, who was almost overwhelmed by her courtesy and understanding. At the convention she sat on the platform, listening to boos, whistles, and catcalls at every mention of Wallace's name. But when chairman Barkley introduced her, the delegates quieted down. Briefly, she told the convention that being president in such troubled times was a great responsibility and urged them not to increase the burden by "considerations which are narrow and partisan." "This is a time," she declared, "when it is the United States we fight for." When she concluded, the balloting for vice president began. On the floor, Hopkins, James Byrnes, and others warned the delegates that Roosevelt would not run without Wallace. When the balloting was over, Wallace had won by a large margin.[14]

On her way to the airport, Eleanor stopped for phone calls from Franklin and Hopkins. Franklin thanked her for her good work. Hopkins also thanked her and apologized for his mistakes. Eleanor made a comment that her years of experience entitled her to make: "You young things don't know politics."[15]

The early weeks of the campaign swung sharply in Roosevelt's favor. Willkie attempted to attack the New Deal, but with defense spending lessening concern about the economy, the voters were not inclined to listen. The fact that Willkie accepted many New Deal reforms such as social security further weakened his appeal. The Republican challenger also seemed as much an internationalist as Roosevelt, supporting the existing neutrality legislation, the destroyers-for-bases deal, and pending legislation for a selective service draft.

In late September, with the polls running heavily against him, Willkie struck a new note. Roosevelt's actions, he charged, were leading the United States into war. Roosevelt's reelection, he predicted, would mean war by the following April. American boys, he declared, were "already almost on the transports." Just where and how they were going to engage the Germans, who now controlled all of Europe, he did not specify. But the polling numbers showed that the public was interested not so much in the specifics as in avoidance of the very thought of war. By the end of October, as Roosevelt's campaign train whistled through New England, Willkie was within four points of the president.

During the campaign, Roosevelt stuck to his explanation that his actions were designed to protect the nation from war. But at each stop his staff loaded on dozens of messages demanding bolder assurances that the country would not fight unless attacked. As a result, on October 30, Roosevelt told a Boston audience: "And while I am talking to you mothers and fathers, I give you one more assurance. I have said this before, but I am going to say it again and again and again: your boys are not going to be sent into any foreign wars."[16]

The election results demonstrated the importance of Roosevelt's assurances. Polls showed that voters favored Roosevelt because of their confidence in his ability to handle the international situation. Since he and Willkie had both pledged to keep the country out of war, and since Roosevelt had a more consistent record as an internationalist, the polls probably showed a combined effect of internationalist support plus a general confidence in Roosevelt's ability to manage a crisis. (The polls also showed that without the international situation, voters favored Willkie.)

Franklin and Eleanor Roosevelt returning to the White House after his inauguration to an unprecedented third term, January 20, 1941. (Ruth Hamilton)

So it was up to Roosevelt to manage the international crisis. He followed the election by continuing his policies of warning the government of unoccupied France in Vichy against active military cooperation with the Nazis and by supporting massive aid to Britain. But now he had to face a new complication. Toward the end of November, British ambassador Lord Lothian informed the president and the nation that Britain could no longer afford to purchase American munitions under the cash-and-carry provisions of the neutrality laws. "Well, boys," he told American reporters, "Britain's broke. It's your money we want."

Lothian's remark raised the specter that had haunted the United States since World War I: that loans to the Allies would drag the nation into the conflict. To this was added the history of irritation, frustration, and anger toward Europe over the war debts issue, which had convinced many Americans that they had been tricked into paying the bill for Europe's war. These were perceptions that Roosevelt felt ill equipped to dispel. While he explored ways to finance the British requests, he refrained from asking Congress to revise the neutrality laws. As he prepared for a two-week vacation cruise early in December, the best he could do was to tell his advisers to "use your imaginations."

On December 9 a seaplane delivered the mail, including a long message from Prime Minister Winston Churchill. In a wide-ranging discussion of Britain's situation, the prime minister outlined measures of "constructive nonbelligerency" by which the United States could support British resistance to Hitler. Included was a suggestion that the United States provide munitions by "gift, loan, or supply." The next day Roosevelt's advisers confirmed that the British would soon be unable to pay for munitions. He now had to decide, and he decided. Without repealing or amending the neutrality acts, the United States could provide war supplies on the condition that after the war Britain would return them. As was his habit, he conceived the idea in homey terms: If your neighbor's house was on fire and he wanted to use your garden hose to put it out, you did not ask him to buy your hose. You merely asked him to return it when the fire was out. That was how Roosevelt explained the policy to the press after he had returned from vacation and put Morgenthau to work on the details. The shorthand name for the policy would be Lend-Lease.

Roosevelt had hoped that military production could be supplied out of the idle plant and manpower capacity of America's depression economy. Now, however, he realized that relaxing financial restraints on Britain's war orders would strain America's economy. In 1940, he had established a National Defense Advisory Commission (NDAC) to coordinate defense programs. At the same time as Lend-Lease was announced, Roosevelt replaced the NDAC with an Office of Production Management (OPM).

Headed by William Knudsen, an executive of the General Motors Corporation and former head of the NDAC, and including Stimson, Knox, and Sidney Hillman of the CIO, the OPM's mandate was to supervise defense production and coordinate it with civilian production. A key department was its Office of Priorities, headed by a steel company executive named Edward Stettinius, Jr.[17]

In one of his most important fireside chats since the early days of the New Deal, Roosevelt explained his policy. Much of his talk repeated the claim that aiding those resisting Hitler was the best way to keep America out of the war. But toward the end, he struck a note of peculiar urgency. In some quarters, businessmen had questioned the wisdom of expanding plant capacity, fearing that expansion would only add to the nation's surplus later on. This fear Roosevelt met head-on. The new defense requirements, he said, would require additional productive capacity. The stakes were too high to do otherwise; the nation was facing "an emergency as serious as war itself." It needed to respond with the same dedication and sacrifice as if it were at war. The United States had to become "the great arsenal of democracy."[18]

The public response indicated how the American people had moved in their thinking. Previous polls had showed about 60 percent of Americans favoring aid to Britain, even at the risk of war. Now a similar 60 percent agreed with Roosevelt's speech, and only 9 percent were opposed. The response indicated that Americans had accepted the results of the election. They seemed willing, within the limits of his speech, to support Roosevelt's leadership.

Roosevelt assigned Morgenthau to draft the Lend-Lease legislation and proposed the policy to Congress in his annual message. Emphasizing lofty objectives that went beyond the mere defense of America, he proclaimed that defeating the dictators would create a world founded on "four essential human freedoms": freedom of speech, freedom of religion, freedom from want, and freedom from fear.[19]

While Lend-Lease was under way, Roosevelt decided to strengthen his ties to Britain. In December, British ambassador Lord Lothian had died, and his replacement, Lord Halifax, had not yet arrived. At about the same time, Roosevelt had recalled his ambassador to Britain, Joseph Kennedy, who had concluded that Britain could not defeat Hitler. To fill the diplomatic gap and to act as his personal representative to Churchill, Roosevelt selected Harry Hopkins.

Roosevelt's decision was a turning point in his administration. During Roosevelt's first term, Hopkins had been a rising star in the New Deal. His performance as federal relief administrator had been imaginative, energetic, and effective. His works projects had employed millions at a low administrative cost. He had upgraded relief administrations at all levels of the federal system. He had spoken eloquently on behalf of the unemployed and during Roosevelt's reelection campaign had straightforwardly and believably defended work relief. All along he had been a loyal New Dealer. He had removed New Deal opponents from his organization; he had channeled relief funds into the hands of Roosevelt's supporters, especially to the big-city bosses. The result had been a certain amount of political favoritism in relief—encouraged by Congress's never appropriating enough money to employ all the unemployed. But Hopkins had also been remarkably successful in convincing state and local politicians that the best politics was a work relief program that gave the unemployed meaningful work that produced things of real social value. In 1937 Roosevelt had called Hopkins to his office and outlined a strategy for the relief administrator to succeed him as president.

But like so many projects of Roosevelt's second term, the promotion of Hopkins came apart at the seams. The personal and political success of work relief—80 percent of WPA workers voted for Roosevelt in 1936—made Hopkins a threat to many congressmen. His loyal support of the Court-packing plan and the party purge further tarnished his reputation. But most important was a disastrous turn in his health. In late 1937 he had gone to the Mayo Clinic in Rochester, Minnesota, where doctors removed a malignant tumor and two-thirds of his stomach. The operation would prove a success beyond all reasonable hope, accomplishing a complete cure of a disease that remains rarely curable. But Hopkins's operation left him permanently debilitated, most likely because it refashioned his digestive system in a way that kept it from absorbing nutrients. Late in 1938 Roosevelt appointed Hopkins secretary of commerce, some thought to improve his image with the business community and his attractiveness as a presidential candidate. But Hopkins could do little with the position because his health continued to deteriorate until he was near starvation. He went again to the Mayo Clinic, where heroic treatments pulled him back from the brink of death.

Hopkins had been married twice. He and his first wife, whom he had met when he was a young social worker in New York City, divorced after their marriage had produced three sons. He left her for the woman who became his second wife and the mother of their daughter. Then she died of cancer only a few months before his own operation at the Mayo Clinic. During his convalescence and subsequent battle with malnutrition, Hopkins was linked with various women, including Missy LeHand and Betsy Cushing Roosevelt, the estranged wife of Franklin's eldest son. But he remained a single parent, living in the quaint Washington suburb of Georgetown. Then, one evening early in 1940, he had dinner at the White House, stayed the night, and was invited by the president to move in. He was on hand during the Nazi blitz and observed Roosevelt's methods as he attempted to devise a way to support the Western democracies against Hitler. Roosevelt sent him to Chicago with instructions to arrange his nomination to a third term. In this capacity, the consensus opinion, which included his own, was that he had performed poorly. His prospects dimmed. That fall he officially resigned his cabinet post and prepared to move back to New York. He participated in the campaign in a desultory fashion and was in Hyde Park to hear the returns. He was with Roosevelt during the cruise when Churchill's decisive letter arrived. He sat in on White House meetings that discussed Lend-Lease and the strategy for selling it to the American people and Congress. It was by these events, so many of them fortuitous, that he became the one person most intimately acquainted with Roosevelt and best qualified to carry out his purposes.

In many ways, Hopkins and Roosevelt were an odd match. Roosevelt was the smooth, confident, urbane leader who soothed people with fireside chats and light, neighborly banter. Hopkins was a wisecracking chain-smoker who tossed off sarcastic one-liners and delivered rough judgments aimed at deflating lofty ideals and puncturing pompous egos. Yet beneath the surface, the two were quite compatible. Both were social reformers who passionately wanted to help the unemployed. Both were activists who kept at problems until they found a solution. Both were extremely sensitive to others and knew how to reach out. More than this, both had a genius for cooperative effort. Roosevelt could inspire loyalty to his vision of a better society and a better world and let it be known that he would not tolerate dissension and bickering. Hopkins could win people's confidence by convincing them that he understood their problems and would do his best to help. Both were adept at forming networks of people they could use as flexible instruments for responding to situations. Both seemed comfortable in unfolding situations, swimming in a stream of events that demanded frequent changes of direction.

In Hopkins, Roosevelt had found the perfect instrument for his style of governance. All along, Roosevelt had sought consensus, but he had often been unable to achieve it except by ordering the disagreeing parties to lock themselves in a room until they resolved their differences. In Hopkins he had found someone capable of achieving consensus by winning people's confidence. Hopkins brought to Roosevelt the added talent of being a shrewd judge of character and ability. It was Hopkins who pressed Roosevelt to name General George C. Marshall the army chief of staff. Roosevelt once told someone that in Hopkins he had a person who existed only to serve him. His statement underestimated Hopkins's abilities.

After conferring with Roosevelt and members of the British embassy, Hopkins flew to England. He was an instant and inevitable hit. Churchill

Roosevelt and his most trusted and effective aide, Harry Hopkins, June 1942. (Franklin D. Roosevelt Library)

rolled out the red carpet and treated Hopkins to long disquisitions on turning the strategic situation to Britain's advantage. Hopkins reciprocated by assuring the prime minister that Roosevelt's only aim was "to beat the son-of-a-bitch in Berlin." They toured defense installations from Dover to Scotland, putting on a kind of Winston-and-Harry show in which Churchill would draw out Hopkins on American intentions and Hopkins would commit the United States to the British cause. Before he left, carrying a list of Britain's ten most vital materiel needs, Hopkins had become a figure in his own right and a man whom Churchill would lionize in his memoirs. The feeling was mutual. "Jesus Christ," Hopkins muttered late one night as he warmed himself in a Scottish hotel, "what a man!" By the end of his visit, Hopkins was spicing his reports to Roosevelt with brave Churchillian rhetoric.

This was all well and good for Hopkins, but for Roosevelt it meant that the man who returned from England in late February had grown immensely in value. Now Hopkins was the man best able to develop the Lend-Lease partnership with Britain. At once he set about establishing his contacts with British military and supply representatives and putting together a network of strategically placed American officials that became known as "the Hopkins Shop." Operating out of an office in the Lincoln bedroom with a bare-bones administrative staff, Hopkins worked to bring the British and Americans together, hoping to balance British war demands with American defense needs. At times it proved an agonizing job, and Hopkins often found himself clarifying misunderstandings and soothing bruised egos, but in the end, he made Lend-Lease the principal instrument of the American-British partnership.[20]

A major step along the road to war: Roosevelt signs the Lend-Lease Bill, March 11, 1941. (© CORBIS/Bettmann)

In March, Congress passed the Lend-Lease bill, and the next month appropriated $7 billion to fund it. The passage of Lend-Lease removed the need for Britain to pay cash for materiel, but it raised the question of how to carry the goods to Britain. Roosevelt's military advisers, led by Secretary of War Stimson, declared that without U.S. military intervention, German submarine attacks would block the supply effort. Roosevelt was unwilling to take that step but worked to increase American and British shipping in the North Atlantic. Then, early in April, he extended American patrolling of its "neutrality zone" to include Greenland and the Azores and promised the British that the patrols would report the presence of German submarines. There his policy rested while German troops slashed through southeastern Europe. In the meantime, a core group of his advisers—Stimson, Knox, Ickes, Morgenthau, and Hopkins—favored stronger leadership and bolder steps.

But where his advisers saw opportunities, Roosevelt saw problems. They argued that his leadership could decisively tip an American opinion that was now almost evenly divided between opposition to and support for a more aggressive policy; he believed that opinion would not change so easily. They wanted him to transfer most of the Pacific Fleet to control the North Atlantic; he worried that weakness in the Pacific would encourage the Japanese to expand farther south. (On April 13, Japan had signed a neutrality pact with the Soviet Union.) They wanted him to order the occupation of strategic Atlantic islands; he worried that his critics would charge him with aggression. When the military chiefs proposed all-out military aid to Britain, he counseled against "any aggressive action until [the military] was fully prepared to undertake it."[21] Roosevelt's responses seemed better suited to recognizing dilemmas than to prescribing action. His call for American preparedness at a time when British Lend-Lease orders were pressing against the American military's defense plans seemed particularly indecisive. Indeed, he had no intention of leading the nation. To him, there seemed to be only one course: let events provide justification for more forceful action. He wanted "to be pushed into war, rather than to lead into it," he told Morgenthau. "Our problem being one of defense," he explained to his ambassador to Tokyo, Joseph Grew, "we cannot lay down hard and fast plans. As each new development occurs we must, in the light of circumstances then existing, decide when and where and how we can most effectively marshal and make use of our resources."[22]

The most he seemed willing to do was to create a climate of opinion ready to perceive almost any incident as a cause for war. Toward the end of May he delivered an address in which he charged Hitler with ambitions of world domination, extended American security far beyond its borders ("our Bunker Hill of tomorrow may be several thousand miles from Boston"), and proclaimed an "unlimited national emergency." At a press conference the next day he assured the nation that he intended to take no further action. Two weeks later, in the wake of news that a German submarine had sunk an American merchant freighter in the South Atlantic, Hopkins, in collaboration with the British, urged him to establish a "security patrol" to protect the sea-lanes by force. Roosevelt shrugged him off.

The problem with Roosevelt's formulation was that it pointed to defeat. By June, Nazi submarines were sinking British ships at three times the rate of replacement. As long as the United States did nothing, Germany would eventually strangle the island democracy. In these circumstances, Hitler had little incentive to provoke the United States.

On June 22, Hitler's invasion of Russia created another critical "development." The diversion of German military to the east temporarily took pressure off Britain. The invasion also afforded Japan the choice of supporting its Axis partner by striking north into Siberia and thus halting its drive to the south and a collision course with the United States. But should the United States respond by stepping up supplies to Britain and China, or should it now divert supplies to the Russians? The issue was complicated by fierce anticommunist sentiment, especially among Irish and Polish Catholics, an important constituency of the Democratic Party, and by U.S. military opinion, which gave the Red Army little chance of holding out against the Germans. For a few days, Roosevelt temporized. Then, at the end of June, he decided to aid Russia. He was not taking much of a risk. A Russian collapse would come before any substantial American resources could arrive, and American supplies might help the Russians hold off the Germans until winter, tying down hundreds of German divisions and relieving the pressure on the British. In July he set up a structure for supplying the Russians and goaded his administrators to make it work. On July 27 he received a message from Harry Hopkins suggesting that Roosevelt send him to Moscow to size up the Russian situation. Hopkins was in London, conferring with Churchill about meeting with Roosevelt in August. Seeing an opportunity for personal diplomacy, Roosevelt approved Hopkins's mission and provided him a letter to Marshal Stalin, informing him that Hopkins had come to scout out ways to provide American aid as rapidly as possible and that the Soviet leader should speak with him "with the identical confidence you would feel if you were talking directly to me." In Moscow, Hopkins accepted Stalin's assurances, as he had earlier accepted Churchill's, and reported to Roosevelt that the Russians could hold out. He suggested a conference with the United States and Britain to arrange the provision of supplies to Russia and acquired Stalin's frank estimate of his country's war needs. From then on, Hopkins remained a passionate advocate of all-out aid to Russia.

In the wake of the German invasion of the USSR, Roosevelt asked the army to come up with a statement of the production requirements for victory by the United States, Great Britain, and the Soviet Union. Working under hothouse conditions, the army produced a $150 billion program that would take until 1944 to complete. Labeled the "Victory Program," it never went into effect but temporarily provided food for isolationist propaganda when the *Chicago Tribune,* bastion of Middle West isolation and anti-Roosevelt politics, published its contents as Roosevelt's plan for war. The *Tribune*'s edition appeared on December 4, 1941, giving its readers little time to reflect on its significance before Japanese bombs began falling on Pearl Harbor.[23]

In the meantime, Roosevelt moved to reconfigure the anti-Nazi coalition. In September a joint British-American supply mission visited Moscow and offered large amounts of aid with no strings attached. The United States went so far as to make Russian supplies a special "protocol" with privileged status in Lend-Lease production. Roosevelt considered these favors payment for the nearly 300 Russian divisions that were keeping the pressure off Britain and chewing up German men and materiel. That fall, all American military estimates ranked the Russian front as the key element in predicting the course of the war.

Roosevelt's opportunity to revise the anti-Nazi coalition came at the Atlantic Conference, where he met secretly with Churchill in Placentia Bay off the coast of Newfoundland. In their conversations, Roosevelt made it plain that he disapproved of British colonialism. After considerable discussion and some wrangling, the two produced a joint declaration that disavowed territorial conquest and committed the two to seeking a world of independent, democratic states and international cooperation to improve working conditions and living standards. It was a decided contrast from Hopkins's assurances in January that Roosevelt's only concern was to "beat that son-of-a-bitch in Berlin." But Churchill was in no position to bring up pointed contrasts.

The Atlantic Conference also served a number of secondary objectives. The American military chiefs came away with a better understanding of the British need for war materiel and a greater willingness to discuss how to allocate American production. At the same time, the Americans questioned the British determination to hold the Middle East against the Germans, fearing that it would weaken their island defenses. The British chiefs gained a more precise appreciation of America's productive capacity and the political difficulties that Roosevelt faced in nudging his nation toward more active engagement.[24]

Roosevelt's desire to drape his defense plans in the mantle of democratic nationalism and social well-being caused him to seek ways to apologize for giving aid to the Soviet Union. He encouraged Pope Pius XII to declare that support for Russia should be separated from support for communism; he encouraged leading Catholics in his administration to speak in favor of aid to Russia. He tried (unsuccessfully) to interpret the Soviet constitution's guarantee of freedom of conscience with the American freedom of religion. He also pointedly characterized Nazism as a greater threat to religious values than communism.

The major purpose of the conference was to build an Anglo-American partnership, looking toward an Anglo-American-Soviet partnership. At the conference, Roosevelt assured Churchill that he "would wage war, but not declare it." As public opinion polls reported deeply divided feelings for and against stronger measures, Roosevelt held firm in believing that only an "incident" would justify them and that only Hitler could supply such an incident. He was unwilling to risk war without the support of a broad and firm public consensus. He was ready, however, to force an "incident." He gave substance to his words by promising to occupy the Azores and to escort British supply convoys in the North Atlantic. As soon as he returned to Washington, he arranged for American ships to perform escort duty as far as Iceland.

Roosevelt's policy involved him in a major public deception. Reading polls that showed that three-fourths of Americans opposed entering the war, he continued publicly to describe the navy's mission as patrolling to defend the Western Hemisphere. Nothing showed his purposes more clearly than his response to the *Greer* incident. In early September a German submarine exchanged fire with the American destroyer *Greer*. In keeping with Roosevelt's escorting policy, a British seaplane had alerted the *Greer* to the presence of a German submarine. The *Greer* chased the submarine, and in two encounters they exchanged depth charges and torpedoes with damage to neither. Two days later, in a national radio address, Roosevelt described the incident as an unprovoked attack on an American vessel that was attempting to maintain freedom of the seas. Magnifying the incident into evidence of Hitler's determination to establish "a permanent world system based on force, on terror, and on murder," Roosevelt declared German submarines "the rattlesnakes of the Atlantic" and announced that henceforth when American vessels encountered them their orders would be to "shoot on sight." Roosevelt had inaugurated an undeclared naval war in the North Atlantic.

But if Roosevelt was deceiving the American people, the American people were also deceiving themselves. Polls showed over 60 percent approval for his "shoot on sight policy," along with over 70 percent who desired to keep out of the war. In other words, they kept their desires for Hitler's defeat and for staying out of the war in separate compartments.

Roosevelt had nurtured this state of mind and indeed used it to justify his steps in aiding Britain. Now in his characterizing the *Greer* incident as an unprovoked attack, he had continued to define his policy within that same context. Americans could support "shoot on sight" as a defensive response of a peaceful nation. When Roosevelt complained, as he often did these days, that the American people did not understand the realities they faced and needed to "wake up," he was describing a condition to which he had regularly contributed. Little changed in the weeks following. Roosevelt asked Congress to revise the neutrality laws to permit him to arm American merchant ships and to permit them to sail into belligerent ports. Congress dallied into mid-November and then passed the legislation by narrow margins. Not even the loss of American lives to torpedo attacks on two navy destroyers could do more than advance this mild response.

Thus, by the fall of 1941, Roosevelt had failed to convince the American people that Germany presented an immediate danger. This was the sum total of his shortcomings of leadership. Those, including Professor Robert Dallek, who have charged him with a larger failure—of setting a precedent of American presidents' misleading their people to support military conflicts—go further than the evidence permits. Franklin Roosevelt was not the first president to lead his country toward a war that a large proportion of the American people were disinclined to accept. Nor was he the first president to take steps that invited war while declaring peaceful purposes. Most presidents who have faced the prospect of war have been strongly influenced by domestic political considerations (a possible exception being Woodrow Wilson). Scholars who see Roosevelt's deceptions as setting a precedent need to make their case on other than historical grounds.

In the meantime, Roosevelt's adjustments seemed to be having little effect on defense production. By October and November, shortages were cropping up everywhere. But the new agencies did provide Roosevelt with instruments for setting priorities and allocating the shortages. Aided by Hopkins, who continually goaded and pressed everyone involved, the president decided to favor short-term aid to Britain and the Soviet Union over the longer-term U.S. defense buildup.

By midautumn, Roosevelt seemed to have run out of momentum. In the North Atlantic, the United States and Germany were waging undeclared war on too small a scale to mobilize public sentiment for sterner measures. Production was creaking along short of Lend-Lease and defense needs, and Harry Hopkins, worn down with his efforts to move things along, was spending his days in a navy hospital.

Roosevelt's Atlantic policy was resting on dead center. Every action had produced a reaction. He could aid the British and the Soviets but could not cooperate with them lest he be accused of following their leadership. His stern warnings and ringing declarations fell flat. His "incidents" failed to stir a warlike spirit. With Lend-Lease taking priority in defense production and with production lagging in every category, he lacked the resources for bolder American moves. He was leading a nation willing to risk war but not to prepare for it.

Roosevelt could not have known that in these circumstances he was following the best course. If he had taken the advice of Hopkins, Morgenthau, and others who argued for a more assertive policy, he might have led a divided nation into the conflict, perhaps a nation more divided than the one Woodrow Wilson had led into the previous war. As it was, however, American opinion provided him just enough room for activity to bring the nation into war under the best political circumstances—but not in the icy waters of the North Atlantic.

By the summer, U.S.-Japanese relations had entered a danger zone. For a time, Japanese leaders had considered honoring their mutual defense obligations in their alliance with Germany and Italy by attacking the USSR, but the Soviet resistance to the Germans proved stiffer than they had anticipated, and the Japanese military did not want to battle the United States, Britain, and the Soviet Union. Moreover, they knew that their ability to prevail in any war depended on reliable supplies of oil, which they could obtain only in the Dutch East Indies. As a result, they decided to move south into French Indochina; to cut off the Burma Road, over which the British and Americans were sending supplies to China; and to establish bases from which to strike at the Dutch. Roosevelt's response was to tell the Japanese that he wanted to improve relations while warning them against further aggression. He had earlier proposed to neutralize Indochina.

Both sides were now on the path to war. To a greater or lesser degree, both sides wanted to keep time on their side. In the United States, the polls showed that Americans wanted to protect their interests in the Pacific, but without going to war. Roosevelt had little reason to believe that relations with Japan could actually improve, but he wanted to play for time, hoping that the Russians would hold out long enough for the British and Americans to strengthen their defenses. In Tokyo the sense of time was somewhat more precise, calculated in part on the effect of reduced petroleum stocks resulting from the American embargo and on the time needed to complete preparations for a war in the Pacific. Tokyo struggled with its options. At a dramatic and unprecedented moment in August, Emperor Hirohito personally intervened to place diplomacy at the top of his nation's agenda.[25]

In September, the Japanese military gave officials until mid-October to improve relations with the United States before it would take action. Negotiations dragged on, with neither side willing to concede anything the other considered vital. When the critical date arrived with no improvement, Prince Konoye resigned as foreign minister. The emperor, accepting advice that the army ought to take responsibility, since it had precipitated the resignation, named General Hideki Tojo to lead the government. In meetings on November 1 and 5, the military decided to pursue diplomacy until midnight, November 30. After that time, the Japanese war plan would go into effect. The Japanese plan called for swift strikes at American, British, and Dutch possessions in the western Pacific. The most daring part of the plan called for a raid on the American naval base at Pearl Harbor, Hawaii.

Roosevelt was aware of a shadowy outline of the Japanese strategy. American intelligence, working under the code name MAGIC, had broken the Japanese diplomatic code. They had not, however, broken the Japanese military codes, which conveyed specific information about military plans. Early in November, Roosevelt received word from MAGIC that Tokyo had given its ambassadors until November 25 to resolve things with the United States diplomatically, which meant, in effect, giving in to all Japanese proposals, including control over Manchuria and much of China. Another message extended the deadline to November 29 but declared that in the absence of a settlement by that date, "things are automatically going to happen."

Now war in the Pacific was an apparent possibility. Although the American and British strategy had called for a "Germany first" priority, it had not ruled out war with Japan. Accordingly, Roosevelt was willing to accept war. Drawing an analogy with his experience in the Atlantic, he assumed that Japan would not attack the United States directly but would move against the British or the Dutch. He was prepared to interpret such a move as a cause for war but realized that he would need to prepare American opinion to accept that interpretation. The consequence of this was that, in the phrase of Eric Larrabee, he "undercalculated" Japanese intentions, not realizing that once they had decided that a move south would probably cause war with the United States, they would minimize their risks by striking directly at the adversary.[26]

On November 27, all Pacific commands received a message from General Marshall, telling them that diplomatic negotiations with Japan were ending and were uncertain to resume. Hostile action could occur "at any moment." The U.S. position was that Japan should commit the first "overt act," but the commands should not be restricted to actions that might jeopardize their defenses. Commanders should undertake reconnaissance or other defensive measures, but in ways that did not alarm the civilian population or "disclose intent." Lieutenant General John DeWitt, commanding the Fourth Army and the Western Defense Command, immediately established a harbor alert at San Francisco, ordered a full alert at Alaska, and initiated cooperative measures with the navy. General Frank M. Andrews of the Caribbean Defense Command promptly set up an interservice twenty-four-hour alert.[27]

On Oahu, General Walter Short interpreted this as continuing business as usual. Thus he confined his reconnaissance to inland observation and took steps to put his radar into full operation. Of all the possible dangers he contemplated, the only one he took seriously was sabotage. At naval headquarters, Admiral Husband E. Kimmel was receiving a similar but more strongly worded set of instructions. Anticipating Japanese movements against the Philippines, Malaya, Thailand, and Borneo, the message conveyed a "war warning" and ordered Kimmel to deploy his forces according to the navy's basic war plan. Kimmel dispatched the message to Short, who downplayed its seriousness. Each of the navy brass in Washington had a specific understanding of how Kimmel should deploy his forces, but in deference to his authority as the commander on the scene, and perhaps to the differences among their own understandings, they left the key decision up to him. Anticipating nothing worse than submarine attacks on his position and expecting that his ships would respond to Japanese advances far to the west, Kimmel ordered depth charge attacks on unauthorized submarines and increased training under his command. Most tellingly, he decided to conserve his aircraft and not to patrol the sector northwest of his command. If he had, he would have discovered the Japanese attack force. Thus, both Short and Kimmel failed to conduct the reconnaissance that Washington believed it had ordered. Short's fear of sabotage caused him to compound the problem by locking up antiaircraft ammunition miles from its guns and clustering aircraft on the interior of the fields to protect them from saboteurs. The result was that the air corps could not respond effectively to the Japanese strike, and the Japanese found themselves attacking clusters of sitting ducks.[28]

So it was that shortly after dawn on December 7, a Japanese torpedo plane roared down on the Pacific Fleet that peacefully rested in Pearl Harbor. Dive-bombers followed. At the same time, other dive-bombers attacked the air forces at Hickham and Wheeler fields. The raid was a complete surprise and struck the American forces with devastating effect. The Pacific Fleet was in ruins except for three aircraft carriers that were absent that day. The nation and Franklin Roosevelt's presidency had sustained a blow that would draw the attention of scholars indefinitely.

Roosevelt learned of the Pearl Harbor attack shortly after 1 P.M., Washington time. He and Harry Hopkins had settled down for a leisurely afternoon, Roosevelt planning to go over his stamp collection. All that changed with a ring of the phone and word from Secretary of the Navy Frank Knox.

Hopkins was shocked at the news, but Roosevelt said that it was just what the Japanese might be expected to do. Seemingly calmed by an event that had clarified everything and given him a definite direction and purpose, he set about consulting with his cabinet and members of Congress and preparing a message to a joint session the next day. He told everyone not to lay blame at this stage but to concentrate on the essential fact that the United States was "in it." The next day he stood before a joint session of Congress and asked for a declaration of war against Japan. He seemed to be back where he had started, facing a nation gripped by crisis and willing to follow his leadership. Only one member, pacifist Jeanette Rankin of Montana, voted no.[29]

Shortly thereafter, Germany and Italy declared war on the United States. Roosevelt's presidency had entered an entirely new phase.

10

★★★★★

FROM UNITY TO PREEMINENCE

Because of Pearl Harbor, Franklin Roosevelt led a united nation into World War II.[1] Pledges of support poured in from every corner of the nation. Roosevelt moved at once to employ the nation's unity as a base on which to build an alliance. When Churchill proposed a meeting, Roosevelt invited him to Washington and arranged for him to stay at the White House. At the meeting, called the Arcadia Conference, Roosevelt pressed for a joint declaration of principles that would confirm the Atlantic Charter. Churchill agreed, and after some adjusting that added the names of small countries, the parties signed the declaration at a White House ceremony on New Year's Day 1942.

Although Roosevelt welcomed the opportunity to fight alongside Britain, he approached their relationship with certain reservations. Although the United States had long been an imperial power, it still harbored suspicions of European colonialism. At this point in the war, Roosevelt anticipated that British colonialism would be a major obstacle to postwar peace. Especially within the State Department, there was the belief that the British were past masters at arranging a world of "balances" and "spheres of influence" to magnify their power and wealth at the expense of others. To many of these people, the key to a successful outcome would be dismantling the British system of trading preferences that limited non-British trade with its imperial and commonwealth states.[2] Among the American military, this attitude first arose as suspicions that the British would use Lend-Lease to build up their power while denuding American defenses. Soon it

Winston Churchill and Roosevelt, May 24, 1943. Roosevelt considered Churchill the lesser of his wartime partners. (U.S. Office of War Information)

would reappear as suspicions that Churchill would dupe Roosevelt into following his strategic designs.

The definition of Britain as a "colonial" power powerfully directed American thinking about the relationship. It led Americans to conclude that most other nations distrusted Britain—in the case of other European nations, because the British had competed against them for imperial gain; in the case of India, because it chafed under British rule; in the case of other colonies or small states, because they feared that the British regarded them as possible spoils of victory; or, in the case of the Soviet Union, because it was ideologically opposed to imperialism. Such thinking prepared the Americans to think of themselves as "honest brokers," able to win the "trust" or "confidence" of others by trumpeting the principles of the Atlantic Charter. It also encouraged them to make deals unilaterally, entirely ignoring British interests.[3] Indeed, it was even possible for the Americans conveniently to assume that the British constituted an obstacle to their selfless aims and that the two were to some degree rivals. A successful partnership would require Roosevelt's balancing these views with the need to establish a productive relationship.

The solution turned out to be allied unity. Again and again the Americans insisted on combining their efforts, thus giving themselves a strong voice, if not always a veto, on war policies.

Discussions of military strategy proceeded more bumpily but still satisfactorily. Roosevelt and Churchill reaffirmed their commitment to defeating Germany first. The president also showed interest in Churchill's proposal to start offensive action in North Africa, where prospects for an early victory that would bolster home-front morale seemed promising. But the U.S. military objected, arguing that the operation would be more difficult than it appeared on the surface and griping behind the scenes that the British were trying to use the Americans to fight the war for British objectives.

Roosevelt had better success in developing mechanisms of Anglo-American cooperation. The conference produced joint boards to manage the allocation of munitions and other supplies. The conference also established a unified command system in a Combined Chiefs of Staff, wherein British and American service chiefs sat together to consider strategy. The first evidence that such an organization would work came over the allocation of munitions. The British had wanted separate systems of allocation, with themselves and the Americans responsible for supplying certain nations. This proposal, sure to prod American suspicions of Britain's "spheres of influence" strategy, provoked General Marshall to threaten to resign unless the conference adopted a unified system. Marshall got his way. The Americans also got the British to agree to establish combined boards to oversee other aspects of war mobilization and operations.[4]

Nothing bedeviled the Anglo-American alliance as issues of colonialism. During the Arcadia Conference, Roosevelt had pressed Churchill to reach an accord with the nationalists in India, both to appease American public opinion and to bolster the Indian defense against a possible Japanese attack. Churchill reluctantly agreed to make the effort but deeply resented Roosevelt's chiding him on the issue. Eventually, Roosevelt, more interested in unity with the British than in reforming British colonial policy, dropped the subject—but only for the moment.

Roosevelt also moved to establish close and supportive ties to China. Domestic politics strongly influenced Roosevelt, since Americans had long held favorable, even romantic, views about China as a land of democracy and enterprise—a kind of United States East. China's suffering at the hands of the Japanese had heightened these feelings. Serious opinion held that if China fell, all of Asia would swing toward Japanese leadership. It was also common wisdom that relations between the British and the Chinese were too sour to permit real cooperation and progress and that American good offices were needed. That spring, Roosevelt established the China, Burma,

India Command and appointed General Joseph Stilwell to head it. At the same time, he appointed Stilwell chief of staff to Chinese president Chiang Kai-shek. Roosevelt had taken an important step toward enlarging his country's influence in the Anglo-American partnership.

Meanwhile, in Washington there were other signs of a strengthening American presence. In this, no one played a larger role than Harry Hopkins. After Pearl Harbor, Hopkins became Roosevelt's right-hand man. He had been a central figure at Arcadia, where he had strongly spoken up for the interests of the American military, especially of Chief of Staff General George Marshall. A stiff, formal, almost totally humorless man but possessing an iron will and unshakable integrity, Marshall had never felt at ease with Roosevelt's lighthearted and discursive bantering and, more important, with his obvious familiarity with and apparent preference for the navy. At the outset of the war, Hopkins encouraged Marshall to take a leading role with the president and became a spokesman for Marshall's point of view.[5]

Now Hopkins extended his reach into the war effort. At Arcadia he became chair of the Munitions Assignments Board, which allocated weaponry among the Allies. When Roosevelt established a War Shipping Administration to oversee ship construction and allocation, Hopkins became a friend and mentor to its chief, Lewis Douglas. Rapidly, his influence spread. Whenever a problem arose—ships for Russia, aircraft for Britain, steel to build warships—Harry Hopkins was at the center of the debate, smoothing ruffled feathers, massaging egos, promising fair treatment, putting together ad hoc "committees" to talk through the problem, and arranging conferences with Roosevelt, before which he primed the president's decision. Before long, everyone—the British included—was paying less attention to the formal machinery of Anglo-American cooperation and focusing on Harry Hopkins. "There are," one British official observed, "no front stairs in Washington."[6]

While Hopkins worked behind to scenes to coordinate the war effort, Roosevelt bolstered home-front morale. When the services brought him a recommendation for aircraft production, he doubled it. He also established a War Production Board, charged with managing the stepped-up demands for war materiel. As the Japanese swept through the Southwest Pacific, he ordered a carrier-based air strike on Tokyo. In the meantime, he promised the American people victories in the near future and publicly criticized those who found fault with the war effort. Privately, he categorized his critics as the prewar isolationists.[7]

Indeed, one of Roosevelt's major activities was to use his new freedom of action against his opponents. He pressed Attorney General Francis Biddle to stop "antiwar talk." He cut off telephone communications with neutral embassies to stymie Axis espionage. He charged J. Edgar Hoover's Federal Bureau of Investigation with tracking down and removing "aliens" from sensitive occupations. Talk around the White House identified his isolationist critics as "Nazis" or "a Nazi-minded person."[8]

To Roosevelt's thinking, no group of "aliens" was more dangerous than Japanese Americans. Motivated by the need to stifle all controversy about the war and to sweep up all Americans in a great consensus of patriotic support for his leadership and the war effort, he permitted the army to remove over 100,000 Japanese Americans from their homes, farms, and businesses on the West Coast to "concentration camps" in the interior of the country. This move was inspired by the hysteria that followed Pearl Harbor and fed by reports and rumors of extensive espionage by Japanese residents of Hawaii, suspicions of Japanese nationals who espoused loyalty to their homeland and the emperor, and stories that magnified Japanese actions into seditious conspiracies. The move was backed by white business interests such as the California Growers Association, by currents of anti-Asian racism that had run through West Coast society since the 1880s, and by political leaders who were as eager as Roosevelt to ride the bandwagon of wartime patriotism. The consequence was to benefit certain white businesses and interests at the expense and suffering of American citizens who had never been charged with any crime or act of disloyalty. Scholars have long since concluded that the relocation was unnecessary and unjustified. In 1988 Congress passed the Civil Liberties Act, which included reparations to families of those who had been interned.[9]

Roosevelt also moved to take command of war strategy. During the latter weeks of winter, there developed in the White House a view that Britain was weakening. Japanese advances in the Pacific were matched by successful German offensives in North Africa. Churchill returned from Washington to face hard questions in Parliament and responded by reorganizing his cabinet. Perceived British weakness opened the door for a planning offensive by the U.S. Army. In February and March the army developed a plan to establish a bridgehead in northern France. The operation would rally British morale with American support; shipping the necessary troops and materiel to Britain would require clearing the Atlantic sea-lanes, and the bridgehead would take pressure off the Russian front. The Russian objective was especially attractive militarily, because the Joint Chiefs placed Russian resistance near the top of their priorities for defeating Germany. It was also attractive diplomatically as a way of diverting attention from territorial issues. Churchill was under pressure in both Moscow and London to recognize Soviet territorial conquests in the Baltic as a way of assuring Stalin's goodwill. Still clinging to the principles of the Atlantic Charter, Roosevelt wanted to avoid sacrificing previously independent states.[10] Pressured by Stalin's demands for his territorial claims, Roosevelt approved a plan to invade France by the spring of 1943 (Operation ROUNDUP). The operation would be accompanied by a huge military buildup in Britain (Operation BOLERO) and by raids along the French coast. In the event of a possible Russian collapse, the Allies would launch an emergency attack (Operation SLEDGEHAMMER). In mid-April, Roosevelt dispatched Harry Hopkins and General Marshall to London to sell the plan to Churchill. In the meantime, he recommended that Churchill allow him to deal with Stalin.[11]

In London, the Hopkins-Marshall mission successfully pressed its case on a reluctant Churchill and his chiefs, obtaining the concession to let circumstances dictate whether to undertake Operation SLEDGEHAMMER. Marshall was delighted, because the decision seemed to concentrate attention on a single major objective and undercut Roosevelt's flirtation with a North Africa operation, which he considered a "dispersal" of military resources. As soon as he heard of the British agreement, Roosevelt persuaded Stalin to send his foreign minister, V. M. Molotov, to Washington. The American offensive seemed about to pay high dividends.

Almost immediately, things began to unravel. The British expressed new reservations about SLEDGEHAMMER. Stalin began to show signs of playing the British and Americans off against each other; he pressed his territorial demands and praised the British when the Americans announced that they were cutting their Russian shipments to support the buildup for SLEDGEHAMMER and ROUNDUP. Feeling their influence slipping away, the Americans increased their investment in SLEDGEHAMMER. What at first had been a secondary, emergency plan now emerged as the centerpiece of U.S. strategy. When Molotov arrived in Washington, Roosevelt promised him offensive action in 1942—which in American terms, meant SLEDGEHAMMER.

But Roosevelt was in no position to carry out his offensive. When he pressed his military chiefs for a commitment to SLEDGEHAMMER, they temporized. Molotov did his part by picturing a Soviet collapse if the Allies failed to establish a second front and to maintain their supply commitments. Irritated but not stymied, Roosevelt ordered his chiefs to consider possibilities other than SLEDGEHAMMER and invited Churchill to Washington to discuss alternatives. Since the prime minister had continued to urge a North African landing, it was likely that this would emerge as the critical issue. But the conference proved inconclusive, and not until Churchill had returned to London did he and his chiefs come down against SLEDGEHAMMER. In turn, Roosevelt instructed Hopkins and Marshall to return to London to pin down "definite plans" for an operation in 1942.

Roosevelt's order sealed the fate of American strategy. By demanding action that year, he handed the initiative to the British. When they rejected SLEDGEHAMMER, they left only the Middle East or North Africa. Although Marshall still tried to hold out, Hopkins informed Roosevelt at once so that he could take the initiative. The result was an agreement to undertake the North African operation (subsequently named Operation TORCH).

Roosevelt's drive for unity with the British had produced not exactly bitter but certainly unappetizing fruit. The American chiefs were disappointed, and Stalin's reaction was problematic. Determined to boost home-front morale, to maintain Anglo-American unity, and to dissuade Stalin and Churchill from territorial deals, Roosevelt had temporarily jeopardized his leadership. Reacting to circumstances, he had permitted his military chiefs to push a strategy that had been designed more for their own political purposes—to undercut British designs for a "peripheral" strategy—than for Roosevelt's.

It was time to pick up the pieces. In the aftermath of the North African landings, Roosevelt fashioned a new plan for U.S. leadership. Roosevelt explored ways to provide the Soviets direct military support by sending American aircraft to the Caucasus Mountains, where the Red Army was fighting a desperate battle for the city of Stalingrad. A Soviet loss on that front would open up strategic oil reserves to the German army and position it to threaten Turkey, establish a new front in the Middle East, and perhaps even swing toward India for a possible linkup with the Japanese. Roosevelt further suggested a top-level military conference with the British and Soviets. He established a Soviet Protocol Committee and charged it to deliver aid to the USSR with no questions asked. He was concerned about complaints from his ambassador to Moscow, William Standley, who had returned to Washington to argue that the United States should ask the Soviets to justify their Lend-Lease requests.[12]

All these moves were part of an emerging design for the postwar world. Ever since the United States had entered the war, various groups and persons had proposed formulas for the world, many of them conflicting and all of them controversial. Wanting to maintain national unity in the face of a dangerous military situation and wary of British and Soviet designs on territorial and, in the British case, colonial spoils that would subvert the ideals of the Atlantic Charter, Roosevelt looked for an alternative. A clue emerged when the Soviets responded favorably to his suggestion that after the war the victorious powers act as "world policemen" to guarantee the peace. What the idea needed was a mechanism for its enforcement, which Roosevelt supplied with the doctrine of "unconditional surrender."

The idea of unconditional surrender had emerged in the spring of 1942, when a subcommittee on security issues had recommended it as a way to avoid the difficulties of a negotiated peace. As Roosevelt interpreted it, unconditional surrender would permit the Allies to occupy the territories of their defeated enemies, disarm them, and establish their own standing as the world's policemen. Operating this way would preserve Allied unity during the war by disallowing negotiations with the enemy, something that Stalin had threatened his Western partners with from time to time. It would also concentrate the Allies' attention on winning the war instead of making territorial deals among themselves.

Most important, unconditional surrender would buy time for the United States to establish its world leadership. As usual, whenever he found himself in a group of friends or allies, Roosevelt was all for equality, as long as he could call the shots. By the end of the war, he expected a much different arrangement of forces from the one that existed in mid-1942. He particularly expected Britain to be more amenable to American anticolonialism. Throughout the year, Harry Hopkins was saying that he expected Churchill to leave office as soon as the war ended. Among other things, Churchill's departure would clear the way for a reorganization of the British empire along lines similar to the United States' supervision of the Philippines—a kind of benign tutelage under international supervision, looking toward independence.[13]

Thus, like Operation SLEDGEHAMMER, unconditional surrender became a means of drawing together various objectives. The question remained whether the doctrine had any more staying power than its predecessor. Much depended on the success of the North African campaign. Roosevelt was elated at the success of the landings, but political consequences clouded the initial success. The president attributed the light resistance of French troops in Algiers to his policy of maintaining diplomatic relations with the collaborationist Vichy regime. This, in his mind, justified not cooperating with the nationalist Free French forces commanded by General Charles de Gaulle and supported by the British. Still, not wanting to cooperate too closely with Vichy, Roosevelt had supported General Henri Giraud, an opponent of Vichy and a well-regarded army officer. But before Giraud could arrive on the scene, the Americans, led by General Dwight Eisenhower and diplomat Robert Murphy, concluded an agreement with French commander Jean Darlan whereby French military resistance ceased in return for Darlan's exercising political authority in French territory. The "Darlan deal" evoked outcries at home, since the general was a well-known fascist sympathizer and Nazi collaborator. Roosevelt justified the deal on military grounds but could not escape the sticky political situation that pitted a Vichy French general, an American-backed French general, and a British-backed French general against one another.[14]

The military picture seemed no less cloudy. American planners wondered whether the effort for TORCH had diverted too much away from ROUNDUP. Churchill began suggesting a Mediterranean campaign to secure the North African victories. Recognizing the prospect of Stalin's anger if the Western Allies again backed out of attacking in Europe, Roosevelt tried to arrange a conference among all three leaders. But Stalin said that he was too busy with the fighting in his own country. Thus, Roosevelt and Churchill agreed to meet near Casablanca in mid-January 1943.

Some of the Americans arrived at Casablanca thinking that the success of the North African campaign and the Soviet defense at Stalingrad had turned the tide decisively in their favor. But what the conference actually achieved was less a decisive move than a forward step. With Roosevelt's assent, the British successfully argued against a landing in France and for an attack on Sicily in the Mediterranean. The Americans argued for a firm commitment to a European landing in 1944 but got no assurance.

Political issues seemed even less certain. A few weeks before the conference, General Darlan had died at the hand of an assassin. But his associates remained on the scene, anxious for power. Giraud, the American protégé, was on hand, all the while seeming less likely to cut a major figure. Missing was General de Gaulle, whose response to being snubbed by Roosevelt was to remain in London. As the conference neared an end with no resolution on the French issue, Roosevelt decided unilaterally to support Giraud. Then at the last minute de Gaulle arrived. Hard negotiating and some maneuvering just before Roosevelt and Churchill appeared before reporters to brief them on the outcome of the conference produced an agreement in which the two Frenchmen agreed to share power. To this degree, Allied unity was preserved.

This was a unity, however, in which Roosevelt had little confidence. He had come to think of France as a weak nation, not suitable for membership in the postwar alliance of world policemen. The French were going to be policed. Roosevelt had the same ambition to dismantle French colonialism as he did British colonialism. While in Casablanca, he met privately with the sultan of Morocco and at dinner ignored Churchill and Giraud to chat with the sultan about improving living conditions for the Moroccan people. The next day, Harry Hopkins made anticolonial remarks to the sultan's grand vizier, who replied that after the war he intended to "throw himself in the arms of Mr. Roosevelt."[15]

At the concluding press conference, Roosevelt struck a more important blow for Allied unity by announcing that the Allied objective was the "unconditional surrender" of their enemies. Roosevelt had discussed the idea with Churchill earlier but probably announced it on his own initiative. The announcement signaled Roosevelt's determination to put his own stamp on the war effort. The context of Roosevelt's remarks indicated the importance of the doctrine. Roosevelt had led off the conference by emphasizing that it was being held to plan future military operations. He then emphasized that Stalin had been invited and was being closely informed. He went on to highlight Anglo-American unity and cooperation in military planning "to maintain the initiative against the Axis powers in every part of the world." He also included aid to the Soviet Union and to China (thereby including them in the nations favored for postwar prominence). It was at this point, in the context of Anglo-American unity on military planning and the importance of the Soviet Union and China, that he announced his and Churchill's "determination that peace can come to the world only by the total elimination of German and Japanese war power." This was the meaning of unconditional surrender, which also included "the destruction of the philosophies in those countries which are based on conquest and the subjugation of other people."[16] Thus, unconditional surrender was to be a bridge from warmaking to peacekeeping, from the Allies to the world policemen. It would be the means by which the victorious powers cleared the decks. It was an assurance to Stalin and to Chiang that they belonged to the club. It was also further encouragement to define the wartime alliance in military terms, to focus Allied unity on winning the war rather than on dividing the spoils of peace.

More than anything, agreement to fight together required agreement on strategy. Here the prospects were not so bright. Across the conference rested the shadow of Stalin's demand for a second front in Europe. During the previous year, the Americans had favored this strategy. But at Casablanca, Roosevelt's prior approval of TORCH and long-standing British plans to attack in the Mediterranean led the Americans to agree to follow up with an attack on Sicily.[17] This meant informing Stalin that there would be no second front in Europe and that supply convoys to the USSR would have to give way to the Mediterranean offensive. Roosevelt and Churchill tried to soften the news with promises to press supplies and to suggest the possibility of a European invasion under the right conditions, but Stalin was unimpressed.

Relations with China were following a similar course. While the British and Americans discussed various strategies for supporting Chiang, the generalissimo complained and threatened to pull up stakes. From Chiang's capital of Chunking, General Joseph "Vinegar Joe" Stilwell derided the Chinese leader's regime as corrupt and his army as worthless. But Roosevelt insisted on supporting Chiang. The president believed that by courting China he would blunt Japanese efforts to turn the war into a racial crusade. Roosevelt also convinced himself that Chiang was moving China rapidly along the path toward liberal democracy. In this regard, he highly rated China's future value to the United States, especially in the event of a conflict with the USSR, and proposed that China be given control of strategic bases from which to police the South Pacific after the war and assume trustee control of Korea and French Indochina.[18]

Roosevelt argued that China was militarily vital to victory in the East. A Pacific Ocean campaign would not defeat Japan, he declared; it could be accomplished only from Chinese bases. But because prospects for a land offensive were unpromising, Roosevelt supported a plan by General Clair Chennault, an American airman who had organized volunteer American pilots into an arm of the Chinese air force. Chennault proposed massive air strikes against Japanese shipping, disrupting their supply lines and diverting Japanese fighters into an air war that Chennault predicted he would win.[19] Because Chennault was close to Chiang, Roosevelt reasoned that supporting his air campaign would bolster Chinese morale and Chiang's goodwill.[20]

The consequences of Roosevelt's thinking were decisive and not altogether promising. Inevitably, China began to slip into the American orbit. As 1943 wore on, the British found the Americans less and less cooperative on matters relating to China and more inclined to adopt a unilateral course, especially in favor of penetration by American business interests. Within the United States, Roosevelt undertook to portray China not only as a loyal ally but also as "one of the great democracies of the world." Here was another instance of Roosevelt's investing in a particular entity a good deal more than it was prepared to bear. Throughout the war, supply shortages, logistical obstacles, and Chiang's decentralized, corrupt, and tyrannical regime thwarted a significant military effort.[21]

Behind Roosevelt's thinking about China lurked some peculiar ideas about the world's racial makeup. Roosevelt had a fascination with what might be called racial ethnography, or the idea that race somehow determined a nation's culture and behavior. For example, the underdevelopment of Japanese skulls indicated that they were a brutal, greedy, and devious people. More than anything, ideas of racial mixing dominated Roosevelt's thinking. He was essentially an adherent of the "melting pot" thesis that the world's populations would eventually become alike. (It was not always clear whether he thought that this would happen because of racial intermarriage or because people would subordinate questions of race to questions of political democracy, self-determination, and economic and social welfare.) In Roosevelt's opinion, some European-Asian racial mixtures produced good results and ought to be encouraged. One of his formulations was that natives of India were a mixture of Aryan and Iranian and thus "cousins" of Western Europeans. He was inclined to apply these formulations in crude, dismissive ways, and not always to nonwhites.[22]

During the first year of American participation in the war, Roosevelt had played alliance politics in New Deal fashion. He created new agencies, announced grand designs and objectives, and invested much political capital in specific enterprises. At the same time, he avoided unshakable commitments, maintained fallback positions, and offered style that lacked substance. Backs were patted, praise lavished, small efforts magnified, unity and high purpose affirmed.

Nothing better represented this approach than the Arcadia Conference, which produced not only the Declaration of the United Nations but also a variety of combined Anglo-American boards to administer the war effort. But almost as soon as the conference adjourned in late January 1942, its promises began to fray. The Combined Chiefs of Staff wrangled over how to create a second front for the USSR. The American Joint Chiefs debated among themselves how much effort to allocate to the Pacific war. Lacking strategic direction, the supplies and allocations boards became pawns in the hands of national interests. During 1942, the trend in the American war effort was toward coordinating its own interests rather than cooperating with the British. By May, British officials in Washington were complaining that the Americans were subordinating strategic issues to "unilateral decisions ruthlessly subjected to political considerations" and were operating through informal, ad hoc, "backstairs" channels that kept them in the dark until the Americans, usually through Harry Hopkins, announced what was to be done.[23]

Some of the British observations overlooked the obvious fact that the American war effort was coming into being and could not be expected to function as smoothly as their own mature system. Roosevelt spent the first quarter of 1942 establishing new agencies for war production, shipping allocations, labor relations, food production, and other areas. Some administrative overlap, friction, and competition were inevitable. These frictions were magnified by the inevitable shortages of war supplies while American production mobilized. Until the ships, planes, tanks, and weapons were rolling off the production lines, all parties were going to have to bid for them and develop ways to share the shortages.

And indeed, the complaints overlooked the ways in which Roosevelt had sought cooperation. Throughout 1942, Harry Hopkins, undoubtedly with Roosevelt's blessing, had prodded the American and British Chiefs of Staff to agree on a strategic directive to guide the war effort. And following Arcadia, Roosevelt had kept up an extensive cable correspondence with Churchill, keeping him informed of his strategic thinking and not moving without his consent. The American decision in June to allocate additional tanks to Britain in the wake of the Tobruk disaster was another example of cooperative action.

Still, the British complaints contained a certain amount of insight. In various ways, Roosevelt had sought to put an American stamp on the Anglo-American war effort. From the beginning of the war, Roosevelt had aimed to enlist American public opinion by putting Americans on the fighting fronts. Hence he had ordered a raid on Tokyo and told the British that American pilots would fly American planes. He had approved Operation TORCH because it provided the best chance to put Americans into action in 1942. His objective necessarily compromised his devotion to Allied cooperation.

Lend-Lease aid illustrated the trend. At Arcadia, the British and Americans had agreed to place their munitions in a "common pool," from which they would be allocated to themselves and to their fighting partners. Only the USSR, which received aid in a special category, was considered exempt. By the end of the year, the Americans were making more and more "unilateral decisions." After a meeting with Hopkins, Edward Stettinius, head of the Office of Lend-Lease Administration, reflected that there "has been a swing on the part of the Administration away from the pooling idea and there is a desire to have the United Nations feel an obligation to the United States."[24] A few months later, Hopkins was declaring that the American "control of shipping would be a powerful weapon at the peace table, and we should not hesitate to use it."[25] When the British tried to gain special guarantees from Lend-Lease, they found themselves negotiating ad hoc agreements with separate American military services and production agencies.[26]

Looking beyond Churchill's leadership, Roosevelt sought to court Foreign Secretary Anthony Eden, who visited Washington in March 1943. The subjects of his visit—postwar peacekeeping and the fate of Germany—provided the Americans with an excellent opportunity to take Eden into their fold. When Eden complained that American shipping policy was hurting Britain's civilian imports, Roosevelt arranged to resolve the issue in Britain's favor.[27] Roosevelt and Eden agreed that Germany should be dismembered and disarmed. They also sketched the outline of a world peacekeeping organization in which Britain, the United States, the USSR, and—at Roosevelt's insistence—China would act as policemen.

Postwar peacekeeping was a ticklish subject. Coincident with Eden's visit, a bipartisan group of internationalist senators, led by Joseph Ball of Minnesota, presented a bill for a peacekeeping organization and proposed to bring it up for a vote on March 16, in the middle of Eden's visit. Fearing that a debate on the resolution would inspire isolationists to attack not only internationalism but also the wartime partnerships with Britain and the Soviet Union, Roosevelt gave the resolution a tepid endorsement and worked with the Senate leadership to bottle it up in committee.[28] In the meantime, Eden and Roosevelt were facing a difference between themselves. Eden had come to Washington with a proposal from Churchill to create a Council of Europe, which would include the United States. (Churchill also proposed a joint "American-Commonwealth" citizenship, cementing their alliance with a kind of domestic identity.) The Americans favored a World Council, composed of representatives from "regional" groups of nations. This council would hear disputes among nations and if it failed to resolve them, the policemen would enforce a decision. Eden also objected to Roosevelt's omitting France from membership in the world peacekeeping organization.[29]

The two also differed over territorial claims. At one point, Eden suggested that the United States take control of certain Pacific islands, hoping that takings by Washington would justify other takings by London. But Roosevelt replied that such lands should be under international supervision. During Eden's visit, the State Department formally presented a draft declaration favoring the eventual "independence" of all colonial peoples.[30]

For the most part, Eden and the British Foreign Office treated the American positions as little more than invitations to further discussion, during which, they hoped, American and British interests would be more precisely balanced. Still, Eden's objections were trivial alongside his more general unease about Roosevelt's behavior. Roosevelt conducted their conversations in his informal, chatty fashion, often tossing out suggestions without indicating how serious he was about them. Eden refused to take seriously Roosevelt's suggestion that nations other than the policemen be armed with nothing more dangerous than rifles. He was flabbergasted at Roosevelt's proposal to combine a part of Belgium, Luxembourg, and districts in France into a state of "Wallonia." Eden found the president's opinions "alarming in their cheerful fecklessness." Roosevelt struck him as "a conjurer, skillfully juggling with balls of dynamite, whose nature he failed to understand." Roosevelt also suggested various "goodwill" gestures that Britain could make by giving up this or that possession without, Eden dryly noted, proposing that the United States give up anything.[31]

Thus, Eden's visit was not quite the success Roosevelt might have wished for. Late on the night before he was to leave Washington, Eden confided to Harry Hopkins that his conversations with Roosevelt had been something of a disappointment. Trying to save the situation, Hopkins assured Eden that Roosevelt had only been "trying out his ideas" and that Hopkins would make sure that the president understood Eden's perspective.[32]

Eden's disappointments posed no obstacle to Roosevelt, who was determined to press his leadership forward. When Churchill expressed concern that the British and Americans were thinking along different lines about how to follow up Operation HUSKY, the invasion of Sicily, Churchill urged another summit meeting, which was held in Washington in May and code-named Trident. The prime minister arrived armed with arguments for following up a success in Sicily with a drive to obtain the surrender of Italy. Roosevelt was not buying it. The president favored active campaigning in the Mediterranean, but he wanted lesser objectives that would not drain resources from his main objective: the cross-channel attack on northern France. All agreed that the attack could not take place in 1943, but Roosevelt wanted a firm commitment to an attack in 1944. He also pressed support for China, declaring the need to undertake operations that would keep the Chinese viable. In their meetings with the British Chiefs, the American Chiefs backed him up, arguing against commitments that would divert resources from the cross-channel operation and favoring a land operation to support China. They carried the point on the cross-channel operation but ran into stiff difficulties on China, with the British raising multiple objections to any land operation. Roosevelt was under pressure from the Chinese ambassador, T. V. Soong, who unswervingly pressed for a land campaign, discounted all objections, and pictured his government as being on the verge of collapse and under imminent threat of a major Japanese offensive. After Churchill and Soong had heatedly disagreed, Roosevelt tried to assuage Soong by allocating support for both an air campaign under General Chennault and preparations for a land operation. But Soong was not satisfied, and in a moment's weakness, Roosevelt promised him a "definite commitment" to a land operation. It took fast work by Hopkins and Marshall to water down the "commitment" to a desire to undertake such an operation. Hopkins then told Soong that the new language was a victory for Roosevelt over British opposition.[33]

It had been Roosevelt's conference. He had dominated the decision for the cross-channel attack and encouraged the Chinese to see him rather than Churchill as their principal backer. Churchill acknowledged Roosevelt's leadership when he reported to his war cabinet that the president had "exercised throughout . . . a dominating influence on the course of Staff discussions."[34] (This, of course, did not stop Churchill from trying to sell a commitment to invading Italy.)

In the months following the Trident Conference, the cross-channel invasion emerged as the key to Roosevelt's leadership. With the British having signed on to unconditional surrender and its guarantee to the Soviets, it was time to commit to the operation that Stalin had been calling for. In August, Roosevelt told the Joint Chiefs that he wanted "a preponderance" of American force in the cross-channel planning so that he could name an American commander. At Casablanca, he had declared that the commander of the invasion should represent the country that contributed the majority of the forces. He now wanted that principle to work in his own favor.[35]

Almost immediately, however, the operation ran into difficulties. Churchill appeared to drag his feet, raising the image of the channel filled with floating Allied corpses. Then the success of the campaign in Sicily (Operation HUSKY) generated an important opportunity in Italy. On July 25, the Italian government deposed Mussolini and raised hopes for a quick Italian surrender. The surrender confronted the American and British chiefs with an issue that they had papered over at Trident. The Americans had argued that any operation in Italy should be strictly limited to keep it from diverting large resources from the cross-channel operation. The British had favored an extensive operation, which, they responded, would divert German resources from the cross-channel area.

Thus was held the Quadrant Conference, at Montreal, Canada. The Americans and the British both swore allegiance to the cross-channel operation, but they differed over how much to commit to an Italian campaign. Roosevelt also opposed Churchill's proposal to deal with a fascist-tinged government led by Mussolini's former chief of staff, Pietro Bagdolio, and King Victor Emmanuel. Only pressure from Churchill, who warned of a total Italian collapse and subsequent anarchy, and from Stalin, who wanted to gain additional support against the Nazis, persuaded him to sign an agreement with Bagdolio in which the Italian leader promised to reenter the war on the side of the Allies and to form a new government based on the consent of the Italian people. As soon as they had agreed on the means of securing the Italian surrender, Roosevelt and Churchill fell to differing over rival candidates for longer-term political leadership. Churchill favored continuing the monarchy, and Roosevelt favored a republic led by Count Carlo Sforza, exiled leader of the Free Italy movement, a strong antifascist and antimonarchist who was popular among Italian Americans. In the meantime, the prime minister continued to press for military strikes in the eastern Mediterranean, again raising doubts about his commitment to the cross-channel attack, now christened Operation OVERLORD. By this time, Roosevelt was accustomed to debating these issues with Churchill, conceding to him here and there, blocking him when necessary, satisfying himself with incremental steps toward his objectives.

But Roosevelt was also capable of grand strokes. By the end of 1943, he was looking to put together his conception of the postwar world in which the United States, Britain, the USSR, and China would cooperate to maintain the peace. He had first raised the subject at Quebec, where he presented Churchill and Eden with a Four-Power Declaration in which the United States, Britain, the Soviet Union, and China would affirm their alliance and their determination to cooperate to keep the peace after victory. The Republicans were threatening to preempt the issue for next year's presidential election, and Roosevelt needed the declaration, he told Churchill and Eden, to head them off. Based on the understanding that the declaration would be provisional only, Churchill and Eden agreed.[36]

In the meantime, Roosevelt worked to develop his grand design. At the Trident conference, Roosevelt had moved to cement a Sino-U.S. bond by supporting Chiang's demand for a land operation in Burma over British objections. But by the fall of 1943, his promises had worn thin and tension had increased between Chiang and the American military commander Joseph Stilwell. Hoping to bolster Chiang and to regain the inside track with him, Roosevelt invited him to a conference at Cairo, Egypt. Roosevelt courted Chiang with endless expressions of support and goodwill, endorsing an amphibious operation in the Bay of Bengal as part of a Burma campaign and rejecting Stilwell's request to put him in charge of all Chinese forces. But such matters were a subtheme in Roosevelt's design for the postwar world. More important, he endorsed Chiang's postwar territorial claims and promised to limit Soviet territorial claims in Asia. He further promised China status as one of the four great powers. He revealed his desire to outflank the British by suggesting that Hong Kong become a free port under Chinese sovereignty and by proposing a system of international mandates and trusteeships that would limit European colonialism. (At one point, Harry Hopkins showed up with a press release promising that territories would be "freed" from Japanese control, suggesting that they might become independent. The British objected, and Churchill successfully substituted the neutral and ambiguous word "expelled.")[37]

Roosevelt's anticolonialism contained generous room for U.S. strategic interests. During the year, he had followed military discussions of what Pacific Ocean bases the United States would need to protect its interests after the war. He expanded the discussion to include ways to enhance U.S. commercial aviation. He had sent the Antarctic explorer Richard E. Byrd on a tour of the South Pacific to identify potential sites. On the eve of the Cairo conference, he and the Joint Chiefs had worked out a detailed plan for U.S. defense in the Pacific.[38]

The keystone in Roosevelt's international architecture was the Soviet Union. Throughout the war, Roosevelt had played up to Stalin and had tried to arrange a meeting where, presumably, he would be able to employ his personal style of diplomacy to its fullest effect. His opportunity finally arrived when Stalin agreed to a meeting at Tehran, Iran. The British would also attend, but Roosevelt saw them as incidental to his main purpose of forging a U.S.-USSR partnership. Roosevelt and his military chiefs had long recognized the Soviets' vital contribution to the war in

Europe and wanted to promote good relations with them so they would keep fighting. (From time to time, Stalin would send out signals that he was exploring a separate peace with Hitler, which invariably sent cold chills down American spines.) Indeed, Roosevelt and his military chiefs so highly valued Soviet fighting skill that after the defeat of Germany they wanted the Soviets to join the war against Japan. Roosevelt also worried about potential Soviet expansionism. Stalin had declared his intention to hold on to the Baltic States, and the prospect of Soviet expansion into the Balkans had caused Roosevelt to consider ways to strengthen British and American influence there. At the same time, Stalin had returned to his style of angry, sarcastic behavior, bitterly complaining that Roosevelt and Churchill were leaving him uninformed about the Italian surrender and future plans in the Mediterranean.[39]

Other signs were pointing toward a more harmonious relationship. At a foreign ministers conference in Moscow, the Soviets had agreed to permit China to sign a Four-Power Declaration, thus accomplishing one of Roosevelt's major diplomatic purposes. Stalin also offhandedly promised that after Germany's defeat the Soviet Union would enter the war against Japan. These achievements, combined with Stalin's willingness to meet with Roosevelt and Churchill, suggested that Roosevelt might be able to establish good relations with the Soviets.

But Roosevelt was unwilling to rely on his charm and goodwill to cajole the Soviet dictator. During 1942 and 1943, and especially after the battle of Stalingrad turned the tide in the Red Army's favor, the White House had experienced a growing concern that the scope of Soviet postwar claims would be proportional to their contribution to victory. Roosevelt wanted to be sure that the United States could share as much of the credit as possible. By the fall of 1943, he was declaring that in the event of a German collapse, he wanted Allied and Soviet troops to enter Berlin at the same time. He also consistently advocated operations aimed at "taking the weight off" the Soviets and strengthening American claims to an equal share of credit for the final victory.[40]

Roosevelt's top priority for coaxing the Soviets remained the cross-channel attack. That fall, as Churchill raised the requirements for carrying out the operation and suggested further strikes east of Italy, the Americans' irritations and suspicions increased to the point of thinking that the prime minister was seeking to sabotage the operation. Roosevelt strongly endorsed the Joint Chiefs' plan to severely restrict Allied aid to military resistance in the Balkans. Stronger operations would have to come on the invitation of the Soviets.[41] As the Americans and British were preparing to depart for Tehran, Hopkins warned the British, "you will find us lining up with the Russians."[42]

Lining up with the Russians meant sorting out military complexities. Churchill was advocating moves farther east in the Mediterranean to capture the island of Rhodes. This, he argued, would encourage Turkey to enter the war, opening up the straits from the Mediterranean to the Black Sea and the southern USSR. The operation would cancel the amphibious landings promised China to support a campaign in Burma and would probably postpone Operation OVERLORD. No one wanted to put off OVERLORD, but Roosevelt and Marshall thought that Stalin might want some action to take the pressure off the Red Army and considered a smaller, commando-style operation on the east coast of the Adriatic to aid the anti-German partisan forces in Yugoslavia fighting under Marshal Tito. The success of such an operation depended on driving the Germans out of Italy, something Roosevelt thought would happen if the British and Americans continued to push north. Roosevelt favored the Burma operation.

Roosevelt wasted no time revealing the American strategy. Persuaded by rumors of a German plot to assassinate the three leaders, he and his party moved from the distant U.S. embassy into the Soviet embassy, which was

Roosevelt's major wartime partner, Joseph Stalin, with Roosevelt at the Tehran Conference, November 29, 1943. (U.S. Army Air Force)

next door to the British embassy. He immediately met privately with Stalin, pledging to support the Soviets militarily and putting out ideas about dismantling the Western European colonial empires. He and Stalin agreed that France should not come out of the war a great power. At the first plenary session, Roosevelt opened by reviewing the military situation, listing a range of possible moves, and concluding with an invitation to Stalin to choose among them. Stalin replied by lining up with the Americans. He endorsed the cross-channel attack as the main operation for 1944. He also promised to enter the war against Japan. When Churchill tried to keep alive action in the eastern Mediterranean by saying that troops for the operation against Rhodes would not come from those for OVERLORD, Stalin replied that such operations would be valuable only if Turkey entered the war, an event he thought unlikely. Roosevelt backed up Stalin with a guess that Turkey's price for entering the war would be so high that it would postpone OVERLORD.

Lining up with the Soviets meant occasionally ganging up on Churchill. Roosevelt used the Joint Chiefs' idea of a commando operation in the eastern Adriatic to neutralize Churchill's calls for action in the eastern Mediterranean. Stalin bluntly asked the prime minister if he truly supported OVERLOAD. Seeing that he was not only outnumbered but also in danger of losing his place in the alliance, Churchill gave in and committed the British to the operation.

Stalin saw his opportunity and took it. At their second plenary session, he demanded that the Allies name a commander of OVERLORD. Nothing would come of the operation, he declared, until someone was placed in charge of its execution. Until then, plans were only plans. He also called for a specific date for the operation and for its reinforcement by a landing in southern France. His demands produced the desired effect. The Combined Chiefs affirmed the two operations, setting May as the date for them to take place. Stalin promised to support the operations with a Red Army offensive. Roosevelt promised to name a commander, which, he informed Stalin at the time, would be General Marshall. When Churchill continued to speak up for other military opportunities, Stalin, backed up by Roosevelt, argued against "diversions."

At length the conference sought to resolve the issue of Turkey's entry into the war, the subject around which the discussion of further Mediterranean operations had revolved. Roosevelt, Churchill, and Stalin agreed to try to persuade Turkey to declare war on Germany. They decided that Roosevelt and Churchill would meet with Turkish president Inonu after the conference. (The meeting, which took place in Cairo on December 4, produced no change in Turkey's attitude. While continually expressing his goodwill and support, President Inonu held to his position that as long as his country was not in the war it was not in danger. A separate meeting, during which Hopkins grilled the Turkish foreign minister, also failed to move the Turks closer to participation.)

Roosevelt found Stalin more cooperative on military strategy than on political arrangements. He tried to get Stalin to negotiate an end to Soviet hostilities with Finland, but the Soviet dictator accused the Finns of refusing to negotiate. He suggested that the Baltic States be allowed some free expression of opinion about being absorbed by the USSR, to which Stalin replied that the subject had not come up when the last Russian czar, an ally of the British and the Americans, had not allowed any such expression, and he did not see why the subject should come up now. Roosevelt adopted a more circumspect stance regarding Poland. There were 6 to 7 million Polish Americans in the United States, Roosevelt observed, and if he ran for reelection in 1944, he would hate to lose their vote. Thus, he told Stalin that he preferred not to discuss territorial matters regarding Poland. He did ask Stalin to reestablish relations with the Polish exile government in London, however. The USSR had broken relations with the London Poles when they had accused the Soviets of murdering hundreds of Polish army officers, whose graves the Germans had uncovered in the Katyn Forest. Again Stalin backed off, charging that Polish supporters of the London government had killed anti-Nazi partisans and hampered the Soviet war effort.

In a private meeting, Roosevelt brought up his idea of the four policemen. Stalin expressed more concern about German resurgence than world security and seemed to favor Churchill's idea of regional security committees. Roosevelt responded that the U.S. Congress would probably oppose sending troops to participate in such arrangements. Stalin then suggested that the powers occupy certain "strong physical points" that would deter future aggression by Germany and Japan. To this Roosevelt agreed "100%." A subsequent foreign ministers meeting, at which Hopkins represented the United States, revealed difficulties with this approach. As Hopkins pointed out, it would be difficult for the great powers to establish bases in friendly nations without impinging on their sovereignty. Establishing bases was also a delicate matter because it had to be done in such a way as to prevent the great powers' arming against one another. The discussion, inevitably, ended inconclusively.

Also inconclusive was a brief discussion of the fate of Germany. All agreed that Germany should be divided into smaller units, with Stalin favoring the smallest ones, Churchill the largest. In the end, they agreed to refer the matter to the European Advisory Commission, which they had created earlier at the foreign ministers conference in Moscow.

Lining up with Stalin also meant realigning priorities. With the Soviets committed to joining the war against Japan and on record against any "diversions," Roosevelt felt less committed to Chiang's Burma operation. When a review found insufficient landing craft to carry out the attack, he called it off.

For all its twists, turns, and improvisations, the Tehran conference had set a pattern for Allied diplomacy. Roosevelt sought to shape a world tolerable to American domestic politics. Wary of the strength of isolationism, he backed away from committing American troops to postwar peacekeeping, favoring instead a system to limit German and Japanese power through political decentralization, trusteeships, and an international organization supported by the four policemen. Hoping to balance Stalin's demands for postwar security with American anticommunism and ethnic voting patterns, he encouraged Stalin to take token steps to reconcile Soviet influence in Eastern Europe with popular will. He coaxed Stalin to be accommodating by permitting him to set the military agenda. To confirm their partnership, he renewed the American request for Soviet participation in the war against Japan and the chance to share in the spoils of that victory.

To draw close to Stalin, Roosevelt also asserted his independence from Churchill. In the process he had, probably without intention, assumed a mediator's role. On many occasions—the postsurrender treatment of Germany, operations in Eastern Europe, the occupation of bases—he had taken the middle ground. Lining up with the Soviets had not meant forsaking the British.

From a structural standpoint, this outcome was precarious. The Anglo-American partnership had developed a solid institutional core, based on the Combined Chiefs of Staff, a network of lesser combined boards, and frequent summit conferences. No such ties linked either the United States or Great Britain to the Soviet Union, and Stalin had shown no inclination to establish them. As a result, relations with the Soviets depended on whatever Roosevelt and Churchill could work out. Roosevelt's desire to establish his own special relationship with Stalin and to relegate Churchill and the British to the status of junior partners, and the result of his playing the mediator's role, gave him a certain amount of leverage—except on issues between him and Stalin. There he had to rely on his powers of charm and persuasion, to which Stalin had considerable immunity.

The conference had also identified a large number of issues that could not be resolved immediately. Roosevelt did not want to settle national boundaries or spheres of influence until either the war or the next presidential election was over. The issue of postwar bases would have to wait until the major powers worked out their own relationship and a world peacekeeping organization was established.

Certain ambiguities were beginning to emerge in Roosevelt's strategy. His anticolonialism looked toward weakening the Western European nations, especially France. With Italy weak and Germany dismembered, there would be little in the way of future Soviet expansion westward. Such a prospect seemed unattractive to Churchill. Indeed, the most prominent element of discord at the conference came in the form of Churchill's spirited defense of the British empire. (As the conference was getting under way, Roosevelt had warned Stalin not to challenge Churchill on India—although he had followed this with a suggestion that he favored "reform from the bottom, somewhat on the Soviet line." When Stalin observed that this would mean revolution, Roosevelt agreed.)

Lining up with the Russians also meant giving up Anglo-American operations in Yugoslavia and the eastern Mediterranean. This made it plain to Stalin that he would have a free hand in whatever territory the Red Army took from the Nazis. Thus he responded ambiguously when Roosevelt appealed for his help in mollifying Polish and Baltic voters in the United States.

We ought to be careful not to interpret such ambiguities through the lens of an approaching Cold War. Roosevelt's approaches to Stalin were based on sound American interests—a desire to focus military grand strategy on the cross-channel attack and to position the United States next to the Soviet Union in the wartime alliance. His anticolonialism was a mixture of his New Deal urge to improve everyone's living standards and opportunities, Secretary of State Hull's wish to dismantle obstacles to American trade, and a desire to punish Nazi collaborators. Each of these motives was open to critical analysis, but none could be said to be naive or contrary to American interests. And since the Soviet Union had yet to establish its system of spheres of influence, puppet regimes, and client states, European colonialism was the available target for American diplomacy.

As much as anything, the Tehran conference was another episode in Roosevelt's improvisational, inventive, and progressive style of governance. In many different ways, his entire presidency had been an experiment in crisis management. Through it all, Roosevelt and his shifting coterie of New Dealers, among whom Harry Hopkins emerged as the prime example, had gained great confidence in their ability to master the tide of events. They had invented the NRA, AAA, WPA, CCC, and others; they had invented Lend-Lease, summit diplomacy, a Joint Chiefs of Staff, and other wartime institutions and practices. Not everything worked as they had planned, but they had adjusted and moved on. They would continue to. In this sense, Tehran's informality and openhandedness had been a triumph of Franklin Roosevelt's belief that relationships were to be built and goals to be reached.

Not surprisingly, the British and the Americans came away from Tehran with differing views of its achievements. Churchill, realizing that he had been outmaneuvered, took a pessimistic view. He left the conference in a black mood, muttering about the bloody Russians and fearing that civilization was heading for disaster. Roosevelt left Tehran in an enthusiastic mood. Stalin had not given him all he wanted, but he had appeared to be realistic, frank, and willing to negotiate. This was enough for Roosevelt the pluralist. He believed that he had laid the groundwork for further negotiations. There would be hard work ahead, but his objectives could be won.

Roosevelt had only one regret. Stalin's badgering to name the commander of OVERLORD had forced him to reevaluate the status of George Marshall. No one knew better than Roosevelt how much Marshall's sound judgment and granite character had meant to the success of the war effort. Time and again he had seen Marshall swallow his pride and dedication to his troops to give aid to an ally whom Roosevelt considered more deserving. Marshall's plain desire to command the war's major operation, his fitness for the command, and his moral claim on it were all unimpeachable. But Roosevelt also realized that the qualities that had given Marshall the claim to command OVERLORD were the qualities that made him so valuable in Washington. They were also the qualities that made it possible for Roosevelt to deny him the honor. Thus at Cairo, where he and Churchill had stopped to tie up Tehran's loose ends, Roosevelt asked Marshall to choose between commanding OVERLORD and remaining in Washington. When Marshall, true to his code of self-denial, replied that the choice should be the president's, Roosevelt declared that he could not sleep well without Marshall in Washington. He then appointed the commander of Allied troops in the Mediterranean, General Dwight D. Eisenhower. For the moment, Roosevelt's war strategy seemed to be on track.

11

★★★★★

WARTIME FRUITS OF PLURALISM

Roosevelt's first domestic priority was to gear up production for war. It seemed a Herculean task. At the time of Pearl Harbor, the United States was lacking in every category of armed strength. Lend-Lease had stimulated production to a degree, but it still lagged behind the most obvious needs. Indeed, the Lend-Lease experience had been as much a lesson in frustration as in achievement. Interested parties—especially the British, the Office of Lend-Lease Administration, the U.S. military, and the Office of Production Management (OPM)—had squabbled over priorities. Short-term needs clashed with long-term planning. Roosevelt had appointed a Supplies, Priorities, and Allocations Board (SPAB) to smooth out the frictions and frustrations, but it had proved ineffective. Just as worrisome, the head of defense production, William Knudsen, chief of OPM and former head of General Motors, seemed complacent, more willing to minimize problems than to attack them. When the torpedoes and bombs were blasting into the Pacific Fleet, an administrative vacuum existed at the heart of American war production.

Into this vacuum rushed the American military. The day after Pearl Harbor, the War Department canceled all Lend-Lease shipments and persuaded Roosevelt to divert Lend-Lease production to it, in effect taking over war production. Cries and complaints from the injured parties caused the department to relax its grip, but the incident showed the need for a more effective structure. The Arcadia Conference produced several "combined boards" to allocate munitions, food, and shipping among the Allies, but they all required administrative support in Washington. Aware that the existing machinery was inadequate, Roosevelt acted boldly. When Congress assembled in January, he announced ambitious (some said astronomical) production goals for 1942 and blandly dismissed the doubters with, "Oh, the production people can really do it if they really try."[1]

Coordinating the effort required a new administrative setup. Just after the Arcadia Conference, Roosevelt established the War Production Board (WPB) and gave it all the necessary powers to stimulate and coordinate war production. But powers were only as effective as those who used them, and Roosevelt had no good ideas as to who should head the agency. For a time, he thought of a combined leadership, apparently hoping that two or more heads would be better than one, but Hopkins talked him out of it. Narrowing the field past Knudsen, to whom he gave an honorary military commission and "special assignment" in the War Department, he appointed Donald Nelson, an executive of the retail chain Sears-Roebuck who had a record of steadfast, loyal, and uncontroversial service in the OPM.

Looming largest among a host of production emergencies was shipping. Engaged in a two-ocean war, committed to aiding its Lend-Lease partners, and with all its shipping now fair game for Nazi and Japanese submarines, the United States desperately needed to step up ship construction. Once again, with so many interested parties, Roosevelt decided to establish a special agency to arbitrate their claims. On February 7, he established the War Shipping Administration (WSA). Roosevelt located the WSA in the U.S. Maritime Commission, the nation's shipbuilding authority, but he appointed Lewis Douglas to make all shipping allocations. Douglas soon formed an effective partnership with Admiral Emory S. "Jerry" Land, the head of the Maritime Commission.

During 1942, Douglas won his spurs in a struggle with the military and the War Production Board over steel allocations. The issue was whether steel should go to the navy to build escorts for transport ships or to the Maritime Commission to build more transports. Behind this issue was the Lend-Lease program, which was falling victim to devastating German submarine attacks, and anxiety over Soviet complaints about the Allies' failure to establish a second front. At first the navy won out, securing an order from Nelson that gave it priority in steel allocations. Near the end of the year, however, Douglas persuaded Roosevelt to reverse the decision and to put the Maritime Commission's program into high gear. This gave the Maritime Commission's creative leadership, which included Vice Admiral Howard Vickery and such hard-driving shipping executives as Henry J. Kaiser, the chance to accomplish one of the great success stories of American war production.[2]

In the meantime, Nelson was fighting his own battles with the military. Led by General Brehon Somerville, the blunt and politically wily head of the Army Service Forces, the Joint Chiefs peppered the WPB with demands for larger proportions of American resources. Nelson, whose top three personality traits someone once described as "patience, patience, and patience," failed to establish the kind of leverage he needed to command the situation. Not until a fiery session in the fall, when Leon Henderson, the head of domestic price control, shouted that either the Joint Chiefs would conform to the WPB's decisions or the country should get a new Joint Chiefs, did the military tone down its demands.

Many thought that the Joint Chiefs bore a larger responsibility for the production difficulties. Since the Arcadia Conference, production and allocation officials had looked to the military for strategic directives to shape their decisions. But until late summer, the Americans and British wrangled over priorities, while the Soviets fumed and hinted that they might collapse or strike a deal with Hitler. The North African campaign shaped strategy to an extent, but not until the Casablanca conference did the Combined Chiefs agree on a long-range strategic plan. In the meantime, Roosevelt had to find some way to tie up the loose ends of production, allocation, and strategy.

This service was performed by Harry Hopkins. During 1941, Hopkins had used his role as expediter of Lend-Lease to build a network among the various interests involved in aid to the Allies. Principal among these was the Office of Lend-Lease Administration, the military services, the defense production agencies, and the Treasury Department. Hopkins coordinated these entities with British claimants for American war materiel and with one another in an informal network familiarly called "the Hopkins Shop." Time and again, conflicting parties agreed to resolve their differences if Hopkins would craft a solution and guarantee that it would hold.

During 1942, Hopkins's abilities were especially valuable. The combined British-American machinery established at the Arcadia Conference almost immediately gave way under the pressure of national objectives, a dominant one being Roosevelt's desire to get Americans into the fighting. Roosevelt occasionally decided to allocate materiel, especially aircraft, to Americans without using the Arcadia machinery, which proved worrisome to the British. Internal squabbles over production priorities further turned American attention inward, forcing the British to protect their interests by making special arrangements with key American officials.[3]

Because of his experience expediting Lend-Lease, Hopkins worked more naturally with allocation problems than with production problems. He rapidly incorporated the WSA into his network and used it as his instrument for balancing British and Soviet war needs and the various domestic claims on American resources. Because Hopkins did not tie in directly to the WPB, Donald Nelson had far less success reconciling the claims he dealt with.[4]

In the process, Hopkins complemented Roosevelt's role as a pluralist leader. Before Hopkins was on the scene, Roosevelt had often resorted to ordering competing subordinates to lock themselves in a room until they had resolved their own differences. With Hopkins living in the White House, the president now had someone who could, in effect, go into the locked room and facilitate a settlement. Because of Hopkins, Roosevelt was able to divert more of his attention to military and diplomatic matters, intervening to decide matters that Hopkins occasionally brought to him.

In the meantime, Roosevelt had to turn to managing the domestic war economy. During the first year of the war, Roosevelt authorized an armed forces of 5 million men. Taking this many men out of the workforce would create labor shortages just when the demands of war production would be straining the nation's productive capacities. In the spring of 1942, Nelson informed him that earlier estimates of $42 billion for production had now increased to $60 billion, with $110 billion projected for 1943 and insufficient resources to meet either target.[5]

This meant that the nation's most pressing economic problem would be inflation, the common malady of wartime nations. Adopting a comprehensive and integrated approach to the problem, Roosevelt proposed to Congress a seven-point program of across-the-board tax increases, wage and price controls, rationing of essential materials, and incentives to buy war bonds. The program also advanced Roosevelt's belief that the war should produce no millionaires. The president wanted no American to end a tax year with more than $25,000.

Roosevelt was soon tussling with Congress over wages and prices. While he waited for Congress to act, Roosevelt put his anti-inflation effort into action. At the end of January 1942, Congress passed an emergency price control act, authorizing the administration to create an Office of Price Administration (OPA) with the power to regulate prices and rents. The interests of farmers, who opposed the control of farm prices, and labor, which opposed wage controls, were protected by pegging farm prices at 110 percent of parity and by denying the agency any authority over wages. Roosevelt responded by creating a War Labor Board to supervise wages and suggested that the Department of Agriculture stabilize farm prices below 110 percent of parity by releasing stored commodities. In reply, the Senate threatened to forbid the administration to release any stored commodities.

Bigger problems were just ahead. After Roosevelt announced his anti-inflation program, the OPA issued a general freeze on prices. This seemed the only practical way to avoid sinking into a morass of detail that would have accompanied any attempt to set individual prices. Still, the OPA had to respond to a flood of petitions for exceptions while it was putting into operation its own supervisory and enforcement machinery. At the same time, it had to print and distribute millions of ration books, forms, regulations, and information bulletins and to organize state and district offices to oversee the program.

The program got off to a predictably lumbering start. Lawyers and economists bickered at the central headquarters, state and district offices waited for instructions while clients lined up, and Democrats complained that Republicans were obtaining appointments and using their offices to attack the president. Congress stalled, wanting to win the war and stop inflation, but without raising taxes. The result was a standoff that lasted through the summer while inflationary pressures mounted. The circumstances produced a political game in which each player responded piecemeal to obvious crises. When a major shortage of rubber loomed, Congress authorized a special agency, but Roosevelt vetoed it and established his own. When labor leaders demanded wage increases to meet rising food prices, the War Labor Board used a labor dispute in the "Little Steel" companies to set a standard for wartime wage increases. Early in September, still with no comprehensive program in place, Roosevelt told Congress to act by October 1 or he would resort to his war powers. Congress passed legislation that fell short of what he wanted but was close enough for him to approve it.[6]

Problems continued to pile up. Prices and wages continued to increase in ways that left everyone discontented. Workers threatened to strike in vital industries. Congress seemed unable to get over its tradition of passing out benefits to special interests without deducting something for the national interest. Military contracts went to big businesses, under the assumption that they were better able to deliver badly needed production in the shortest time. To this, Congress reacted with pressure to distribute war contracts to smaller firms. Whenever executive agencies tried to limit wages or prices, their orders contained gaps and exceptions that seemed to favor some over others. Inevitably, these conflicts arrived on Roosevelt's desk. For a time, Roosevelt responded in piecemeal fashion, creating special committees to deal with problems as they arose. Then he would create committees to reconcile the differences that arose between these. With no end of the bickering and complaining in sight, and wishing to lessen his burdens, Roosevelt decided to create the Office of Economic Stabilization under James Byrnes, who had been an effective Senate ally in the later years of the New Deal. Byrnes's job would be to broker the war's domestic interests, as Hopkins's was brokering its international ones.[7]

Roosevelt also presented himself as America's political broker. By this time, the congressional elections were on the horizon. Roosevelt decided to adopt his 1933–1934 strategy of being president of all the people, emphasizing the need for a united citizenry. "Politics is out," he declared to a press conference. Behind the scenes, he courted Wendell Willkie, who spoke up against isolationism, racism, and colonialism. At one point, Roosevelt tried to bring Willkie into his administration by offering him a labor mediation job, but Willkie refused. Roosevelt contributed little to the campaign. When he took a two-week trip outside Washington in late September, he went "off the record" with no fanfare and only three press people. He visited war plants and training facilities. His train headed west through Wisconsin to Idaho and Washington, then down the Pacific coast to San Diego and back east through Texas. His radio address on this trip concentrated on the national effort, avoided political asides, and criticized only those who were not doing their best for the war effort, especially those who were refusing to hire women, blacks, and older persons.

But these chidings drew no political distinctions, and with every candidate supporting the war effort, Roosevelt's nonpartisanship was an invitation to political apathy. The man who had worked so hard throughout his presidency to make himself the issue was now telling the voters that there was nothing political to worry about. On election day, millions of voters stayed home, more of them Democrats than Republicans. As a result, the Republicans registered their greatest gains of any Roosevelt election, picking up forty-four House and nine Senate seats and the governorships of New York and California.[8]

In the wake of the election, Roosevelt met with House and Senate leaders for a postmortem. Having already heard how much the voters resented price and rent controls, he promised to get rid of Leon Henderson, head of the OPA. He then sat back and listened to complaints about "bureaucrats demanding so many things of the people," "long-haired professors in Washington," "too many useless questionnaires," and "too many young smart lawyers in OPA." There were complaints about too many jobs going to Republicans, who responded to public complaints by blaming Washington.

Southern congressmen complained about race. The administration, they charged, was promoting "social equality." Roosevelt and Senator Guffey of Pennsylvania denied this and were willing to say so publicly. But the Democrats, they warned, could not carry New York or Pennsylvania without the black vote. Further discussion revealed that, by southern standards, "social equality" meant equal opportunity for government employment.

The congressmen warned Roosevelt against recommending a "huge social program" to the next Congress. Representative Clifton Woodrum of Virginia, chair of the powerful House Appropriations Committee, warned that a "social program extending from birth to death would probably cause repercussions and ultimate defeat." Roosevelt replied that he intended his message to the new Congress to concentrate on the progress of the war. He then proposed a social program, couched in terms of what the returning soldiers would expect. It included jobs in private industry, supplemented with government employment; education for those up to sixteen years of age; medical care "at certain prices they can afford"; and security against unemployment and want in old age. The congressmen remained skeptical.[9]

In his State of the Union Address, Roosevelt stuck to the course he had laid out. He began with a long review of the war effort, including an optimistic report on war production. He tipped his hat to the farmers, workers, and others who were striving on behalf of the war effort. He then ran down the list of social objectives for which the war was being waged and that the returning soldiers had a right to expect. "I have been told that this is no time to speak of a better America after the war," he declared. "I am told it is a grave error on my part. I dissent."[10]

Roosevelt did what he could to show Congress he meant business. The resignation of OPA chief Leon Henderson led many to believe that Roosevelt was relaxing his anti-inflation commitment. During the first three months of 1943, prices rose menacingly. At the same time, Congress passed legislation refiguring parity in a way that would have boosted farm prices substantially. Roosevelt vetoed the bill and followed with a "hold the line" order, freezing wages and prices at their current levels. He strengthened the powers of the major price and wage agencies. The OPA followed with a program that rolled back the prices of thirty-nine commodities and set dollars-and-cents prices on approximately 1,000 grocery items in 200 cities. More important, it decentralized its administrative structure by appointing community volunteers who defended price controls and rationing to their neighbors. The WPB was also authorizing the rationing of a growing list of consumer goods. Eventually, rationing covered 20 percent of the consumer price index. When soft coal miners went on strike for higher wages, Roosevelt took over the mines, and the union ordered the workers back on the job. The combination of price controls, rationing, and government takeovers proved remarkably effective. Between April 1943 and June 1946, when controls were removed, the annual rate of inflation was 1.6 percent.[11]

Roosevelt's leadership produced long-term economic benefits but a short-term political backlash. Stung by Roosevelt's initiatives, Congress passed the Smith-Connally bill, restricting the right to strike by requiring advance notice and a thirty-day wait before a strike vote could be taken. Roosevelt favored other provisions of the bill that essentially restated labor powers he was already exercising, but he vetoed the bill, charging that the waiting period might actually encourage strikes by creating frustration that might boil over. Congress decisively overrode his veto.[12]

Congressional relations continued to produce frustration and mixed results. A case in point was the effort to reform the process of collecting taxes. In mid-1942, Beardsley Ruml, a freelance social policy adviser who was chairman of the board of the New York Federal Reserve Bank, had proposed a pay-as-you-go system whereby the Treasury would deduct income taxes on a regular basis from workers' paychecks. The problem was that it would require forgiving the previous year's taxes, which, under the current system of paying at the end of each tax year, would have been paid out of income subject to withholding. This feature angered Morgenthau, who rightly pointed out that forgiveness would mean a windfall for the wealthiest taxpayers. The ensuing legislative struggle indicated how the congressional elections had limited Roosevelts ability to lead. House and Senate, Republicans and Democrats, wrangled over how much tax forgiveness should go into the new system. Roosevelt held himself aloof until the Senate passed a bill including total forgiveness of 1942 taxes. He then denounced the Senate bill and set the stage for wrangling over how to set a lower rate. The result was a formula that he had influenced but was nothing close to what Morgenthau preferred.[13]

Reforming tax collection was difficult, but raising revenue from the taxes turned out to be even worse. Roosevelt calculated that holding down inflation would require about $12 billion in new tax revenues and suggested that the Treasury ask for $18 billion to leave room for compromise. By the time the proposal reached Congress, however, it had gone down to $10.5 billion. Senate Finance Committee chair Walter George agreed to this figure, but his committee slashed it to $2.1 billion. When Morgenthau complained, George charged him with "exceedingly bad grace." The final bill, passed after much congressional hand-wringing for the overburdened taxpayer, was a Swiss cheese of loopholes. Roosevelt's advisers urged him to veto it, and the president, who had called for strong fiscal measures in his State of the Union Address, went along, calling the bill "relief not for the needy but for the greedy." But Congress was in no mood to listen. Senate majority leader Alben Barkley, who had been one of Roosevelt's most loyal lieutenants and for whom Roosevelt had successfully campaigned in 1938, called the veto "a calculated and deliberate assault upon the integrity of every member of Congress." Then, urging a vote to override veto, he resigned his post. The result was an overwhelming vote to override, followed by Barkley's reelection as majority leader.[14]

Roosevelt had little better success limiting war profiteering. Ever since his days as Woodrow Wilson's assistant secretary of the navy, Roosevelt had hated the idea that a few could become rich while so many others sacrificed. During the New Deal years, Congress had done its part by limiting profits in naval and aircraft construction while leaving profits untouched in other war industries. To these restrictions Roosevelt contributed his own leadership. The first president with actual experience with war contracts, Roosevelt watched over the defense buildup of the late 1930s and early 1940s, assuring the American people that he was spending their dollars for necessary defense.

The defense buildup produced new realities. A rapidly worsening world emergency required fast action, and fast action required big incentives. American business, hostile to Roosevelt and gun-shy from the shocks of the depression, wanted assurances that defense contracts would produce profits that could guard against future losses on new plants and equipment. Nor did the administration want to penalize companies that reaped large profits from efficient management or deny American voters the benefits of defense-created prosperity.[15] As with price controls, the solution seemed to be an across-the-board policy that would limit all profits by imposing a ceiling on all tax exemptions. But Congress balked, unwilling to reduce profits to constituents. In the end, Roosevelt compromised on a tax bill that imposed steeply graded tax rates on corporations but softened the blow with attractive amortization schedules.

These constraints ultimately determined the approach to profiteering. To spur production, Congress and the administration added new incentives that further boosted profits. In 1940 Congress created the Defense Plant Corporation, which built war plants and leased them to private contractors. Toward the end of the war, Congress authorized selling off these plants and their equipment to the highest bidders. Congress further provided that the value of property used for war production could be written off against federal taxes. The result was reminiscent of the previous century's sale of federal land with the addition of a tax break. Corporate America came out of the war stronger than ever, and the wealth and income of corporate executives skyrocketed.[16]

Administrative problems continued into 1943, until two things forced Roosevelt's hand. Congress considered legislation to create an office to oversee the domestic war effort, and Bernard Baruch showed up in Roosevelt's office ready to volunteer for the job. Anxious to steer clear of congressional interference, Roosevelt was tempted by Baruch's offer. The elderly speculator had gained a carefully scripted reputation as an administrative genius who supposedly dispensed timeless wisdom from a park bench across from the White House. Appointing Baruch would satisfy many of Roosevelt's conservative critics. The only problem was that at his advanced age, Baruch was not going to be up to the job. So Roosevelt did the natural thing and elevated Byrnes, who had been exercising similar powers in a limited way, to become director of the Office of War Mobilization (OWM).[17]

In this position, Byrnes acted as a referee. He began by asking the agencies to submit reports on their operations and future plans. He carefully avoided managing the war agencies and deferred to regular cabinet and executive offices. By letting the agencies know that he would not interfere with their administrative responsibilities, he encouraged them to solve their own problems. When disagreements came to his attention, he assigned authority and specified processes of decision making. He facilitated communication between conflicting parties and brought them together to compromise their differences. He directed agency personnel to investigate problems in the field. When he saw a need to intervene in a dispute, he acted. By letting the operating agencies run their own affairs, by facilitating good relations among them, and by husbanding his authority to act decisively, Byrnes established himself as the agencies' superior, even above the Joint Chiefs of Staff. Almost inevitably, the OWM evolved into a planning agency for postwar "reconversion."[18]

This arrangement did not guarantee administration unity. When Roosevelt met with his economic advisers to plan his revenue request for 1944, he followed Morgenthau's recommendations until Byrnes declared that he would not support any revenue bill unless he had a say in it. Angry with one member of his administration speaking against another, Roosevelt banged the table. "I am the boss," he said with emphasis. "I am the one who gets the rap if we get licked in Congress and I am the one who is in control. You people have to get together on a tax bill and then we can work it the way I want which is for the Treasury to present it . . . and the other people to work behind the scenes."[19]

At least one more particularly messy squabble was to come. Roosevelt had appointed Vice President Wallace to head the Board of Economic Warfare (BEW). The board engaged in "preclusive buying," that is, offering high prices for strategic materials. But Wallace had to get his money from the Reconstruction Finance Corporation. Heading the RFC was Jesse Jones, a conservative Texas banker totally out of sympathy with Wallace's agency. "The Reconstruction Finance Corporation," he declared, "does not pay $2 for something it can buy for $1." An executive order from Roosevelt temporarily clarified their relationship. Then things blew up. When Roosevelt issued another order asking his agencies to eliminate overlapping and duplicating functions, Wallace issued a directive in which the BEW made all the purchasing commitments and the RFC wrote the checks. Jones grumbled and fought back, and by the spring of 1943, he and Wallace were exchanging potshots in the press. Roosevelt asked Byrnes to get them to work out their differences, but he failed. Roosevelt then abolished the BEW, created a new Office of Economic Warfare, and transferred some of Jones's key responsibilities to it.[20]

The next year, Roosevelt narrowly avoided another public embarrassment when Donald Nelson had a falling out with his second in command over proposals to convert war industries to civilian production. This time, Roosevelt did not have to create new agencies, but he had to send Nelson on a special mission to China and then arrange an appointment for him in the State Department in exchange for his resignation.[21]

Roosevelt was managing conflicts by pounding tables, creating offices, and reassigning administrators. They were not good solutions, but as long as not everyone was going to act like Harry Hopkins, he had little other choice.

In the meantime, the New Deal was succumbing to the combination of wartime prosperity and congressional conservatism. The Civilian Conservation Corps was an early casualty, followed by the Works Progress Administration, the National Youth Administration, and the National Resources Planning Board. Congress allowed the Farm Security Administration and the Rural Electrification Administration to survive in shadowed forms. By 1944, even Hopkins, who had been the central spokesman and symbol of New Deal liberalism, was declaring that "our past domestic policies" had turned many voters against Roosevelt.[22]

Yet, amid what looked like chaos, frustration, and backtracking, the Roosevelt presidency was fashioning a war effort. Under the direction of often-clashing or dumbfounded agencies, war materiel rolled off assembly lines, recruits filled induction centers, and trains and ships carried them to the battlefields. Behind the lines, American agriculture prospered as never before, prices rose, and production boomed. The number of farms decreased at the same rate as before and after the war, mechanization proceeded apace (with help from Congress, which prodded the military to release steel for tractor production), and income soared. At the end of the war, the farmer's return on his labor had increased 30 percent, the number of mortgaged farms had declined by 27 percent, and the value of farm real estate had increased 79 percent.[23]

To a remarkable degree, wartime management furthered Roosevelt's goal of economic democracy. Economic historian Harold Vatter calculated that between 1941 and 1945 the average pretax income of American families increased at all five levels, each of which represented 20 percent of all families. But with the exception of the lowest 20 percent, which was just slightly below the next highest level, every increase up to the top was smaller than the one below it. One major cause was increased farm income, resulting from higher farm prices (which nearly doubled between 1940 and 1945) and farmers' receiving a higher proportion of the return on the commodities they produced.[24]

No part of war production would have greater historic importance than national research into atomic weapons. In 1939 Roosevelt first learned of the possibility that splitting an atom of uranium—atomic fission—could release enormous amounts of energy, sufficient to destroy an entire transportation center. Such was the estimation of Albert Einstein. The pioneer in theoretical physics had learned of research that supported such a possibility, and he wanted to warn Roosevelt before the Nazis were able to develop such a weapon themselves. Roosevelt responded by creating a scientific-military committee that limped along for about a year, after which he established the National Defense Research Committee (NDRC) and later the Office of Scientific Research and Development (OSRD). In October 1941, Roosevelt assigned responsibility for atomic research and development to Secretary of War Henry Stimson and to Vannevar Bush and James Conant of the OSRD. Roosevelt's initiative was vital to developing the atomic bomb. Its attention diverted by fighting to obtain funding for other munitions, the army was skeptical about the prospects for atomic energy. It was the scientific expertise that Roosevelt had assembled that convinced it to go forward.[25] Word that the British were making progress on fission led to an agreement to exchange information with them, ratified in June 1942 at the second Washington conference, and to various experiments with uranium-235. In the meantime, Roosevelt's top atomic advisers had turned over development of the project to the army, which established the Manhattan Engineering District.

Under General Leslie R. Groves, the Manhattan District assumed a structure similar to the engineering districts with which Groves was familiar. Principal sites were located in Oak Ridge, Tennessee, Hanford, Washington, and Los Alamos, New Mexico, with major research and development programs at Columbia University, the University of Chicago, the University of California–Berkeley, and Rochester University. On December 2, 1942, scientists at the University of Chicago, led by Enrico Fermi, achieved a self-sustaining reaction of nuclear fission with U-235. Shortly afterward, Roosevelt approved a request for $400 million out of the War Department appropriation to carry on the project. This kind of funding continued until 1944, when Stimson, General George Marshall, and Bush visited Speaker Sam Rayburn and other House leaders to inform them of the project and its cost. Rayburn agreed to channel the appropriation in a way to keep it secret. A subsequent meeting with Senate leaders had the same result.[26]

By this time, major research work on the bomb had been established at Los Alamos under the direction of Dr. J. Robert Oppenheimer, who headed a theoretical physics group at the University of California–Berkeley. Its scientists and engineers gathered to convert Fermi's laboratory experiment into a military weapon. They fashioned the processes developed at Hanford (plutonium-generating reactors) and Oak Ridge (gaseous diffusion) into nuclear devices.

In other areas of domestic life, Roosevelt preferred to swim in the mainstream of majority values. He had created a Fair Employment Practices Committee to head off a protest march by African Americans. During the war he gave it little attention and placed it in the War Manpower Commission, where it languished. At the same time, he allowed others to associate a war against Nazi racism with the cause of equal rights at home.[27]

Demographic trends indicated a new direction for African Americans. The war accelerated their urbanization, as they moved from the farms to the war plants. Between 1940 and 1947, the out-migration of African American males from seven southern states amounted to 20 percent of that population. Accompanying these shifts was an overall increase in the standard of living and a sense of upward momentum that many African Americans were disinclined to see reversed. Black membership in the NAACP, the nation's most conspicuous civil rights organization, rose dramatically. In 1942, white members of the religious Fellowship of Reconciliation formed the Congress of Racial Equality and began a campaign to integrate public facilities in interstate commerce.

Roosevelt was still tinkering and maneuvering as the 1944 elections rolled around. His desire to retire to Hyde Park was stronger than it had been in 1940, but the countervailing pressures were stronger yet. He waited until just before the Democratic convention opened in Chicago on July 16 to announce that he would be a candidate for reelection. His announcement brought smiles to Democratic candidates everywhere. Like him or not, they had come to count on Franklin Roosevelt's record of leading their ticket to victory.

Roosevelt continued to hope to realign the parties along liberal and conservative lines. This meant not only a continuation of New Deal domestic policies but also more immediately an internationalist foreign policy. This drew Roosevelt toward his 1940 opponent Wendell Willkie. Willkie had become an outspoken advocate of internationalism, touring the globe and publishing a book, *One World,* in which he called on Americans to participate in international peacekeeping. Published in 1943, Willkie's book had been so popular that Republican congressional leaders had issued a "Mackinac Declaration," warning that the United States should not give up its national sovereignty. Willkie had run for the Republican nomination but dropped out after a disastrous defeat in the Wisconsin primary. Roosevelt sent speechwriter Sam Rosenman to confer with Willkie about uniting Democratic and Republican liberals. Willkie responded enthusiastically. But news of a possible Roosevelt-Willkie alliance was leaked to the press, and during that fall's presidential campaign, Roosevelt shelved the idea.

Courting Willkie was another of Roosevelt's fantasies about reorganizing the party system from the top down. Over the years, he had been far more successful by sponsoring policies that moved blocs of voters behind liberal Democratic policies. His attempts to change party leadership in 1938 and 1940 had brought defeat and acrimony. Roosevelt's choice of a vice presidential running mate showed his ambivalence. Early on, he ruled out renominating Henry Wallace, recalling the acrimony in 1940 and fearing that a move to renominate him would split the party. Other leading candidates included Director of War Mobilization James Byrnes, Senator Harry Truman, who had chaired a special Senate committee that investigated waste and profiteering in war industries, and Supreme Court Associate Justice William O. Douglas. Each appealed to a constituency within the party, with Douglas, who had headed the Securities and Exchange Commission, the liberal favorite. Alben Barkley had support for standing up to Roosevelt over the veto of the tax bill.

At a meeting of party leaders the week before the convention, Roosevelt concluded that either Truman or Douglas would be the strongest candidate and scribbled a statement to that effect on a piece of paper and handed it to Robert Hannegan, chair of the Democratic National Committee. But in order to preserve as much preconvention harmony as possible, Roosevelt pledged his support to both Wallace and Byrnes. He wrote a letter to the convention tepidly endorsing Wallace and personally encouraged Byrnes, causing the latter to mount a strenuous campaign. When Roosevelt stopped briefly in Chicago on his way from Hyde Park to Hawaii for a meeting with Pacific theater commanders, he told Hannegan that Byrnes would be an acceptable candidate, but he should be sure that Byrnes was acceptable to Sidney Hillman, the chief political strategist of the CIO. Convinced that Byrnes was Roosevelt's choice, Hannegan went forward with plans to nominate him.[28]

What followed had all the qualities of a bad novel. Hannegan continued to insist on Byrnes, but Hillman and Ed Flynn, Democratic boss of the Bronx, would not accept him. Flynn declared that Roosevelt wanted Truman. The bewildered politicians decided to call Roosevelt, now in San Diego. Roosevelt told them to go for Truman and to release his letter approving Truman and Douglas. Byrnes called Roosevelt, who confirmed his choice; Byrnes dropped his candidacy and left town in a fury.[29] Wallace said that he would stay in the race, but Roosevelt's mind was made up. It would be Truman, if he could be persuaded to take the job. When Truman hesitated, Hannegan placed a call to Roosevelt, who declared loudly enough for all to hear: "Well, you tell the Senator that if he wants to break up the Democratic party in the middle of the war, that's his responsibility." With that he banged down the phone. Truman it was.[30]

The convention proceedings hardly improved on the hotel proceedings. Wallace supporters packed the convention hall and staged a raucous demonstration that they hoped would stampede the delegates; Hannegan had to adjourn the convention to put a stop to them. After the balloting began the next afternoon, Hannegan kept it going to keep out Wallace supporters, who had evening tickets. In the middle of the second ballot, states began switching to Truman, and he was over the top.[31]

It was Democratic Party politics Franklin Roosevelt style. He sparked ambitions, flattered egos, sent mixed signals, covered his tracks, and in the end got what he wanted. He bruised some egos, but he could always make that up later. He had lined up the bosses and kept the party together. Once when he was discussing the vice presidential nomination with some of his assistants, he recalled that Boss Charles Murphy of New York had always said, "the convention will decide" who would be nominated for lieutenant governor. "And," Roosevelt continued, "he got away with it for years." Whatever Murphy got away with, it was peanuts compared with what Franklin Roosevelt got away with. If only Joe Stalin was as easily maneuvered as Jimmy Byrnes, Henry Wallace, or Bob Hannegan.[32]

The major issue, as it had been since 1932, was Roosevelt himself. Now, however, neither his policies nor his personality dominated the campaign. Attempting to use Roosevelt's success against him, Republicans charged that he and his New Dealers were old and tired, a message that pointed directly at Roosevelt's health. The president was clearly not his former self. There were, indeed, many flashes of his old vigor and animation; his face was expressive, his voice strong and resonant, his shoulders solid and powerful. But there were many other occasions on which his face seemed slack, his expression uncomprehending, his grip weak and trembling. When Harry Truman had lunch with him (the first time the two met) on the south lawn of the White House, he was shocked to see Roosevelt's hand shake so much that he could not pour cream in his coffee.[33] On a couple of occasions Roosevelt embarrassed his listeners by unknowingly repeating himself.

He experienced warning symptoms. On his return from discussing Pacific war strategy in Hawaii, he delivered a speech at a shipyard at Bremerton, Washington. During the speech he experienced an attack of angina, a sharp, paroxysmal pain that extended from his chest to his shoulders. Gripping the lectern, already in great discomfort from his leg braces, he continued the speech during the fifteen minutes it took for the pain to subside. It was another instance of his supreme physical courage. An electrocardiogram a few minutes later was negative. Roosevelt's only worry was that the speech had not gone over well.[34] In this conclusion he was correct, and as the campaign moved into September, the Republicans seemed to be taking advantage. The Republicans had nominated Governor Thomas E. Dewey of New York, a crime-fighting district attorney who had won the governorship in 1942. Although his boyish looks, mustache, and slicked curly hair made him look like the groom on top of a wedding cake, he was an intelligent and able executive and a Republican moderate. Adopting a strategy that later would be called "Modern Republicanism," Dewey proposed to accept many New Deal policies but to administer them more efficiently and with better results. Through spokesman John Foster Dulles, he arranged with Secretary Hull to agree on the need for a postwar United Nations and to leave out of the debate whether the international body could commit American troops without the consent of Congress. He also accepted the principles of New Deal labor and social security legislation but promised to carry them out with less government bureaucracy and better cooperation with private business. He drove home his points by highlighting the conflicts, squabbles, and confusions of Roosevelt's administration and accused him of failing to achieve economic recovery and preparedness for war. By mid-September, he had reduced Roosevelt's lead in the polls from nine points to five. But he had also failed to spark enthusiasm and was running out of money.

Then Roosevelt jarred the campaign onto a new track. He scheduled his first campaign address for September 23, after he wrapped up the second Quebec conference and a subsequent Hyde Park meeting with Churchill. He appeared before the International Brotherhood of Teamsters and spoke over a national radio hookup. His veteran speechwriter Sam Rosenman called this speech the greatest of his career. Roosevelt began by pointing out that Republicans had tried to thwart and subvert all the New Deal legislation whose principles they now embraced, and he charged them with having obstructed American preparedness. As for Dewey's claim that the nation had still been in a depression in 1940, Roosevelt brought up "an old and somewhat lugubrious adage" that you should "'never speak of rope in a house of a man who's been hanged.'" On more contemporary issues, he praised labor's contribution to the war effort, supported the right of labor to contribute to political campaigns, and denounced Republican opposition to federal legislation allowing soldiers to vote. Then Roosevelt uttered the remarks that would place this speech into the annals of American political oratory. A Minnesota congressman had charged, falsely, that on his return to the United States from Alaska, Roosevelt had forgotten his Scottie dog Fala and had sent a destroyer to retrieve the pet at a cost of millions of taxpayer dollars. So, with mock seriousness tinged with indignation, Roosevelt responded:

> The Republican leaders have not been content to make personal attacks upon me—or my wife—or my sons—they now include my little dog Fala. Unlike the members of my family, Fala resents this. When he learned that the Republican fiction writers had concocted a story that I had left him behind on an Aleutian Island and had sent a destroyer back to find him, at a cost to the taxpayer of two or three or twenty million dollars, his Scotch soul was furious. He has not been the same dog since. I am accustomed to hearing malicious falsehoods about myself but I think I have a right to object to libelous statements about my dog.[35]

The teamsters loved it, Roosevelt partisans loved it, and the radio audience was appreciative. One columnist opined that from now on the race would be between Dewey and Fala. Dewey was outraged. Believing that Roosevelt had engaged in falsehoods and misrepresentations, he struck back with a fighting speech in Oklahoma City, quoting sources from Roosevelt's administration to back up his charges. He goaded his audience into a frenzy, charging Roosevelt with communist sympathies for having commuted the prison sentence of Earl Browder, executive secretary of the American Communist Party, for draft evasion; for working hand in glove with labor bosses; and for surrounding himself with "long-haired braintrusters." The next month his anger boiled again when he learned that U.S. intelligence had broken the Japanese diplomatic code prior to Pearl Harbor. In his mind, this elevated the Pearl Harbor disaster from a tragedy of unpreparedness to treason by Franklin Roosevelt. But warnings from the War Department that revealing the secret would hurt the war effort forced him to keep silent. Lacking other issues, he hammered on labor and communism, using Hillman and Browder as his keywords.[36]

Roosevelt returned to the stump during the last two weeks of the campaign, giving four speeches. By this time, he had come to take Dewey's attacks personally and was declaring his "unvarnished contempt" for him and the Republicans generally for running a low and vicious campaign.[37]

In New York City he rode for hours in an open car in a bitter wind and stabbing rain, calming fears about his health and enjoying the stimulation of the campaign trail. Addressing the Foreign Policy Association, he called for an advance U.S. commitment to use its troops to back up postwar peace-keeping, violating Dewey's understanding that the issue would stay out of the campaign and courting internationalist Republicans. (Roosevelt continued to hope that he could strengthen liberalism in the Democratic Party by bringing in liberal, internationalist Republicans. Early in the campaign he had sent Rosenman to court Wendell Willkie. Willkie had responded favorably to Rosenman but had also responded similarly to Dewey. In October Willkie died of a heart attack without endorsing either candidate.) In Philadelphia Roosevelt took advantage of the American victory in the Philippines and General Douglas MacArthur's triumphal return to the islands to ask whether the quarrelsome and tired old men of Dewey's portrayal could have put together such a successful war effort. He responded to Dewey's charge of domestic failure by predicting 60 million new jobs after the war (a figure reached in 1947). He continued on to Soldier Field in Chicago and wound up the campaign at Fenway Park in Boston, both outdoor locations that gave him additional opportunities to appear in vigorous good health.

More calmly than four years earlier, Roosevelt and his party switched on the election returns on November 8. Roosevelt had thought that a poor turnout might defeat him, and reports of a large vote in New York set a favorable trend. In the end, he managed a large electoral vote, but for the first time he had to rely on narrow victories in several states. Still, his coat-tails significantly increased Democratic strength—and, presumably, pro-Roosevelt strength—in Congress, and his internationalism swept away most isolationist candidates of both parties.[38]

Those who wondered about Roosevelt's direction after the election were kept guessing. Shortly after the election, Roosevelt oversaw a reorganization of the State Department. Roosevelt authorized Edward Stettinius to reorganize the department, and the new secretary turned to Hopkins for advice. The result was a series of designations largely of conservative internationalists. Eleanor thought that the lineup looked similar to "what it might have been under Dewey."[39] With Hopkins advising how to apply some liberal makeup and Roosevelt promising to remove any nominee who did not follow his policies, the nominations won confirmation by the Senate.[40] After the inauguration, with larger Democratic majorities in Congress, Roosevelt switched to the liberal side by nominating Henry Wallace to replace the conservative Jesse Jones as secretary of commerce and nominating Hopkins's aide in federal relief, Aubrey Williams, to head the Rural Electrification Administration. But nothing came easy. Roosevelt had to trade with Senate conservatives to get Wallace approved. The Senate then blocked Williams's appointment.[41] It was clear that, increased Democratic majority or not, Roosevelt was heading for rough times on Capitol Hill as the war wound toward its conclusion.

In the White House, Eleanor and Franklin continued their partnership. It had always been Eleanor's lot to shift out of areas into which Franklin moved. Her initial commitment to bettering the lives of the unemployed and destitute shifted to a concern for youth when Franklin proposed the WPA and brought Harry Hopkins into his inner circle. She continued her support for the young, but the flirtation of the American Youth Congress with Soviet isolationism dampened her enthusiasm. With the defense buildup, she moved into civilian defense work and support for efforts to aid war refugees. She convened a White House conference to promote civilian defense and accepted an official position recruiting volunteers in the Office of Civilian Defense. She had done it all before when she had recruited women for the New York Democratic Party. She knew the drill: surveys of available talent, training programs, jobs for the volunteers to do. She built her network: the Red Cross, the Department of Agriculture, the Federal Security Agency, mayors, deans, social workers. When she learned that the State Department was willing to grant visitor's visas to refugees but that the consuls were slow to issue them, she pressed Sumner Welles to "do something" about it and to send her a "report" about the situation. She was going full steam ahead when the news arrived that Japan had bombed Pearl Harbor. At once she was off to the West Coast to tour civilian defense operations.[42]

Eleanor's experience in civilian defense taught her a harsh lesson. Wherever she went, she attracted attention. This fact, once the bane of her life during the early New Deal, no longer bothered her. But the more conspicuous her public stature, the more she served as a target for political opponents. As criticism of her mounted, she decided that she would have to resign from civilian defense. Characteristically, she announced to others that she was doing it for Franklin; her public stature made her a target for his opponents. "I realize," she said, "how unwise it is for a vulnerable person like myself to try a government job." She was soon off to Britain to tour war plants and military bases, to meet with Churchill and the press, and to show the American colors.[43]

She continued to be a voice for liberal causes. Reflecting on a visit to her son James's training camp, she felt "deeply resentful" that some of those boys would fight and die for a way of life that a few years ago "we didn't want to tax ourselves to give them a chance to make a living in." The war intensified her commitment to equal rights for black Americans. Fighting

Hitler and his Aryan creed would mean little, she believed, unless America fought racism at home. She considered equal rights the basis of American democracy. In magazine articles and radio messages she conveyed this message. She persuaded Franklin to meet with African American leaders to get advice on combating white supremacy in the armed forces. Her influence led to orders desegregating military recreation areas and government buses. She continued to entertain African Americans at the White House. She fought for integrated public housing in Detroit, Michigan, persuading Franklin to reverse a whites-only policy. When a riot followed shortly after integration, many blamed her for stirring up "racial unrest." In 1944, Republicans accused her of advocating racial intermarriage, a charge that at the time was an ideological bulwark of white supremacy. Undeterred, she campaigned hard to include a civil rights plank in the Democratic platform.[44]

Eleanor continued to press for opportunities for women. She encouraged young women to defer marriage for war work. She toured war plants with Franklin and issued public statements praising the work of the women and reporting appreciative comments from supervisors. She attended a rally to raise money for war bonds by praising "women in war work." When she learned that both production and families were suffering because women were trying to juggle factory work and homemaking, she called for day-care centers and nursery schools near the factories. Because of her efforts, the Kaiser shipyards established a model day-care center that became the incentive for others.[45]

In the summer of 1943, she took an extended trip through the Southwest Pacific. Some of the military brass resented her coming and tested her fortitude by driving on steep roads and giving her the benefit of their opinions about "race mixing." She took it all with wry skepticism, observing that the general who opposed racial integration "would sleep with a Maori woman" if he had the chance. When Admiral William F. "Bull" Halsey cautioned her that "Guadalcanal is no place for you, Ma'am," she replied: "I'm perfectly willing to take my chances. I'll be entirely responsible for anything that happens to me." Halsey then explained that because of action in the area he would have to provide a fighter escort for her but had none to spare. Saddened at not having the chance to be near danger, but with a clearer idea of what the men were going through, she set off on round after round of visits to hospitals and camps. She stopped at every bed and visited with the men, ate in mess halls, rode in jeeps, walked mile after mile. Her most difficult moments came when she reviewed troops in full battle dress and imagined what war would be like for them. Whenever she met the troops she wished she could stop being the First Lady and become instead the mother or sister of each. She seems not to have guessed that this

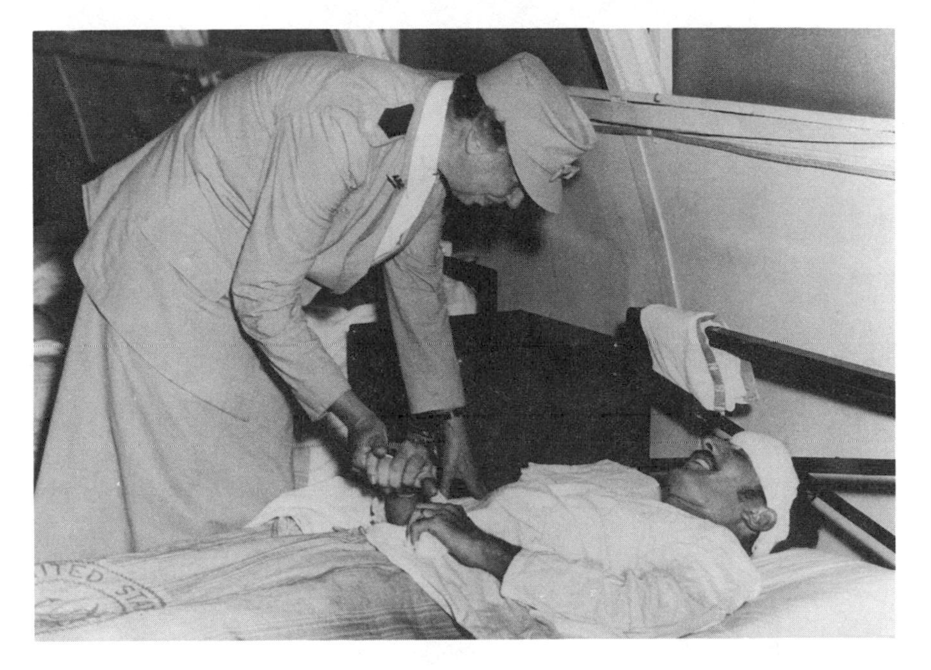

Eleanor Roosevelt encouraging a wounded GI in the South Pacific, August 1943. Wanting to experience war's dangers, Eleanor had to experience some of its consequences. (Franklin D. Roosevelt Library)

was exactly the impression she was making. Eventually, she made it to Guadalcanal.[46]

On her trip she consistently observed that officers were better off than their men and that the natives were often mistreated. She was still the New Deal liberal, unreconstructed and proud of it. She had smiled broadly when Franklin announced the four freedoms, and she was not going to let him forget them. She consulted with Walter Reuther, president of the United Auto Workers, about how to maintain full employment after the war and passed his ideas along to James Byrnes. She also worked on Bernard Baruch, who had proposed a plan for "reconversion" from war production to civilian production that would benefit big business. She had hoped Franklin would keep Henry Wallace as vice president in 1944, but after meeting Harry Truman she felt "much more satisfied."[47]

After the election, Eleanor met with Franklin and Harry Hopkins to discuss the future. Eleanor warned him against making too much of his international successes. The American people, she said, wanted him to keep his promises to them. He was under "a moral obligation" to carry through with his domestic reforms, especially the need to maintain full employment. What counted was action, she reminded him, not just "making speeches."[48]

Their relationship never mended. Franklin was self-contained and unable to let go emotionally, and Eleanor was wary and self-protective. Wartime proved especially trying for them. Eleanor found time to bring her issues to him during moments, such as the cocktail hour, that he wanted for relaxation. But their relationship continued to be one of ebb and flow, of distance and tension balanced against respect and affection. Franklin continued to regard her as his surrogate and to value her advice, when he was prepared to receive it. In times of hurt, such as when his mother and her brother died, they could reach out to each other. But jealousy and bitter memories constantly intruded. Eleanor never lost her bitterness at his betrayal of her with Lucy Mercer. Franklin especially resented her attachment to Joseph Lash. In 1943, when military intelligence reported that Lash had spent time with Eleanor in her room at the Blackstone Hotel in Chicago, he ordered Lash, who was in the air corps, shipped to the South Pacific. He also disbanded the intelligence unit but permitted the military to intercept Lash's letters to Eleanor and deliver them to him. In return, he arranged for Lucy Mercer Rutherford, recently widowed, to visit him in the White House.[49]

The tension wore on those around them. In 1942, Harry Hopkins married for the third time. His wife, Louise, took a job with the Red Cross, but since Harry continued to live at the White House, she became part of the Roosevelt family. Occasionally, Franklin would ask her to serve as hostess at his evening cocktail parties or to arrange the settings for dinner. Eleanor resented these intrusions on her domain and on at least one occasion spoke strongly to Franklin about it. Late in 1943, Harry and Louise bought a house in Georgetown. The move, Harry wrote to a friend, "will suit me no end."[50]

There were other departures. In the summer of 1941, Missy LeHand suffered a stroke. She never returned to work. In 1944, while returning from Hawaii, where he had conferred with the Pacific commanders, Roosevelt learned that she had died. He did not show any emotion.[51]

12

★★★★★

AMBIGUOUS VICTORIES

The year 1944 opened with positive prospects for the American war effort. In the Pacific, two thrusts had won impressive if often costly victories. One was commanded by General Douglas MacArthur in New Guinea and the Admiralty Islands; the other, commanded by Admiral Chester W. Nimitz, had captured the Gilbert Islands and caused devastating submarine damage, hindering Japan's ability to support its forces. In Europe, a similar dual strategy was developing. Despite his pledges to concentrate on OVERLORD, Roosevelt found himself committed to the Italian front as the Allied offensive, designed in September 1943 to capture Rome, bogged down south of its objective. By now, the United States had the resources to advance on all fronts. In the Pacific, Nimitz captured the Marshall and Mariana Islands and MacArthur returned to the Philippines, provoking a desperate Japanese response in which the U.S. Navy destroyed their surface capabilities at the battle of Leyte Gulf. The big news of the year was the Allied invasion of northern France, commenced on June 6. As the troops were struggling on the beachheads, Roosevelt went on the radio to deliver a prayer for the success of the operation.

Other aspects of the year were less reassuring. Early in January, Harry Hopkins fell ill with the flu and was soon hospitalized with complications stemming from his cancer operation years before. In March he went to the Mayo Clinic for surgery. He would not return to Washington until July. Hopkins's departure deprived Roosevelt of his most intimate adviser and the man he had groomed to represent him at the highest-level diplomatic talks. It also left him without the personal comfort that Hopkins's good-natured, sympathetic personality provided. While Hopkins was experiencing his difficulties, Roosevelt had a checkup in which his doctors found an enlarged heart, high blood pressure, and congestive heart failure. He was sixty-two years old and in very bad shape. But Roosevelt never asked about his condition, and he and his personal physician, Admiral Ross McIntire, assured the public that he was fighting a respiratory infection and nothing more. The doctors prescribed digitalis, which relieved the symptoms and appeared to confirm the public diagnosis.[1] Nevertheless, Roosevelt spent most of April resting at Bernard Baruch's estate in South Carolina. Toward the end of his stay he was joined by Lucy Mercer Rutherford, whose husband had died a few weeks before. They would be companions on and off for the next year, always without Eleanor's knowing.

As news of Hitler's Holocaust leaked out, proposals came forward to aid Europe's Jews. Although the United States accepted thousands of Jewish immigrants—more than any other nation in the Western Hemisphere—that saved only a small fraction of the millions that would eventually perish.

A certain number owed their survival to Eleanor Roosevelt. In 1940 she had begun by organizing a committee to coordinate the different agencies to care for refugee children; to pressure the State Department to be more generous in granting visitor's visas, which were not restricted by the numerical quotas of the immigration laws; and to find families to take in the refugee children. She succeeded in getting Franklin to override State Department reluctance to admit British children, but he refused her request to extend the program to Jewish children.[2]

Roosevelt sympathized with the plight of the Jews, but as was so often the case, he was more acutely sensitive than Eleanor to the competing priorities and political pressures that restricted his range of movement. He agreed with the State Department's concern that more immigrants would mean more enemy sympathizers and a greater threat to the war effort. In a White House that felt under siege from its domestic opponents, this was a powerful argument—one that was tenaciously reinforced by the FBI and Breckinridge Long, the man in charge of the State Department's visa section. When Roosevelt called him in to discuss the visa situation, Long spun tales of German agents posing as refugees to undermine the war effort. (At one time, Eleanor called Long a fascist. When Franklin admonished her never to say that again, she agreed but observed that her silence would not change what he was.) Roosevelt let Long go his way, piling up mountains of obstacles to refugee immigration. Roosevelt also felt the sting of congressional opinion. When he asked for authority to set aside immigration procedures that were obstructing the free travel of experts with skills vital to the war effort, Congress, fearing that the law would open immigrant floodgates, turned him down decisively.[3] Eleanor continued to badger him about the issue, and he continued to put her off with dismissive retorts.

Wartime strategy also militated against initiatives on behalf of Europe's Jews. The Anglo-American offensive in North Africa needed the sympathy of its Arabs, who asked for and received assurances from Roosevelt that he would not press for Jewish settlements in Palestine.[4]

The consequence of this, as historian David Wyman noted, was to turn Hitler toward his policy of mass murder. Originally, the Nazis had sought to solve the "Jewish question" through mass emigration. But when the rest of the world, including the United States, closed its doors to the refugees, Hitler turned to a policy of extermination. News of this policy began to arrive in the United States in the summer of 1942, where it encountered a massive State Department effort to discredit it. But evidence continued to mount, and by late fall 1942, Roosevelt was aware of Hitler's extermination policy. In December the United States joined with the Soviet Union and Great Britain (the latter of which had pressed for this action) to issue a declaration condemning Germany's intention to exterminate the Jewish people and promising retribution on those who did so.[5]

The resolution typified Roosevelt's response to the Holocaust. Personally sympathetic to the plight of the European Jews, he preferred to respond to events. He permitted his Jewish friend Secretary of the Treasury Henry Morgenthau to pressure the State Department for more vigorous action to save Europe's Jews. In November 1943 a vigorous advertising campaign on behalf of European Jews was under way, and Congress seemed to be on the verge of demanding a special commission to rescue as many Jews as possible and to establish special camps in neutral nations to guarantee their safety. Roosevelt suggested similar steps to his undersecretary of state, but he soon left for the Tehran conference, and little was done. When Congress persisted after his return, he established a War Refugee Board, which was left to make its way though the labyrinth of competing Washington bureaucracies. Wyman estimates that the War Refugee Board "played a crucial role in saving approximately 200,000 Jews," although he points out that it could have been even more effective if the rest of the Roosevelt administration had provided the assistance required by the executive order that created it.[6]

Roosevelt's other response to the Nazi extermination program was to urge other nations to welcome Jewish refugees. But his efforts got no further abroad than they had at home. Latin America said no. Africa said no. When Roosevelt approached the Vatican to stir up sympathy among the world's Roman Catholics, Pope Pius XII said no.

When it came to saving Jews, everyone had other priorities. When the War Refugee Board appealed to the army to bomb the Auschwitz death camp, the army said that it could not spare the planes. Appeals for shipping to transport Jewish refugees ran into declarations of a shipping shortage, which somehow failed to exist for non-Jews, who were shipped by the thousands.[7]

Minor explanations for this record abounded: building the alliance, avoiding "favoritism" to one group, quibbles over proper procedures and documentation, bureaucratic bungling. Democrats, who had been stung by charges that the New Deal amounted to a "Jew Deal," hesitated to lay themselves open to more charges. What made all this possible was that American society—and much of the Western world—had been infected with a kind of passive anti-Semitism similar to the attitudes that gave lynchers and race-baiters free rein in many parts of the country. Much could have been accomplished if the secretary of state had replaced the anti-Semite Breckinridge Long with someone who favored saving the Jews and had established in 1940 the rescue machinery that two years later was up against the formidable priorities of the war effort.

Roosevelt placed saving Jews second to winning the war. Within this context, his record was far from dismal, but it may benefit from a more precise analysis. When he thought that he could move to help Europe's Jews, he acted. For the most part, however, he acted in a political sphere severely circumscribed by other values and priorities. He was undoubtedly right, as Abraham Lincoln had been, that winning the war was the first priority and that others needed to be subordinated to it or subsumed under it. Franklin Roosevelt's difficulty was that, unlike Lincoln's decision to attack slavery, he did not formulate a premise that winning the war depended on saving the Jews. If he had, he would have moved much more decisively, and many of the obstacles he found in the way of rescuing the Jews would have disappeared. When, for example, Roosevelt pushed Lend-Lease as a way to protect the nation by aiding Hitler's enemies, the military and civilian agencies had no trouble locating those who were best qualified to organize and expedite the program. Similar drive and initiative informed many of his New Deal programs. But saving the Jews languished because Roosevelt chose not to press the issue and followed instead a passive policy of small efforts, gestures, tokenism, and inattention.[8]

Meanwhile, Roosevelt strove to keep intact the alliance he had started to construct at Tehran. As he had anticipated at the conference, this meant balancing the need for military cooperation with clashing international and domestic political forces. As the Red Army neared the Polish frontier, he and Churchill encouraged the London Poles to accept Soviet territorial claims on eastern Poland. But Stalin refused to hold discussions with the Poles and made statements indicating that he favored an entirely new government. To boot, he accused Churchill of trying to "intimidate" him.

In response, Roosevelt sent signals that he would be willing to see a different, pro-Soviet government in Poland. When Polish Americans began to express concern over the fate of their native land, he invited the head of the London Poles to Washington for a show of support, at the same time assuring Stalin that he had designed the meeting to persuade the Poles to accommodate the Soviets.

Polish-Soviet relations seemed briefly to improve. Then, on August 1, with the Red Army near the outskirts of Warsaw, the Polish underground rose up against the Germans. Instead of aiding the insurgents, the Soviet forces stayed in place, limited in part by overextended supply lines and a German counterattack, but also influenced by Stalin's decision to leave the Germans free to fight it out with the Poles, who would probably side with the London government. Churchill urgently proposed to help the Warsaw fighters, but Roosevelt held back, not wanting to jeopardize Soviet entry into the Pacific war. Only when the Nazis had crushed the Poles did Stalin agree to cooperate in supplying them.

Roosevelt responded warily to a Soviet-British proposal to assign postwar influence in Romania to the USSR and in Greece to Great Britain. Fearing that the deal would spark tension and controversy within the alliance and threaten the principles of national self-determination, he agreed only to a brief trial of the arrangement.

Roosevelt also decided to treat General Charles de Gaulle with a grudging flexibility. He not only distrusted de Gaulle's haughty, imperious attitude but also wished to minimize the role of France in postwar Europe by stripping it of its colonies. Allowing de Gaulle to claim the French government would threaten his postwar system. His solution was to insist on an expression of the preferences of the French people, whom, be believed, wanted neither the pro-Nazi Vichy regime of Pétain and Laval nor the Free French organization of de Gaulle. At the same time, Roosevelt had to accept the fact that de Gaulle commanded French troops that were necessary for the success of Operation ANVIL, the landing in southern France that complemented OVERLORD. So he staged a visit to Washington by the French leader, requiring that de Gaulle ask to be invited and using the occasion to outline his plan for a weak postwar France. Roosevelt also handed down stiff terms for his recognition of de Gaulle's organization as a de facto French government: that he accept General Eisenhower's supreme military authority and that he yield to the authority of the French people to choose their own leaders. De Gaulle protested but went along. In October the United States officially recognized de Gaulle's government.[9]

Overshadowing these issues was the growing rift in U.S.-Soviet relations. On one issue after another—Poland, planning for Soviet entry into the Pacific war, the forming of a United Nations security organization—the Soviets were taking unilateral, obstructionist positions. Especially worrisome to Roosevelt was the Soviet demand that in the United Nations all sixteen of its republics have individual votes and that the great powers have an absolute veto on all security matters, including issues to which they were a party. Roosevelt warned the Soviets that he could never persuade the Senate to ratify the organization under such conditions, but got nowhere. The conference, which had been meeting at the Dumbarton Oaks estate in Washington, closed at an impasse.

These matters influenced the last of the wartime Anglo-American conferences. For the second time, Roosevelt and Churchill met in Quebec. For Roosevelt, it was a chance to mend a relationship that had been somewhat battered and neglected in his effort to line up with Stalin. He found the prime minister fretting about the expansion of Soviet power in Eastern Europe and the Balkans and determined to take action. Roosevelt agreed to insert British troops in Greece as soon as the Germans left in order to preserve order and check communist influence. He also approved plans for military interventions in Yugoslavia, Istria, and Trieste and a strike to occupy Vienna. He hoped that Hungary would surrender to the United States and Britain to avoid a communist takeover.

Roosevelt also took steps to shore up the British economy. He agreed to continue Lend-Lease aid while Britain converted to a peacetime economy. He proposed that Britain gain economic dominance in Europe by putting forward a proposal for the deindustrialization of Germany. The proposal had come from Secretary of the Treasury Morgenthau, who suspected that the British were planning to build their postwar prosperity on German reparations payments that could only come from an industrial economy. Morgenthau also discovered a War Department "Handbook of Military Government," which suggested that Germany was to be treated gently. Fearing that an economically strong Germany would again threaten world peace, he assigned his staff to propose an alternative and showed the handbook to Roosevelt, who indignantly rejected its proposals. He saw "no reason for starting a WPA, PWA, or a CCC for Germany when we go in with our Army of Occupation." The Germans must be made to feel that theirs was a defeated nation. Treasury's plan for achieving this sense of defeat was to deprive Germany of the industrial capacity to become a military power in the future. Taking this as his starting point, Roosevelt asked Churchill how he would like to have the steel business of Europe for the next twenty or thirty years. Churchill was excited by the prospect, but not enough to persuade him to accept all of Morgenthau's prescriptions. Still, he and Roosevelt agreed on a modified plan that denied Germany many vital resources.[10]

Once the Morgenthau plan was in place, Roosevelt agreed that American troops should occupy the southwest sector of Germany instead of the northwest, as he had previously demanded. The shift would allow Britain to sustain its position more easily and to assume the main responsibility for policing German industry. Strengthening Britain, he believed, would further check Soviet influence.[11]

Roosevelt played a double game with the atomic bomb. In 1942 word of British atomic research had inspired gestures of Anglo-American cooperation and sharing of scientific knowledge. Early in 1943, however, Roosevelt decided that the British should receive only information that would help them build a bomb, presumably excluding postwar industrial uses. Churchill responded by playing his Hopkins card, protesting to Harry Hopkins that Roosevelt was breaking a commitment he had made during the summer of 1942 at the second Washington conference. Churchill stressed the need for postwar Anglo-American unity in case the Soviets developed the bomb. In August 1943 Roosevelt again reversed himself and signed an agreement with Churchill specifying the conditions under which they would use atomic weapons and setting up a committee to maintain collaboration. The implication, as Martin Sherwin suggests, was that Roosevelt was adding new strength to his nation's postwar role as one of the world's policemen. "There could still be four policemen [the United States, Great Britain, the USSR, and China]," Sherwin writes, "but only two of them would have the bomb."[12]

But, as usual, Roosevelt was hedging his policies. Earlier in 1944, and now at Quebec, he struck up an acquaintance with the Danish physicist Niels Bohr, who had helped to develop a bomb and who strongly advocated international cooperation and control of atomic energy. Bohr had contacts with both British and Soviet scientists, and Roosevelt undoubtedly realized that his remarks would be passed along. Shortly before he left for Quebec, Roosevelt told Bohr that he wanted to work with Stalin to use atomic energy for the benefit of all humankind. Then, having sent this message of goodwill and international cooperation, he expressed his determination to keep critical information out of Soviet hands. He and Churchill signed an agreement specifically rejecting any "international agreement regarding [the] control and use" of atomic energy.[13]

Roosevelt's new design soon began to crumble. When the Morgenthau plan became public, Republicans attacked it, claiming that it would strengthen Nazi resistance and cost American lives. The press picked this up and added the War Department's warning that postwar European prosperity would depend on a revived German industry. By the end of September, Roosevelt had disavowed the Morgenthau plan and shifted postwar planning from the Treasury Department to the State Department.[14]

The death of the Morgenthau plan was the rebirth of Harry Hopkins. After his return to Washington from his convalescence, Hopkins had operated on the fringes of the administration. Roosevelt sympathetically welcomed his advice, then ignored it. But Hopkins had continued to work behind the scenes, keeping up his contacts with the British and trying to reconcile differences among departments. When Roosevelt scuttled the Morgenthau plan, Hopkins pulled out an alternative directive, an approach he had worked out weeks earlier with the War and Treasury Departments and bearing the innocuous title "JCS 1067." The document called for military control of Germany, political decentralization, strict limits on economic reconstruction, and an emphasis on treating the Germans as a conquered people. (All thought the document a master stroke and advised its publication as a face-saving maneuver during the election campaign. But the British objected, and it did not surface again until Germany surrendered and it became the working document for the American occupation.)

When he had been in the White House, Hopkins's power base had been in Lend-Lease and the War Department. Now it reached into the State Department. In November, ill health forced Cordell Hull to resign. Roosevelt replaced him with Edward Stettinius, former head of Lend-Lease, recently undersecretary of state, and close friend and ally of Hopkins. At once, Hopkins was advising him on reorganizing the department with a series of new assistant secretaries, a mixture of old New Dealers, liberals, conservatives, and career diplomats. Hopkins supplemented these moves by appointing Charles "Chip" Bohlen as the liaison between the White House and State. A specialist in Soviet affairs, Bohlen had been Roosevelt's interpreter at Tehran and was then the head of the East European desk at State. Hopkins had often consulted with Bohlen in the past, and he now capitalized on their relationship by making sure that Bohlen reported directly to him.[15]

The return of Harry Hopkins not only brought Roosevelt back in touch with his former principal adviser; it also provided new institutional strength to his policies. Hopkins had never been comfortable with Roosevelt's freewheeling style of summit diplomacy, especially his tendency to make promises of which no record survived. He now worked with Stettinius to provide Roosevelt with expert advice and solid documentation. The next conference would be the best staffed and briefed of any to date.

The question was whether staffing could solve the problems that were piling up. After its pause to permit the devastation of the Warsaw underground, the Red Army continued to advance into Poland and the Balkans. Churchill, anxious to forestall Soviet gains, urged Roosevelt to agree to another summit, but Roosevelt declined. Determined to do what he could on his own, Churchill visited Moscow, where he bargained with Stalin to parcel out Soviet-British influence in southeastern Europe. It was not the sort of arrangement that Roosevelt, who had spent the war developing his arguments for an inclusive postwar framework with the major nations' sharing equally in keeping the peace, could be expected to accept. In Washington, Hopkins warned him against endorsing Churchill's negotiations, and from Moscow, Averell Harriman denounced the Churchill-Stalin deal. In the meantime, Roosevelt and Churchill squabbled over establishing a new government in Italy and over British intervention in Greece to put down a communist effort to control the liberation government. Roosevelt had actually encouraged British intervention in Greece to stop possible Soviet expansion. But the American press interpreted both the Italian and the Greek incidents as British efforts to establish its own sphere of influence, and the State Department reasserted its opposition to interference with internal matters that each nation should be free to decide democratically.[16]

Nor were events in China moving in an encouraging direction. Roosevelt's plans to award China the status of a great power were running into Generalissimo Chiang Kai-shek's lack of appetite for the role. During most of 1944, Roosevelt had pressured Chiang to undertake a North Burma offensive, as advocated by General Stilwell. But Chiang continued to temporize with promises and no action. Roosevelt tried everything he could, sending preemptory, sarcastic messages and a series of personal representatives: Vice President Wallace and Donald Nelson, recently deposed from the War Production Board, and Patrick Hurley, a wealthy corporation lawyer and secretary of war under Herbert Hoover. Roosevelt hoped that in addition to smoothing relations between Chiang and Stilwell, Hurley would be able to broker an accord between Chiang and Mao Tse-tung's communist forces. As bad as a feckless defense against Japan might be for China's great-power prospects, civil strife with the communists would be even worse. Chiang responded by launching an offensive not against the Japanese but against Stilwell, whose removal he now demanded. Faced with Chiang's determination, now backed up by Hurley, who as a negotiator was proving more gullible than adroit, Roosevelt finally gave in, recalled Stilwell, and ordered Hurley to work out an agreement between Chiang and Mao. Mao seemed willing, but again Chiang stalled, and the process broke down. Roosevelt turned to Stalin, hoping that together the Americans and the Soviets could achieve political stability in China.[17]

Roosevelt was navigating in crosscurrents that unpredictably rushed and subsided. Fears of isolationism encouraged him to refrain from public political entanglements, concerns about Soviet expansionism made him seek means of encouraging British intervention, and opposition to British-sponsored people and regimes drove him to cut deals and risk political entanglements. Whenever he steered in one direction, a wave pushed him in another. In such situations, he typically shifted his ground while proclaiming that he was holding a steady course.

Those who watched him move from issue to issue, from crisis to crisis, from one personal allegiance to another, might give in to confusion or cynicism or even mistrust. But for those who, like Harry Hopkins, stayed with him and always believed in him, there would inevitably come a moment of insight and a realization that his actions made sense and even bespoke a kind of genius. Roosevelt's alliance politics were of this character. Given the realities he faced, he had come to see himself, as in so many previous instances, in the broker's role. If for domestic purposes he had to maintain the appearance of independence and dedication to the high ideals of the Atlantic Charter, he could present himself as an impartial judge, an honest broker between Churchill and Stalin. This pose would enable him to switch sides to support and to chide in ways that encouraged the parties to turn to him to resolve their differences.

And so Roosevelt's plan for the four policemen was turning into a balance-of-power strategy. Britain and the Soviet Union would balance each other in Europe, China and the Soviet Union in Asia. In each area the balancing parties would turn to the United States to resolve their differences, to maintain the balance. Presumably, American independence and the U.S. role as "honest broker" would provide a stability that other balance-of-power arrangements had lacked. But would anyone balance the United States in the Western Hemisphere?

In the absence of a formal United Nations structure, Roosevelt had to continue to rely on the technique of summit diplomacy. While his reelection campaign was in progress, he had to put off a Big Three meeting. But planning for the next meeting started in October and continued into December, when it was decided that Roosevelt, Churchill, and Stalin would meet in February at the Crimean city of Yalta.

During the weeks between the election and the conference, Roosevelt's health waned and waxed. In late November his blood pressure went up and he lost his appetite. A trip to Warm Springs failed to reinvigorate him; he seemed drawn and weak. His conversation lacked its usual spark and gaiety and often wandered off the point. Then there would be times when the old Roosevelt returned—the agile, expressive features, the sharp and pertinent observation, the colorful anecdote, the obvious enjoyment of the occasion. He seemed his old self when the new Congress assembled on January 2 and two and a half weeks later at his inauguration. One could have imagined a certain symmetry to the occasion. His first inauguration had occurred in the midst of a desperate crisis, his second on the rising tide of successful struggle. His third had taken place on the brink of war, and now his fourth in its final victorious moments. In keeping with what in the affluent United States passed for wartime austerity, Roosevelt held the ceremony on the south lawn, speaking from a small porch. Attended by his son James, he took the oath, again on the Dutch family Bible, from Chief Justice Harlan Fiske Stone. Gripping the lectern, in raw January weather in front of some 8,000 guests shivering in snow and slush, he spoke briefly, emphasizing his faith in progress and better days ahead and declaring that the United States would have to see its peace and prosperity intimately linked to the peace and prosperity of other nations.[18]

Roosevelt focused his hopes on establishing a United Nations security organization. On January 11, 1945, he told a group of seven senators that nations whose armies controlled a given territory were able to establish a sphere of influence and that the Soviets had such power in Eastern Europe. Because the United States did not want a break with the Soviets, its best hope was to try to improve relations. In his view, such improvement would have the best chance of working through the machinery of the United Nations. Without such an organization, the United States would retreat into isolation, and the system of spheres of influence and balances of power—the system that had now caused two horrible wars—would reappear.[19]

Roosevelt's remarks defined his expectations for the Yalta conference. He would do what he could to moderate Soviet domination in Eastern Europe but would put his hopes on a United Nations to modify whatever result he had to accept. Indeed, he had no interest in confronting Stalin over Eastern Europe. He and his military chiefs still wanted Soviet participation in the Pacific war and to support a strong and independent China.

Establishing a United Nations peacekeeping organization was proving surprisingly difficult. Congress worried that through the organization the president would be able to send American troops into battle without its consent. The Soviets demanded votes for all sixteen Soviet republics and an absolute veto over all actions of the Security Council. Roosevelt protested directly to Stalin but got nowhere. Solving the problem was hindered by disagreement among the Americans; some favored the Soviet position, and others supported a British proposal that members abstain from voting in matters to which they were a party. Eventually, the negotiators adjourned with the issue unresolved.

The voting issue, of course, affected the issue of enforcement and became the center of American debate over postwar security. Journalists and politicians easily recognized the United Nations structure as a big-power alliance that pinned the hopes for world peace on their ability to get along. Before the election, Roosevelt had supported the British proposal that members abstain from voting on matters that concerned them. On November 15 he recommended a compromise formula that would require members to abstain on matters of procedure and decisions to investigate breaches of the peace but would permit them to veto any enforcement actions. The American people, he had concluded, would insist that the United States vote on "serious" matters.[20] A month later, Stalin agreed to eliminating the veto on procedural matters but remained firm on all other points. The difference between the United States and the Soviet Union had narrowed, but Roosevelt was perplexed as to how to proceed other than to insist on the American formula. There the matter rested.

Before he could address these or any other issues with Stalin, however, Roosevelt had to settle things with Churchill. It would be wrong to think that Roosevelt saw relations with the Soviet Union as his only problem. By this time, it was firm American doctrine that Churchill's strategy of dividing Eastern Europe into spheres of influence would only spark more of the rivalries that had produced war. Among Roosevelt's advisers, none believed this more firmly than his Joint Chiefs of Staff. In May 1944, as American and British troops were preparing for the cross-channel invasion, the Joint Chiefs forecast the postwar situation. The most likely conflict, they concluded, would arise between Britain and the Soviet Union. In this conflict the British would be overmatched, and even help from the United States could not defeat the Soviets. "In other words," the estimate continued, "we would find ourselves engaged in a war which we could not win even though the United States would be in no danger of defeat and occupation." The goal of American policy, the chiefs urged, was to promote cooperation among the Allies and avoid efforts by either "to attach to herself parts of Europe to the disadvantage and possible danger of her potential adversary."[21] When the Yalta meeting had been set, Churchill urged Roosevelt to confer with him, encouraging him with dark foreboding of a divided alliance and a "disappointing" postwar period.[22] Roosevelt agreed only to a brief meeting on the Mediterranean island of Malta but dispatched Hopkins to London to confer with Churchill. As he had done so often during the war, Hopkins was able to identify some key issues and to set the Americans and British to work on solving them. Thus, by the time they arrived at Yalta, Eden and Stettinius had agreed on a strategy for establishing zones of occupation in Germany, a strategy for countering Soviet demands for extra votes in the United Nations organization, and a commitment to support Roosevelt's proposal for a coalition government in China and a similar coalition followed by free elections in Poland. Still, all did not go smoothly. Churchill complained about U.S. criticism of his Italian policy. His remarks convinced Hopkins that the United States should take steps to counter British influence. When Hopkins arrived in Rome, he held a news conference at which he criticized British intervention in Italy. In the meantime, he had stopped in Paris, where General de Gaulle, now installed as head of the French provisional government, was angry over being left out of the conference. Hopkins got him to accept a postconference meeting with Roosevelt and reported that the United States and Britain now favored giving France an occupation zone in Germany and big-power status in the United Nations organization.[23] Hopkins's efforts complemented those of the State Department in making Yalta the best prepared of the wartime summit conferences.

In the aftermath of the Morgenthau plan, Roosevelt spent a good deal of time considering the postwar treatment of Germany. With no agreement among the Allies, the Americans had to craft a policy that would coordinate with those of the British and the Soviets. As usual, Roosevelt preferred to react to circumstances. He did not want to make policies for a nation that the United States was not occupying. Although he had consistently favored dividing Germany politically, in October he wanted "no decision" on the subject. This left him favoring demilitarization, de-Nazification, and "extensive controls" over the German media and educational systems.[24] Worried that the military might not be tough enough on Germany, he wanted to include "some outstanding civilian" on the Allied control commission that would administer German affairs after the surrender. As his thinking developed, he came to oppose reparations and to support only enough economic reconstruction to sustain the native population but not to sustain exports.[25]

The State Department's briefing book followed Roosevelt's prescriptions. Immediately after Germany's surrender, the briefing book emphasized the need for unity in Allied control so that the victors would not adopt different policies in their occupation zones. The principal long-range objectives were to create a Germany with a peaceful, democratic government organized along federal lines and an economy focused on supplying domestic demand. The department thus rejected previous plans to partition Germany into several states, believing that as long as Germany was capable of an integrated economy, such partition would not be effective unless the Allies committed themselves to prolonged and detailed supervision. Yielding to anticipated Soviet and British demands, the department accepted reparations but recommended that they be provided "in kind" (rather than in capital or productive goods), be taken from all production above the subsistence needs of the population, and be limited to five years to prevent their interfering with restoring "normal" trading.[26]

Settling the future of Poland continued to be a knotty problem. The two issues were Poland's boundaries and the composition of its government. In October the new head of the London Poles, Stanislaw Mikolajczyk, rejected the British and Soviet proposals to establish Poland's eastern border at the so-called Curzon Line, which would surrender many square miles to the Soviets. In June 1944 Mikolajczyk had met with Roosevelt, who had disassociated himself from the Curzon Line proposal. In October Mikolajczyk appealed to Roosevelt to ask Stalin to permit Poland to retain key trade and production areas. Roosevelt responded evasively. Mikolajczyk then resigned as prime minister, and in Parliament Churchill criticized the United States for creating difficulties over Poland. Roosevelt at once solicited Churchill's advice about Poland and proposed asking Stalin to postpone decisions on Poland until the next summit meeting. Churchill approved, and the State Department released a statement that paraphrased Roosevelt's evasive reply to Mikolajczyk. Stalin then called for recognition of a pro-Soviet regime in Lublin and repeated his usual charge that the London government was a screen for anti-Soviet terrorists. "Disturbed and deeply disappointed," Roosevelt renewed his entreaty to Stalin, who replied that the Soviet presidium had already decided to recognize the Lublin government and therefore his hands were tied.[27]

The briefing book sought to rationalize the U.S. position by supporting the Curzon Line, with modifications requested by Mikolajczyk; encouraging Mikolajczyk to take a leading role in establishing a new Polish government; and, to fulfill the expectations of the American people, demanding a vigorous role in Poland's political reconstruction. The most important objective was to form a government supported by the Polish people and a Poland characterized by peace and internal harmony and stability. It called for very limited territorial compensation for Poland in the west, fearing that including too much German territory would lead to massive relocations of populations, causing irredentism.[28]

Running through the briefing book analyses was the desire to avoid spheres of influence and divisions among the Allies. In considering the economic reconstruction of Eastern Europe, the State Department acknowledged that the Soviets would want those states "oriented to the East, both politically and economically." It continued to hope that it would be able to work within that framework, that if the Soviets felt confident of the fundamental orientation, they would be receptive to American economic aid and to American participation in "territorial settlements of questions involving general security."[29]

The role of American economic aid in this mixture of political and economic issues was especially intriguing. From Moscow, Ambassador Averell Harriman reported a request from Foreign Minister Molotov for $6 billion in long-term credits, to run thirty years on terms exceedingly favorable to the Soviet Union. The credits would cover Lend-Lease items ordered but not delivered, with a special discount on items ordered before the end of the war. Harriman passed along the request, with the recommendation that it be the basis for U.S.-Soviet relations, with the United States controlling the credits in ways that would influence Soviet behavior.[30] The proposal, the timing of which was designed to ensure a place on the Big Three agenda, set off a flurry of activity in Washington. Secretary of the Treasury Morgenthau proposed to expand the credit to $10 billion and to structure it to gain access to Soviet strategic materials and create American jobs. Leo Crowley, head of the Foreign Economic Administration, which had taken over Lend-Lease, proposed to delay until the Soviets had responded to a long-standing American proposal to expand Lend-Lease aid by permitting the Soviets to acquire industrial plants. The State Department supported Crowley and Harriman's idea of using long-term credits for political leverage over the Soviets, as opposed to Morgenthau's proposal to use it to support the American postwar economy. Roosevelt responded by deferring a commitment on the credits, which would require congressional approval, "until we get what we want."[31] In the meantime, he demonstrated goodwill toward the Soviets by ordering a maximum effort to fill their pending Lend-Lease orders.[32]

In its briefing book on China, the State Department recommended that the United States seek a coalition between Chiang Kai-shek's government and the communist forces of Mao Tse-tung. That failing, as appeared likely, it recommended establishing a U.S. commander of all Chinese armed forces under Chiang. Thus the U.S. policy was to prop up Chiang's government by unifying its military under an American general. This would both strengthen Chiang politically and ensure his cooperation with the Soviets when they entered the Pacific war.[33]

High on the U.S. agenda was Soviet military support. The Red Army had made the major contribution to winning the war in Europe, and the Americans were counting on it for a substantial role against Japan, which still had hundreds of thousands of troops on the Asian mainland. The Joint Chiefs continued to desire Soviet entry into the Pacific war "at the earliest possible date" and were at work with the Combined Chiefs and the Red Army to work out the Soviets' specific role in the fighting.[34]

Two days after his inauguration, Roosevelt boarded the cruiser *Quincy* to travel to the conference. In contrast to previous conferences, a full staff of diplomatic advisers would accompany him. (Secretary of State Stettinius and his team flew ahead to Naples, where they joined up with Harry Hopkins.) He also had access to the bulging briefing book of State Department recommendations. Hopkins had preceded him to London, Paris, and Rome. Roosevelt also took along his daughter Anna, who had become his companion and White House hostess during Eleanor's absences. Rounding out his substantial entourage were a number of special guests: James Byrnes, receiving a consolation prize for losing the vice presidency; Emory

S. Land, director of the War Shipping Administration; and Ed Flynn, Democratic boss of the Bronx and key player at the party convention. Because Congress was in session, he took along his appointments secretary Pa Watson and press secretary Steve Early. Thus this conference, which all expected to be a momentous one that would set the course of the postwar world, was the best staffed and best prepared of all and, consequently, the one at which Roosevelt's style of personal diplomacy would have the least effect.

On February 2, the *Quincy* entered the harbor on the Mediterranean island of Malta. In another step of preconference planning, Roosevelt was to meet Churchill and his staff before the final leg to Yalta. The meeting did not go particularly well. Roosevelt seemed physically drained. He had slept ten hours a night on the *Quincy* but still felt tired. Flesh hung around his face, and dark circles shadowed his eyes. As was so often the case now, his bright, optimistic manner compensated for his appearance. Churchill arrived in a dark mood, downcast over the state of the world, grousing about American criticism of his actions in Italy and Greece, brooding about Stalin's intentions, and feeling the need to establish a common Anglo-American front before the conference.[35]

By the time Roosevelt arrived, the Americans and the British had agreed on military strategy, on the zones of occupation following Germany's defeat, and on giving France a permanent seat on the United Nations Security Council and an occupation zone in Germany. Stettinius, Hopkins, and Eden also discussed various subjects, including United Nations voting and the government of Poland. Beyond these agreements and discussions Roosevelt was unwilling to go. He was following his usual practice of not making it appear to the Soviets that their allies were ganging up on them. When Churchill and Eden tried to steer him onto conference strategy, he responded with chatty evasions. For some reason—perhaps their experience with Roosevelt's preference for improvising, or his success in asserting American leadership in the Western alliance—this behavior seemed to undermine British confidence in the understandings they had worked out with Stettinius and Hopkins. As they were preparing to depart for Yalta, Eden expressed concern to Hopkins that they were going to the conference unprepared to meet "a Bear who would certainly know his mind."[36]

On the evening of February 2, Roosevelt went to the Luqua Airfield to depart for Yalta. The army had outfitted a transport plane for his convenience, including a special elevator to lift him from the runway and private living and sleeping quarters. He boarded shortly after 11 P.M. and went directly to bed. Through the night, planes roared off the runway carrying the some 700 members of the British and American delegations. At 3:30 A.M., Roosevelt's plane took off. The flight took seven hours, arriving in Saki around noon, local time. Roosevelt had slept poorly and looked weak and haggard. He and Churchill reviewed troops, and he tried to rest during the eighty-mile drive to the conference site. The Soviets had arranged for him to stay at Lividia Palace, formerly a royal residence and site of the scheduled plenary sessions.

According to Professor Robert Dallek, Roosevelt had a complex strategy for the Yalta conference. He planned to "bargain" with Stalin about the Far East and to "split the differences" remaining over forming the United Nations. He had little hope that he could deflect the Soviets from controlling the governments of Eastern Europe, but he hoped that he could avoid having to concede their domination of Poland. This meant that it was all-important to get a working formula for the United Nations.[37]

As the Yalta conference got under way, Roosevelt, as he had at Tehran, moved quickly to distance himself from Churchill. Meeting privately with Stalin, he alluded to their previous desire for a hard peace with Germany and sneered at the British desire to arrange a settlement whereby they could "have their cake and eat it too." In return, Stalin downplayed recent Soviet military gains, which he had emphasized to Churchill, and played along with Roosevelt's slighting comments about de Gaulle and the French in general.

But Roosevelt had not gone to Yalta simply to conciliate the Soviets. His principal objective was to establish a system of cooperation among the major Allies. Voting formulas and territorial political settlements would be the outcome of such a system, but they would be less important than the cooperative process. As much as anything, Roosevelt hoped that Yalta would produce not so much a static division of Europe, as had the Versailles conference of 1919, but rather a mood and spirit conducive to continued negotiation. His own strategy for achieving this would be to act as the intermediary, the "honest broker" between Churchill and Stalin. In his New Deal days, he had ordered those with opposing views to lock themselves in a room until they had reconciled their differences. Now at Yalta, he would seek the same outcome by making himself the catalyst for settling differences.

Roosevelt's position attached great significance to the United Nations organization. His great hope was that the United Nations would provide the forum for postwar cooperation. Early in the conference, voting procedures became the major issue as the Soviets reduced their request for additional seats in the general assembly from sixteen to three. This reduced the area of concern to the veto. Stalin was wary that the United States and Britain might use voting procedures to relegate the Soviet Union to a permanent minority. In a lengthy exchange, Churchill assured Stalin that only on discussion items would the veto be ruled out; on all action items it would apply. None of the major powers, now expanded to include China and France, would be able to impose actions on another power without its consent. After overnight consideration, Stalin accepted the voting formula.[38]

Stalin's acceptance came in the middle of tense wrangling over the future of Poland. After the first discussion of Poland, during which Stalin had called for the Polish government to be based on the pro-Soviet Lublin government, Roosevelt had written him a letter proposing that representatives of Lublin and noncommunist Polish nationals form an interim government that would hold free elections to form a legitimate government. At the following session, Stalin declared that the Soviets were printing their response, and during the interval before its delivery, he approved the Anglo-American voting formula. After some further discussion of the United Nations organization, the Soviets presented a proposal to invite non-London Poles to meet with the Lublin Poles to form an interim government that would hold elections. The difference was that Roosevelt wanted a new government, Stalin an "enhanced" Lublin government. Roosevelt had wanted to bring the Poles to Yalta to set up the interim government, but Molotov and Stalin claimed to be unable to find the noncommunists. The sticking point for Churchill was Stalin's request that the three powers all recognize the new interim government. That, Churchill declared, would mean breaking with the London Poles, whom Britain had supported for five years. Doing this would cost him too dearly at home. The only way to save the situation and to avoid a break among the Allies would be to organize a new government. With these differences in the open, Roosevelt moved to occupy the center, suggesting that they all now agreed on free elections and downplaying the importance of how to govern "in the meantime for a relatively few months."[39] But Stalin was not backing away. The liberation of Poland by the Red Army, he declared, had magnified the Lublin government's popularity and diminished that of the London government. But Roosevelt was not having any of it and persisted in emphasizing the commitment to free elections, this time joined by Churchill. The result was that the subject was referred to the foreign ministers. Stettinius proposed to create a new interim government that the three powers would then recognize. Molotov resisted this proposal, claiming that the Lublin government was needed to provide stability in the rear of the Red Army. At the plenary session, however, Molotov proposed that the Lublin government should be "reorganized on a wider democratic basis" and would be called "the National Provisional Government of Poland." This satisfied

Roosevelt and Churchill, who now turned to guarantees that the subsequent elections would be free. Roosevelt emphasized the point by saying that the elections would have to be as above suspicion as Caesar's wife. Stalin observed that Caesar's wife's reputation was better than her actual character. This caused the next issue to arise. In the foreign ministers meeting, Molotov objected to guarantees of free elections as an insult to the Poles and suggested that this be worked out in Moscow with Polish representatives. Eden and Stettinius accepted this, as did Churchill and Roosevelt. After some discussion about the form in which to put the revision of the Polish boundaries, the matter ended. The result was that Roosevelt and Churchill agreed to help organize and then to recognize a new interim government for Poland.

On certain points, the language of the Polish formula was unclear. Nothing short of a voluminous, step-by-step protocol for organizing an interim government and conducting elections would have caused subsequent events to unfold differently. At the moment, however, Roosevelt was pleased by the direction the negotiations had taken. At one point, he had been so upset by Stalin's hard line that his blood pressure had risen erratically. Now, however, his spirit had returned.

Shortly after they concluded the discussions on Poland, Stalin exploded when Roosevelt seemed to support Churchill's objections to Soviet claims for reparations from Germany. Challenging Roosevelt directly for running out on a previous agreement, Stalin rose from his seat and bitterly reviewed his nation's losses at the hands of the Nazis. While did spoke, Hopkins mentally reviewed the results of the conference: the Soviets had accepted the American plan for United Nations voting, included France as a major power, supported a coalition government in China headed by Chiang, agreed to enter the war against Japan, and agreed to reorganize their Polish government and to hold free elections in Poland. "Mr. President," he scrawled in a note, "the Russians have given in so much at the conference that I don't think we should let them down. Let the British disagree if they want to—and continue their disagreement in Moscow."[40] His words summed up the American estimate of the conference. Yalta had not so much settled the peace as provided an approach to settling it through further discussion.

Roosevelt carried through his thrust at colonialism, helped in part by Hopkins, who assured the British that Roosevelt would not, in Eden's words, "press too hard" on the subject.[41] Conferring with Stalin, Roosevelt worked out plans to provide "trusteeships" for "unstable" areas such as Korea and French Indochina. When the subject surfaced at the plenary session, Churchill exploded with a vigorous defense of the British empire. Mollified by a response from Stettinius that the United Nations would create trusteeships for detached enemy possessions, he supported an expanded formula that placed under United Nations supervision all League of Nations mandates, including British mandates, and territories that "voluntarily" requested it. The result was that Roosevelt got the principle of trusteeships in return for narrowing its scope by excluding the possessions of the big powers.[42]

In Far East matters, Stalin agreed to enter the Pacific war and to support a coalition government in China under Chiang's leadership. In return, Stalin asked for certain Japanese Island territories. When Roosevelt suggested that the USSR be granted use of the warm water port to Dairen, on the Kwantung Peninsula, Stalin added to the request the use of the Manchurian railways.[43]

Like Tehran, Yalta produced its effusions of goodwill. At dinner following the fifth plenary session, Stalin praised Churchill's courage for standing alone against Germany and Roosevelt for having a broad conception of national interest and for establishing Lend-Lease to mobilize opposition to Hitler. In response, Roosevelt emphasized Allied unity, characterizing the atmosphere of the dinner as that of a family. He then continued to show how much his New Deal values remained at the heart of his character. "He said that each of the leaders represented here were working in their own way for the interests of their people. He said that fifty years ago there were vast areas of the world where people had little opportunity and no hope, but much had been accomplished, although there were still great areas where people had little opportunity and little hope, and their objectives here were to give to every man, woman, and child on this earth the possibility of security and wellbeing."[44]

Roosevelt returned from Yalta determined to put the most optimistic face on the results of the conference. Although he privately acknowledged the conference's shortcomings, especially those that might expand Soviet influence, he omitted such thoughts from his public statements. The conference, he told Congress in a jam-packed joint session, had produced "the beginnings of a permanent structure of peace."

He did not have to wait long before the conference's shortcomings began to manifest themselves. Early in March, Churchill began pointing out Soviet tactics to dominate Romania and urged a joint protest. About the same time, the United States and the Soviet Union collided over the issue of American ex–prisoners of war now in Soviet custody. When Roosevelt raised the issue of their treatment and repatriation with Stalin, the marshal replied that there were no such persons. Stalin also informed the United States that Ambassador Gromyko instead of Foreign Minister Molotov would represent the Soviet Union at the conferences scheduled for San

Francisco to establish the United Nations, a snub at Roosevelt's principal Yalta accomplishment.[45]

More serious was a Soviet charge of bad faith against the Americans and British. In mid-March, German officers had contacted American intelligence in Bern, Switzerland, about negotiating a surrender of German forces in Italy. Suspicious that the Soviets might interfere to delay the surrender, Roosevelt and Churchill authorized further discussions and put off sending word to Stalin. When he learned of it, Stalin was furious, charging the Americans and British with striking deals that would permit the Germans to shift troops to the eastern front. In his sharpest response, Roosevelt expressed "bitter resentment" toward those responsible for "such vile misrepresentations of my actions or those of my trusted subordinates." Soon, he wired Churchill, the advance of their armies would make it possible for them to be "tougher" with Stalin.[46]

In the meantime, the Polish problem was overshadowing all other difficulties. After Yalta, instead of implementing the procedure to form a new interim government, the Soviets moved to solidify the Lublin regime. American and British efforts to the contrary were unavailing. Molotov suggested that if the Americans accepted the Lublin regime as the basis of the interim government, the Soviets would accommodate the United States' position on ex–prisoners of war. As usual, Churchill initiated calls for a strong response to Stalin, but also as usual, Roosevelt temporized, hoping that calm diplomacy would straighten out the situation. By the end of March, however, Roosevelt had lost patience. "We can't do business with Stalin," he declared to Anna. "He has broken every one of the promises he made at Yalta." On March 29, fearing that public disapproval of events in Poland would turn into disapproval of all postwar collaboration, including the United Nations, he cabled Stalin that his policy was "unacceptable."[47]

On April 7, Stalin replied by charging that the American and British ambassadors were trying to subvert the Yalta understanding that the Lublin government was to be the core of the interim regime. For the moment, Roosevelt's commitment to the success of the San Francisco conference restrained him. Thus, while he pondered his next move, he sent the American people brave and optimistic words. "The only limit to our realization of tomorrow will be our doubts of today. Let us move forward with strong and active faith." On April 11, he encouraged Churchill to mute his anxieties. "I would minimize the general Soviet problem as much as possible," he cabled the prime minister, "because these problems, in one form or another, seem to arise every day and most of them straighten out as in the case of the Bern meeting. We must be firm, however, and our course thus far is correct."[48] Now, as he had throughout his life, he continued to look for ways in which people could compromise on their differences and move on to larger objectives. At this moment, the objective of a peace based on cooperation among the victors depended on the success of the United Nations.

To a certain degree, Roosevelt had not appreciated the strains and contradictions in his own vision. His was, indeed, a grand design. What he sought was essentially a harmonious world order based on strategic balances and a world organization that would reconcile the inevitable tensions. But it was not a vision that took much account of the real and serious interests that history had produced. The principles of the Atlantic Charter and American domestic politics, by which he proposed to steer the world, were of only limited utility. He might want to use these devices to reform the British and to civilize the Soviets, but he could not disentangle himself from the realities he encountered. Thus he found himself shoring up colonial empires for the sake of big-power unity. It was unlikely that Stalin would find the votes of 6 or 7 million Polish Americans more compelling than his nation's security needs, nor that any policy could maintain the regime of Chiang Kai-shek.

Roosevelt's policies were, as much as anything, his attempt to reconstruct the world along New Deal lines. His were the policies of liberal nationalism: democratic political institutions and open markets, underpinned by a faith in social engineering. Harry Hopkins, who understood him as well as anyone, once remarked that Roosevelt really believed in the liberal democratic clichés he was so fond of coining. But here, once again, a comparison with Abraham Lincoln seems appropriate. Lincoln's reconstruction of the nineteenth-century American Union could proceed apace as long as it relied on a victorious military force. But as postwar Reconstruction was to demonstrate, his policies rapidly became immersed in the complexities of peacetime politics, where they lost their momentum and their clarity and became a source of frustration and disillusion. Roosevelt's policies suffered a similar fate. To the extent that they failed to take into account others' national interests, they condemned him to play a game of adjustment and maneuver. But this was a game he had always played, and at which he had often succeeded in spectacular fashion.

Maybe he could have pulled it off. At the end of the war, there was probably no person who stood higher in the estimation of the world than Franklin Roosevelt. Maybe through the United Nations, world tours, and other summit conferences he could have marshaled the resources necessary to moderate the brutalities of Soviet expansionism and Western colonialism.

But these were complexities he would not face, efforts he would not make. Upon his return from Yalta, as for many months now, he continued to have good and bad moments. He would drift in and out of attention. During moments of stress, his blood pressure would rise, causing the veins on his forehead to stand out. Toward the end of March, he decided to relax at Warm Springs. Eleanor remained in Washington. He received some official visitors and kept in touch with business on the phone. Among his guests was Lucy Mercer Rutherford. On April 12, 1945, a little after 1 P.M., he said, "I have a terrific headache" and slumped forward.

In Washington, Vice President Harry Truman was called to the telephone in Speaker Sam Rayburn's hideaway in the Capitol. He listened to a brief message and hung up the phone. "Jesus Christ and General Jackson," he said.

When he arrived at the White House, he was ushered into the presence of the staff, who were standing on either side of Eleanor.

"Harry," she said, "the president is dead."

Instinctively, Truman asked if there was anything he could do for her.

"Is there anything we can do for you?" she replied. "For you are the one in trouble now."[49]

13

★★★★★

CONCLUSION

The first thing to notice about the presidency of Franklin D. Roosevelt is its length. Of the thirty-one elections held before 1932, ten had conferred a second term. Fourteen incumbent presidents had declined to run, had failed to be renominated, or had been defeated. Of the ten two-term presidents, only Ulysses Grant had considered a third term. Roosevelt ran for a third term only because he believed that the dangerous international situation required his leadership. In this sense, his third term, which the length of the war prolonged into a fourth term, was a historical accident. Still, Roosevelt's reelection in 1940 followed precedent. Two previous presidents, Madison in 1812 and Wilson in 1916, had sought reelection during an international crisis and in each case had been reelected. The unique feature of Roosevelt's reelection was its third-term character.

Roosevelt's political opponents lacked this perspective. It was enough for them that a president they disliked had been elected to four terms. Thus, the Eightieth Congress, dominated by Republicans and conservative Democrats, passed and sent to the states a Twenty-second Amendment, providing that no person, save incumbent president Harry Truman, could be elected to the presidency for more than two terms. At this writing we have yet to see whether this limitation will deprive the nation of continuous leadership at a critical moment.

The debate on the amendment yielded little additional substance. Supporters quoted George Washington and other presidents on the virtues of a two-term limitation. A few charged that Roosevelt had accumulated executive powers and used them to secure reelection. It was a curious echo of the turn-of-the-century Progressive charge that political bosses used patronage and payoffs from special interests to dominate the electoral process.

Still, one can understand why Roosevelt's detractors wanted to eliminate his four-term precedent. Roosevelt's enormous personal popularity—at the time unique in presidential history—had so dominated electoral politics that only in his last campaign had his challenger stood even a slim chance of defeating him. Against the possibility that Roosevelt might have set a precedent on which other liberal presidents could capitalize, his opponents retreated to the bulwarks of the Constitution. It was not the first time the Constitution had been used to thwart popular majorities, but it was the first time a constitutional amendment had been employed for that purpose. The constitutional bulwarks have remained intact, but they have not been able to restrain the developing scholarly consensus that Franklin Roosevelt was a great president.

Professor Barry D. Karl, a major student of administrative history, provides a focus for understanding the basis of Roosevelt's greatness. Karl has claimed that Roosevelt's choice of political rather than administrative means to carry out his objectives kept the United States from developing an administrative state independent from the political process. He writes: "Calling Congress into special session immediately [in 1933], rather than governing by executive order, was perhaps the most crucial decision of Roosevelt's presidency and the most characteristic. Roosevelt was essentially a professional politician." In other words, Roosevelt relied on the traditional institutions and methods of American democracy.[1]

We may debate whether Roosevelt's decision to govern by means of his political skills was truly a critical moment in American history. It seems clear, however, that his preference for political maneuvering decisively affected his approach to administration. Instead of setting up a "rational" chain of command, he created a system that depended on free flows of communication and a desire to achieve consensus. He used such bodies as the National Emergency Council less to "govern" his administration than to help his administrators share experiences and learn the political ropes. His tendency to dismiss anyone who aspired to the title "assistant president" showed that he was not at all interested in establishing a chain of command. (He got along much better with Harry Hopkins, who referred to himself as an "office boy.")

Karl's insight has informed much of the recent discussion of Roosevelt's administrative presidency. Although Roosevelt receives low marks on a scale of rational management, he has been praised for using his staff and cabinet as instruments of acquiring information and conveying his authority. The major result of this approach was multiple arrangements, serving multiple functions. Roosevelt was never able to construct a system that would "coordinate" his programs, but he was able to create networks that could balance interests and adjudicate conflicts while, most important of all, reserving the power of decision for himself. One searches the record of Roosevelt's presidency in vain to find a major issue that "got away" from him. The failures of his presidency resulted from bad judgment, not inattention. Nor does one find Roosevelt spending time supervising his staff. He simply relied on them to carry out his policies and to bring him issues they could not resolve. In the meantime, he moved them about like pieces on a chessboard, assigning them duties that suited his purposes and not always theirs. He wanted staff members to compete with one another to keep them on their toes and motivate them to improve their performance.[2]

Positive and negative evaluations of Roosevelt's presidency run through the spectrum of his activities. Some praise his vision of a cooperative pluralism, a humane and just American society, and a world order of independent states whose security was guaranteed by the major powers and especially by the United States. Some see virtues in his managerial style, especially in his ability to keep command of his presidential office and to maximize his sources of information. Others find his vision either too "liberal" or too "conservative," usually concluding that his New Deal failed to eliminate the shortcomings and injustices of free-market capitalism or retarded economic recovery by improperly intervening in the economy. Still others decry his mercurial methods, his tendency to follow public opinion or congressional politics, his willingness to accommodate big-city bosses and party plutocrats, his preference for indirection, his moments of hesitation and lassitude, and his preference for subterfuge and prevarication.

Both Roosevelt's favorable and unfavorable critics have constructed a fairly consistent image: a president who had great confidence in his leadership skills and who believed that his personality was his major political asset. Roosevelt kept himself in the spotlight to get the maximum advantage of his ability to affect people on a personal level. His successes, shortcomings, and failures resulted less from any weakness in his vision or his management of government than from the quality of his political judgments.[3]

It seems clear that one of Roosevelt's major achievements was to create an institutional structure for the modern welfare state. Although many of his New Deal agencies, most notably the WPA, disappeared with wartime prosperity, programs for farm prices, retirement income, unemployment compensation, labor-management relations, and financial management remained. Just as important, his presidency removed psychological and political obstacles to using government to protect people from the vicissitudes of the marketplace.

Because of Roosevelt's New Deal, subsequent presidents were freer than ever to use government in creative ways. The New Deal made possible Truman's Fair Deal, Kennedy's New Frontier, and Johnson's Great Society. Even Ronald Reagan's jobs legislation echoed the WPA. These were achievements of major historical importance. But the greatest importance of Roosevelt's presidency was how it demonstrated the indispensable ingredient of political leadership. The New Deal was uniquely Roosevelt's creation. He did not conceive of all or even most of it, but his social values encouraged it, and he recruited people who were able to conceive it. He then provided the political muscle to enact it. (Even when Roosevelt followed Congress's initiative in establishing a Federal Emergency Relief Administration, he refashioned it into the more significant WPA.) Though never as successful as he hoped to be, he left behind a new political structure that would return Democratic majorities to both houses in fifteen of the next seventeen Congresses and to twenty-two of twenty-four Houses of Representatives. During this time, successive presidents reconfigured his New Deal legacy, but none subverted it. Without his ability to keep himself in the spotlight and to generate and maintain his popularity with the voters, Roosevelt's presidency would have concluded in as dismal a fashion as that of Herbert Hoover.

The Pearl Harbor attack permitted Roosevelt to pursue his vision of a world order of independent states whose security would be guaranteed by the major powers. Roosevelt recognized that the strongest postwar nations would be the United States and the Soviet Union. Not surprisingly, he sought to position the United States in the superior position, aiming to construct a world order in which the Soviets would be hemmed in by Britain and France in Europe and by China in Asia. To achieve this balance, he had to compromise his desire to dismantle European colonialism. He backed down before Churchill's explosive defense of British India, agreed to return Indochina to France, and generally circumscribed his anticolonialism with realpolitik.[4] But in the end, history accomplished what he did not, and during the postwar years the world witnessed an ever-increasing number of independent states.

Roosevelt also left behind a dynamic personal legacy. If his programs and his political values survived him, so did his image. For most of Roosevelt's successors, this legacy was a burden. Harry Truman so resented being constantly compared with Roosevelt, especially by Roosevelt's sons and Eleanor, that he laced his journals and private conversations with anti-Roosevelt statements. Dwight Eisenhower pointedly surrounded himself with anti–New Dealers and made it his personal mission to disparage the Tennessee Valley Authority. John Kennedy, whose father Joseph P. Kennedy had become a virulent Roosevelt hater, struggled with the Roosevelts on his way to the White House and once in office tried to minimize the difficulties of Roosevelt's presidency in relation to his own. Only Lyndon Johnson enthusiastically embraced Roosevelt, and, with a Congress as sympathetic as Roosevelt's early ones, he enacted the most far-reaching social legislation since the New Deal. Yet, in one of history's characteristically tragic ironies, his attempt to apply the lesson of Roosevelt's internationalism—that "democracies" should stand up to "aggression"—he led the nation into the quagmire of Vietnam and a war that ultimately ruined his presidency. A typically ambivalent Richard Nixon praised Roosevelt publicly while trying to dismantle his programs. And so it went: each president establishing his own relationship to Roosevelt while trying to establish his own identity.[5]

This book's portrayal of Roosevelt as a pluralist leader owes much to the perceptions of his contemporaries, many of whom tried to interpret his achievements for their own and future generations. No one was more impressed by Roosevelt's achievements than Paul Appleby. Appleby, who, along with Chester Davis, Florence Kerr, and Hallie Flanagan, had been a contemporary of Harry Hopkins at Grinnell College in Iowa, had entered the New Deal as an assistant secretary of agriculture under Henry Wallace. In this capacity he had acted as an office manager or executive secretary, in effect controlling the flow of information in and out of the secretary's office. When Wallace became vice president, Appleby held various positions, increasingly involved in international agricultural policy. In 1944 he became an assistant director in the Bureau of the Budget, a position he held until 1947, when he resigned to enter academic life and to become one of the nation's leading students of administration. In 1945 he reflected on Franklin Roosevelt's presidency in a book entitled *Big Democracy*.[6]

Appleby wanted to show how sound administration could advance the public good. He believed that the increasing complexity of society made it impossible for the average citizen to influence public policy directly. The mastery of complexity required specialization and expertise. It also required centralization, a focal point where experts could gather to work out policy. Appleby believed that this kind of development was inevitable. The only question was whether centralization served special interests or the general welfare, whether it subverted or preserved democracy. In Appleby's thinking, only government was capable of defining and providing for the general welfare by democratic means. Thus the government administrator or bureaucrat became a key person in that process, because only the bureaucrat made decisions continually, whereas legislatures and courts decided things occasionally.

Thus Appleby tried to reconcile democracy and expertise. He rejected the notion that people who were removed from the political process should manage society. Bureaucrats should always consider themselves involved in politics and should be held politically accountable. Because democracy worked best when it resolved controversial issues, the bureaucrat carried on the process of balancing and reconciling competing claims and interests.

Good bureaucrats also encouraged democracy within their offices. They stood up for the welfare of their subordinates and encouraged them to form a team, to be creative, and to resolve their own differences. Good bureaucrats had to assemble a staff that would take account of their individual peculiarities so that they could most objectively provide the necessary information.

A bureaucracy functioned at different levels. The central department established general rules and facilitated operations, and the lower levels put policies into effect. The basic concept was federalism, a sharing of power and responsibility by different parts of government.

Appleby saw administration as a constant interaction between different levels of bureaucracy. He also saw it as fundamentally political in nature, a constant interaction between the bureaucrat and the public. The logic of events, he wrote, is superior to the logic of the mind. Politics, the competition between parties and the interaction between government and its citizens, makes bureaucracies able to both change with the times and be responsive to the citizenry. An agency run by politicians, he asserted, would be more efficient than one run by professional administrators.

Appleby's formulation was built around relationships. A democratic institution was interactive, both internally and externally; its bureaucrats were cooperative. Its interactions were continual because it had to stay in touch with its constituents. And, above all, it kept its focus on the common good. Here was a bit of an unresolved issue in Appleby's formulation. It was not entirely clear whether the common good was the inevitable result of an open, flexible, interactive, continuously operating institution or whether the common good resulted from the organization's always keeping in mind that its purpose was the common good. What was clear, however, was Appleby's belief that the objective of big democracy was a whole that was greater than the sum of its parts.

Appleby's was the classic formulation of the pluralistic administration and politics that Franklin Roosevelt had conducted. It was the intellectual fruit of Roosevelt's New Deal and wartime administration.

Of all his possible lessons, this was the one Franklin Roosevelt seems to have taught the best. Even by the end of his second term, there had developed a kind of celebration of executive leadership and government by administration. Bureaucracy seemed the wave of the future. The task of the present was to employ pluralistic methods to make bureaucracy an instrument of democracy. A first step was to incorporate bureaucracy into the organic development of society. Legal scholars routinely observed that the growth of government bureaucracy was a necessary consequence of the nation's economic and social development, specifically, of industrialization and urbanization. So that bureaucracy could serve a growing and changing society, its methods should be flexible and based on consensus building. In 1939 the noted scholar of public administration Leonard D. White published a revised edition of his 1926 textbook on government administration. The new edition no longer characterized administration in abstract, mechanistic terms but emphasized the need for flexibility so that the administrator could mediate or facilitate the achievement of large objectives. "The duties of public office," White wrote, "can be adequately performed only by permanent officials, with suitable professional and technical training, acting under the direction of department heads of broad vision who are able by the personal leadership to mediate between the technician, the politician, and the public."[7]

Administrative law adopted a similar vision. The New Deal seemed to make administrative agencies subject to the law, yet free to make their rulings according to actual circumstances and conditions. The Supreme Court, which in its anti–New Deal phase had expressed alarm at broad delegations by legislatures to administrative agencies, now viewed the practice with an encouraging attitude. In 1940 Justice Felix Frankfurter, who considered himself an architect of the New Deal and whom Roosevelt had nominated to the Supreme Court, expressed this view in the *Phelps Dodge* case. The issue in the case was whether the National Labor Relations Board had the authority to order employers to rehire workers they had dismissed for union activity after those employees had found other jobs. It was an issue the Wagner Act had not addressed. But Frankfurter had no trouble ruling for the workers. The "great national purpose" of the Wagner Act had been to promote industrial peace through worker "self-organization" and collective bargaining. History showed that "an embargo against employment of union labor was notoriously one of the chief obstructions to collective bargaining through self-organization." Neither statutory law nor judicial precedent should prevent the government from carrying out its purposes. "Attainment of a great national policy through expert administration in collaboration with limited judicial review," Frankfurter wrote, "must not be confined within narrow canons." In acting on behalf of such a policy, the board should have the authority to avail "itself of the freedom given it by Congress to attain just results in diverse, complicated situations." Still, Frankfurter's decision remanded the case to the board for a clearer ruling while at the same time emphasizing his own support for the board's authority. "All we ask of the Board," he wrote, "is to give clear indication that it has exercised the discretion with which Congress had empowered it. This is to affirm most emphatically the authority of the Board."[8] In another decision, Frankfurter declared for the Court that the judiciary could not limit regulatory agencies by writing its own principles into the congressional statutes. That, he wrote, "would mean that for practical purposes . . . judicial review . . . rather than the public interest, [would] be decisive factors in" administration. "Interference by the courts," he declared, "is not conducive to the development of habits of responsibility in administrative agencies."[9]

In 1944 Robert H. Jackson, who had served as attorney general before Roosevelt elevated him to the High Court, affirmed the need in wartime for a transportation policy based on "informed, expert and unbiased judgment" and argued for judicial restraint in dealing with administrative agencies. It was "not for the Court to set aside, without legislative command, its slow-wrought general principles which protect the finality and integrity of decisions by administrative tribunals."[10] "The survival of democracy," another scholar of public administration wrote, "may well depend upon an orderly development of administrative law and tribunals to give effective direction to the administrative process."[11]

The key to effective administration was less its expertise than its ability to connect with the public. As Appleby noted, Franklin Roosevelt's presidency employed administration to activate citizen participation. The furthest thing from his mind was to create an administrative or bureaucratic state that would operate apart from the American people. In both the New Deal and wartime, his government was remarkably inventive in devising ways to keep the people and their government in touch with each other. The New Deal breathed new life into American federalism, employing all levels of national, state, and local jurisdictions in operating its programs. Its conception of regionalism and regional planning added a new dimension to the federal structure. The major New Deal programs relied heavily on local participation, from local jurisdictions' applying for WPA work relief projects to AAA votes to approve subsidy programs to Indian self-government, rural electrification cooperatives, greenbelt communities, union representation, and collective bargaining contracts. Wartime programs encouraged citizen participation by devices such as draft boards, ration boards, war bond and scrap collection drives, "victory gardens," and price control committees. Administrators energetically sought out individuals with ideas to increase war production and created incentives to spur creative approaches. More than any previous administration, Roosevelt's managed the war effort in the public interest. Roosevelt's war policies held inflation to the lowest levels in wartime history and produced a more equitable distribution of income than any time before or since.

Citizen participation in the New Deal and the war differed qualitatively. Roosevelt's New Deal programs involved citizens as voters and policy makers. The New Deal's effort to create and invigorate local citizenship created intermediating institutions that connected to the grassroot level while leaving much to the initiative of the locals. Local responses varied, but some New Deal programs were notably successful. Among working-class Americans in northern cities, the New Deal created a unified culture of commitment to industrial unionism, the Democratic Party, and Franklin Roosevelt. Wartime programs incorporated citizens into an administrative system that was less voluntary and provided a narrow range of choice.

Roosevelt also relied on Congress. All New Deal programs originated with congressional legislation and were subject to congressional oversight and investigation. Roosevelt's popularity and voter approval of his programs softened—indeed, often muted—congressional criticism of his programs, although they did not eliminate it entirely. Throughout the war he relied on Congress to create agencies for economic management and stabilization. He crafted his executive orders to conform to congressional statutes.

Because he relied so heavily on his own powers of persuasion, Roosevelt failed to develop effective institutional links to Congress. His advice to his agency heads ran along the lines of keeping congressmen happy by not upsetting their agendas, by compromising with their patronage desires, and by making sure that they carefully followed the law. He allowed members of his inner circle, most notably Corcoran and Cohen, to bargain with congressmen, but he essentially relied on his own popularity and the popularity of his programs to pressure Congress into following his wishes. It seems clear that during the war, Roosevelt's leverage with congressional Democrats depended largely on the need for a unified war effort and on his popularity with the voters.

The attempt by Roosevelt's presidency to work with Congress and to mobilize citizen participation revealed the complexities of pluralism. The New Deal sought to create an administrative system that would delegate lawmaking power to socially important private groups while at the same time preserving the state's neutrality, flexibility, and superiority. This the New Deal tried to do by converting into public rights what the law had previously defined as private rights. Farmers could vote to assign their rights to control planting to local committees that functioned by majority vote under the supervision of the AAA and the Department of Agriculture. Employee rights, which courts had defined as an individual contract between employee and employer, were now decided by majority vote under the supervision of the National Labor Relations Board. These and other "regulations" and "interventions" on the part of the state were made in the name of free enterprise and market capitalism. Agricultural policy was designed to "stabilize" markets, not to abolish them; labor policy was designed to "equalize" bargaining between employees and employers, not to abolish the contract system. Thus the New Deal sought to create a new kind of federalism in which the national government would establish goals that those at lower levels would seek to achieve by "democratic" methods that both regulated their conduct among themselves and legitimated them as "constituents" of governmental bodies. By these means the New Deal sought to absorb hitherto private groups into a system for defining and protecting the public interest.[12]

The New Deal approach gave citizen constituencies an opportunity to use government resources for their own purposes. Two examples provide some idea of the range of their response. Philosopher Michael Walzer provides evidence that the initiative that working men and women took to unionize under the New Deal carried forward into their civic lives. He recalls that in his hometown of Johnstown, Pennsylvania, New Deal labor law made it possible for the CIO to organize the steel mills. The result was what he calls "a separation of economy and polity." The city officials no longer took orders from the mill owners. This caused both a decline in deference and an increase in civic participation. Children were more equal in the educational system, working-class churches were more active in the community's social and philanthropic life, deference was less visible in everyday life.[13] When Robert and Helen Lynd, who had written a celebrated study of Muncie, Indiana, during the 1920s, returned in the mid-1930s, they found what might be called pluralist confusion rather than pluralist consensus. They found a "solidly Republican" political culture that voted for Democrats, a class-dominated and politically shady social structure in which nonunion factory hands left work happily joshing with one another and planning weekend recreations on their way home to mow their lawns, paint their garages, and play catch with their kids. For civic pride and duty, Muncie had substituted an insipid boosterism that saw New Deal construction and employment projects as objects of local achievement.[14] It was a picture of civic action without much civic consciousness: George Babbitt voting for Roosevelt.

Examples such as Muncie gave pluralism a bad name. In the years following the war, scholars, most of them political scientists, concluded that pluralism merely enlarged the number of special interests that had access to government and that the stronger of these interests were able to use government for their own purposes. As a result, the New Deal became an example of "corporate liberalism," in which government and business reached an accommodation that, on the whole, turned government into the protector of corporate property and a supporter of expanding its power. Corporate wealth had prevailed by taking advantage of the "flexible" and "evolutionary" nature of New Deal administrative practices. If "democracy" was to survive, administrative agencies would have to be circumscribed by a legal formalism of rigid rules and legislative restrictions. Instead of broad authority to use their discretion and to decide on a case-by-case basis, administrative agencies needed to be guided by rules that were based on great moral principles, preferably principles of "democracy."[15]

Franklin Roosevelt had entertained a different vision. To him, democracy meant bringing more groups into the public arena where they could obtain government recognition and support. As long as government remained the senior partner, charged with defining the "public interest" or "national purpose," and as long as the "constituents" of the interest groups—the farmers, the workers, the community residents, the WPA workers, and the state and local governments—made their choices "democratically," pluralistic methods would create a cooperative pluralism in which all interests realized their interdependence and identified their welfare with the common welfare.

There turned out to be no way that Roosevelt could avoid pluralism's ambiguities and complexities. All too often, he found that his achievements were no better than the instruments through which he worked: city bosses, racist planters, patronage-hungry congressmen, profit-driven business executives. Try and hope as he might, he could not create a political-administrative structure that would securely and predictably achieve his vision. During his presidency, he continually maneuvered, reordered, charmed, admonished, inspired, dodged, and prevaricated to keep his hands on the reins of power. His behavior replicated the dimensions of his pluralist vision—complex, varied, praise- and blameworthy, but always underpinned by his faith in the "four freedoms" and similar expressions of the democratic ideal. Not surprisingly, his achievements were mixed. His New Deal programs did as much to enlarge the field of competition for special advantage as they did to encourage cooperation for the general welfare. His wartime diplomacy failed to prevent the Cold War. But these outcomes did not measure his true achievement. Roosevelt could not create a utopia of domestic and international peace and prosperity. But he could demonstrate the qualities needed to achieve them. No president in our history has faced such critical problems with the courage, vision, and stamina that Roosevelt displayed. The reality that he faced and from which he never retreated was that the role of the pluralist leader in modern society is to be constantly at work. Pluralism always assumed that today's problems grew out of yesterday's solutions. Thus, unable to create a world of cooperative pluralism, Roosevelt constantly worked to create it. The result was the largest and most varied social legislation the United States had seen to that date.

Working with the political instruments at hand, Roosevelt fashioned a New Deal that reconfigured the relationship between the national government and the American people, extending regulations, building the nation's capital base, and constructing welfare and fiscal policies that, until recently, succeeding generations took for granted. Although other presidents, most notably Dwight Eisenhower, more substantially built the presidential office, Roosevelt started the momentum. Roosevelt's wartime management left behind a similarly rich legacy: the summit conference, the partnership with science, the Joint Chiefs of Staff, and the United Nations. Although Roosevelt would not have intended it, each of these in its own way provided tools that the United States would use to stabilize the West in its long encounter with the Soviet Union.

In important ways, Franklin Roosevelt's presidency was also Eleanor Roosevelt's presidency. It would be a mistake to emphasize the stresses and frictions in their relationship. These were more often personal and emotional than political. Nor would it be correct to refer to Eleanor as the "conscience" of Franklin's presidency. Instead, she was his complement, acting on issues that he hesitated to take up and pressing him to follow her initiatives. Perhaps even better than he, Eleanor understood the routine, gritty, and persistent effort that practical politics required. She also understood the importance of loyalty and the need to avoid burning bridges. Although she moved in and out of friendships during the presidential years, she never lost contact with anyone who might be a useful political ally. Perhaps if she had held the political power and the responsibilities of office, she would have been less direct and outspoken, but it is unlikely that she would have been as devious and evasive as Franklin. As it was, her directness, candor, and pressure often caused him to be less devious and evasive and to take chances he might have preferred to avoid. Because of Eleanor, Franklin was less willing to play the game with only the cards in his hand but was willing to take a chance and draw from the deck.

Because Eleanor took on issues on the margins of Franklin's agenda, hers was necessarily the more prophetic role. While he established programs that carried into the future, she highlighted causes and issues that her successors would turn into programs. This was her contribution to the American civil rights tradition. But her contribution went beyond merely raising issues in the abstract. From time to time she persuaded Franklin to take actions that showed how the president could use executive powers—

nominations to office, creation of special committees and task forces, executive orders—to advance the cause. She did the same with other administrative leaders, especially Harold Ickes and Harry Hopkins. If she occasionally nagged and scolded, she did so because that was how the process worked and because, after all, that has long been the prophet's method. Those who dismissed her as a nag and a scold were usually those who disliked her message to begin with.

By working on the margins to include groups such as African Americans, Eleanor kept alive the New Deal's pluralistic objectives. By advocating civil rights, she made a major contribution to the wartime redefinition of liberalism as social democracy as well as economic democracy.[16] Like her husband, she died before the civil rights acts of 1964 and 1965 fulfilled her mission.

In many ways, the presidency of Franklin D. Roosevelt was a historical phenomenon, rooted in its own time and place and in a set of assumptions about social interaction and problem solving that would not endure. The issues and the peculiar mixture of politics, leadership, and talent that made up his presidency cannot recur in the same combinations. Still, viewed in its own time and setting, it provides a fascinating example of a creative response by an American presidency to crises of unprecedented scope and duration. How successive generations choose to understand its example depends on conditions and values that are similarly peculiar to their times. No one would have understood and approved of this result more than Franklin and Eleanor Roosevelt. To paraphrase Eleanor's warning to Harry Truman, we are the ones in trouble now.

NOTES

CHAPTER 1
FRANKLIN ROOSEVELT IN THE SPOTLIGHT

1. *Historical Statistics of the United States, Colonial Times to 1957* (Washington, D.C.: U.S. Government Printing Office, 1961), pp. 17–67; *Statistical Abstract of the United States* (Washington, D.C.: U.S. Government Printing Office, 1989), p. 8.

2. Robert S. McElvaine, *The Great Depression: America, 1929–1941* (New York: Times Books, 1984), pp. 92–93.

3. Ibid. , pp. 47–48.

4. Albert U. Romasco, *The Poverty of Abundance: Hoover, the Nation, the Depression* (New York: Oxford University Press, 1965), chap. 7.

5. Josephine C. Brown, *Public Relief, 1929–1939* (New York: Henry Holt and Company, 1940), pp. 43–59.

6. Romasco, *Poverty of Abundance,* chap. 8.

7. Brown, *Public Relief,* pp. 55–57.

8. Clifford E. Olmstead, *History of Religion in the United States* (Englewood Cliffs, N.J.: Prentice-Hall, 1960), pp. 563–64; Robert T. Handy, "The American Religious Depression, 1925–1935," in *Religion in American History: Interpretive Essays,* ed. John M. Mulder and John F. Wilson (Englewood Cliffs, N.J.: Prentice-Hall, 1978).

9. *Historical Statistics,* pp. 207–10; Lawrence Cremin, *American Education: The Metropolitan Experience, 1870–1980* (New York: Harper and Row, 1988), p. 545; Malcolm M. Willey, *Depression, Recovery and Higher Education: A Report by Committee Y of the American Association of University Professors* (New York and London: McGraw-Hill, 1937), pp. 22–30, 53–63, 155–64, 209, 234; quote, p. 276. See also *Higher Education in the Forty-eight States: A Report to the Governors' Conference* (Chicago: Council of State Governments, 1952).

10. Jeffrey A. Charles, *Service Clubs in American Society: Rotary, Kiwanis, and Lions* (Urbana and Chicago: University of Illinois Press, 1993), pp. 104–10.

11. Paul Kleppner, *Who Voted? The Dynamics of Electoral Turnout, 1870–1980* (New York: Praeger Publishers, 1982), pp. 43–54, 68, 73–82.

12. Robert E. Park, "Human Nature and Collective Behavior," *American Journal of Sociology* 32 (1926–1927): 734.

13. The best statement of pluralism in its historical setting is in Alan I. Marcus and H. P. Segal, *American Technology: A Brief History* (San Diego: Harcourt, Brace, Jovanovich, 1988), pp. 255–60. Other works that illuminate the role of pluralism as an organizing principle of social analysis include Hamilton Cravens, *The Triumph of Evolution: The Heredity-Environment Controversy, 1900–1941* (Baltimore: Johns Hopkins University Press, 1988); Hamilton Cravens, *Before Head Start: The Iowa Station and America's Children* (Chapel Hill: University of North Carolina Press, 1993); Henry D. Shapiro, *Appalachia on Our Mind: The Southern Mountains and Mountaineers in the American Consciousness* (Chapel Hill: University of North Carolina Press, 1978); Barry Karl, *Charles E. Merriam and the Study of Politics* (Chicago: University of Chicago Press, 1974); Eric Goldman, *Rendezvous with Destiny* (New York: Harcourt, Brace, Jovanovich, 1953); William Graebner, *The Engineering of Consent: Democracy and Authority in Twentieth Century America* (Madison: University of Wisconsin Press, 1987). Original sources include Walter B. Cannon, *The Wisdom of the Body* (New York: Norton, 1932) (physiology); Margaret Mead, *Coming of Age in Samoa* (New York: William Morrow, 1928) (anthropology); Robert E. Park, Ernest W. Burgess, and Roderick D. McKenzie, *The City* (Chicago: University of Chicago Press, 1925) (sociology).

14. The following account of Franklin Roosevelt is based on the following sources: Kenneth Sydney Davis, *FDR: The Beckoning of Destiny, 1882–1928, a History* (New York: Putnam, 1972); Frank Freidel, *Franklin D. Roosevelt: A Rendezvous with Destiny* (Boston: Little, Brown, 1990); Geoffrey Ward, *A First-Class Temperament: The Emergence of Franklin Roosevelt* (New York: Harper and Row, 1989).

15. Davis, *Beckoning of Destiny*, p. 73.

16. Ibid., pp. 142–43.

17. Ward, *First-Class Temperament*, pp. 165–66; Freidel, *Rendezvous with Destiny*, pp. 19–20, 21, 257.

18. Blanche Wiesen Cook, *Eleanor Roosevelt*, vol. 1, *1884–1933* (New York: Viking, 1992), pp. 228–30.

19. Ward, *First-Class Temperament*, pp. 771–72; Samuel Rosenman and Dorothy Rosenman, *Presidential Style: Some Giants and a Pygmy in the White House* (New York: Harper and Row, 1976), p. 299; Freidel, *Rendezvous with Destiny*, p. 190.

20. Bernard Bellush, *Franklin D. Roosevelt as Governor of New York* (New York: Columbia University Press, 1955), pp. 83–84, 88–99, 110–22, 136–49, 208–22.

21. Frank Freidel, *Franklin D. Roosevelt: The Triumph* (Boston: Little, Brown, 1957), chap. 16.

22. Ibid., pp. 91–94, 255–60, 333–37.

23. Rayburn to Will G. Stephens, April 29, 1932, Rayburn Papers, microfilm, series 1, reel 2, Sam Rayburn Library, Bonham, Tex.

24. Freidel, *Rendezvous with Destiny*, 70–73.

25. Freidel, *Triumph*, pp. 313–15.

26. Rexford Tugwell, *The Brains Trust* (New York: Viking Press, 1968), p. 304.

27. Ibid., pp. 308, 411; Frank Freidel, *Franklin D. Roosevelt: Launching the New Deal* (Boston: Little, Brown, 1973), p. 64.

28. Raymond Moley, *After Seven Years* (New York and London: Harper and Brothers, 1939), pp. 23–24.

29. Jordan A. Schwarz, *Liberal: Adolf A. Berle and the Vision of an American Era* (New York: Free Press; London: Collier Macmillan, 1987), pp. 70–80; Elliot A. Rosen, "The Brain Trust and the Origins of the New Deal," in *Franklin D. Roosevelt: The Man, the Myth, the Era, 1882–1945*, ed. Herbert D. Rosenbaum and Elizabeth Bartelme (New York: Greenwood Press, 1987), pp. 156–57; Tugwell, *Brains Trust*, p. 96.

30. Tugwell, *Brains Trust*, pp. 34–35, 42–44, 57–58.

31. Freidel, *Launching the New Deal*, pp. 71, 74–75, 79.

32. David E. Hamilton, *From New Day to New Deal: American Farm Policy from Hoover to Roosevelt, 1928–1933* (Chapel Hill: University of North Carolina Press, 1991), pp. 226–27.

33. Ibid., p. 220.

34. Samuel I. Rosenman, ed., *The Public Papers and Addresses of Franklin D. Roosevelt*, vol. 1 (New York: Random House, 1938), pp. 625–27, 629.

35. Ibid., pp. 646, 703.

36. Ibid., pp. 642–44, 679.

37. Ibid.

38. Ibid., pp. 742–55.

39. Ibid., p. 782.

40. Ibid., pp. 856–59.

41. Moley, *After Seven Years*, pp. 98–101; Martin Fausold, *The Presidency of Herbert Hoover* (Lawrence: University Press of Kansas, 1985), pp. 216–25.

42. Frank Freidel, "The Interregnum Struggle between Hoover and Roosevelt," in *The Hoover Presidency: A Reappraisal*, ed. Martin L. Fausold and George T. Mazuzan (Albany: State University of New York Press, 1974), pp. 142–45.

43. Moley, *After Seven Years*, p. 123.

44. *New York Times*, February 16, 17, 18, 1933.

45. George Whitney Martin, *Madam Secretary, Frances Perkins* (Boston: Houghton Mifflin, 1976), pp. 235–37.

46. Richard Lowitt, *Bronson M. Cutting, Progressive Politician* (Albuquerque: University of New Mexico Press, 1992), pp. 231–32.

47. Freidel, *Rendezvous with Destiny*, pp. 88–91; Fausold, *Hoover Presidency*, p. 231.

48. Fausold, *Hoover Presidency*, p. 234.

49. Rosenman, *Papers*, vol. 2, pp. 11–16.

CHAPTER 2
A HUNDRED DAYS

1. Bernstein, Irving, *Turbulent Years: A History of the American Worker, 1933–1941* (Boston: Houghton Mifflin, 1970), p. 15; Thomas W. Gavett, *Development of*

the Labor Movement in Milwaukee (Madison and Milwaukee: University of Wisconsin Press, 1965), p. 153; John L. Shover, *Cornbelt Rebellion: The Farmers' Holiday Association* (Urbana and London: University of Illinois Press, 1968), pp. 9, 11, 41; R. T. Dunn and J. R. Handy to Sam Rayburn, June 13, 1932, microfilm reel 2, Sam Rayburn Papers, Sam Rayburn Library, Bonham, Tex.; Raymond Moley, *After Seven Years* (New York and London: Harper and Brothers, 1939), p. 143.

2. James E. Sargent, *Roosevelt and the Hundred Days: Struggle for the Early New Deal* (New York: Garland, 1981), pp. 20–21.

3. Ibid., pp. 55, 96.

4. Raymond Moley, *The First New Deal* (New York: Harcourt, Brace and World, 1966), pp. 171–77; Sargent, *Roosevelt and the Hundred Days*, pp. 96–99.

5. William E. Leuchtenburg, *Franklin D. Roosevelt and the New Deal, 1932–1940* (New York: Harper and Row, 1963), pp. 43–44.

6. At the end of his first press conference, the reporters spontaneously applauded. Sargent, *Roosevelt and the Hundred Days*, p. 101. Roosevelt's fireside chat on banking was dictated by him from a draft written by Arthur Ballantine, former undersecretary of the treasury under Hoover and a major consultant on writing the banking bill. Moley, *First New Deal*, pp. 194–95.

7. Sargent, *Roosevelt and the Hundred Days*, p. 102.

8. Robert Paul Browder and Thomas G. Smith, *Independent: A Biography of Lewis W. Douglas* (New York: Alfred A. Knopf, 1986), pp. 82, 87.

9. Sargent, *Roosevelt and the Hundred Days*, pp. 112, 118.

10. Browder and Smith, *Biography of Lewis W. Douglas*, pp. 84–86.

11. Sargent, *Roosevelt and the Hundred Days*, pp. 110–11, 114.

12. Ibid., pp. 115, 125, 160–61.

13. David E. Hamilton, *From New Day to New Deal: American Farm Policy from Hoover to Roosevelt, 1928–1933* (Chapel Hill: University of North Carolina Press, 1991), pp. 189–90; Jordan A. Schwarz, *The Speculator: Bernard M. Baruch in Washington, 1917–1965* (Chapel Hill: University of North Carolina Press, 1981), pp. 283, 284. Arthur M. Schlesinger, Jr., *The Coming of the New Deal* (Boston: Houghton Mifflin, 1958), p. 55; Sargent, *Roosevelt and the Hundred Days*, pp. 162–68.

14. Moley, *First New Deal*, pp. 300–2.

15. Sargent, *Roosevelt and the Hundred Days*, pp. 167–77; Schlesinger, *Coming of the New Deal*, p. 196; Browder and Smith, *Biography of Lewis W. Douglas*, pp. 91–92.

16. Schlesinger, *Coming of the New Deal*, p. 205.

17. Sargent, *Roosevelt and the Hundred Days*, pp. 109–11, 131–32; Moley, *First New Deal*, pp. 267–69.

18. Sargent, *Roosevelt and the Hundred Days*, pp. 133–35.

19. Quoted in Frank Freidel, *Franklin D. Roosevelt: A Rendezvous with Destiny* (Boston: Little, Brown, 1990), p. 87; Schlesinger, *Coming of the New Deal*, pp. 321–24.

20. Frank Freidel, *Franklin D. Roosevelt: Launching the New Deal* (Boston: Little, Brown, 1973), pp. 351, 352.

21. Michael E. Parrish, *Securities Regulation and the New Deal* (New Haven, Conn.: Yale University Press, 1970), pp. 48–56.

22. Joseph P. Lash, *Dealers and Dreamers: A New Look at the New Deal* (New York: Doubleday, 1988), p. 125.

23. Freidel, *Launching the New Deal,* pp. 344–45, 347.

24. Sargent, *Roosevelt and the Hundred Days,* pp. 217–19; Parrish, *Securities Regulation,* pp. 72–91.

25. Sargent, *Roosevelt and the Hundred Days,* pp. 197–203; Freidel, *Launching the New Deal,* pp. 417–19.

26. Robert Himmelberg, *The Origins of the National Recovery Administration* (New York: Fordham University Press), pp. 189–96.

27. Moley, *First New Deal,* pp. 286–87.

28. Himmelberg, *Origins of the NRA,* pp. 201–4; Ellis Wayne Hawley, *The New Deal and the Problem of Monopoly: A Study in Economic Ambivalence* (Princeton, N.J.: Princeton University Press, 1966), pp. 24–25.

29. Freidel, *Launching the New Deal,* p. 425.

30. J. Joseph Huthmacher, *Senator Robert F. Wagner and the Rise of Urban Liberalism* (New York: Atheneum, 1968), pp. 145–47; Himmelberg, *Origins of the NRA,* pp. 195, 197–200.

31. Himmelberg, *Origins of the NRA,* pp. 201–5.

32. Moley, *First New Deal,* pp. 284–85; Raymond Moley, *After Seven Years* (New York and London: Harper and Brothers, 1939), pp. 186–88.

33. John Kennedy Ohl, *Hugh S. Johnson and the New Deal* (DeKalb: Northern Illinois University Press, 1985), pp. 96–99.

34. Sargent, *Roosevelt and the Hundred Days,* pp. 205–6.

35. Freidel, *Launching the New Deal,* p. 423.

36. Ibid., p. 424; Ohl, *Hugh S. Johnson,* pp. 101–2.

37. Himmelberg, *Origins of the NRA,* pp. 205–8.

38. Sargent, *Roosevelt and the Hundred Days,* pp. 133–35.

39. Freidel, *Launching the New Deal,* pp. 430–33.

40. Martha H. Swain, *Pat Harrison: The New Deal Years* (Jackson: University of Mississippi Press, 1978), pp. 46–49.

41. Kenneth Sydney Davis, *FDR, the New Deal Years, 1933–1937: A History* (New York: Random House, 1986), p. 123.

42. Robert Dallek, *Franklin D. Roosevelt and American Foreign Policy, 1932–1945* (New York: Oxford University Press, 1979), pp. 47–48.

43. Freidel, *Rendezvous with Destiny,* p. 100.

44. Schlesinger, *Coming of the New Deal,* p. 197.

45. Dallek, *Roosevelt and American Foreign Policy,* p. 45.

46. Browder and Smith, *Biography of Lewis W. Douglas,* p. 100.

47. Charles P. Kindleberger, *The World in Depression, 1929–1939* (London: Allen Lane, Penguin Press, 1973), pp. 204–7, 211; Dallek, *Roosevelt and Foreign Policy,* p. 46.

48. Leuchtenburg, *Roosevelt and New Deal,* pp. 201–4.

49. Dallek, *Roosevelt and American Foreign Policy,* pp. 50–55.

50. The text of the draft is printed in Moley, *First New Deal,* p. 481.

51. Moley, *After Seven Years,* pp. 208–9, 215, 235–36.

52. Schlesinger, *Coming of the New Deal,* pp. 224–25; Kindleberger, *World in Depression,* pp. 220, 224; Davis, *FDR, the New Deal Years,* p. 198.

53. Barry J. Eichengreen, *Golden Fetters: The Gold Standard and the Great Depression, 1919–1939* (New York: Oxford University Press, 1992), pp. 318, 321–22.

CHAPTER 3
STRATEGIES FOR ECONOMIC RECOVERY

1. David E. Hamilton, *From New Day to New Deal: American Farm Policy from Hoover to Roosevelt, 1928–1933* (Chapel Hill: University of North Carolina Press, 1991), pp. 228–32.

2. John Morton Blum, *From the Morgenthau Diaries,* vol. 1 (Boston: Houghton Mifflin, 1959–1967), pp. 63, 66–71, 120–29; Arthur M. Schlesinger, Jr., *The Coming of the New Deal* (Boston: Houghton Mifflin, 1959), p. 237.

3. Theodore Saloutos, *The American Farmer and the New Deal* (Ames: Iowa State University, 1982), pp. 88–96.

4. For a full discussion of the mystical aspects of Wallace's character, see Graham White and John Maze, *Henry A. Wallace: His Search for a New World Order* (Chapel Hill and London: University of North Carolina Press, 1995).

5. Peter H. Irons, *The New Deal Lawyers* (Princeton, N.J.: Princeton University Press, 1982), pp. 123, 130, 131.

6. The following account is drawn from Saloutos, *American Farmer,* pp. 66–68, 70–85.

7. Gilbert C. Fite, *Cotton Fields No More: Southern Agriculture, 1865–1980* (Lexington: University Press of Kentucky, 1984), pp. 134–35.

8. Schlesinger, *Coming of the New Deal,* pp. 58–60.

9. Donald H. Grubbs, *Cry from the Cotton: The Southern Tenant Farmers' Union and the New Deal* (Chapel Hill: University of North Carolina Press , 1971), p. 59; Irons, *New Deal Lawyers,* p. 163.

10. Ibid., pp. 171–72.

11. Richard Lowitt, "Henry A. Wallace and the 1935 Purge in the Department of Agriculture," *Agricultural History* 53 (1979): 612; Roger Biles, *The South and the New Deal* (Lexington: University Press of Kentucky, 1994), p. 46; Saloutos, *American Farmer,* pp. 117–22.

12. Grubbs, *Cry,* p. 138.

13. Saloutos, *American Farmer,* pp. 124–27, 134–35, 140–41.

14. Philip J. Funigiello, *Toward a National Power Policy: The New Deal and the Electric Utility Industry, 1933–1941* (Pittsburgh: University of Pittsburgh Press, 1973), pp. 135–37.

15. Ibid., chap. 6.

16. Clayton D. Brown, *Electricity for Rural America: The Fight for the REA* (Westport, Conn.: Greenwood Press, 1980), pp. 210–21.

17. Fite, *Cotton Fields,* pp. 176–79; Grubbs, *Cry,* pp. 150–51; Paul E. Mertz, *New Deal Policy and Southern Rural Poverty* (Baton Rouge: Louisiana State University Press, 1978), chaps. 9–10.

18. Grubbs, *Cry,* pp. 140–61.

19. Richard Stewart Kirkendall, *Social Scientists and Farm Politics in the Age of Roosevelt* (Ames: Iowa State University Press, 1982), chaps. 4–5, conclusion.

20. Saloutos, *American Farmer*, pp. 245–48.

21. Ibid., pp. 275–79.

22. Rainer Schickele, *Agricultural Policy: Farm Programs and National Welfare* (New York, Toronto, and London: McGraw-Hill, 1954), pp. 165, 175, 199–201, 275; Theodore Schultz, *Agriculture in an Unstable Economy* (New York and London: McGraw-Hill, 1945), pp. 171–78.

23. On the contrast between the agriculture program and the industrial program, see Theda Skocpol and Kenneth Finegold, "State Capitalism and Economic Intervention. . . ," *Political Science Quarterly* 97 (1982): 255 ff.

24. Theodore Rosenof, *Dogma, Depression, and the New Deal: The Debate of Political Leaders over Economic Recovery* (Port Washington, N.Y.: Kennikat Press, 1975), p. 87; Donald Robert Brand, *Corporatism and the Rule of Law: A Study of the National Recovery Administration* (Ithaca, N.Y.: Cornell University Press, 1988), p. 94.

25. Ellis Wayne Hawley, *The New Deal and the Problem of Monopoly: A Study in Economic Ambivalence* (Princeton, N.J.: Princeton University Press, 1966), pp. 29, 33–56.

26. Quoted in Rosenof, *Dogma*, p. 83.

27. Leverett S. Lyon et al., *The National Recovery Administration: An Analysis and Appraisal* (Washington, D.C.: Brookings Institution, 1935), pp. 34–40.

28. John Kennedy Ohl, *Hugh S. Johnson and the New Deal* (DeKalb: Northern Illinois University Press, 1985), pp. 103–4.

29. Ibid., p. 104; Jordan A. Schwarz, *The Speculator: Bernard M. Baruch in Washington, 1917–1965* (Chapel Hill: University of North Carolina Press, 1981), pp. 286–89; Irons, *New Deal Lawyers*, pp. 27–28.

30. Ohl, *Johnson*, pp. 110–12.

31. Schlesinger, *Coming of the New Deal*, pp. 112–15.

32. Frank Freidel, *Franklin D. Roosevelt: A Rendezvous with Destiny* (Boston: Little, Brown, 1990), pp. 126–27.

33. Lyon et al., *National Recovery Administration*, pp. 95–112.

34. Ohl, *Johnson*, pp. 115–36.

35. Lyon et al., *National Recovery Administration*, p. 58.

36. Hawley, *Problem of Monopoly*, pp. 56–57, 63, 68.

37. Ibid., pp. 78–82.

38. Walton Hale Hamilton, ed., *Current Economic Problems* (Chicago: University of Chicago Press, 1914), p. 143.

39. Brand, *Corporatism and the Rule of Law*, pp. 108, 110–14, 159–62; Hugh Johnson, *The Blue Eagle from Egg to Earth* (Garden City, N.Y.: Doubleday, 1935).

40. Brand, *Corporatism and the Rule of Law*, p. 114.

41. Hawley, *Problem of Monopoly*, pp. 94–101.

42. Lyon et al., *National Recovery Administration*, pp. 613–14; Brand, *Corporatism and the Rule of Law*, pp. 116–17.

43. Brand, *Corporatism and the Rule of Law*, chaps. 7–8.

44. George E. Paulsen, *A Living Wage for the Forgotten Man: The Quest for Fair Labor Standards, 1933–1941* (Selinsgrove, Pa.: Susquehanna University Press; London: Associated University Presses, 1996), p. 50.

45. Brand, *Corporatism and the Rule of Law*, pp. 122–36.

46. Joseph P. Lash, *Dealers and Dreamers: A New Look at the New Deal* (New York: Doubleday, 1988), pp. 180–86, 194; Arthur M. Schlesinger, Jr., *The Politics of Upheaval* (Boston: Houghton Mifflin, 1960), pp. 303–6.

47. Lash, *Dealers and Dreamers*, pp. 199–214.

48. Schlesinger, *Politics of Upheaval*, pp. 318–24.

49. Irons, *New Deal Lawyers*, pp. 35–45.

50. Ibid., pp. 54–57, 82–85.

51. Brand, *Corporatism and the Rule of Law*, pp. 196–206.

52. Schlesinger, *Coming of the New Deal*, pp. 136–37.

53. Irons, *New Deal Lawyers*, pp. 28–30; Stanley Vittoz, *New Deal Labor Policy and the American Industrial Economy* (Chapel Hill: University of North Carolina Press, 1987), pp. 93, 95.

54. Lyon et al., *National Recovery Administration*, pp. 464–65; Irons, *New Deal Lawyers*, p. 204.

55. Lyon et al., *National Recovery Administration*, chap. 32.

56. Vittoz, *New Deal Labor Policy*, pp. 94, 97–100.

57. Ibid., pp. 108–15.

58. Ibid., pp. 124–27.

59. Irons, *New Deal Lawyers*, p. 205.

60. Irving Bernstein, *Turbulent Years: A History of the American Worker, 1933–1941* (Boston: Houghton Mifflin, 1970), pp. 172–75; Irons, *New Deal Lawyers*, p. 206.

61. Bernstein, *Turbulent Years*, pp. 177–79; Irons, *New Deal Lawyers*, pp. 208–9.

62. Bernstein, *Turbulent Years*, pp. 186–89; Irons, *New Deal Lawyers*, pp. 209–11.

63. Sidney Fine, "President Roosevelt and the Automobile Code," *Mississippi Valley Historical Review* 45 (1958): 23–50; Irons, *New Deal Lawyers*, pp. 212–13; Bernstein, *Turbulent Years*, pp. 180–85.

64. Schlesinger, *Coming*, pp. 398ff.

65. Melvyn Dubofsky, *The State and Labor in Modern America* (Chapel Hill and London: University of North Carolina Press, 1994), pp. 122–23; Lyon et al., *National Recovery Administration*, pp. 467–69; Vittoz, *New Deal Labor Policy*, pp. 142–46; J. Joseph Huthmacher, *Senator Robert F. Wagner and the Rise of Urban Liberalism* (New York: Atheneum, 1968), pp. 166–85.

66. Kenneth S. Davis, *FDR: The New Deal Years, 1933–1937* (New York: Random House, 1986), pp. 326–35.

67. Dubofsky, *The State and Labor*, p. 125.

68. James A. Gross, *The Making of the National Labor Relations Board: A Study in Economics, Politics, and the Law* (Albany: State University of New York Press, 1981), chap. 4.

69. Irons, *New Deal Lawyers*, p. 231.

70. Paulsen, *Living Wage*, pp. 58–62.

71. Ellis W. Hawley, "The New Deal State and the Anti-Bureaucratic Tradition," in *The New Deal and Its Legacy: Critique and Appraisal*, ed. Robert Eden (New York: Greenwood Press, 1989); Christopher L. Tomlins, *The State and the Unions: Labor*

Relations, Law, and the Organized Labor Movement in America, 1880–1960 (Cambridge: Cambridge University Press, 1985), pp. 103–9, 134–40.

72. Theda Skocpol and Kenneth Finegold, "Explaining New Deal Labor Policy," *American Political Science Review* 84 (1990): 1297–1315.

73. Karl E. Klare, "Judicial Deradicalization of the Wagner Act and the Origins of Modern Legal Consciousness, 1937–1941," *Minnesota Law Review* 62 (1978): 265–339.

74. Robert E. Williams, *NLRB Regulation of Election Conduct*, Labor Relations and Public Policy Series, No. 8 (Philadelphia: Wharton School, Industrial Research Unit, 1985), pp. 29–31.

75. Davis, *New Deal Years*, p. 528.

76. Alan Dawley, "Workers, Capital, and the State in the Twentieth Century," in *Perspectives on American Labor History: The Problems of Synthesis*, ed. J. Carroll Moody and Alice Kessler-Harris (DeKalb: Northern Illinois Press, 1989).

CHAPTER 4
STRATEGIES FOR SOCIAL RECOVERY

1. Louis Jaffe, "Law Making by Private Groups," *Harvard Law Review* 51 (1937): 201–53.

2. Jean Wittick Pearson, "Arthurdale," master's thesis, Iowa State University, pp. 27–31, 76.

3. Odum wrote prolifically on regionalism. One of his major statements was *American Regionalism; A Cultural-Historical Approach to National Integration* (New York: H. Holt and Company, 1938). His quoted statements are from Merrill Jensen, ed., *Regionalism in America* (Madison: University of Wisconsin Press, 1951), pp. 403, 405.

4. *I'll Take My Stand: The South and the Agrarian Tradition* (New York and London: Harper, 1930), Herbert Agar, *The People's Choice, from Washington to Harding: A Study in Democracy* (Boston and New York: Houghton Mifflin, 1933).

5. Paul Conkin, *Tomorrow a New World: The New Deal Community Program* (Ithaca, N.Y.: Cornell University Press, 1959), pp. 34, 70–71, 307; Harry McDean, "Western Thought in Planning Rural America: The Subsistence Homesteads Program, 1933–1935," *Journal of the West* 31 (1992): 17.

6. Franklin D. Roosevelt, *Looking Forward* (New York: John Jay Company, 1933), pp. 10–13, 30–36, 55–57.

7. Michael J. McDonald and John Muldowny, *TVA and the Dispossessed: The Resettlement of Population in the Norris Dam Area* (Knoxville: University of Tennessee Press, 1982), pp. 8–9; Walter L. Creese, *TVA's Public Planning: The Vision, the Reality* (Knoxville: University of Tennessee Press, 1990), pp. 95, 99.

8. Creese, *TVA's Public Planning*, pp. 105–7.

9. FDR quoted in Kenneth S. Davis, *FDR: The New Deal Years: 1933–1937* (New York: Random House, 1986), p. 430.

10. Erwin C. Hargrove and Paul Conkin, eds., *TVA: Fifty Years of Grass-Roots Bureaucracy* (Urbana and Chicago: University of Illinois Press, 1983), p. 50; McDonald and Muldowny, *TVA and the Dispossessed,* p. 286.

11. Creese, *TVA's Public Planning,* pp. 280–83.

12. The following account relies heavily on Francis Paul Prucha, *The Great Father: The United States Government and the American Indians* (Lincoln: University of Nebraska Press, 1986), pp. 808–12, 921–39, 940–50.

13. Kenneth R. Philp, *John Collier's Crusade for Indian Reform, 1920–1954* (Tucson: University of Arizona Press, 1977), pp. 140–45.

14. Ibid., pp. 132–33; Graham D. Taylor, *The New Deal and American Indian Tribalism: The Administration of the Indian Reorganization Act, 1934–45* (Lincoln: University of Nebraska Press, 1980), pp. 105–10, 114–17.

15. Philp, *Collier's Crusade,* pp. 155–60.

16. Ibid., pp. 163–64.

17. Prucha, *Great Father,* p. 976.

18. Philp, *Collier's Crusade,* pp. 138–39.

19. Taylor, *New Deal and American Indian Tribalism,* p. 132.

20. Ibid., pp. 29, 37–40.

21. Ibid., pp. 93–94, 139–50.

22. Davis, *New Deal Years,* p. 375.

23. McDean, "Western Thought in Planning Rural America," pp. 21–22.

24. Arthur M. Schlesinger, Jr., *The Coming of the New Deal* (Boston: Houghton Mifflin, 1958), pp. 368–71.

25. Joseph L. Arnold, *The New Deal in the Suburbs: A History of the Greenbelt Town Program, 1935–1954* (Columbus: Ohio State University Press, 1971), pp. 158, 182, 195, 198, 203–5, 208–9, 244–46.

26. Conkin, *Tomorrow a New World,* pp. 326–31.

27. Arnold, *New Deal in the Suburbs,* pp. 208–9.

28. Hopkins address, September 23, 1933, Hopkins Papers, Franklin D. Roosevelt Library, Box 9.

29. George McJimsey, *Harry Hopkins: Ally of the Poor and Defender of Democracy* (Cambridge: Harvard University Press, 1987), pp. 53–55.

30. Ibid., pp. 56–59; Searle F. Charles, *Minister of Relief: Harry Hopkins and the Depression* (Syracuse, N.Y.: Syracuse University Press, 1963), pp. 149–52; Bonnie Fox Schwartz, *The Civil Works Administration, 1933–1934: The Business of Emergency Employment in the New Deal* (Princeton, N.J.: Princeton University Press, 1984) pp. 39–52, 182–87.

31. McJimsey, *Hopkins,* pp. 59–66.

32. Lester G. Seligman and Elmer E. Cornwell, Jr., eds., *New Deal Mosaic: Roosevelt Confers with his National Emergency Council, 1933–1936* (Eugene: University of Oregon Press, 1965), p. 76.

33. McJimsey, *Hopkins,* pp. 78–79, 83–85.

34. Anthony Badger, *The New Deal: The Depression Years, 1933–40* (Houndmills, England: Macmillan, 1989), pp. 203–4.

35. McJimsey, *Hopkins,* chaps. 5–6; Charles, *Minister of Relief,* p. 144.

36. Hallie Flanagan, *Arena* (New York: Duell, Sloan and Pearce, 1940), pp. 115–29.
37. McJimsey, *Hopkins*, pp. 111–12.
38. John Morton Blum, *From the Morgenthau Diaries* (Boston: Houghton Mifflin, 1959), pp. 238–49, 265.
39. Albert U. Romasco, *The Poverty of Abundance: Hoover, the Nation, the Depression* (London and New York: Oxford University Press, 1965), pp. 230–34.
40. Robert Leupold, "The Kentucky WPA: Relief and Politics, May–November, 1935," *Filson Club Historical Quarterly* 49 (1975): 152–68.
41. Florence Kerr, oral history interview, June 1974, Columbia University Oral History Project.
42. Frank Freidel, *Franklin D. Roosevelt: A Rendezvous with Destiny* (Boston: Little, Brown, 1990), p. 189.
43. Arthur M. Schlesinger, Jr., *The Politics of Upheaval* (New York: Houghton Mifflin, 1960), p. 603.
44. McJimsey, *Hopkins*, p. 110.
45. Raymond Wolters, *Negroes and the Great Depression: The Problem of Economic Recovery* (Westport, Conn.: Greenwood Press, 1970), pp. 203–9.
46. *Old Age Security: Report of the New York State Commission* (Albany, N.Y.: J. B. Lyon Company, 1930), pp. 234–35.
47. Colin Gordon, *New Deals: Business, Labor, and Politics in America, 1920–1935* (Cambridge: Cambridge University Press, 1994), pp. 242–43; Roy Lubove, *The Struggle for Social Security, 1900–1935* (Cambridge: Harvard University Press, 1968), chaps. 7–8.
48. Ann Shola Orloff, *The Politics of Pensions: A Comparative Analysis of Britian, Canada, and the United States, 1880–1940* (Madison: University of Wisconsin Press, 1993), pp. 278–82.
49. FDR message in Daniel Nelson, *Unemployment Insurance: The American Experience, 1915–1935* (Madison: University of Wisconsin Press, 1969), p. 204; Samuel I. Rosenman, ed., *The Public Papers and Addresses of Franklin D. Roosevelt* (New York: Random House, 1938), vol. 3, pp. 321–22.
50. George Whitney Martin, *Madam Secretary, Frances Perkins* (Boston: Houghton Mifflin, 1976), p. 294; Orloff, *Politics of Pensions*, pp. 285–87.
51. Orloff, *Politics of Pensions*, pp. 287–89.
52. Gordon, *New Deals*, pp. 268–79; Orloff, *Politics of Pensions*, pp. 289–93.
53. Schlesinger, *Coming of the New Deal*, pp. 313–14, Orloff, *Politics of Pensions*, p. 295.
54. Schlesinger, *Coming of the New Deal*, pp. 308–9.
55. Bruno Stein, "Funding Social Security on a Current Basis: The 1939 Policy Change in the United States," in *Nationalizing Social Security in Europe and America*, ed. Douglas E. Ashford and E. W. Kelley (Greenwich, Conn., and London: JAI Press, 1986), pp. 112–20.
56. Orloff, *Politics of Pensions*, p. 297.
57. Brian Balough, "The Social Security Board as Political Actor," in *Federal Social Policy: The Historical Dimension*, ed. Ellis Hawley (University Park: Pennsylvania State University Press, 1988).

CHAPTER 5
RESOURCES FOR RECOVERY

1. Speech at Commerce Building, April 24, 1934, in Edgar Nixon, ed., *Franklin D. Roosevelt and Conservation, 1911–1945,* 2 vols. (Hyde Park, N.Y.: General Services Administration, National Archives and Records Service, Franklin D. Roosevelt Library, 1957), vol. 1, p. 273.

2. Richard White, *"It's Your Misfortune and None of My Own": A New History of the American West* (Norman: University of Oklahoma Press, 1991), pp. 477–81.

3. Press conference, February 14, 1934, in Nixon, *FDR and Conservation,* pp. 255–58.

4. White House statement, July 3, 1934, in ibid., pp. 317–18.

5. Thomas, K. McCraw, *TVA and the Power Fight, 1933–1939* (Philadelphia, New York, and Toronto: J. B. Lippincott, 1971), pp. 27–30, 33–36; Philip J. Funigiello, *Toward a National Power Policy: The New Deal and the Electric Utility Industry, 1933–1941* (Pittsburgh: University of Pittsburgh Press 1973), pp. 36–38.

6. McCraw, *TVA,* pp. 29–30, 54–55.

7. Ibid., pp. 57–62, 74.

8. Ibid., pp. 79–80.

9. Ibid., pp. 125–43.

10. Ibid., pp. 174–76, 188–93.

11. Ibid., p. 274.

12. William E. Leuchtenburg, "Roosevelt, Norris and the 'Seven Little TVA's,'" *Journal of Politics* 14 (1952): 418–41.

13. White, *"It's Your Misfortune and None of My Own,"* pp. 477–81.

14. R. Douglas Hurt, *The Dust Bowl: An Agricultural and Social History* (Chicago: Nelson-Hall, 1984), chap. 8.

15. Paul J. Culhane, *Public Lands Politics: Interest Group Influence on the Forest Service and the Bureau of Land Management* (Baltimore: Published for Resources for the Future by Johns Hopkins University Press, 1981), pp. 75–90.

16. White, *"It's Your Misfortune and None of My Own,"* pp. 477–81.

17. Ibid., pp. 487–88; Daniel Yergin, *The Prize: The Epic Quest for Oil, Money, and Power* (New York: Simon and Schuster, 1991), pp. 255–58.

18. Robert Kelley Schneiders, "Dams across the Wide Missouri: Water Transportation, the Corps of Engineers, and Environmental Change along the Lower Missouri Valley, 1803–1993," doctoral diss., Iowa State University, 1997.

19. Richard Lowitt, *The New Deal and the West* (Bloomington: Indiana University Press, 1984).

CHAPTER 6
ROOSEVELT'S POLITICAL BASE

1. Grace G. Tully, *FDR, My Boss* (New York: C. Scribner's Sons, 1949), pp. 6–19.

2. Lester G. Seligman and Elmer E. Cornwell, Jr., eds., *New Deal Mosaic: Roosevelt Confers with His National Emergency Council, 1933–1936* (Eugene: University of

Oregon Press, 1965), January 23, 1934, p. 168; March 20, 1934, pp. 166, 171. Hereafter cited as *NEC*, with dates and page numbers following.

3. Elliott Roosevelt, ed., *FDR: His Personal Letters* (New York: Duell, Sloan and Pearce, 1947–1950), pp. 342, 372, 415, 419, 613, 419, 613.

4. James McGregor Burns, *Roosevelt: The Soldier of Freedom* (New York: Harcourt Brace Jovanovich, 1970), p. 350.

5. Kenneth Sydney Davis, *FDR, the New Deal Years, 1933–1937: A History* (New York: Random House, 1986), p. 204.

6. *NEC*, pp. 281–82.

7. Eleanor Roosevelt, *This I Remember* (New York: Harper, 1949), pp. 69–70, 346–47.

8. Robert E. Sherwood, *Roosevelt and Hopkins, an Intimate History* (New York: Harper, 1948), p. 266.

9. Ibid., p. 3.

10. Arthur M. Schlesinger, Jr., *The Coming of the New Deal* (Boston: Houghton Mifflin, 1958), pp. 541–42.

11. William E. Leuchtenburg, *In the Shadow of FDR: From Harry Truman to Ronald Reagan* (Ithaca, N.Y.: Cornell University Press, 1983), p. 49.

12. George McJimsey, *Harry Hopkins: Ally of the Poor and Defender of Democracy* (Cambridge: Harvard University Press, 1987), p. 332.

13. Hugh Gregory Gallagher, *FDR's Splendid Deception* (New York: Dodd, Mead, 1985), pp. 128–29.

14. Raymond Moley, *After Seven Years* (New York and London: Harper and Brothers, 1939), p. 51.

15. Frances Perkins, *The Roosevelt I Knew* (New York: Viking Press, 1946), p. 112.

16. Frank Freidel, *Franklin D. Roosevelt: A Rendezvous with Destiny* (Boston: Little, Brown, 1990), pp. 370–71.

17. Tully, *FDR*, pp. 6, 65.

18. Rexford G. Tugwell, *The Democratic Roosevelt* (New York: Harper, 1957), pp. 44, 293–94, 304, 332; Perkins, *The Roosevelt I Knew*, pp. 156, 162.

19. Perkins, *The Roosevelt I Knew*, pp. 411, 444–45, 490–93.

20. *NEC*, December 1, 1933, pp. 3, 23; January 23, 1934, p. 73; December 11, 1934, pp. 351–52, 375; February 5, 1935, pp. 435–37.

21. Ibid., December 17, 1935, p. 484.

22. Tugwell, *Democratic Roosevelt*, p. 361.

23. *NEC*, August 21, 1934, pp. 282–88; December 17, 1935, pp. 484–86; Freidel, *Rendezvous with Destiny*, p. 204; Tugwell, *Democratic Roosevelt*, p. 236; Perkins, *The Roosevelt I Knew*, p. 113.

24. Betty Houchin Winfield, *FDR and the News Media* (Urbana: University of Illinois Press, 1990), pp. 82–94, 110; *NEC*, December 11, 1934, pp. 378–80.

25. Samuel Irving Rosenman, *Presidential Style: Some Giants and a Pygmy in the White House* (New York: Harper and Row, 1976), p. 334.

26. Winfield, *FDR and the News Media*, pp. 115, 132–35.

27. Ibid., p. 196.

28. Ibid., pp. 215–18, 220, 222–25.

29. Otis Graham, *An Encore for Reform: The Old Progressives and the New Deal* (New York: Oxford, a Galaxy Book, 1967), pp. 34–43, 48–49, 68–69, 86–90. For a similar analysis that emphasizes the personal independent style of progressive Republicans, see Ronald L. Feinman, *Twilight of Progressivism: The Western Republican Senators and the New Deal* (Baltimore and London: Johns Hopkins Press, 1981).

30. George Feinman and John A. Hudson, *All but the People: Franklin D. Roosevelt and His Critics, 1933–39* (London: Macmillan, 1969), pp. 148–60.

31. Ibid., pp. 160–66; Schlesinger, *Coming of the New Deal,* pp. 486–88.

32. T. Harry Williams, *Huey Long* (New York: Knopf, 1969); Alan Brinkley, *Voices of Protest: Huey Long, Father Coughlin, and the Great Depression* (New York: Knopf, 1982).

33. David H. Bennett, *Demagogues in the Depression; American Radicals and the Union Party, 1932–1936* (New Brunswick, N.J.: Rutgers University Press, 1969), pp. 120–22.

34. Ibid., pp. 41–47, 174.

35. Brinkley, *Voices of Protest,* pp. 124–27; Bennett, *Demagogues in the Depression,* p. 178.

36. Everett Carll Ladd, *Transformations of the American Party System: Political Coalitions from the New Deal to the 1970s* (New York: Norton, 1978), p. 50.

37. Jerome M. Ladd, William H. Flanigan, and Nancy Zingale, *Partisan Realignment: Voters, Parties, and Government in American History* (Beverly Hills, Calif.: Sage Publications, 1980), p. 258.

38. Courtney Brown, *Ballots of Tumult: A Portrait of Volatility in American Voting* (Ann Arbor: University of Michigan Press, 1991), pp. 47–48, 52–53.

39. Robert S. Erikson and Kent L. Tedin, "The 1928–1936 Partisan Realignment: The Case for the Conversion Hypothesis," *American Political Science Review* 75 (1981): 951–62.

40. Paul Kleppner, *Who Voted? The Dynamics of Electoral Turnout, 1870–1980* (New York: Praeger Publishers, 1982), pp. 85, 89.

41. Kristi Andersen, *The Creation of a Democratic Majority, 1928–1936* (Chicago: University of Chicago Press, 1979), pp. 26–38, 60–61, 69–72, 119; David W. Prindle, "Voter Turnout, Critical Elections, and the New Deal Realignment," *Social Science History* 3 (1979): 144–70.

42. David W. Brady, *Critical Elections and Congressional Policy-Making* (Stanford, Calif.: Stanford University Press, 1988), pp. 89–92.

43. They also gained in states west of the North Dakota–Texas longitude. Courtney Brown, *Ballots of Tumult,* pp. 62–63, 67; see also Duncan MacRae, Jr., and James Meldrum, "Critical Elections in Illinois: 1888–1958," *American Political Science Review* 54 (1960): 669–83, who show a shift in urban and foreign-born areas, although less "wet."

44. Lizabeth Cohen, *Making a New Deal: Industrial Workers in Chicago, 1919–1939* (Cambridge: Cambridge University Press, 1990).

45. Ladd, Flanigan, and Zingale, *Partisan Realignment,* p. 258.

46. R. R. Dykstra and D. R. Reynolds, "In Search of Wisconsin Progressivism," in *The History of American Electoral Behavior,* ed. Joel Silbey, Alan Bogue, and William H. Flanigan (Princeton, N.J.: Princeton University Press, 1978).

47. James L. Sundquist, *Dynamics of the Party System: Alignment and Realignment of Political Parties in the United States,* rev. ed. (Washington, D.C.: Brookings Institution, 1983), chap. 11. Nancy Zingale, "Third Party Alignments: Minnesota," in Silbey, Bogue, and Flanigan, *History of American Electoral Behavior.*

48. Ladd, *Transformations of the American Party System,* pp. 61–62, 115; Lawrence H. Fuchs, *The Political Behavior of American Jews* (Glencoe, Ill.: Free Press, 1956), pp. 71–79.

49. Brown, *Ballots of Tumult,* pp. 62–66.

50. Sundquist, *Dynamics of the Party System,* pp. 215–39.

51. Ibid., chap. 11. Zingale, "Third Party Alignments: Minnesota."

52. Brady, *Critical Elections and Congressional Policy-Making,* p. 93.

53. Calculated from the voting results reported in Arthur M. Schlesinger, *History of American Presidential Elections* (New York: Chelsea House, 1971).

54. Kleppner, *Who Voted?* p. 110.

55. Democratic margins were: 1933–1935, 60–35 Senate and 310–117 House; 1935–1937, 69–25 Senate and 319–103 House; 1937–1939, 76–16 Senate and 331–89 House; 1939–1941, 69–23 Senate and 261–164 House; 1941–1943, 66–28 Senate and 268–162 House; 1943–1945, 58–37 Senate and 218–208 House; 1945–1947, 56–38 Senate and 242–190 House.

56. Brady, *Critical Elections and Congressional Policy-Making,* pp. 153–55.

57. Milton C. Cummings, *Congressmen and the Electorate: Elections for the U.S. House and the President, 1920–1964* (New York: Free Press, 1966), p. 48.

58. V. O. Key, *Southern Politics in State and Nation* (New York: Knopf, 1949), chaps. 16–17.

59. James T. Patterson, *Congressional Conservatism and the New Deal: The Growth of the Conservative Coalition in Congress, 1933–1939* (Lexington: University of Kentucky Press, 1967), pp. 6 n. 16, 70–71, 160.

60. Clyde P. Weed, *The Nemesis of Reform: The Republican Party during the New Deal* (New York: Columbia University Press, 1994), pp. 148, 165, 172–73, 176–79, 184–86, 192–95.

61. Richard Bensel, *Sectionalism and American Political Development, 1880–1980* (Madison: University of Wisconsin Press, 1984), pp. 149–50, 206–7.

62. Brady, *Critical Elections and Congressional Policy-Making,* pp. 128–33.

63. Patterson, *Congressional Conservatism,* pp. 70–71, 160; Freidel, *Rendezvous with Destiny,* p. 166.

64. Patterson, *Congressional Conservatism,* pp. 80, 83, 85, 98, 155.

65. Patterson, *Congressional Conservatism,* pp. 66–67, 125–27.

66. Sean J. Savage, *Roosevelt: The Party Leader, 1932–1945* (Lexington: University of Kentucky Press, 1991), chap. 2; McJimsey, *Hopkins,* pp. 89–93.

67. Savage, *Party Leader,* pp. 83, 90–97.

68. Steve Fraser, "The 'Labor Question,'" in *The Rise and Fall of the New Deal Order, 1930–1980,* ed. Steve Fraser and Gary Gerstle (Princeton, N.J.: Princeton University Press, 1989), pp. 70–71.

69. Freidel, *Rendezvous with Destiny,* pp. 190, 223–24.

CHAPTER 7
ELEANOR ROOSEVELT AND A NEW DEAL FOR WOMEN

1. For an excellent statement of this point, see William H. Chafe, "Women's History and Political History: Some Thoughts on Progressivism and the New Deal," in *Visible Women*, ed. Nancy A. Hewitt and Susan Lebsock (Urbana and Chicago: University of Illinois Press, 1993), pp. 106–8.

2. Lois Scharf, *Eleanor Roosevelt: First Lady of American Liberalism* (Boston: Twayne Publishers, 1987), pp. 136–37; 142–43; Winifred Wandersee, "The Economics of Middle-Income Family Life: Working Women during the Great Depression," in *Decades of Discontent: The Women's Movement, 1920–1940*, ed. Lois Scharf and Joan M. Jensen (Westport, Conn.: Greenwood Press, 1983), pp. 54–56.

3. Blanche Wiesen Cook, *Eleanor Roosevelt*, vol. 1, *1884–1933* (New York: Viking, 1992), pp. 38–39, 46–67.

4. Ibid., pp. 102–19.

5. Ibid., pp. 154–60.

6. Ibid., pp. 288–301.

7. Joseph P. Lash, *Eleanor and Franklin: The Story of Their Relationship, Based on Eleanor Roosevelt's Private Papers* (New York: W. W. North, 1971), p. 348; Elisabeth Israels Perry, "Training for Public Life: ER and Women's Political Networks in the 1920s," in *Without Precedent: The Life and Career of Eleanor Roosevelt*, ed. Joan Hoff and Marjorie Lightman (Bloomington: Indiana University Press, 1984).

8. Joseph P. Lash, *Love, Eleanor: Eleanor Roosevelt and Her Friends* (Garden City, N.Y.: Doubleday, 1982), pp. 106–8.

9. Ann Davis, "The Character of Social Feminism in the Thirties: Eleanor Roosevelt and Her Associates in the New Deal," in *Franklin D. Roosevelt: The Man, the Myth, the Era, 1882–1945*, ed. Herbert D. Rosenbaum and Elizabeth Bartelme (New York: Greenwood Press, 1987).

10. Cook, *Eleanor Roosevelt*, pp. 320–32; 422–23.

11. Ibid., p. 337.

12. Ibid., pp. 429–47.

13. Ibid., pp. 478–79. Eleanor's relation with Lorena Hickok is described in Doris Faber, *The Life of Lorena Hickok, ER's Friend* (New York: Morrow, 1980).

14. Lash, *Eleanor and Franklin*, pp. 367–68; Cook, *Eleanor Roosevelt*, pp. 463, 472.

15. Kenneth Sydney Davis, *FDR, the New Deal Years, 1933–1937: A History* (New York: Random House, 1986), p. 377.

16. Lash, *Eleanor and Franklin*, pp. 361–64.

17. Ibid., p. 367; Scharf, *Eleanor Roosevelt*, p. 89.

18. Lash, *Love, Eleanor*, pp. 182–224.

19. Jean Wittick Pearson, "Arthurdale," master's thesis, Iowa State University, pp. 54–56.

20. "Subsistence Farmsteads," *Forum* 91 (1934): 199–201; Pearson, "Arthurdale," pp. 88–90.

21. James R. Kearney, *Anna Eleanor Roosevelt: The Evolution of a Reformer* (Boston: Houghton Mifflin, 1968), chap. 4.

22. Pearson, "Arthurdale," pp. 60, 81; "Subsistence Farmsteads."
23. Kearney, *Anna Eleanor Roosevelt,* chap. 3; Lash, *Eleanor and Franklin,* p. 364.
24. Scharf, *Eleanor Roosevelt,* pp. 90–93.
25. Ingrid Winter Scobie, "Helen Gahagan Douglas and the Roosevelt Connection," in Hoff and Lightman, *Without Precedent.*
26. John A. Edens, ed., *Eleanor Roosevelt: A Comprehensive Bibliography* (Westport, Conn.: Greenwood Press, 1994), pp. 20, 22, 76.
27. Lois Scharf, "ER and Feminism," in Hoff and Lightman, *Without Precedent.*
28. Ibid., pp. 21, 73, 75.
29. Ibid., pp. 73, 74.
30. Ibid., p. 75.
31. Lash, *Eleanor and Franklin,* pp. 545–54.
32. Lash, *Love, Eleanor,* pp. 266–67.
33. Lash, *Eleanor and Franklin,* p. 599.
34. Ibid., pp. 585–96, chap. 49.
35. Ibid., pp. 513–19.
36. Scharf, *Eleanor Roosevelt,* pp. 106–7; Lash, *Eleanor and Franklin,* p. 526.
37. Scharf, *Eleanor Roosevelt,* p. 109.
38. Lash, *Eleanor and Franklin,* pp. 530–33.
39. Harvard Sitkoff, *A New Deal for Blacks: The Emergence of Civil Rights as a National Issue* (New York: Oxford University Press, 1978), pp. 62, 77–79, 289–94, 307–10.
40. Lash, *Eleanor and Franklin,* pp. 525–26, 533–35.
41. Sitkoff, *New Deal for Blacks,* pp. 69–79.
42. Lash, *Eleanor and Franklin,* pp. 386, 461, 464–65; Lash, *Love, Eleanor,* p. 296.
43. Maurine Beasley, "Eleanor Roosevelt and 'My Day': The White House Years," in Rosenbaum and Bartelme, *The Man, the Myth, the Era,* pp. 257–61.
44. Eleanor Roosevelt, *This Is My Story* (New York and London: Harper and Brothers, 1937).
45. George Whitney Martin, *Madam Secretary, Frances Perkins* (Boston: Houghton Mifflin, 1976), pp. 260–71, 294–305, 420–21.
46. Ibid., p. 328.
47. Ibid., pp. 367–68, 389.
48. Susan Ware, *Partner and I: Molly Dewson, Feminism, and New Deal Politics* (New Haven, Conn.: Yale University Press, 1987), pp. 194, 196–97, 198–204.
49. Martha H. Swain, *Ellen S. Woodward: New Deal Advocate for Women* (Jackson: University Press of Mississippi, 1995), pp. 42–44, 96–97.
50. Ibid., p. 179.
51. Ware, *Partner,* p. 192.
52. Swain, *Woodward,* pp. 91–93; Linda Gordon, *Pitied but Not Entitled: Single Mothers and the History of Welfare, 1890–1935* (New York: Free Press 1994), pp. 185–89, 193–95; Mimi Abramovitz, *Regulating the Lives of Women: Social Welfare Policy from Colonial Times to the Present* (Boston: South End Press, 1988), pp. 280–87.
53. Abramovitz, *Regulating the Lives of Women,* pp. 250–56.

CHAPTER 8
THE NEW DEAL REACHES ITS LIMIT

1. The account of the Supreme Court incident is based on William E. Leuchtenburg, *The Supreme Court Reborn* (New York: Oxford University Press, 1995), chaps. 4–5; Frank Freidel, *Franklin D. Roosevelt: A Rendezvous with Destiny* (Boston: Little, Brown, 1990), chap. 18.

2. John Morton Blum, *From the Morgenthau Diaries: Years of Crisis, 1928–1938* (Boston: Houghton Mifflin, 1959), pp. 382, 385.

3. Albert U. Romasco, *The Politics of Recovery: Roosevelt's New Deal* (New York: Oxford University Press, 1983), p. 181; Alan Brinkley, *The End of Reform: New Deal Liberalism in Recession and War* (New York: Knopf, 1995), pp. 25–27.

4. Brinkley, *End of Reform*, pp. 32–43.

5. James M. Landis, *The Administrative Process* (New Haven, Conn.: Yale University Press, 1938).

6. Alan Brinkley, *Voices of Protest: Huey Long, Father Coughlin, and the Great Depression* (New York: Knopf, 1982), pp. 49–57; Theodore Rosenof, *Dogma, Depression, and the New Deal: The Debate of Political Leaders over Economic Recovery* (Port Washington, N.Y.: Kennikat Press, 1975), p. 102.

7. Alvin H. Hansen, *Business-Cycle Theory* (Boston: Ginn and Company, 1927).

8. Dean L. May, *From New Deal to New Economics: The Liberal Response to the Recession of 1937* (New York: Garland, 1981), pp. 131–33; Richard V. Gilbert, George H. Hildebrand, Jr., Arthur W. Stuart, Maxine Yaple Sweezy, Paul M. Sweezy, Dorrie Tarshis, and John D. Wilson, *An Economic Program for American Democracy* (New York: Vanguard Press, 1938).

9. George McJimsey, *Harry Hopkins: Ally of the Poor and Defender of Democracy* (Cambridge: Harvard University Press, 1987), pp. 74–75; Brinkley, *End of Reform*, pp. 66–97.

10. Brinkley, *End of Reform*, pp. 132–36; Rosenof, *Dogma, Depression, and the New Deal*, pp. 30–31.

11. Arthur M. Schlesinger, Jr., *The Politics of Upheaval* (Boston: Houghton Mifflin, 1960), pp. 285–92; Rosenof, *Dogma, Depression, and New Deal*, p. 88; Brinkley, *End of Reform*, p. 87.

12. Joseph P. Lash, *Dealers and Dreamers: A New Look at the New Deal* (New York: Doubleday, 1988), pp. 317–30.

13. Brinkley, *End of Reform*, p. 58; Samuel I. Rosenman, ed., *The Public Papers and Addresses of Franklin D. Roosevelt*, 13 vols. (New York: Random House, 1938), vol. 6, pp. 436, 493.

14. Herbert Stein, *The Fiscal Revolution in America* (Chicago and London: University of Chicago Press, 1969), pp. 105–6.

15. Quoted in Herman E. Kroos, *Executive Opinion: What Business Leaders Said and Thought on Economic Issues, 1920s–1960s* (Garden City, N.Y.: Doubleday, 1970), p. 184.

16. Freidel, *Rendezvous with Destiny*, p. 253.

17. Stein, *Fiscal Revolution*, p. 109.

18. Blum, *Years of Crisis,* pp. 388–95, 404–5, 410.

19. May, *From New Deal to New Economics,* pp. 128–34.

20. Rosenman, *Public Papers,* vol. 7, pp. 221–35.

21. Roger J. Sandilands, *The Life and Political Economy of Lauchlin Currie* (Durham, N.C., and London: Duke University Press, 1990), pp. 92–95.

22. Mark Gelfand, *A Nation of Cities: The Federal Government and Urban America, 1933–1965* (New York: Oxford, 1975), pp. 56–65, 90–91, 96–99, 110–111; J. Joseph Huthmacher, *Senator Robert F. Wagner and the Rise of Urban Liberalism* (New York: Atheneum, 1968), pp. 207–30. For a view that New Deal housing policy was unduly restrained, see Roger Biles, "FDR, the New Deal, and Public Housing," in *The New Deal and Public Policy,* ed. Byron Daynes, William D. Pederson, and Michael P. Riccards (New York: St. Martin's Press, 1998).

23. William E. Leuchtenburg, *Franklin D. Roosevelt and the New Deal* (New York: Harper and Row, 1963), pp. 259–60.

24. Ibid., p. 265; Kenneth S. Davis, *FDR, into the Storm* (New York: Random House, 1993), pp. 239–41.

25. Barry Dean Karl, *Executive Reorganization and Reform in the New Deal* (Cambridge: Harvard University Press, 1965), pp. 261–65. See also Richard Polenberg, *Reorganizing Roosevelt's Government: The Controversy over Executive Reorganization, 1936–1939* (Cambridge: Harvard University Press, 1966), pp. 20–27.

26. Polenberg, *Reorganizing Roosevelt's Government,* pp. 41–42, 47–50.

27. Davis, *Into the Storm,* pp. 19–28, 32–37, 213–15, 222–23, 419–23; Polenberg, *Reorganizing Roosevelt's Government,* chaps. 4–5, pp. 139–40.

28. Polenberg, *Reorganizing Roosevelt's Government,* pp. 162–72. Polenberg also cites concern among House Democrats that if they sent the bill to a conference committee, Roosevelt would remove certain concessions he had made and trick them into taking the original bill.

29. Herman Miles Somers, *Presidential Agency: OWMR, the Office of War Mobilization and Reconversion* (Cambridge: Harvard University Press, 1950), pp. 208–9.

CHAPTER 9
FROM ISOLATION TO WAR

1. Waldo H. Heinrichs, *Threshold of War: Franklin D. Roosevelt and American Entry into World War II* (New York: Oxford University Press, 1988), p. 8; Akira Iriye, *The Origins of the Second World War in Asia and the Pacific* (London and New York: Longman, 1987), "Introduction."

2. The following account is drawn from Robert Dallek, *Franklin D. Roosevelt and American Foreign Policy, 1932–1945* (New York: Oxford University Press, 1979).

3. Wayne S. Cole, *Roosevelt and the Isolationists, 1932–45* (Lincoln: University of Nebraska Press, 1983), pp. 6–9.

4. Ibid., chap. 17; Roosevelt quote, p. 260.

5. James Thomas Emmerson, *The Rhineland Crisis, 7 March 1936: A Study in Multilateral Diplomacy* (Ames: Iowa State University Press, 1977).

6. A. J. P. Taylor, *English History 1914–1945* (Oxford: Oxford University Press, 1965), pp. 373–88; Donald Cameron Watt, *How War Came: The Immediate Origins of the Second World War, 1938–1939* (London: Heinemann, 1989), pp. 244–50, chap. 8.

7. Dallek, *Roosevelt and American Foreign Policy*, p. 144.

8. Ibid., p. 164.

9. Ibid., p. 198.

10. Iriye, *Origins of the Second World War*, pp. 108–10.

11. James McGregor Burns, *Roosevelt: The Lion and the Fox* (New York: Harcourt, Brace and World, 1956), pp. 411–14.

12. Kenneth S. Davis, *FDR, into the Storm* (New York: Random House, 1993), pp. 576–83.

13. Ibid., p. 597.

14. Joseph P. Lash, *Eleanor and Franklin: The Story of Their Relationship, Based on Eleanor Roosevelt's Private Papers* (New York: W. W. North, 1971), pp. 619–24; Frank Freidel, *Franklin D. Roosevelt: A Rendezvous with Destiny* (Boston: Little, Brown, 1990), pp. 345–46.

15. Lash, *Eleanor and Franklin*, p. 624.

16. Robert E. Sherwood, *Roosevelt and Hopkins: An Intimate History* (New York: Harper and Brothers, 1948), p. 191.

17. R. Elberton Smith, *The Army and Economic Mobilization* (Washington, D.C.: Office of the Chief of Military History, 1959), pp. 98–103.

18. Samuel I. Rosenman, ed., *The Public Papers and Addresses of Franklin D. Roosevelt*, 13 vols. (New York: Random House, 1941), vol. 9, pp. 230–40.

19. Ibid., pp. 366–67.

20. George McJimsey, *Harry Hopkins: Ally of the Poor and Defender of Democracy* (Cambridge: Harvard University Press, 1987), chap. 10.

21. Eric Larrabee, *Commander in Chief: Franklin Delano Roosevelt, His Lieutenants, and Their War* (New York: Harper and Row, 1987), p. 49.

22. Dallek, *Roosevelt and American Foreign Policy*, p. 271.

23. Smith, *The Army and Economic Mobilization*, pp. 134–39.

24. McJimsey, *Hopkins*, pp. 177–78.

25. Gordon Prange, *At Dawn We Slept: The Untold Story of Pearl Harbor* (New York: McGraw-Hill, 1981), pp. 169–71, 177–78, 208–12.

26. Larrabee, *Commander in Chief*, p. 91.

27. Mark Skinner Watson, *Chief of Staff: Prewar Plans and Preparations* (Washington, D.C.: Office of the Chief of Military History, 1964), p. 505. See also Stetson Conn, Rose C. Engleman, and Byron Fairchild, *The Western Hemisphere: Guarding the United States and Its Outposts* (Washington, D.C.: Office of the Chief of Military History, 1964), p. 250.

28. Prange, *At Dawn*, chap. 50.

29. James McGregor Burns, *Roosevelt: The Lion and the Fox* (New York: Harcourt, Brace, 1956), p. 461.

CHAPTER 10
FROM UNITY TO PREEMINENCE

1. This chapter is drawn from Robert Dallek, *Franklin D. Roosevelt and American Foreign Policy, 1932–1945* (New York: Oxford University Press, 1979).

2. William Roger Louis, *Imperialism at Bay 1941–1945: The United States and the Decolonization of the British Empire* (Oxford: Clarendon Press, 1977), pp. 21–26.

3. Christopher Thorne, *Allies of a Kind: The United States, Britain and the War against Japan, 1941–1945* (London: H. Hamilton, 1978), pp. 172–78.

4. Alan Wilt, *War from the Top: German and British Military Decision Making during World War II* (Bloomington: Indiana University Press, 1990), p. 40. Wilt points out that the Americans insisted on assigning military responsibilities to specific geographic areas, with both nations responsible for Western Europe; the British finally agreed.

5. Forrest Pogue, *George C. Marshall, Organizer of Victory* (New York: Viking Press 1979), pp. 175–78; George McJimsey, *Harry Hopkins: Ally of the Poor and Defender of Democracy* (Cambridge: Harvard University Press, 1987), pp. 156–57, 214, 216, 219–21.

6. Ibid., p. 236.

7. Dallek, *Roosevelt and American Foreign Policy*, pp. 330–34.

8. McJimsey, *Hopkins*, p. 320.

9. Roger Daniels, *Concentration Camps North America: Japanese in the United States and Canada during World War II* (Malabar, Fla.: R. E. Krieger, 1981), chap. 3; Page Smith, *Democracy on Trial: The Japanese-American Evacuation and Relocation in World War II* (New York: Simon and Schuster, 1995), chap. 8.

10. Dallek, *Roosevelt and American Foreign Policy*, pp. 337–38.

11. Ibid., pp. 338–39; McJimsey, *Hopkins*, p. 245.

12. McJimsey, *Hopkins*, p. 263.

13. Louis, *Imperialism at Bay*, pp. 147–50, 154–58.

14. Dallek, *Roosevelt and American Foreign Policy*, pp. 366–68.

15. McJimsey, *Hopkins*, pp. 276–77; Dallek, *Roosevelt and American Foreign Policy*, pp. 378–79.

16. Samuel I. Rosenman, ed., *The Public Papers and Addresses of Franklin D. Roosevelt*, 13 vols. (New York: Random House, 1950), vol. 12, pp. 37–48.

17. Wilt, *War from the Top*, pp. 197–99.

18. Thorne, *Allies of a Kind*, pp. 307, 308; Dallek, *Roosevelt and American Foreign Policy*, p. 389.

19. Richard Leighton and Robert Coakley, *Global Logistics and Strategy*, 2 vols. (Washington, D.C.: Office of the Chief of Military History, 1955, 1959), vol. 1, pp. 541–42.

20. Dallek, *Roosevelt and American Foreign Policy*, pp. 384–87.

21. Thorne, *Allies of a Kind*, pp. 312–15; Dallek, *Roosevelt and American Foreign Policy*, p. 391.

22. Thorne, *Allies of a Kind*, pp. 157–59, 167–69, 242–43, 426–40.

23. McJimsey, *Hopkins*, pp. 233–36.

24. Ibid., p. 239.
25. Ibid., p. 281.
26. Leighton and Coakley, *Global Logistics and Strategy,* vol. 1, pp. 282–84.
27. Ibid., pp. 616–23.
28. Robert Divine, *Second Chance, the Triumph of Internationalism in America during World War II* (New York: Atheneum, 1967), pp. 91–96.
29. E. Llewellyn Woodward, *British Foreign Policy during the Second World War* (London: Her Majesty's Stationery Office, 1970–), pp. 437–42; Anthony Eden, *The Reckoning* (Boston: Houghton Mifflin, 1965), pp. 430–43.
30. Louis, *Imperialism at Bay,* pp. 228–29, 231–32.
31. Eden, *Reckoning,* p. 433.
32. Ibid., p. 441. Hopkins's own notes, however, say that Eden considered his visit a success in all respects. Robert E. Sherwood, *Roosevelt and Hopkins, an Intimate History* (New York: Harper and Brothers, 1948), p. 719.
33. McJimsey, *Hopkins,* p. 286; Pogue, *Organizer of Victory,* pp. 205–9; *Foreign Relations of the United States: Conferences at Washington and Quebec, 1945* (Washington, D.C.: U.S. Government Printing Office, 1955), pp. 29–32, 44, 46, 53–54, 56, 61–62 (hereafter *FRUS*).
34. Quoted in Dallek, *Roosevelt and American Foreign Policy,* p. 395.
35. *FRUS, Conferences at Washington and Quebec,* pp. 496–501.
36. Dallek, *Roosevelt and American Foreign Policy,* pp. 419–20.
37. Ibid., pp. 426–29; McJimsey, *Hopkins,* pp. 303–4.
38. Louis, *Imperialism at Bay,* pp. 259–73.
39. Frank Freidel, *Franklin D. Roosevelt: A Rendezvous with Destiny* (Boston: Little, Brown, 1990), p. 473.
40. *FRUS, Conferences at Washington and Quebec,* p. 32.
41. Dallek, *Roosevelt and American Foreign Policy,* pp. 430–31.
42. McJimsey, *Hopkins,* p. 305.

CHAPTER 11
WARTIME FRUITS OF PLURALISM

1. Robert E. Sherwood, *Roosevelt and Hopkins, an Intimate History* (New York: Harper and Brothers, 1948), pp. 473–74.
2. Frederic C. Lane, *Ships for Victory, a History of Shipbuilding under the United States Maritime Commission in World War II* (Baltimore: Johns Hopkins Press, 1951), chap. 5.
3. George McJimsey, *Harry Hopkins: Ally of the Poor and Defender of Democracy* (Cambridge: Harvard University Press, 1987), chap. 15.
4. James McGregor Burns, *Roosevelt: The Soldier of Freedom* (New York: Harcourt Brace Jovanovich, 1970), pp. 246–47; Civilian Production Administration, *Industrial Mobilization for War* (Washington, D.C.: U.S. Government Printing Office, 1946), chap. 2.
5. Burns, *Soldier of Freedom,* p. 256.

6. *The United States at War: Development and Administration of the War Program by the Federal Government* (Washington, D.C.: Bureau of the Budget Publication, 1946), pp. 235–73.

7. Frank Freidel, *Franklin D. Roosevelt: A Rendezvous with Destiny* (Boston: Little, Brown, 1990), pp. 438–40.

8. Burns, *Soldier of Freedom*, pp. 268–70, 273–81.

9. Wright Patman to Sam Rayburn, December 17, 1942, Rayburn Papers, microfilm, ser. 1, reel 12, Sam Rayburn Library, Bonham, Tex.

10. Samuel I. Rosenman, ed., *The Public Papers and Addresses of Franklin D. Roosevelt*, 13 vols. (New York: Harper and Brothers, 1950), vol. 12, pp. 21–34.

11. *United States at War*, pp. 386–91; Rosenman, *Public Papers*, vol. 12, pp. 185–99; Harold Vatter, *The U.S. Economy in World War II* (New York: Columbia University Press, 1985), pp. 93–95; Hugh Rockoff, *Drastic Measures: A History of Wage and Price Controls in the United States* (Cambridge: Cambridge University Press, 1984), pp. 85–176.

12. Rosenman, *Public Papers*, vol. 12, pp. 268–72.

13. John Morton Blum, *From the Morgenthau Diaries: Years of War, 1941–1945* (Boston: Houghton Mifflin, 1959–1967), pp. 58–64.

14. Ibid., pp. 73–76.

15. R. Elberton Smith, *The Army and Economic Mobilization* (Washington, D.C.: Office of the Chief of Military History, 1959), pp. 134–35.

16. Stuart D. Brandes, *Warhogs: A History of War Profits in America* (Lexington: University of Kentucky Press, 1997), pp. 211, 228–29, 238–47, 249–65.

17. *United States at War*, pp. 371–99; Burns, *Soldier of Freedom*, pp. 339–40, 354.

18. Examples of Byrnes's activities are in Civilian Production Administration, *Industrial Mobilization for War*, pp. 721–23, 738–40, 770, 787, 801. See also Herman Miles Somers, *Presidential Agency OWMR: The Office of War Mobilization and Reconversion* (Cambridge: Harvard University Press, 1950), pp. 58–74.

19. Blum, *Morgenthau Diaries*, p. 70.

20. Burns, *Soldier of Freedom*, pp. 340–41; *United States at War*, pp. 421–28.

21. Civilian Production Administration, *Industrial Mobilization for War*, pp. 739–41.

22. McJimsey, *Hopkins*, p. 334.

23. Vatter, *U.S. Economy in World War II*, pp. 49–55.

24. Ibid., pp. 54, 142–44.

25. Vincent C. Jones, *Manhattan: The Army and the Atomic Bomb* (Washington, D.C.: Office of the Chief of Military History, 1985), pp. 21–26.

26. Ibid., pp. 273–74.

27. Burns, *Soldier of Freedom*, p. 262.

28. Robert Ferrell, *Choosing Truman: The Democratic Convention of 1944* (Columbia: University of Missouri Press, 1994), pp. 19–38.

29. Ibid., pp. 42–50.

30. David McCulloch, *Truman* (New York: Simon and Schuster, 1992), pp. 294–314; Freidel, *Rendezvous with Destiny*, pp. 533–37; Ferrell, *Choosing Truman*, pp. 57–62.

31. McCulloch, *Truman*, pp. 316–20; Ferrell, *Choosing Truman*, pp. 73–88.
32. Freidel, *Rendezvous with Destiny*, p. 533.
33. McCulloch, *Truman*, p. 327.
34. Freidel, *Rendezvous with Destiny*, pp. 545–46.
35. Sherwood, *Roosevelt and Hopkins*, p. 821.
36. Richard Norton Smith, *Thomas E. Dewey and His Times* (New York: Simon and Schuster, 1982), pp. 410–35.
37. Sherwood, *Roosevelt and Hopkins*, p. 829.
38. Robert Divine, *Second Chance, the Triumph of Internationalism in America during World War II* (New York: Atheneum, 1967), p. 241.
39. Quoted in Freidel, *Rendezvous with Destiny*, p. 570.
40. McJimsey, *Hopkins*, pp. 348–49; Freidel, *Rendezvous with Destiny*, pp. 570–71.
41. Freidel, *Rendezvous with Destiny*, pp. 575–76.
42. Joseph P. Lash, *Eleanor and Franklin: The Story of Their Relationship, Based on Eleanor Roosevelt's Private Papers* (New York: W. W. North, 1971), pp. 636–37, 640–46.
43. Ibid., pp. 652, 662–70.
44. Joseph P. Lash, *Love, Eleanor: Eleanor Roosevelt and Her Friends* (Garden City, N.Y.: Doubleday, 1982), p. 381; Doris Kearns Goodwin, *No Ordinary Time: Franklin and Eleanor Roosevelt: The Home Front in World War II* (New York: Simon and Schuster, 1994), pp. 626–28; Allida M. Black, "Defining Eleanor, Defining Power: World War II, Racism and a Preoccupied White House," in *FDR and the Modern Presidency: Leadership and Legacy*, ed. Mark J. Rozell and William D. Pederson (Westport, Conn.: Praeger, 1997).
45. Goodwin, *No Ordinary Time*, pp. 365, 369, 393, 413–18.
46. Lash, *Eleanor and Franklin*, pp. 682–91; Goodwin, *No Ordinary Time*, pp. 463–64.
47. Lash, *Eleanor and Franklin*, pp. 701, 708.
48. Sherwood, *Roosevelt and Hopkins*, p. 831.
49. Freidel, *Rendezvous with Destiny*, pp. 508–12.
50. McJimsey, *Hopkins*, p. 333.
51. Freidel, *Rendezvous with Destiny*, pp. 370–71, 542.

CHAPTER 12
AMBIGUOUS VICTORIES

1. Doris Kearns Goodwin, *No Ordinary Time: Franklin and Eleanor Roosevelt: The Home Front in World War II* (New York: Simon and Schuster, 1994), pp. 491–97.
2. Richard Breitman, "Roosevelt and the Holocaust," in *FDR and the Holocaust*, ed. Verne W. Newton (New York: St. Martin's Press, 1996).
3. David S. Wyman, *The Abandonment of the Jews: America and the Holocaust, 1941–1945* (New York: Pantheon Books, 1984), pp. 56–57.
4. Breitman, "Roosevelt and the Holocaust."
5. Wyman, *Abandonment of the Jews*, pp. 72, 75.

6. Ibid., pp. 155–56, 209–15, 285.
7. Ibid., pp. 335–36.
8. See Goodwin, *No Ordinary Time*, pp. 101–4, 173–75, 396–97, 453–55, 515–16; Robert Dallek, *Franklin D. Roosevelt and American Foreign Policy, 1932–1945* (New York: Oxford University Press, 1979), pp. 444–48.
9. Frank Freidel, *Franklin D. Roosevelt: A Rendezvous with Destiny* (Boston: Little, Brown, 1990), pp. 527–28.
10. Ibid., pp. 550–53.
11. Dallek, *Roosevelt and American Foreign Policy*, pp. 475–76.
12. Martin Sherwin, *A World Destroyed: The Atomic Bomb and the Grand Alliance* (New York: Knopf, 1975), pp. 73–89.
13. Freidel, *Rendezvous with Destiny*, pp. 553–55.
14. Dallek, *Roosevelt and American Foreign Policy*, pp. 476–77; George McJimsey, *Harry Hopkins: Ally of the Poor and Defender of Democracy* (Cambridge: Harvard University Press, 1987), p. 346.
15. McJimsey, *Hopkins*, pp. 347–49.
16. Ibid., pp. 357–59; Dallek, *Roosevelt and American Foreign Policy*, pp. 468–70, 504–6.
17. Dallek, *Roosevelt and American Foreign Policy*, pp. 485–502.
18. Freidel, *Rendezvous with Destiny*, pp. 573–74.
19. Dallek, *Roosevelt and American Foreign Policy*, pp. 507–8.
20. *Foreign Relations of the United States: The Conferences at Malta and Yalta, 1945* (Washington, D.C.: U.S. Government Printing Office, 1955), pp. 50–51, 56–57, (hereafter *FRUS*).
21. Ibid., pp. 107–8.
22. E. Llewellyn Woodward, *British Foreign Policy in the Second World War* (London: Her Majesty's Stationery Office, 1962), pp. 484–85.
23. McJimsey, *Hopkins*, pp. 361–63.
24. *FRUS, The Conferences at Malta and Yalta*, pp. 158–59.
25. Ibid., pp. 171–72, 174–75.
26. Ibid., pp. 178–97.
27. Ibid., pp. 202–27.
28. Ibid., pp. 230–34.
29. Ibid., pp. 237–38.
30. Ibid., pp. 310–15.
31. John Morton Blum, *From the Morgenthau Diaries: Years of War, 1941–1945* (Boston: Houghton Mifflin, 1959–1967), pp. 304–5.
32. Lloyd C. Gardner, *Spheres of Influence: The Great Powers Partition Europe, from Munich to Yalta* (Chicago: I. R. Dee, 1993), p. 223.
33. *FRUS, The Conferences at Malta and Yalta*, pp. 351–58.
34. Ibid., pp. 388–96.
35. McJimsey, *Hopkins*, p. 363.
36. Anthony Eden, *The Reckoning* (Boston: Houghton Mifflin, 1965), p. 562.
37. Dallek, *Roosevelt and American Foreign Policy*, pp. 509–10.
38. Diane Shaver Clemens, *Yalta* (New York: Oxford University Press, 1970), pp. 216–26.

39. *FRUS, The Conferences at Malta and Yalta,* p. 788.
40. Robert E. Sherwood, *Roosevelt and Hopkins, an Intimate History* (New York: Harper and Brothers, 1948), p. 860.
41. Eden to Churchill, quoted in William Roger Louis, *Imperialism at Bay 1941–1945: The United States and the Decolonization of the British Empire* (Oxford: Clarendon Press, 1977), p. 455.
42. Ibid., 458–60; Dallek, *Roosevelt and American Foreign Policy,* pp. 510–13.
43. Dallek, *Roosevelt and American Foreign Policy,* pp. 516–18.
44. *FRUS, The Conferences at Malta and Yalta,* pp. 797–98.
45. Dallek, *Roosevelt and American Foreign Policy,* pp. 523–24; Freidel, *Rendezvous with Destiny,* pp. 600–601.
46. Dallek, *Roosevelt and American Foreign Policy,* pp. 526–27; Freidel, *Rendezvous with Destiny,* p. 602.
47. Dallek, *Roosevelt and American Foreign Policy,* p. 525; Freidel, *Rendezvous with Destiny,* p. 601.
48. Dallek, *Roosevelt and American Foreign Policy,* pp. 526–27; Freidel, *Rendezvous with Destiny,* p. 602.
49. David McCulloch, *Truman* (New York: Simon and Schuster, 1992), pp. 341–42.

CHAPTER 13
CONCLUSION

1. Barry D. Karl, *The Uneasy State: The United States from 1915 to 1945* (Chicago and London: University of Chicago Press, 1983), p. 232.
2. Matthew J. Dickinson, *Bitter Harvest: FDR, Presidential Power and the Growth of the Presidential Branch* (Cambridge: Cambridge University Press, 1997), chap. 8.
3. The major works about Roosevelt's presidency usually acknowledge both his positive and his negative traits. Classification of the following works as "positive" or "negative" views of Roosevelt's presidency represents the author's subjective judgment. Positive evaluations include Arthur M. Schlesinger, Jr., *The Coming of the New Deal* (New York: Houghton Mifflin, 1959); William E. Leuchtenburg, *Franklin D. Roosevelt and the New Deal* (New York: Harper and Row, 1963); Clinton Rossiter, *The American Presidency,* rev. ed. (New York: Harcourt, Brace and World, 1956); Frank Burt Freidel, *Franklin D. Roosevelt: A Rendezvous with Destiny* (Boston: Little, Brown, 1990); and Morton J. Fritsch, *Franklin D. Roosevelt: The Contribution of the New Deal to American Political Thought and Practice* (Boston: Twayne Publishers, 1975). Generally positive but with a significant negative substance are James McGregor Burns, *Roosevelt: The Lion and the Fox* (New York: Harcourt Brace Jovanovich, 1956); and Patrick J. Maney, *The Roosevelt Presence: The Life and Legacy of FDR* (Berkeley: University of California Press, 1998 [1993]). Somewhat more difficult to classify, since they go from being balanced toward the positive side to being rather strongly negative, are Kenneth Sydney Davis's *FDR, the New Deal Years, 1933–1937: A History* (New York: Random House, 1986) and *FDR, into the Storm* (New York: Random House, 1993). There have been several studies of how

Roosevelt's presidency affected the national economy. An important one that sees a shift in Roosevelt's policies from reform to accommodation with market capitalism is Alan Brinkley, *The End of Reform: New Deal Liberalism in Recession and War* (New York: Knopf, 1995). A similar approach informs Theodore Rosenof's *Dogma, Depression, and the New Deal: The Debate of Political Leaders over Economic Recovery* (Port Washington, N.Y.: Kennikat Press, 1975) and *Economics in the Long Run: New Deal Theorists and Their Legacies, 1933–1993* (Chapel Hill: University of North Carolina Press, 1997).

4. Christopher Thorne, *Allies of a Kind: The United States, Britain and the War against Japan, 1941–1945* (London: Hamish Hamilton, 1978), pp. 240–48, 596–97, 622–33.

5. William E. Leuchtenburg, *In the Shadow of FDR: From Harry Truman to Ronald Reagan* (Ithaca, N.Y.: Cornell University Press, 1983).

6. Paul Appleby, *Big Democracy* (New York: Knopf, 1945).

7. Leonard D. White, *Introduction to the Study of Public Administration* (New York: Macmillan, 1939), p. 17.

8. *Phelps Dodge Corporation v. National Labor Relations Board,* 313 U.S. 177 (1940).

9. *Federal Communications Commission v. Pottsville Broadcasting,* 309 U.S. 117 (1940).

10. *Interstate Commerce Commission v. Jersey City,* 322 U.S. 503 (1944).

11. Rinehart John Swenson, *Federal Administrative Law, a Study of the Growth, Nature and Control of Administrative Action* (New York: Ronald Company, 1952), p. 33.

12. Louis Jaffe, "Law Making by Private Groups," *Harvard Law Review* 51 (1937): 201–53; Karl E. Klare, "Judicial Deradicalization of the Wagner Act and the Origins of Modern Legal Consciousness, 1937–1941," *Minnesota Law Review* 62 (1978): 265–339.

13. Michael Walzer, "Response," in *Pluralism, Justice, and Equality,* ed. David Miller and Michael Walzer (Oxford and New York: Oxford University Press, 1995), p. 283.

14. Robert S. Lynd and Helen Merell Lynd, *Middletown in Transition: A Study in Cultural Conflicts* (New York: Harcourt, Brace and Company, 1937), pp. 120–21, 125–26, 248–49, 426–28, 452–53.

15. Donald Robert Brand, *Corporatism and the Rule of Law: A Study of the National Recovery Administration* (Ithaca, N.Y.: Cornell University Press, 1988), pp. 297–312; Rosenof, *Dogma, Depression, and the New Deal,* pp. 8–17.

16. This redefinition of liberalism is noted by Brinkley, *End of Reform,* pp. 167–70.

BIBLIOGRAPHICAL ESSAY

This book is based on both published primary sources and secondary sources. The following essay is divided into two parts. The first part discusses the published primary sources and those secondary sources that provide a general view of Franklin D. Roosevelt's presidency. The second part discusses works that were especially useful for the book's chapters. The works cited in the general section are not repeated under the chapter headings. Works that pertain to more than one chapter are discussed in the first chapter in which they appear.

PUBLISHED PRIMARY SOURCES

There is no "definitive" collection of Franklin D. Roosevelt's papers. The holdings of the Franklin D. Roosevelt Library in Hyde Park, New York, are so extensive that it is impossible to imagine anyone preparing such a collection. Elliot Roosevelt, ed., *FDR, His Personal Letters,* 4 vols. (New York: Duell, Sloan and Pearce, 1947–1950), helps one understand some of Roosevelt's personality, especially his hesitancy to write about his deeper feelings and motives—personal, political, and presidential. Samuel I. Rosenman, ed., *The Public Papers and Addresses of Franklin D. Roosevelt,* 13 vols. (New York: Random House, 1938), vol. 1, contains his major speeches and executive orders and excerpts from his press conferences. Roosevelt's handling of the press is comprehensively documented in *The Complete Press Conferences of Franklin D. Roosevelt,* 25 vols. (New York: De Capo Press, 1972). One gains some appreciation of Roosevelt's ability to reach the American people in Russell D. Buhite and David W. Levy, eds., *FDR's Fireside Chats* (Norman: University of Oklahoma Press, 1992). Publications that focus on domestic aspects of Roosevelt's presidency include Edgar B. Nixon, ed., *Franklin D. Roosevelt and Con-*

servation, 1911–1945, 2 vols. (Washington, D.C.: U.S. Government Printing Office, 1957), which publishes Roosevelt's speeches, letters, press conference statements, and executive orders dealing with natural resource policy as well as communications to Roosevelt on these matters. The record of Roosevelt's foreign policy is much more complete. An excellent documentary record of Roosevelt's diplomacy is Edgar B. Nixon, Donald Schewe, and Daryl L. Revoldt, eds., *Franklin D. Roosevelt and Foreign Affairs,* 17 vols. (Cambridge: Belknap Press of Harvard University Press, New York: Clearwater, 1969–1983). An essential source is Warren F. Kimball, ed., *Churchill and Roosevelt: The Complete Correspondence,* 3 vols. (Princeton, N.J.: Princeton University Press, 1984). The volumes in the series *Foreign Relations of the United States* provide a detailed documentary record of Roosevelt's foreign policy. The volumes on the wartime conferences are especially valuable.

Neither is there a "definitive" publication of Eleanor Roosevelt's papers. Joseph Lash, *Love, Eleanor: Eleanor Roosevelt and Her Friends* (Garden City, N.Y.: Doubleday, 1982), purports to be a selection of her letters but often lacks specific citations and too often provides paraphrases instead of direct quotations. With these limitations, however, the book offers insights into Eleanor Roosevelt's friendships and personal and political views. Bernard Asbell, ed., *Mother and Daughter: The Letters of Eleanor and Anna Roosevelt* (New York: Coward, McCann and Geoghegan, 1982), contains letters between Eleanor and daughter Anna and complements Lash's book. Maurine H. Beasley, *The White House Press Conferences of Eleanor Roosevelt* (New York: Garland, 1983), provides information about Eleanor's activities and views on public issues. Selections from her popular newspaper column "My Day" are printed in Rochelle Chadakoff, ed., *Eleanor Roosevelt's "My Day": Her Acclaimed Columns, 1936–1945* (New York: Pharos Books, 1989). An excellent bibliography of Eleanor's writings is John A. Edens, ed., *Eleanor Roosevelt: A Comprehensive Bibliography* (Westport, Conn.: Greenwood Press, 1994).

Documentary sources from those who worked closely with Roosevelt include Harold Ickes's massive *The Secret Diary of Harold Ickes,* 3 vols. (New York: Simon and Schuster, 1953–1954), which is useful if the reader concentrates on what Roosevelt said and not on Ickes's interpretation of what he meant. John Morton Blum, *From the Morgenthau Diaries,* 3 vols. (Boston: Houghton Mifflin, 1959–1967), masterfully condenses the huge amount of material in the office record of Roosevelt's Dutchess County neighbor, friend, and secretary of the treasury into a useful narrative of paraphrases and quotations. William D. Hassett, *Off the Record with FDR: 1942–1945* (New Brunswick, N.J.: Rutgers University Press, 1958), is a straightforward account by an experienced journalist who was Roosevelt's correspondence secretary.

There are several good biographical studies of Franklin D. Roosevelt. The best scholarly biography is Frank Burt Freidel, *Franklin D. Roosevelt: A Rendezvous with Destiny* (Boston: Little, Brown, 1990), which is balanced in its treatment of subjects, insightful regarding the political context in which Roosevelt operated, and sympathetic to Roosevelt without being hero-worshipping. Freidel had previously published four volumes of a projected and then abandoned multivolume biography. The first three volumes, *Franklin D. Roosevelt: The Apprenticeship, The Ordeal,* and *The Triumph* (Boston: Little Brown, 1952–1960), portray Roosevelt through his election to the presidency and focus on his political views and political career. The fourth volume, *Franklin D. Roosevelt: Launching the New Deal* (Boston: Little Brown, 1973), is a densely written, scholarly account of the planning of the New Deal and the Hundred Days that put its first version into practice. Freidel emphasizes Roosevelt's commitment to public service and his political liberalism (the use of government power to solve social problems, sympathy for the less fortunate in society, distrust of the wealthy and economically powerful, and openness to new ideas and practices), as well as his complex, mercurial personality. Freidel views Roosevelt's political tactics with a realist's eye that credits his many successes and tends to attribute his failures to the limitations of the political situations in which he operated rather than his own misjudgments. Freidel credits Roosevelt's skill as a wartime leader, especially his commitment to a liberal internationalism of anticolonialism, political and economic democracy, and a world of independent nations. At the same time, Freidel consistently portrays Roosevelt as operating within a context of constraining political, diplomatic, and military conditions.

James McGregor Burns, *Roosevelt: The Lion and the Fox* (New York: Harcourt Brace Jovanovich, 1956), and *Roosevelt: The Soldier of Freedom* (New York: Harcourt Brace Jovanovich, 1970), provide a political analysis of Roosevelt written by a political scientist interested in the study of leadership and in advancing a liberal political agenda. Burns's first volume faults Roosevelt for lacking the vision necessary to construct a liberal political party capable of prevailing against the forces of conservatism, primarily those in Congress. His second volume is similar to Freidel's in attributing Roosevelt's limitations more to the situations he faced than to his own judgments.

A much briefer but valuable biography is Patrick J. Maney, *The Roosevelt Presence: The Life and Legacy of FDR* (Berkeley: University of California Press, 1998 [1993]). Maney credits Roosevelt with enacting government programs that stabilized American capitalism, building a majority Democratic coalition that persisted for decades, and revitalizing the presidency. At the same time, he detected in Roosevelt traits of deception, vindictiveness, and unwarranted optimism that detracted from his achievements. Another significant biography is Rexford G. Tugwell, *The Democratic Roosevelt* (New York: Harper, 1957), by a one-time member of Roosevelt's inner circle that combines the intellectual rigor and balance of the scholar with the personal insights of an associate and admirer. Another good study is Nathan Miller, *FDR: An Intimate History* (Garden City, N.Y.: Doubleday, 1983).

Other major works include Kenneth S. Davis, *FDR: The Beckoning of Destiny, 1882–1928* (New York: Putnam, 1972); *The New York Years, 1928–1933; The New Deal Years, 1933–1937;* and *Into the Storm, 1937–1940* (New York: Random House, 1985–1993). Davis subtitles his volumes *A History*, enabling him to provide massive contextual detail and to portray those around Roosevelt in their individual complexity, including Eleanor. Davis is generally favorable to Roosevelt and less inclined than Burns or Maney to highlight his personal failings. In "FDR as a Biographer's Problem," *American Scholar* 53 (1983–1984), Davis described Roosevelt as a man of intellectual limitations but with the confidence and political skill to lead the nation in times of crisis. Volumes by Geoffrey C. Ward, *Before the Trumpet: Young Franklin Roosevelt, 1883–1905,* and *A First-Class Temperament: The Emergence of Franklin Roosevelt* (New York: Harper and Row, 1985, 1989), take Roosevelt up to the time he became governor of New York. The Davis and Ward volumes are gold mines of detail on Roosevelt's life.

The interest in Roosevelt has reached encyclopedic proportions. Otis L. Graham, Jr., and Megan Robinson Wander edited *Franklin D. Roosevelt: His Life and Times, an Encyclopedic View* (Boston: G. K. Hall, 1985), which contains informative essays on all aspects of Roosevelt's personal and public life and the context of his times.

Studies of the New Deal form the first major context for Roosevelt's presidency. William E. Leuchtenburg, *Franklin D. Roosevelt and the New Deal* (New York: Harper and Row, 1963), is the classic one-volume study. Anthony J. Badger, *The New Deal: The Depression Years, 1933–1940* (New York: Farrar, Straus and Giroux, 1989), is a superior synthesis of the scholarly literature. Robert S. McElvaine, *The Great Depression: America 1929–1941* (New York: New York Times Books, 1984), is excellent. Albert U. Romasco, *The Politics of Recovery, Roosevelt's New Deal* (New York: Oxford, 1983), is less substantial than either Leuchtenburg or Badger but is still brisk and intelligent. A major critique that emphasizes Roosevelt's political opportunism is Paul K. Conkin, *The New Deal* (Arlington Heights, Ill.: AHM Publishing Co., 1967).

Still in a class by themselves are the volumes by Arthur M. Scheslinger, Jr., *The Crisis of the Old Order, The Coming of the New Deal,* and *The Politics of Upheaval* (New York: Houghton Mifflin, 1957–1960). Although his favorable view of Roosevelt is no longer in keeping with the scholarly tendency to highlight Roosevelt's faults, Schlesinger provides a readable and intelligent discussion of the complexities of the issues Roosevelt faced during his first term. The volumes carry Roosevelt through his first term and his election to a second term in 1936.

The great volume of historical writing on the New Deal has formed a base for important essays of synthesis on its features. John Braeman, Robert H. Bremner, and David Brody, eds., *The New Deal,* vol. 1, *The National Level,* vol. 2, *The State and Local Levels* (Columbus: Ohio State University Press, 1975), is excellent, as are Harvard Sitkoff, ed., *Fifty Years Later: The New Deal Evaluated* (New York: Knopf, 1985), and Steve Fraser and Gary Gerstle, eds., *The Rise and Fall of the New Deal Order, 1930–1980* (Princeton, N.J.: Princeton University Press, 1989). Another important collection is Herbert D. Rosenbaum and Elizabeth Bartelme, eds., *Franklin D. Roosevelt: The Man, the Myth, the Era, 1882–1945* (New York: Greenwood Press, 1987).

The best book on Roosevelt's foreign policy is Robert Dallek, *Franklin D. Roosevelt and American Foreign Policy, 1932–1945* (New York: Oxford University Press, 1979), which covers the scope of Roosevelt's diplomacy using primary sources. The circumstances leading to the United States' entry into World War II receive detailed analysis in William L. Langer and S. Everett Gleason, *The Challenge to Isolation* and *The Undeclared War* (New York: Harper and Row, 1952, 1953).

Important general studies of Roosevelt's wartime diplomacy are Gaddis Smith, *American Diplomacy during the Second World War* (New York: John Wiley and Sons,

1965); Warren F. Kimball, *The Juggler: Franklin Roosevelt as Wartime Statesman* (Princeton, N.J.: Princeton University Press, 1991); and Robert Divine, *Roosevelt and World War II* (Baltimore: Johns Hopkins Press, 1969). Roosevelt's role as commander in chief is discussed in Eric Larrabee, *Commander in Chief: Franklin D. Roosevelt, His Lieutenants and Their War* (New York: Harper and Row, 1987); William R. Emerson, "FDR (1941–1945)," in *The Ultimate Decision: The President as Commander in Chief*, ed. Ernest R. May (New York: Brazillier, 1960); and Maurice Matloff and Edwin M. Snell, *Strategic Planning for Coalition Warfare*, 2 vols. (Washington, D.C.: Office of the Chief of Military History, 1953).

This volume interprets Roosevelt's presidency within the framework of pluralism. The author has attempted to define this term historically, that is, as a word that describes the way people in the 1930s organized their understanding of social reality and how they approached problem solving. The principal secondary work that describes pluralism in this way is Alan I. Marcus, *Technology in America*, 2d ed. (New York: Harcourt Brace Jovanovich, 1998). Because Marcus interprets the history of technology as part of the history of ideas, he identifies large themes that apply to different kinds of activities, such as politics and government. Another work that illuminates an important aspect of pluralist decision making is William Graebner, *The Engineering of Consent: Democracy and Authority in Twentieth Century America* (Madison: University of Wisconsin Press, 1987). Also influential is Michael Walzer, *Spheres of Justice: A Defense of Pluralism and Equality* (New York: Basic Books, 1983). Walzer argues that in a pluralistic society no one should be able to translate an advantage in one social area into an advantage in another. Thus, in a good society, most people would have some advantage that others would recognize and honor, so social deference would be widely distributed. Walzer also argues that in such a society all political decisions would have to be made democratically, which evokes the New Deal's preference for "grassroots democracy" but only hints at Roosevelt's elaborate organizational schemes to bring about consensus. Because Walzer is trying to establish the proper relations among different social groups, he pays little attention to the pluralist assumption that making decisions was a continuous process. The noted political scientist Luther Gulick explains the pluralist idea that a whole can be greater than the sum of its parts in "Notes on the Theory of Organization," in *Papers on the Science of Administration*, ed. L. Gulick and L. Urwick (New York: Institute of Public Administration, 1937).

The pluralist approach focuses on Roosevelt's administrative and political style and pays less attention to his economic policies. The present author is, however, aware of the considerable amount of historical literature that focuses on Roosevelt's economic policies and often measures them in relation to earlier reforms of the Progressive era of Theodore Roosevelt and Woodrow Wilson and in relation to the formulations of the seminal British economist John Maynard Keynes. Recent studies addressing this aspect of the New Deal are Theodore Rosenof, *Dogma, Depression, and the New Deal: The Debate of Political Leaders over Economic Recovery* (Port Washington, N.Y.: Kennikat Press, 1975), and *Economics in the Long Run: New Deal Theorists and Their Legacies, 1933–1993* (Chapel Hill: University of North Carolina Press, 1997), and Herbert Stein, *The Fiscal Revolution in America* (Chicago and

London: University of Chicago Press, 1969). Two studies by economists, E. Cary Brown, "Fiscal Policy in the Thirties: A Reappraisal," *American Economic Review* 46 (1956), and Larry Peppers, "Full-Employment Surplus Analysis and Structural Change: The 1930s," *Explorations in Economic History* 10 (1973), have demonstrated that Roosevelt followed a path of fiscal conservatism so that the New Deal never really tried to stimulate recovery through government spending. Richard P. Adelstein, "The Nation as an Economic Unit: Keynes, Roosevelt, and the Managerial Ideal," *Journal of American History* 78 (1991), argues that because Roosevelt preferred to appeal to the mass of voters and to work through the federal system, he was unable to exercise the control necessary to establishing Keynesian reforms.

CHAPTER 1

The economic causes of the Great Depression are discussed in John A. Garraty, *The Great Depression* (San Diego, New York, and London: Harcourt Brace Jovanovich, 1986); Susan Estabrook Kennedy, *The Banking Crisis of 1933* (Lexington: University Press of Kentucky, 1973); Charles P. Kindleberger, *The World in Depression, 1929–1939* (London: Allen Lane the Penguin Press, 1973), and Michael A. Bernstein, *The Great Depression: Delayed Recovery and Economic Change in America, 1929–1939* (Cambridge and New York: Cambridge University Press, 1987).

The condition of the nation during the early years of the depression and the response of the Hoover administration is brilliantly analyzed in Albert U. Romasco, *The Poverty of Abundance: Hoover, the Nation, the Depression* (New York: Oxford University Press, 1965), and Martin Fausold, *The Presidency of Herbert Hoover* (Lawrence: University Press of Kansas, 1985). Jordan A. Schwarz, *The Interregnum of Despair: Hoover, Congress, and the Depression* (Urbana: University of Illinois Press, 1970), is an excellent study of its title subject.

The trial of social welfare agencies during the early years of the depression is described in Josephine C. Brown, *Public Relief, 1929–1939* (New York: Henry Holt and Company, 1940).

Sources that define pluralism, other than those cited in the general section of the bibliography, include Hamilton Cravens, *The Triumph of Evolution: The Heredity-Environment Controversy 1900–1941* (Baltimore: Johns Hopkins Press, 1988), and *Before Head Start: The Iowa Station and America's Children* (Chapel Hill: University of North Carolina Press, 1993); Henry D. Shapiro, *Appalachia on Our Mind: The Southern Mountains and Mountaineers in the American Consciousness* (Chapel Hill: University of North Carolina Press, 1978); Barry Karl, *Charles E. Merriam and the Study of Politics* (Chicago: University of Chicago Press, 1974); and Eric Goldman, *Rendezvous with Destiny* (New York: Harcourt, Brace, Jovanovich, 1953). Original sources include Walter B. Cannon, *The Wisdom of the Body* (New York: Norton, 1932) (physiology); Margaret Mead, *Coming of Age in Samoa* (New York: William Morrow, 1928) (anthropology); and Robert E. Park, Ernest W. Burgess, and Roderick D. McKenzie, *The City* (Chicago: University of Chicago Press, 1925) (sociology).

On Roosevelt's governorship, Bernard Bellush, *Franklin D. Roosevelt as Governor of New York* (New York: Columbia University Press, 1955), is the standard work.

Studies of Roosevelt's planning the New Deal include Rexford Tugwell, *The Brains Trust* (New York: Viking Press, 1968), and Raymond Moley, *After Seven Years* (New York and London: Harper and Brothers, 1939), books by two members of the Brains Trust. Also important are Jordan A. Schwarz, *Liberal: Adolf A. Berle and the Vision of an American Era* (New York: Free Press; London: Collier Macmillan, 1987); Elliot A. Rosen, "The Brain Trust and the Origins of the New Deal," in *Franklin D. Roosevelt: The Man, the Myth, the Era, 1882–1945*, ed. Herbert D. Rosenbaum and Elizabeth Bartelme (New York: Greenwood Press, 1987); and Elliot A. Rosen, *Hoover, Roosevelt, and the Brains Trust: From Depression to New Deal* (New York: Columbia University Press, 1977).

A suggestive analysis of the difference between Hoover's approach to the depression and Roosevelt's is Ellis Hawley, *The Great War and the Search for a Modern Order: A History of the American People and Their Institutions, 1917–1933* (New York: St. Martin's Press, 1979). David E. Hamilton, *From New Day to New Deal: American Farm Policy from Hoover to Roosevelt, 1928–1933* (Chapel Hill: University of North Carolina Press, 1991), focuses on Hoover's farm policies but includes an insightful chapter on the contrast with Roosevelt's.

CHAPTER 2

The best account of the Hundred Days that shaped the early New Deal is James E. Sargent, *Roosevelt and the Hundred Days: Struggle for the Early New Deal* (New York: Garland, 1981). Also excellent is Raymond Moley, *The First New Deal* (New York: Harcourt, Brace and World, 1966). The conservative influence on Roosevelt's early New Deal thinking is revealed in Robert Paul Browder and Thomas G. Smith, *Independent: A Biography of Lewis W. Douglas* (New York: Knopf, 1986), and Jordan A. Schwarz, *The Speculator: Bernard M. Baruch in Washington, 1917–1965* (Chapel Hill: University of North Carolina Press, 1981).

Important accomplishments of the Hundred Days are treated in Michael E. Parrish, *Securities Regulation and the New Deal* (New Haven, Conn.: Yale University Press, 1970); Robert Himmelberg, *The Origins of the National Recovery Administration* (New York: Fordham University Press, 1976); Ellis Wayne Hawley, *The New Deal and the Problem of Monopoly: A Study in Economic Ambivalence* (Princeton, N.J.: Princeton University Press, 1966); and Van L. Perkins, *Crisis in Agriculture: The Agricultural Adjustment Administration and the New Deal, 1933* (Berkeley: University of California Press, 1969).

An insightful analysis of international monetary issues and the World Economic Conference is Barry J. Eichengreen, *Golden Fetters: The Gold Standard and the Great Depression, 1919–1939* (New York: Oxford University Press, 1992).

CHAPTER 3

The best account of New Deal agricultural policy is Theodore Saloutos, *The American Farmer and the New Deal* (Ames: Iowa State University, 1982). Other important studies include Gilbert C. Fite, *Cotton Fields No More: Southern Agriculture, 1865–1980* (Lexington: University Press of Kentucky, 1984); Donald H. Grubbs, *Cry from the Cotton: The Southern Tenant Farmers' Union and the New Deal* (Chapel Hill: University of North Carolina Press, 1971); Pete Daniel, *Breaking the Land: The Transformation of Cotton, Tobacco, and Rice Cultures since 1880* (Urbana: University of Illinois Press, 1985); and Paul E. Mertz, *New Deal Policy and Southern Rural Poverty* (Baton Rouge: Louisiana State University Press, 1978). An excellent treatment of midwestern agriculture is Sally H. Clarke, *Regulation and the Revolution in United States Farm Productivity* (Cambridge and New York: Cambridge University Press, 1994).

There is still a need for a fully satisfactory biography of Henry A. Wallace. Edward L. Schapsmeier and Frederick H. Schapsmeier, *Henry A. Wallace of Iowa: The Agrarian Years, 1910–1940* (Ames: Iowa State University Press 1968), and *Prophet in Politics: Henry A. Wallace and the War Years, 1940–1965* (Ames: Iowa State University Press, 1971), are workmanlike and useful. For a full discussion of the mystical aspects of Wallace's character, see Graham White and John Maze, *Henry A. Wallace: His Search for a New World Order* (Chapel Hill and London: University of North Carolina Press, 1995).

The legal aspects of agricultural policy receive attention in Peter H. Irons, *The New Deal Lawyers* (Princeton, N.J.: Princeton University Press, 1982), which also treats the National Recovery Administration. Rainer Schickele, *Agricultural Policy: Farm Programs and National Welfare* (New York, Toronto, and London: McGraw-Hill, 1954), and Theodore Schultz, *Agriculture in an Unstable Economy* (New York and London: McGraw-Hill, 1945), discuss New Deal agricultural policy from the perspective of agricultural economics. Richard Stewart Kirkendall, *Social Scientists and Farm Politics in the Age of Roosevelt* (Ames: Iowa State University Press, 1982), discusses the role of New Deal agricultural economists.

A dramatic incident in the politics of the agricultural program is elucidated by Richard Lowitt, "Henry A. Wallace and the 1935 Purge in the Department of Agriculture," *Agricultural History* 53 (1979).

The program to provide electric service to rural America is discussed by Philip J. Funigiello, *Toward a National Power Policy: The New Deal and the Electric Utility Industry, 1933–1941* (Pittsburgh: University of Pittsburgh Press, 1973), and Clayton D. Brown, *Electricity for Rural America: The Fight for the REA* (Westport, Conn.: Greenwood Press, 1980).

An interesting contrast between the administrative histories of the New Deal's program for agricultural recovery and its program for industrial recovery is Theda Skocpol and Kenneth Finegold, "State Capacity and Economic Intervention in the Early New Deal," *Political Science Quarterly* 97 (summer 1982).

An important modern study of the National Recovery Administration is Donald Robert Brand, *Corporatism and the Rule of Law: A Study of the National Recovery Administration* (Ithaca, N.Y.: Cornell University Press, 1988). An older but very useful analysis is Leverett S. Lyon et al., *The National Recovery Administration: An Analysis and Appraisal* (Washington, D.C.: Brookings Institution, 1935). The story of the NRA's unsuccessful leader is told in John Kennedy Ohl, *Hugh S. Johnson and the New Deal* (De Kalb: Northern Illinois University Press, 1985), and Hugh

Johnson, *The Blue Eagle from Egg to Earth* (Garden City, N.Y.: Doubleday, 1935). Ellis Hawley, whose previously cited book is the best study of the NRA, provides the best overview in "The New Deal and Business," in *The New Deal: The National Level*, ed. John Braeman, Robert H. Bremner, and David Brody (Columbus: Ohio State University Press, 1975). Bernard Bellush, *The Failure of the NRA* (New York: Norton, 1975), attributes the failure to its control by big business and its consequent failure to address the problems of labor.

Joseph P. Lash, *Dealers and Dreamers: A New Look at the New Deal* (New York: Doubleday, 1988), provides a political narrative of the New Deal's regulation of the electric utilities industry.

The development of New Deal labor policy receives an excellent overall treatment in Melvyn Dubofsky, *The State and Labor in Modern America* (Chapel Hill and London: University of North Carolina Press, 1994). Another masterful treatment is Irving Bernstein, *Turbulent Years: A History of the American Worker, 1933–1941* (Boston: Houghton Mifflin, 1970). Stanley Vittoz, *New Deal Labor Policy and the American Industrial Economy* (Chapel Hill: University of North Carolina Press, 1987), is an incisive class analysis. J. Joseph Huthmacher, *Senator Robert F. Wagner and the Rise of Urban Liberalism* (New York: Atheneum, 1968), is an excellent biography of the man who shaped New Deal and American labor policy.

James A. Gross, *The Making of the National Labor Relations Board: A Study in Economics, Politics, and the Law* (Albany: State University of New York Press, 1981), discusses Roosevelt's twists and turns in developing his labor policy; Christopher L. Tomlins, *The State and the Unions: Labor Relations, Law, and the Organized Labor Movement in America, 1880–1960* (Cambridge: Cambridge University Press, 1985), looks more generally at the administrative and legal significance of the New Deal, as does Robert E. Williams, *NLRB Regulation of Election Conduct*, Labor Relations and Public Policy Series, No. 8 (Philadelphia: Wharton School, Industrial Research Unit, 1985).

Excellent syntheses of New Deal labor policy include Ellis W. Hawley, "The New Deal State and the Anti-Bureaucratic Tradition," in *The New Deal and Its Legacy: Critique and Appraisal*, ed. Robert Eden (New York: Greenwood Press, 1989); Theda Skocpol and Kenneth Finegold, "Explaining New Deal Labor Policy," *American Political Science Review* 84 (1990); Karl E. Klare, "Judicial Deradicalization of the Wagner Act and the Origins of Modern Legal Consciousness, 1937–1941," *Minnesota Law Review* 62 (1978); and Alan Dawley, "Workers, Capital, and the State in the Twentieth Century," in *Perspectives on American Labor History: The Problems of Synthesis*, ed. J. Carroll Moody and Alice Kessler-Harris (De Kalb: Northern Illinois University Press, 1989).

CHAPTER 4

Contemporary expressions of "regionalism," an important aspect of New Deal pluralistic thinking, include Howard Odum, *American Regionalism: A Cultural-Historical Approach to National Integration* (New York: H. Holt and Company, 1938), and *I'll Take My Stand: The South and the Agrarian Tradition* (New York and London: Harper, 1930); and Herbert Agar, *The People's Choice, from Washington to Harding: A Study in Democracy* (Boston and New York: Houghton Mifflin, 1933).

New Deal efforts to reshape American communities are explored in Paul Conkin, *Tomorrow a New World: The New Deal Community Program* (Ithaca, N.Y.: Cornell University Press, 1959); Harry McDean, "Western Thought in Planning Rural America: The Subsistence Homesteads Program, 1933–1935," *Journal of the West* 31 (1992); and Joseph L. Arnold, *The New Deal in the Suburbs: A History of the Greenbelt Town Program, 1935–1954* (Columbus: Ohio State University Press, 1971).

Aspects of the New Deal's most ambitious regional development program are studied in Michael J. McDonald and John Muldowny, *TVA and the Dispossessed: The Resettlement of Population in the Norris Dam Area* (Knoxville: University of Tennessee Press, 1982); Walter L. Creese, *TVA's Public Planning: The Vision, the Reality* (Knoxville: University of Tennessee Press, 1990); and Erwin C. Hargrove and Paul Conkin, eds., *TVA: Fifty Years of Grass-Roots Bureaucracy* (Urbana and Chicago: University of Illinois Press, 1983). Roy Talbert, *FDR's Utopian: Arthur Morgan of the TVA* (Jackson: University Press of Mississippi, 1987), is a biography of TVA's principal social reformer. Nancy Grant, *TVA and Black Americans: Planning for the Status Quo* (Philadelphia: Temple University Press, 1990), shows that TVA social planning excluded African Americans.

New Deal Indian policy is treated masterfully within a broad historical context in Francis Paul Prucha, *The Great Father: The United States Government and the American Indians* (Lincoln: University of Nebraska Press, 1986). Graham D. Taylor, *The New Deal and American Indian Tribalism: The Administration of the Indian Reorganization Act, 1934–45* (Lincoln: University of Nebraska Press, 1980), discusses the specific aspects of New Deal policy. Kenneth R. Philp, *John Collier's Crusade for Indian Reform, 1920–1954* (Tucson: University of Arizona Press, 1977), portrays the author of the policy, as does Lawrence C. Kelly, *The Assault on Assimilation: John Collier and the Origins of Indian Policy Reform* (Albuquerque: University of New Mexico Press, 1983).

There is no general history of New Deal unemployment relief. Donald S. Howard, *The WPA and Federal Relief Policy* (New York: Russell Sage Foundation, 1943), exhaustively studies the New Deal's principal relief agency from the perspective of a policy analyst. The best historical study is Searle F. Charles, *Minister of Relief: Harry Hopkins and the Depression* (Syracuse, N.Y.: Syracuse University Press, 1963). The Civil Works Administration receives a good treatment that emphasizes its inner administrative history from Bonnie Fox Schwartz, *The Civil Works Administration, 1933–1934: The Business of Emergency Employment in the New Deal* (Princeton, N.J.: Princeton University Press, 1984). Biographies of Harry Hopkins, who emerged as the leader of federal relief for the unemployed, are Robert E. Sherwood, *Roosevelt and Hopkins, an Intimate History* (New York: Harper and Brothers, 1948, 1953), and George McJimsey, *Harry Hopkins: Ally of the Poor and Defender of Democracy* (Cambridge: Harvard University Press, 1987). The Sherwood biography emphasizes Hopkins's dynamic and goading leadership style; McJimsey emphasizes his collegial and inspirational style.

Special studies of relief include Monty Noam Penkower, *The Federal Writers' Project: A Study in Government Patronage of the Arts* (Urbana : University of Illinois

Press, 1977); Joanne Bentley DeHart, *Hallie Flanagan: A Life in the American Theatre* (New York: Knopf, 1988); Richard A. Reiman, *The New Deal and American Youth: Ideas and Ideals in a Depression Decade* (Athens and London: University of Georgia Press, 1992); Jerre Mangione, *The Dream and the Deal: The Federal Writers' Project, 1935–1943* (Boston: Little, Brown, 1972); Hallie Flanagan, *Arena* (New York: Duell, Sloan and Pearce, 1940).

The New Deal did not have a "policy" toward African Americans in the same sense that it had a policy for American Indians. But the role of African Americans was important, both as an "issue" within New Deal circles and for the political history of the Roosevelt presidency. The best survey is Harvard Sitkoff, *A New Deal for Blacks: The Emergence of Civil Rights as a National Issue* (New York: Oxford University Press, 1978). Also very good is Raymond Wolters, *Negroes and the Great Depression: The Problem of Economic Recovery* (Westport, Conn.: Greenwood, 1970).

There have been several excellent studies of New Deal social security policy: Colin Gordon, *New Deals: Business, Labor, and Politics in America, 1920–1935* (Cambridge: Cambridge University Press, 1994); Roy Lubove, *The Struggle for Social Security, 1900–1935* (Cambridge: Harvard University Press, 1968); Ann Shola Orloff, *The Politics of Pensions: A Comparative Analysis of Britain, Canada, and the United States, 1880–1940* (Madison: University of Wisconsin Press, 1993); Daniel Nelson, *Unemployment Insurance: The American Experience, 1915–1935* (Madison: University of Wisconsin Press, 1969); Linda Gordon, *Women, the State, and Welfare* (Madison: University of Wisconsin Press, 1990); and Gwendolyn Mink, *The Wages of Motherhood: Inequality in the Welfare State, 1917–1942* (Ithaca, N.Y.: Cornell University Press, 1995). Helpful on the fiscal aspects of social security is Bruno Stein, "Funding Social Security on a Current Basis: The 1939 Policy Change in the United States," in *Nationalizing Social Security in Europe and America*, ed. Douglas E. Ashford and E. W. Kelley (Greenwich, Conn., and London: JAI Press, 1986).

CHAPTER 5

The best general history of the American West, which includes an incisive treatment of the New Deal's effects, is Richard White, *"It's Your Misfortune and None of My Own," A New History of the American West* (Norman: University of Oklahoma Press, 1991). A treatment that stresses the benefits of New Deal programs is Richard Lowitt, *The New Deal and the West* (Bloomington: Indiana University Press, 1984).

The public power aspects of the TVA are spelled out briefly and clearly in Thomas K. McCraw, *TVA and the Power Fight, 1933–1939* (Philadelphia, New York, and Toronto: J. B. Lippincott, 1971). Roosevelt's plans to expand the TVA concept and the unwillingness of Congress to embrace his plan are presented by William E. Leuchtenburg, "Roosevelt, Norris and the 'Seven Little TVAs,'" *Journal of Politics* 14 (1952).

The best study of the "dust bowl" is R. Douglas Hurt, *The Dust Bowl: An Agricultural and Social History* (Chicago: Nelson-Hall, 1984). See also Donald Worster, *Dust Bowl: The Southern Plains in the 1930s* (New York: Oxford University Press, 1979).

Paul J. Culhane, *Public Lands Politics: Interest Group Influence on the Forest Service and the Bureau of Land Management* (Baltimore: Published for Resources for the Future by Johns Hopkins University Press, 1981), explains the tangled bureaucratic struggles to control western lands and resources.

A model study of how New Deal dam building on the Missouri River first arose and then essentially failed is Robert Kelley Schneiders, "Dams across the Wide Missouri: Water Transportation, the Corps of Engineers, and Environmental Change along the Lower Missouri Valley, 1803–1993," doctoral dissertation, Iowa State University, 1997.

CHAPTER 6

Sources that describe Roosevelt's working routine and administrative and political style include Grace G. Tully, *FDR, My Boss* (New York: C. Scribner's Sons, 1949), by one of his secretaries, and Samuel I. Rosenman, *Working with Roosevelt* (New York: Harper, 1952), by his principal speechwriter. Samuel I. Rosenman, *Presidential Style: Some Giants and a Pygmy in the White House* (New York: Harper and Row, 1976), compares Roosevelt favorably with other presidents of the twentieth century. See also Michael F. Reilly, *Reilly of the White House* (New York: Simon and Schuster, 1947), by the head of the Secret Service detail that guarded Roosevelt; and Francis Biddle, *In Brief Authority* (Garden City, N.Y.: Doubleday, 1962), by an administration insider and wartime attorney general. Roosevelt's son Elliott contributed a memoir of his selective experiences in Elliott Roosevelt and James Brough, *A Rendezvous with Destiny: The Roosevelts of the White House* (New York: Putnam, 1975). Frances Perkins, *The Roosevelt I Knew* (New York: Viking Press, 1946), is a memoir by one of Roosevelt's continuously serving cabinet members. Another important memoir is Eleanor Roosevelt, *This I Remember* (New York: Harper, 1949). All these memoirs are favorable to Roosevelt's presidential leadership but provide objective and useful descriptions of his personality and working habits.

Hugh Gregory Gallagher, *FDR's Splendid Deception* (New York: Dodd, Mead, 1985), describes how Roosevelt dealt with his disability.

The best discussion of Roosevelt's dealings with the press and public is Betty Houchin Winfield, *FDR and the News Media* (Urbana: University of Illinois Press, 1990).

Roosevelt's relation with Progressive politicians of the Theodore Roosevelt and Woodrow Wilson eras is analyzed in Otis Graham, *An Encore for Reform: The Old Progressives and the New Deal* (New York: Oxford, a Galaxy Book, 1967). For a similar analysis that emphasizes the personal independent style of progressive Republicans, see Ronald L. Feinman, *Twilight of Progressivism: The Western Republican Senators and the New Deal* (Baltimore and London: Johns Hopkins Press, 1981). Related to these studies but broader in its coverage is Douglas B. Craig, *After Wilson: The Struggle for the Democratic Party, 1920–1934* (Chapel Hill: University of North Carolina Press, 1992).

George Wolfskill and John A. Hudson, *All but the People: Franklin D. Roosevelt and His Critics, 1933–39* (London: Macmillan, 1969), covers Roosevelt's detractors, from those on the fringe of sanity to his most powerful political adversaries. Specific works about Roosevelt's major fringe critics are Alan Brinkley, *Voices of Protest: Huey Long, Father Coughlin, and the Great Depression* (New York: Knopf, 1982); and David Harry Bennett, *Demagogues in the Depression: American Radicals and the Union Party, 1932–1936* (New Brunswick, N.J.: Rutgers University Press, 1969). Huey Long, Roosevelt's most serious third-party adversary, is the subject of an exemplary biography in T. Harry Williams, *Huey Long* (New York: Knopf, 1969).

The best analysis of Roosevelt's voting strength is Jerome M. Clubb, William H. Flanigan, and Nancy Zingale, *Partisan Realignment: Voters, Parties, and Government in American History* (Beverly Hills, Calif.: Sage Publications, 1980), which argues that Roosevelt's popularity restructured American voting patterns. Kristi Andersen, *The Creation of a Democratic Majority, 1928–1936* (Chicago: University of Chicago Press, 1979), identifies Roosevelt's majority with new voters rather than with switching voters. David W. Prindle, "Voter Turnout, Critical Elections, and the New Deal Realignment," *Social Science History* 3 (1979); Everett Carll Ladd, *Transformations of the American Party System: Political Coalitions from the New Deal to the 1970s* (New York: Norton, 1978); Courtney Brown, *Ballots of Tumult: A Portrait of Volatility in American Voting* (Ann Arbor: University of Michigan Press, 1991); Robert S. Erikson and Kent L. Tedin, "The 1928–1936 Partisan Realignment: The Case for the Conversion Hypothesis," *American Political Science Review* 75 (1981); James L. Sundquist, *Dynamics of the Party System: Alignment and Realignment of Political Parties in the United States*, rev. ed. (Washington, D.C.: Brookings Institution, 1983); and Paul Kleppner, *Who Voted? The Dynamics of Electoral Turnout, 1870–1980* (New York: Praeger Publishers, 1982), discuss aspects of voter behavior, emphasizing the gradual drift of some Roosevelt voters, mostly in the Middle West, to the Republican party.

The influence of Roosevelt's popularity on congressional elections is discussed by James E. Campbell, *The Presidential Pulse of Congressional Elections* (Lexington: University Press of Kentucky, 1993); David W. Brady, *Critical Elections and Congressional Policy-Making* (Stanford, Calif.: Stanford University Press, 1988); Duncan MacRae, Jr., and James Meldrum, "Critical Elections in Illinois: 1888–1958," *American Political Science Review* 54 (1960); and Milton C. Cummings, *Congressmen and the Electorate: Elections for the U.S. House and the President, 1920–1964* (New York: Free Press 1966).

The role of Congress in Roosevelt's presidency receives attention in James T. Patterson, *Congressional Conservatism and the New Deal: The Growth of the Conservative Coalition in Congress, 1933–1939* (Lexington: University of Kentucky Press, 1967), which emphasizes the gradual development of a conservative opposition capable of frustrating Roosevelt's legislative agenda. Clyde P. Weed, *The Nemesis of Reform: The Republican Party during the New Deal* (New York: Columbia University Press, 1994), argues that Republican congressmen were more successful opposing Roosevelt's administrative and Supreme Court reforms than his economic reforms. Richard Bensel, *Sectionalism and American Political Development, 1880–1980*

(Madison: University of Wisconsin Press, 1984), discusses the institutional development of Congress and the shifting balances in its votes to distribute resources among the nation's regions.

Sean J. Savage, *Roosevelt: The Party Leader, 1932–1945* (Lexington: University of Kentucky Press, 1991), is the best discussion of Roosevelt as a practical politician and shows that the Democratic Party reorganized itself to pay special attention to groups directly helped by New Deal policies.

CHAPTER 7

The best biography of Eleanor Roosevelt is Joseph P. Lash, *Eleanor and Franklin: The Story of Their Relationship, Based on Eleanor Roosevelt's Private Papers* (New York: W. W. North, 1971), a book that combines a close friend's sympathy with a scholar's commitment to evidence. Another excellent treatment is Lois Scharf, *Eleanor Roosevelt: First Lady of American Liberalism* (Boston: Twayne Publishers, 1987), which emphasizes her political commitments. The best study of Eleanor's pre–First Lady years is Blanche Wiesen Cook, *Eleanor Roosevelt,* vol. 1, *1884–1933* (New York: Viking, 1992). Ann Davis, "The Character of Social Feminism in the Thirties: Eleanor Roosevelt and Her Associates in the New Deal," in *Franklin D. Roosevelt: The Man, the Myth, the Era, 1882–1945,* ed. Herbert D. Rosenbaum and Elizabeth Bartelme (New York: Greenwood Press, 1987), places Eleanor in her network of liberal women. Notably less favorable but still scholarly is James R. Kearney, *Anna Eleanor Roosevelt: The Evolution of a Reformer* (Boston: Houghton Mifflin, 1968).

In *This Is My Story* (New York and London: Harper and Brothers, 1937), Eleanor presented her life as an example to those women who wanted greater independence and influence.

The condition of women at the dawn of the New Deal and their relative lack of organization and political influence are described in William H. Chafe, "Women's History and Political History: Some Thoughts on Progressivism and the New Deal," in *Visible Women,* ed. Nancy A. Hewitt and Susan Lebsock (Urbana and Chicago: University of Illinois Press, 1993), and Winifred Wandersee, "The Economics of Middle-Income Family Life: Working Women during the Great Depression," in *Decades of Discontent: The Women's Movement, 1920–1940,* ed. Lois Scharf and Joan M. Jensen (Westport, Conn.: Greenwood Press, 1983).

Eleanor's relationship with Lorena Hickok is described in Doris Faber, *The Life of Lorena Hickok, ER's Friend* (New York: Morrow, 1980).

Eleanor's popular writings are discussed by Maurine Beasley, "Eleanor Roosevelt and 'My Day': The White House Years," in *Franklin D. Roosevelt: The Man, the Myth, the Era, 1882–1945,* ed. Herbert D. Rosenbaum and Elizabeth Bartelme (New York: Greenwood Press, 1987).

Susan Ware provides the best history of women in and out of the New Deal in *Beyond Suffrage, Women in the New Deal* (Cambridge: Harvard University Press, 1981), and *Holding Their Own: American Women in the 1930s* (Boston: Twayne, 1982). Important women in the New Deal are portrayed by George Whitney Martin, *Madam Secretary, Frances Perkins* (Boston: Houghton Mifflin, 1976); Susan Ware,

Partner and I: Molly Dewson, Feminism, and New Deal Politics (New Haven, Conn.: Yale University Press, 1987); and Martha H. Swain, *Ellen S. Woodward: New Deal Advocate for Women* (Jackson: University Press of Mississippi, 1995).

CHAPTER 8

An excellent analysis of the origin of Roosevelt's plan to reform the Supreme Court is William E. Leuchtenburg, *The Supreme Court Reborn* (New York: Oxford University Press, 1995).

An excellent account of Roosevelt's decision to increase spending and the effect of that decision on New Deal policy is Dean L. May, *From New Deal to New Economics: The Liberal Response to the Recession of 1937* (New York: Garland, 1981). Contemporary justification for the spending program is provided by Richard V. Gilbert, George H. Hildebrand, Jr., Arthur W. Stuart, Maxine Yaple Sweezy, Paul M. Sweezy, Dorrie Tarshis, and John D. Wilson, *An Economic Program for American Democracy* (New York: Vanguard Press, 1938). Roger J. Sandilands, *The Life and Political Economy of Lauchlin Currie* (Durham, N.C., and London: Duke University Press, 1990), discusses one of the leading advocates of spending, as does Sidney Hyman, *Marriner S. Eccles, Private Entrepreneur and Public Servant* (Stanford, Calif.: Graduate School of Business, Stanford University, 1976).

The New Deal housing program is discussed in Mark Gelfand, *A Nation of Cities: The Federal Government and Urban America, 1933–1965* (New York: Oxford, 1975), and Gail Radford, *Modern Housing for America: Policy Struggles in the New Deal Era* (Chicago: University of Chicago Press, 1996).

Roosevelt's plan to reorganize the executive branch is discussed by Barry Dean Karl, *Executive Reorganization and Reform in the New Deal* (Cambridge: Harvard University Press, 1965), which emphasizes the administrative thinking behind the plan, and by Richard Polenberg, *Reorganizing Roosevelt's Government: The Controversy over Executive Reorganization, 1936–1939* (Cambridge: Harvard University Press, 1966), which stresses the political struggle it caused. A recent study that attributes later disappointments with presidential performance to the administrative reforms of the Progressive and New Deal periods is Matthew J. Dickinson, *Bitter Harvest: FDR, Presidential Power and the Growth of the Presidential Branch* (Cambridge: Cambridge University Press, 1997). Placing the reorganization issue in a broad historical context is Barry Dean Karl, *The Uneasy State: The United States from 1915 to 1945* (Chicago and London: University of Chicago Press, 1983).

CHAPTER 9

Studies of the United States' entry into World War II have produced several shelves of books. Excellent summaries are Waldo H. Heinrichs, *Threshold of War: Franklin D. Roosevelt and American Entry into World War II* (New York: Oxford University Press, 1988); Akira Iriye, *The Origins of the Second World War in Asia and the Pacific* (London and New York: Longman, 1987); and Jonathan G. Utley,

Going to War with Japan, 1937–1941 (Knoxville: University of Tennessee Press, 1985). The best global view of how the European war originated is Donald Cameron Watt, *How War Came: The Immediate Origins of the Second World War, 1938–1939* (London: Heinemann, 1989). Good reviews of the recent literature are Mark M. Lowenthal, "Roosevelt and the Coming of the Second World War: The Search for United States Policy," *Journal of Contemporary History* 16 (1981), and J. Garry Clifford, "Both Ends of the Telescope: New Perspectives on FDR and American Entry into World War II," *Diplomatic History* 13 (1989).

Roosevelt's principal foreign policy opponents are expertly and exhaustively analyzed by the master scholar of the isolationist movement in Wayne S. Cole, *Roosevelt and the Isolationists, 1932–45* (Lincoln: University of Nebraska Press, 1983).

United defense preparations are detailed in Mark Skinner Watson, *Chief of Staff: Prewar Plans and Preparations* (Washington, D.C.: Office of the Chief of Military History, 1959); R. Elberton Smith, *The Army and Economic Mobilization* (Washington, D.C.: Office of the Chief of Military History, 1959); and Stetson Conn, Rose C. Engleman, and Byron Fairchild, *The Western Hemisphere: Guarding the United States and Its Outposts* (Washington, D.C.: Office of the Chief of Military History, 1964).

Historians continue to investigate the Japanese attack on Pearl Harbor. The best account to date is Gordon Prange, *At Dawn We Slept: The Untold Story of Pearl Harbor* (New York: McGraw-Hill, 1981). Also important is Roberta Wohlstetter, *Pearl Harbor; Warning and Decision* (Stanford, Calif.: Stanford University Press, 1962).

CHAPTER 10

The number of studies dealing with the first two years of American participation in World War II is just as formidable as the number of studies about American entry into the war. In addition to the sources cited earlier, principal military studies include R. W. Coakley and R. M. Leighton, *Global Logistics and Strategy*, 2 vols. (Washington, D.C.: Office of the Chief of Military History, 1955, 1959), and Forrest Pogue, *George C. Marshall, Organizer of Victory* (New York: Viking Press, 1979). A very useful study of command relations between the United States and Britain is Alan Wilt, *War from the Top: German and British Military Decision Making during World War II* (Bloomington: Indiana University Press, 1990).

The Roosevelt-Churchill relationship will always attract historians. Joseph Lash, *Roosevelt and Churchill, 1939–1941: The Partnership that Saved the West* (New York: W. W. Norton, 1976), stresses the similar strategic thinking of the two during the years before U.S. entry into the war. Warren Kimball, *Forged in War: Roosevelt, Churchill, and the Second World War* (New York: William Morrow, 1997), is an excellent and well-balanced study that recognizes the tensions and frictions in their relationship but concludes that their similarities and common objectives outweighed their differences. Churchill tells his side of the story in the finest memoirs in the English language in *The Second World War*, 6 vols. (Boston: Houghton Mifflin, 1948–1953). Churchill's biographer Martin Gilbert offers encyclopedic treatment in *Winston S. Churchill*, vol. 4, *Finest Hour*, and vol. 5, *Road to Victory* (Boston: Houghton Mifflin, 1983, 1986).

Special issues in the wartime alliance are treated in several studies. William Roger Louis, *Imperialism at Bay 1941–1945: The United States and the Decolonization of the British Empire* (Oxford: Clarendon Press, 1977), highlights Roosevelt's anticolonialism and shows it to be one of the continuing themes of his war leadership. Christopher Thorne, *Allies of a Kind: The United States, Britain and the War against Japan, 1941–1945* (London: H. Hamilton, 1978), is an excellent study of a subject often overlooked because of American predominance in the Pacific. Thorne provides admirable detail to indicate the substantial involvement of the British and misses few occasions to point out Roosevelt's intellectual shortcomings. Anthony Eden, *The Reckoning* (Boston: Houghton Mifflin, 1965), is similarly inclined to minimize Roosevelt's qualities but is very useful for the detail it provides about British attitudes and policies. A less partisan and almost encyclopedic amount of detail is presented in E. Llewellyn Woodward, *British Foreign Policy during the Second World War* (London: Her Majesty's Stationery Office, 1970–).

Three excellent accounts of the decision to "relocate" Japanese Americans and Japanese immigrants are Roger Daniels, *Concentration Camps North America: Japanese in the United States and Canada during World War II* (Malabar, Fla.: R. E. Krieger, 1981); Page Smith, *Democracy on Trial: The Japanese-American Evacuation and Relocation in World War II* (New York: Simon and Schuster, 1995); and Peter Irons, *Justice at War: The Story of Japanese American Internment Cases* (New York: Oxford University Press, 1983).

CHAPTER 11

There are a number of excellent studies of the United States' home front during World War II. A good public source is *The United States at War: Development and Administration of the War Program by the Federal Government* (Washington, D.C.: Bureau of the Budget Publication, 1946). The official story of the War Production Board is provided in Civilian Production Administration, *Industrial Mobilization for War* (Washington, D.C.: U.S. Government Printing Office, 1946). Mobilization from the army's standpoint is told in R. Elberton Smith, *The Army and Economic Mobilization* (Washington, D.C.: Office of the Chief of Military History, 1959). Another official history that illuminates mobilization in the shipping industry is Frederic C. Lane, *Ships for Victory: A History of Shipbuilding under the United States Maritime Commission in World War II* (Baltimore: Johns Hopkins Press, 1951).

Other general histories include Alan S. Milward, *War, Economy, and Society, 1939–1945* (Berkeley: University of California Press, 1979); Richard Overy, *Why the Allies Won* (New York: Norton, 1995); Richard Polenberg, *War and Society: The United States, 1941–1945* (Philadelphia: Lippincott, 1972); and John Morton Blum, *V Was for Victory* (New York: Harcourt Brace Jovanovich, 1976).

Special aspects of the home front receive treatment in Harold Vatter, *The U.S. Economy in World War II* (New York: Columbia University Press, 1985); Stuart D. Brandes, *Warhogs: A History of War Profits in America* (Lexington: University of Kentucky Press, 1997); Hugh Rockoff, *Drastic Measures: A History of Wage and Price Controls in the United States* (Cambridge: Cambridge University Press, 1984);

Herman Miles Somers, *Presidential Agency OWMR: The Office of War Mobilization and Reconversion* (Cambridge: Harvard University Press, 1950); Allan M. Winkler, *The Politics of Propaganda: The Office of War Information* (New Haven, Conn.: Yale University Press, 1978); Nelson Lichtenstein, *Labor's War at Home: The CIO in World War II* (New York: Cambridge University Press, 1982); and Keith Olson, *The G. I. Bill, the Veterans, and the Colleges* (Lexington: University of Kentucky Press, 1974).

The development of the atomic bomb is thoroughly covered in Richard Rhodes, *The Making of the Atomic Bomb* (New York: Simon and Schuster, 1986). The official history from the army's point of view is Vincent C. Jones, *Manhattan: The Army and the Atomic Bomb* (Washington, D.C.: Office of the Chief of Military History, 1985). The diplomatic aspects of the bomb are treated in Martin Sherwin, *A World Destroyed: The Atomic Bomb and the Grand Alliance* (New York: Knopf, 1975).

Wartime politics, including the election of 1944, are discussed in works previously cited and in Roland Young, *Congressional Politics in the Second World War* (New York: Columbia University Press, 1956); Polly Davis, *Alben W. Barkley: Senate Majority Leader and Vice President* (New York: Garland, 1979); Allen Drury, *A Senate Journal, 1943–1945* (New York: McGraw-Hill, 1963); David McCulloch, *Truman* (New York: Simon and Schuster, 1992); Richard Norton Smith, *Thomas E. Dewey and His Times* (New York: Simon and Schuster, 1982); and Robert Ferrell, *Choosing Truman: The Democratic Convention of 1944* (Columbia: University of Missouri Press, 1994).

Additional insight into the Roosevelt White House during the war comes from John Morton Blum, *From the Morgenthau Diaries: Years of War, 1941–1945* (Boston: Houghton Mifflin, 1959–1967), and Doris Kearns Goodwin, *No Ordinary Time: Franklin and Eleanor Roosevelt: The Home Front in World War II* (New York: Simon and Schuster, 1994).

CHAPTER 12

The last years of the war and of Roosevelt's presidency are treated in sources previously cited. Sources specifically relevant to the material in this chapter include studies of Roosevelt's dealing with the Holocaust: Verne W. Newton, ed., *FDR and the Holocaust* (New York: St. Martin's Press, 1996), and David S. Wyman, *The Abandonment of the Jews: America and the Holocaust, 1941–1945* (New York: Pantheon Books, 1984). On the Yalta Conference, see Lloyd C. Gardner, *Spheres of Influence: The Great Powers Partition Europe, from Munich to Yalta* (Chicago: I. R. Dee, 1993); Russell D. Buhite, *Decisions at Yalta: An Appraisal of Summit Diplomacy* (Wilmington, Del.: Scholarly Resources, 1986); and Diane Shaver Clemens, *Yalta* (New York: Oxford University Press, 1970).

CHAPTER 13

Most of the works discussed in the conclusion have been cited earlier. The essays in Mark J. Rozell and William D. Pederson, *FDR and the Modern Presidency:*

Leadership and Legacy (Westport, Conn.: Praeger, 1997), provide an up-to-date appreciation of Roosevelt by contemporary scholars, as does Steve Fraser and Gary Gerstle, eds., *The Rise and Fall of the New Deal Order, 1930–1980* (Princeton, N.J.: Princeton University Press, 1989).

William E. Leuchtenburg, *In the Shadow of FDR: From Harry Truman to Ronald Reagan* (Ithaca, N.Y.: Cornell University Press, 1983), is the only study to examine how following presidents evaluated Roosevelt's legacy. It will be hard for anyone to surpass.

As the text indicates, the classic statement of New Deal pluralism is Paul Appleby, *Big Democracy* (New York: Knopf, 1945). Since Roosevelt's presidency, the discussion of pluralism has flourished. Some of the major contributions, not previously cited, are Theodore J. Lowi, *The Politics of Disorder* (New York: Basic Books, 1971), and *The End of Liberalism: The Second Republic of the United States* (New York: Norton, 1979). Other studies include Wayne C. Booth, *Critical Understanding: The Powers and Limits of Pluralism* (Chicago: University of Chicago Press, 1979); Reginald J. Harrison, *Pluralism and Corporatism: The Political Evolution of Modern Democracies* (London and Boston: Allen and Unwin, 1980); and Robert A. Dahl, *Dilemmas of Pluralist Democracy: Autonomy vs. Control* (New Haven, Conn.: Yale University Press, 1982).

The theme of "corporate liberalism," which had a moment of prominence in the critique of pluralism, is discussed and essentially disposed of in Ellis W. Hawley, "The Discovery of a 'Corporate Liberalism,'" *Business History Review* 52 (1978).

INDEX